I0127090

Land and Life in Timor-Leste

Ethnographic Essays

Land and Life in Timor-Leste

Ethnographic Essays

Edited by Andrew McWilliam and Elizabeth G. Traube

ANU
THE AUSTRALIAN NATIONAL UNIVERSITY

E PRESS

ANU
E PRESS

Published by ANU E Press
The Australian National University
Canberra ACT 0200, Australia
Email: anuepress@anu.edu.au
This title is also available online at http://epress.anu.edu.au/

National Library of Australia Cataloguing-in-Publication entry

Title: Land and life in Timor-Leste : ethnographic essays /
                 Andrew McWilliam and Elizabeth G. Traube, editors.

ISBN: 9781921862595 (pbk.) 9781921862601 (ebook)

Notes: Includes bibliographical references.

Subjects: Ethnology--Timor-Leste.
                 Timor-Leste--Social life and customs--21st century.
                 Timor-Leste--Social conditions--21st century.
                 Timor-Leste--Rural conditions--21st century.

Other Authors/Contributors:
                 McWilliam, Andrew.
                 Traube, Elizabeth G.

Dewey Number: 301.295986

All rights reserved. No part of this publication may be reproduced, stored in a retrieval system
or transmitted in any form or by any means, electronic, mechanical, photocopying or otherwise,
without the prior permission of the publisher.

Cover design and layout by ANU E Press

Cover image: 'Uma Lulik Borolaisoba, Watulari, Viqueque' by Josh Trindade.

This edition © 2011 ANU E Press

Contents

Contributors

Susana Barnes

Susana Barnes is a PhD candidate in anthropology at Monash University. Previously, she undertook fieldwork as part of an ANU interdisciplinary anthropological–legal study of customary land-tenure systems in Timor-Leste. Her research interests are East Timorese ethnography, customary land and resource tenures, ritual and religion, social transformation and state and society. Email: <susanabarnes@gmail.com>

Judith Bovensiepen

Judith Bovensiepen is a Lecturer in Social Anthropology at the University of Kent in Canterbury (UK). Her research interests include place, landscape and displacement, kinship and exchange, as well as religious transformations and anthropological approaches to history and social change. Email: <J.M.Bovensiepen@kent.ac.uk>

James J. Fox

James J. Fox is Emeritus Professor of Anthropology at The Australian National University. His current affiliation is with the Resource Management in the Asia Pacific Program. He did his first fieldwork on Timor in 1965-66 and has continued to do research in both East and West Timor on a wide range of topics. His most recent field trip to Timor-Leste was in April 2011. Email: <james.Fox@anu.edu.au>

Andrew McWilliam

Andrew McWilliam is a Senior Fellow in Anthropology at The Australian National University. He has published widely on the ethnography of Timor and has continuing research interests in Timor-Leste and eastern Indonesia. Recent work has focused on issues of governance, community economies and ritual exchange, customary resource tenures and plantation histories. Email: <andrew.mcwilliam@anu.edu.au>

Laura Meitzner Yoder

Laura Meitzner Yoder is Associate Professor in the graduate and undergraduate programs at Merry Lea Environmental Learning Center of Goshen College, Indiana, USA. Her work centres on environmental history and political ecology. Email: <Lsmyoder@goshen.edu>

Andrea Katalin Molnar

Andrea Katalin Molnar is Professor of Anthropology and Faculty Associate of the Center for Southeast Asian Studies at Northern Illinois University (USA). She is the author of *Timor-Leste: Politics, history, and culture* (2010), and is the current Executive Editor (SEA) for the journal *Asian Affairs: An American Review*. Her research and teaching interests include Indonesia, Timor-Leste, Southern Thailand, political anthropology, social structure, development, gender and language, conflict and peace, anthropology of religion, Islam, and religions of South-East Asia. Email: <akmolnar@niu.edu>

Lisa Palmer

Lisa Palmer is a senior lecturer in the School of Resource Management and Geography at the University of Melbourne where she teaches and researches in the fields of indigenous and local peoples' natural and cultural resource management. Since 2006 she has conducted fieldwork in Timor-Leste. She is currently chief investigator on an Australian Research Council research project in Timor-Leste entitled 'Reconnecting with Water: Lessons from a diverse economy'. Email: <lrpalmer@unimelb.edu.au>

Sandra Pannell

Sandra Pannell has a doctorate in anthropology from the University of Adelaide and works as a consultant anthropologist in native title and cultural heritage research. She has held positions at the University of Adelaide, James Cook University, The Australian National University, and the Rainforest Cooperative Research Centre in Cairns. She is the author of two books, one on World Heritage and the other on Indigenous environmental histories. She is editor of a book on violence, society and the state in Indonesia and co-editor of volumes on resource management in eastern Indonesia and Indigenous planning in northern Australia. Email: <sandra.pannell@bigpond.com>

Antoinette Schapper

Antoinette Schapper is based at the University of Leiden and works on Papuan and Austronesian languages on Timor and Alor. Her research focuses on grammatical description and understanding of the (pre-)history of languages in eastern Indonesia. Currently, she is writing a grammar of the central Alorese language Kamang and investigating spatial patterns of several Alorese languages. Email: <a_schapper@hotmail.com>

Elizabeth G. Traube

Elizabeth G. Traube is Professor of Anthropology at Wesleyan University (USA). She has longstanding research interests in Timor-Leste and is the author of *Cosmology and Social Life: Ritual exchange among the Mambai of East Timor* (1986). Recent publications have focused on contemporary perspectives of the legacy of resistance and the independence struggle. Email: <etraube@wesleyan.edu>

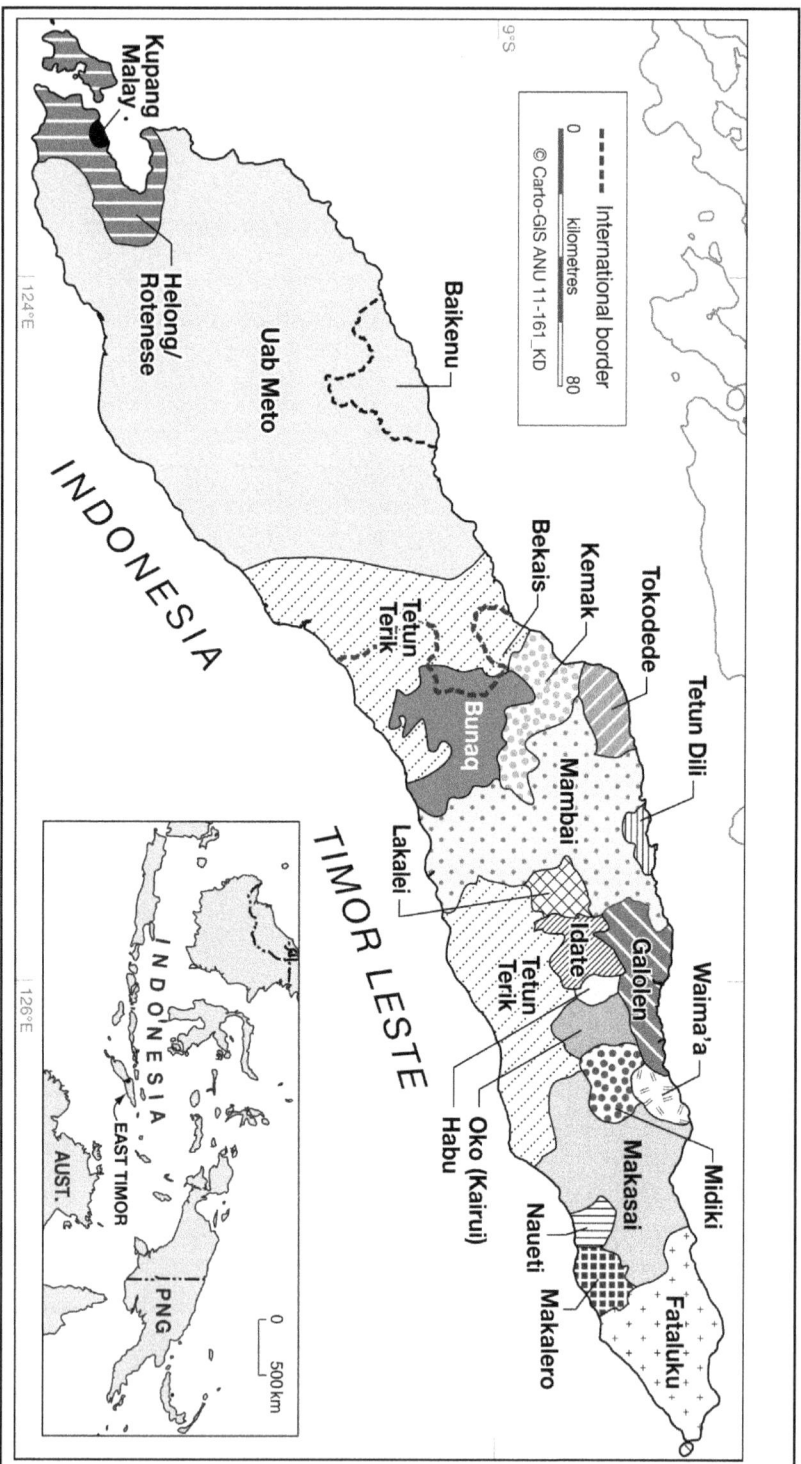

Ethno-linguistic map of Timor

The Australian National University, Carto-GIS

1. Land and Life in Timor-Leste: Introduction

Andrew McWilliam and Elizabeth G. Traube

Post Occupation

In the aftermath of the Indonesian occupation (1975–99) and the bittersweet triumph of the resistance struggle, Timor-Leste emerged as the first new nation of the twenty-first century.[1] The path to independence, however, was a rocky one and left a deep legacy of suffering and social dislocation. In the chaotic withdrawal of Indonesian forces, a final bout of violence, property destruction and population displacement left the half-island nation a smoking ruin under the protection of a multinational peacekeeping force: the International Force for East Timor (Interfet).

Ten years on, the process of rebuilding continues. A constitutional democratic system of parliamentary government has been established, oil and gas revenues now provide sustainable funds for much needed infrastructure, and government services are gradually being reinstated to support economic livelihoods for a growing population. Social life in the villages and scattered settlements is once again focused on the seasonal rhythm of agriculture and the rituals of exchange that mark life-cycle ceremonies and the conduct of rural sociality. Still, the path to a peaceful prosperity has not been without setbacks—most dramatically exemplified in the round of inter-communal violence and property destruction that erupted in the capital, Dili, during 2006. The intense period of civil disorder was fuelled by a powerful mix of ethnicised political and economic rivalries, corrosive youth unemployment and tensions over housing. If independence was built on the unity of struggle and shared suffering, the post-independence landscape is a more fragmented mosaic of crosscutting positions, competing claims and aspirations.

In the wake of these events and the opportunities afforded an open political environment for the first time in a generation, Timor-Leste has attracted the attention of a new wave of social-science researchers. Most are drawn to the island with a shared interest in exploring and documenting the aftermath of occupation and the diverse challenges of renewed nation building. The result is a growing body of anthropological research and analysis that charts the shifting

---

1   The Democratic Republic of Timor-Leste (RDTL) was officially declared (restored) on 20 May 2002.

fortunes of Timor-Leste society through the micro-politics of local communities adapting to changing circumstances (see Gunn 2007 for a preliminary review). In bringing together a selection of this work, the present volume marks the enthusiastic resumption of comparative ethnographic research in Timor-Leste following a long hiatus, or 'ethnographic gap' as Gunn describes it, when social research under Indonesian rule was actively discouraged.

The present volume is designed as a comparative appreciation of contemporary post-independence social life in Timor-Leste. It brings together a group of anthropologists and established researchers from Europe, the United States and Australia who have been pursuing extended ethnographic research among the diverse language communities of the island. Each of the contributing papers provides a unique perspective on situated processes of social renewal, emphasising the multiple ways that Timorese people are rebuilding connections with one another and their emplaced communities of origin and entitlement.

Central to these efforts of social renewal are the enduring associations that people assert and sustain with the land of their ancestors and the life-giving resources on which all families depend. These connections provide a common theme throughout the papers of the volume and one that underlines the long-term impact of internal displacement and resettlement policies that were widely practised under Indonesian military rule and previous Portuguese colonial governments. Independence has, for the first time in decades, provided opportunities for settlement choice and the possibility of return. At the same time, across Timor-Leste, people have heightened expectations of receiving public goods and services from the new nation-state. Thus, the theme of land and life also brings into view a series of salient framing questions as points of comparative analysis across Timor-Leste society. We interrogate, for instance, the complex ways that Timorese households are making and remaking their ties to land, whether in terms of mythically constituted places of ancestral origin, or to resettlement lands of more recent familiarity where investments in housing and construction preclude easy return to former village lands even if new land security remains uncertain. More generally, we ask what is the status of emplaced tradition and social authority for the majority of the rural population? To what extent do ritually maintained social alliances still guide the production of localities, inscribing connection and informing entitlement? How are different relationships to land implicated in nationalist discourse and the often-contested claims that coalesce around contributions to the national struggle for independence? These and related ideas of social connection and the production of emplaced relationships inform the contributing papers of the collection, providing comparative insights into the everyday worlds of diverse Timorese communities.

The Flow of Life in Timor-Leste

In exploring the theme of land and life in Timor-Leste, we seek to make explicit comparative association with the now classic volume edited by James J. Fox (1980) entitled *The Flow of Life: Essays on eastern Indonesia*. The book marked a significant shift in the direction of ethnographic research on eastern Indonesian societies, moving from a concern with prescriptive organisational structures of the kind developed under Dutch structural anthropology (Josselin de Jong 1977; van Wouden 1968) to an emphasis on more dynamic, shared categories of social reproduction expressed as 'metaphors for living' and typically encoded in pervasive dyadic forms. In his introduction to the volume, Fox noted that the contributing essays converged on a number of crucial social categories, many of them recognisably cognate and forming part of a much broader and shared Austronesian-language cultural heritage. This heritage included ideas around the traditional house and its architectural expressions of social and cosmic principles of order, the role of exchange and social alliance in the reproduction of community, and the general significance of symbolic classification and of certain prominent binary cultural categories expressed in social dynamics.[2]

Six of the 16 papers in *The Flow of Life* dealt with indigenous language communities of Timor—for the most part based on ethnographic research undertaken during the 1960s and early 1970s. This geographical emphasis reflected an increased anthropological attention accorded Timorese ethnography during the period, particularly among French and US-based researchers. Their work was informed by the prevailing style of structuralist theory, which encouraged a comparative appreciation of the common cultural heritage across the island and the complex patterns of alliance and classification that sustained the 'flow of life' among these communities. The contributors to that collection of papers included many of the prominent ethnographers of Timor at the time: Brigitte Clamagirand writing on the Marobo Kemak people of highland Bobonaro; Elizabeth Traube working with Mambai speakers in Aileu; Shephard Forman on Makassae social orders in highland Baucau; Claudine Friedberg on Bunak cultural practices in central Timor;[3] Gerard Francillon among Tetun speakers of Wehali (central West Timor); and the Dutch anthropologist Schulte Nordholt revisiting his earlier work among Atoni (Meto) speaking communities of West Timor, which encompassed the region of Oecussi—historically part of East Timor.[4] Taken

---

2 Elaborating upon what Needham (1978:12–13) once described as 'primary factors' in a society's symbolic classification and which Fox (1989:45) later expressed as 'symbolic operators'.

3 Friedberg collaborated with her husband, Louis Berthe, on Lamaknen Bunak ethno-botanical research in the border region between East and West Timor.

4 Notable omissions from the list of contributors to *The Flow of Life*, however, included Maria Lameiras-Campagnolo (1975), who pursued pioneering doctoral research among Fataluku speakers in Lautem district; David Hicks (1976), who completed research in Viqueque during the 1960s; and Clark Cunningham, who undertook long-term ethnographic work in West Timor about the same time. The legacy of other active

together, their contributions provided a sustained appreciation of social practices clustered around the mesh of cultural ideas and forms that connected each of the indigenous language communities of Timor into what has become a recognisably shared Austronesian cultural heritage.

It is also notable that *The Flow of Life* reported on a period of relative political stability in Timor. Despite increasing connections to the outside world, local communities in the still comparatively remote hinterlands and highlands had not been radically transformed by intrusions of modern politico-economic forces and communication technologies. To a significant degree, the depiction of rural Timorese society presented by *The Flow of Life* remained organised around predominantly ancestral principles and protocols, where the influence of the colonial state had a significant but limited impact on practices of social reproduction.

Much has changed in the interim, with 30 years of dynamic political history and economic change, and an aborted decolonisation process followed by a foreign invasion and sustained military occupation with its accompanying repressive simplifications. There have also been large investments in government services such as roads, communications, health and education, as well as the formation, persistence and eventual victory of a grassroots resistance movement. These factors have all contributed to a substantially altered cultural landscape and the kind of questions that might be asked of the contemporary ethnographic context.

The contributors to this contemporary companion volume to *The Flow of Life* offer a comparative appreciation of these earlier studies, but they also expand its ethnographic reach both in terms of incorporating new ethno-linguistic regions of Timor into the ethnographic record and in ways that extend and revisit some of the ideas and patterns of practice highlighted in the earlier work. The fact that among the contributors is one of the anthropologists whose research bridges the 'ethnographic gap' between pre and post- Indonesian occupation of Timor-Leste underlines the comparative relevance of the earlier work. Elizabeth Traube has re-engaged her research in Timor-Leste after many years of electing not to pursue field access. She is therefore uniquely placed to reflect on both continuities and transformations in customary communities over this period.

At the conclusion of his introduction to *The Flow of Life* (1980), Fox noted that the volume marked a new development in the comparative analysis of Austronesian societies. But he cautioned that while the forms of comparison in the papers had concentrated on a few prominent shared social categories, there

---

Portuguese anthropologists during the period, such as Antonio de Almeida and Ruy Cinatti, while not addressed here, represented the contemporary expression of a longstanding Lusophone research engagement with Timorese society—one that continues in sometimes convergent ways to the present.

was also a material basis to the societies under study, a basis on which other forms of productive comparison might be made (Fox 1980:18). This observation provides another point of departure for the present collection of papers, which, each in their different ways, integrate perspectives on the material conditions of social life in the sovereign Republic of Timor-Leste. More specifically, they address the different ways that Timorese people assert attachments and claims to place and landscapes of memory and belonging in the contemporary world.

In the process, the papers also engage the legacy of an expanded field of comparative analysis and understanding that developed out of the intellectual lead of *The Flow of Life*, but which was never specifically applied to questions of ethnography in the politically closed world of Indonesian-occupied Timor. The rapid expansion of ethnographic research from an appreciation of comparative Austronesian cultural ideas and meanings both in eastern Indonesia from the 1980s and in the pan-Pacific field of Austronesian-speaking societies highlighted the remarkable extent of a shared cultural heritage of common language origins. Ideas about the production of place, of topogeny,[5] precedence, stranger kings and the discourse of origins ramified across the expanded field of comparative Austronesian studies and found diverse application in areas such as prehistoric interpretations (see Bellwood 1996) as well as contemporary articulations of the cultural field (for example, Barraud and Platenkamp 1989; Fox 1989, 1993, 1995, 1997; Fox and Sather 1996; Vischer 2009). As Reuter has noted in a recent comparative collection of Austronesian-based ethnography that focuses on material and emplaced conditions of social life, 'territorial and social categories are often closely interlinked. Founders and newcomers are afforded a place in Austronesian cosmological models, and their harmonious interaction is no less integral to society than male and female is to the perpetuation of life itself' (2006:35). In the long-deferred return to ethnography in Timor-Leste, the contributors to this volume use these fundamental Austronesian ideas of place and place making, land and social connection as a critical lens through which to observe and investigate contemporary Timorese society and to explore their continuing relevance within a vibrant and politically transformed cultural landscape.

Portuguese Colonial Intervention

The complex mix of peoples on Timor is the product of multiple histories of migration and expansion into new territories. Archaeological, linguistic and cultural evidence suggests that the earliest inhabitants of the island were Papuan-

---

5   Topogeny is defined by Fox (1997:8, 91) as 'the recitation of an ordered series of place names', which is analogous with the recitation of a genealogy that indicates precedence in relation to an origin or starting point.

language speakers. Today Papuan-language speakers are located in central Timor (Bunaq) and in the eastern reaches of the island (including Fataluku, Makassai and Makalero speakers). These groups have interacted with, borrowed from and displaced as well as been displaced by Austronesian newcomers (see Schapper, this volume). Austronesian-speaking peoples first arrived in the region some 3000 years ago. From these, and probably subsequent, migrations of Austronesian speakers derive the majority of the languages now spoken on Timor (Fox 2000:3).

While the Austronesian immigrants came as settlers, other outsiders came to Timor for commercial purposes. By the fourteenth century, the island was already famous for its sandalwood and was visited regularly by Chinese and Javanese traders. The sandalwood trade also attracted Europeans. The Portuguese were the first to arrive and would be the last to leave. During the sixteenth century, Portuguese traders and missionaries established bases on the islands of Solor, Flores and Timor. Unions between the traders and native women gave rise to a Portuguese-speaking mestizo population, variously known as Topasses or Larantukans, who became the dominant force in the sandalwood trade. While the Dutch established themselves in Kupang, on the western tip of Timor, the Portuguese attempted, with little success, to assert control over the Topasses from Goa. In 1701, the first governor appointed by the Portuguese Crown took up residence in Lifao, originally a Topass-controlled settlement, on the north-western coast of Timor. But the Portuguese position remained precarious, as successive colonial governments faced opposition from the Dutch, the Topasses and indigenous groups. In 1769, besieged by the Topasses, the Portuguese Governor, Antonio José Telles de Menezes, abandoned Lifao and fled eastward to Dili.

From their new base in Dili, the Portuguese established fortresses along the northern coast and began looking eastward and southward, into the interior. But while the transfer of the capital brought some measure of security from Dutch and Topass attacks, the handful of Portuguese in Dili remained dependent on fragile alliances with local chiefs.[6] Until well into the twentieth century colonial rule was largely 'indirect', with the Portuguese endeavouring to insert themselves into local tributary arrangements. This required identifying local political authorities—a project that proved challenging for the colonisers and consequential for the local systems. Both the Dutch and the Portuguese had perceived western Timor as divided into the two 'empires' of Sonba'i and Belu (or Servião and Bello in Portuguese orthography). Leaving the accuracy of that characterisation aside, the situation was still more fluid in the east, where dozens of small local political communities were materialised through

---

6   Indeed, missionisation efforts were set back by the transfer, as they had to be begun again, with the peoples surrounding Dili (Durand 2004:57).

ritual performances and tributary arrangements. These communities were conceptualised as hierarchical orderings of named ancestral origin houses, which played determinate roles in annual seasonal rituals, the collection of harvest tribute and warfare. Leadership was dyadically distributed between symbolically immobile sacral authorities, oriented to the cosmic powers of the inside, and active executives oriented to the outside, responsible for regulating human affairs and protecting the boundaries of the realm. Not surprisingly, the Portuguese dealt primarily with the latter, who better fit European conceptions of rule. They contracted alliances with local leaders by distributing military patents, ranked from colonel to lieutenant, and insignia of rule, such as staffs, flags and military drums. The recipients pledged loyalty to the Crown and agreed to send tribute in kind (amassed from their 'subjects') to the Portuguese in Dili and to raise troops to assist them in punitive expeditions against 'rebellious' rulers. The Portuguese referred to such executive figures as 'kings' (*rei*) or 'rulers' (*regulo*) and to the territories perceived to be under their jurisdiction as 'kingdoms' or *reino*; the last term entered into and remains common in indigenous vernaculars. The term *rei* was later partially replaced with the Tetun title *liurai*—literally, 'he who crosses over the land'.

For Timorese executive leaders, both the military titles and the relationship to the outsiders they signified were a valuable political currency, while the obligation to help suppress rebellions could be used pragmatically in putting down one's own rivals. For the Portuguese, however, the system of tributary alliances became increasingly inefficient and unreliable. Today's loyal ally might be tomorrow's rebel, and no matter how many punitive expeditions they mounted, another revolt always ensued, leaving a legacy of periodic havoc with violent blood-letting including headhunting, the destruction of settlements and the enslavement of war captives (see Pélissier 1996). During the latter half of the nineteenth century, as Lisbon and The Hague negotiated a treaty that would formally assign to the Portuguese the eastern half of the island, as well as the enclave of Oecusse, the actual Portuguese ability to control this territory remained tenuous at best (Fox 2000:16).

Beginning in the late nineteenth century, however, the Portuguese implemented a series of initiatives designed to solidify, extend and rationalise colonial control. Administrative reforms linked Timor more tightly with Goa and Macau, and, after 1896, to Portugal as a direct colonial dependency. The introduction of coffee cultivation by Governor Affonso de Castro (1859–63) anticipated a shift away from the tributary economy and the development of an export plantation economy, which would require the 'pacification' of the interior (Gunn 2001:8–9). At the turn of the century, Governor José Celestinho da Silva (1894–1908) initiated a military campaign aimed at ending the chronic rebellions and transforming Timor into a properly civilised, Europeanised colony (Pélissier 1996:190); the military task was inherited and completed by his successor, Filomeno de Câmara. The two governors faced a common adversary in the 'kingdom' of Manufahi, where two successive rulers, Dom Duarte and his son, Dom Boaventura, resisted the tightening of colonial controls. Among Boaventura's grievances was the replacement in 1909 of tribute in kind with a cash-based head tax—a key element in colonial visions of socioeconomic development. Resentment of the head tax was widespread and resistance to it would prove long lived. Nevertheless, the defeat of the second Manufahi Revolt of 1911–12 marked a transition in Timorese–Portuguese political relations. If the rebellion had given expression to a deeply rooted anti-colonial sentiment—a persistent desire to expel the Europeans from the land—the Timorese collaborators mobilised in the campaign to suppress it became witnesses to the heightened level of military technology available and the extreme brutality directed against the defeated.[7] Between 15 000 and 25 000 people are estimated to have died in the 1911–12 campaigns—approximately 5 per cent of the population at the time (Durand 2009:73). The Manufahi Revolt thus taught Timorese that the potential costs of rebellion had risen sharply.

For the Portuguese, the rebellious Manufaistas confirmed their mistrust of the indigenous leadership. Over the next decades, the colonial government intervened more intensively in Timorese political affairs, replacing many traditional ruling families with their own appointees (Pélissier 1996:297–8). Intensified efforts to educate the sons of rulers created a small Europeanised, Catholic, Portuguese-speaking elite, who were recruited into an expanding colonial bureaucracy. Following the military pacification of the colony, the Portuguese imposed a uniform system of administration across the territory. The colony was divided into 10 administrative districts (*conçelhos*), each of which was divided into subdistricts (*postos*). In most subdistricts, the old 'kingdoms' were preserved as the next level of organisation, but they were conceived as purely administrative units, the leaders of which would receive and relay directives from the district and subdistrict administrators. Ignoring the local hierarchies of origin villages, the Portuguese treated these 'kingdoms' as fixed territories composed of residential villages, which were designated by the Tetun term *suku* (in Portuguese, *suco*) and further subdivided into hamlets (*aldéia*). The district and subdistrict heads were appointed from Dili and were typically European or mestizo; they in turn appointed the village and hamlet heads; the former, the *chefe de suco*, came to be addressed as *liurai*, though few of them came from traditional ruling lines.

While the administrative system was designed to fix individuals to specific territories, at least for purposes of taxation, the twentieth century also saw

---

7   Gunn (2001:7) observes that the implementation of the steam gunboat was crucial to Portugal's defeat of the Manufaistas.

a number of involuntary displacements of populations. The most dramatic took place during World War II, when the Japanese invaded and occupied Portuguese Timor (1941–45); some 60 000 Timorese are estimated to have died during the occupation, in reprisals for Timorese support given to Australian commandos, as well as in renewed intra-Timorese hostilities incited by the Japanese occupiers. After the war, when West Timor became part of the new Republic of Indonesia, Portugal, with Allied support, resumed colonial control of its easternmost province. The postwar decades of Portuguese colonial rule on Timor were characterised by mounting political repression (enforced through Prime Minister Salazar's secret police, the Polícia Internacional de Defesa do Estado or PIDE) and somewhat erratic projects of economic development, such as the Government's efforts in the 1960s to induce a shift of population to the south-east coast—a terrain seen as hospitable to intensive rice cultivation (Fox 2000:24).

In 1974 the abrupt overthrow of the Estado Novo in Portugal made decolonisation an imminent necessity. Without discounting its violence, Portuguese colonial rule would be taken to task more for neglect than for direct exploitation of the subject population. As a non-settler colonial power, the Portuguese had depended historically on mobilising some Timorese against others (Robinson 2001:283), and even the major twentieth-century 'pacification' campaigns were waged with indigenous support. The idea of transforming the Timorese into industrious, productive, civilised modern subjects was a persistent theme in Portuguese colonial ideology, but efforts at its realisation were lacklustre, while neither the massive relocation nor the extermination of the population was ever part of the Portuguese colonial vision. In a terrible irony, the people of Timor-Leste would experience the 24-year Indonesian occupation of their land as a greater threat to their existence than had 400 years of disparate Portuguese colonial rule.

Mobility, Origins, Displacement and Return

One of the enduring legacies of Indonesian occupation is the degree to which local Timorese populations were displaced and resettled as part of a sustained policy to reorganise Timorese society and promote compliant allegiance to Indonesian rule, what Philpott describes as the 'state articulated goals of prosperity' (2000:173). The actual extent of displacement and resettlement is not documented in detail, but it clearly affected the whole population at different times and in varying degrees.[8] Its impact and consequences continue to inform social and political agendas in contemporary Timor-Leste.

---

8   *Chega!* (CAVR 2005) provides a litany of emotional testimonies to the impact of these events across the country. In the absence of official documentation, more precise records of the impact of displacement and forced resettlement across Timor- Leste during the Indonesian occupation would require detailed field research to at least the level of each subdistrict to determine which hamlets (*aldeia*) were moved, where they were resettled and to what extent there has been a return to former settlement areas.

The early years following the military invasion were the most keenly felt in this respect. Fitzpatrick (2002:135), for example, cites Indonesian military statistics from 1978, reporting that 372 921 people were relocated into more easily controllable areas. Up to 150 camps, known as 'settlement areas' (*daerah pemukiman*), were established across the territory, with an average camp population of 2000 people. Budiardjo and Liem (1984:81) cite the example of Baucau, where, of the estimated 74 000 resident population of the largely rural district at the time, 61 000 people were forced to live in cramped conditions around the town of Baucau proper. A report of the situation noted that 'villages (*povoção*) as we knew them before the Indonesian invasion simply don't exist any more. All village life has stopped. Everyone has been brought together in the settlements around the *postos* [subdistrict centres]' (TAPOL report cited in Budiardjo and Liem 1984:76). Widespread food shortages and malnutrition were also common at the time and contributed substantially to a high number of reported deaths.

These excesses moderated over time as the territory was gradually brought under general Indonesian military control, but restrictive policies on settlement locations, population movements and cultural practices remained a constraining feature on social life for decades. Settlement relocation policies, particularly to roadsides and the edges of townships, facilitated surveillance and control of the population while permitting economies of scale in the provision of services. These strategies were consciously deployed in an effort to undermine political resistance by weakening perceived allegiances to oppositional cultural networks and authority. Ultimately, however, both coercive and persuasive techniques of rule failed to control the subject population, who, from 1983 on, expressed their disaffection via an increasingly effective clandestine resistance movement.

While these recent experiences of coercive displacement loom large in the dynamics of contemporary Timorese social contexts, they are not without precedent in the historical experiences of Timorese peoples. As we have noted, during the Portuguese colonial period, repeated expeditions to punish rebellious rulers, as well as a succession of militarised occupations in the form of the early twentieth-century Portuguese pacification campaigns, Japanese wartime occupation and the subsequent return of the Portuguese, have all contributed to periods of population upheaval and resettlement.

Although displacement took new and intensified forms under successive foreign occupations, it is not irreconcilable with traditional models of social life. On Timor, as throughout the Austronesian world, mobility is culturally constructed as an inevitable feature of social existence and is interwoven with ideas about origins. Ancestral narratives preserved in Timorese societies recount a potentially endless process of human migration and dispersal, as ancestors set out from named origin places to open up and settle new lands. Such stories of mobility revolve around separations and encounters. On the one hand, male ancestors divide their origin houses when they leave them and found new houses that stand to the source house as younger to elder sibling or, in a pervasive botanic idiom, as branch/tip to trunk. Such male-ordered ties between houses are ideally commemorated in rites that reverse the outward movements and reunite scattered house members at acknowledged origin sites. On the other hand, migration stories also describe encounters between earlier settlers and newcomers. These stories, which might be told from both perspectives, commonly conclude with the parties establishing a marital alliance in which immigrant men marry daughters of the original/earlier inhabitants and obtain rights in land in return for their labour and political support as co-residents.

To this extent, Timorese society is predicated on mobility and a cultural preparedness to relocate residence and adjust group relationships in the face of changing circumstances, while preserving connections to ancestral origin places left behind. Reuter (2006:14) describes the interplay of displacement and emplacement as central to defining identity and status in the Austronesian world, arguing that 'no matter how much displacement they might experience, their relationships with the land, their place of origin and their place of residence are matters of utmost importance to all people, and no less so to a people on the move'. In this context, the important consideration is less the nature of involuntary displacement, and rather more the particular conditions under which in-migrants and host communities reach (or fail to reach) negotiated agreements for shared arrangements.

Ironically, the massive displacement precipitated by the Indonesian invasion might have reinforced the cultural value of origin places. In 1975, many administratively created districts and subdistricts 'emptied out', people say, as civilians fled from the invaders behind Falintil.[9] While people conventionally speak of spending the years of exile in 'the forest' (Tetun: *ai laran*), they alternated between wild and settled spaces and called on their respective spirit guardians, the spirits of the outside associated with mountains and forest groves, and those of the inside who look after ancestral origin villages, where many people took refuge from the invading Indonesian forces. Moreover, after 1978, when Fretilin ordered the 'surrender' of civilians and turned its armed wing, Falintil, into a guerrilla force, resistance fighters continued to solicit help from the 'hidden world,' by way of its recognised human representatives; as we discuss later, many people regard the ultimate victory of the resistance as at least in part made possible by an alliance between the human and non-human realms. In short, under extraordinary political circumstances, many people might have come to feel an intensified connection to the sacred powers of the land and their human guardians.

---

9   Forças Armadas de Libertação Nacional de Timor Leste.

Ritual life was disrupted but not completely suspended during the occupation. While regular physical returns to ancestral origin villages were rendered difficult or impossible, the historical culture of mobility provided considerable flexibility. Indeed, the importance attributed to origin places encourages symbolic strategies for adapting to displacement. Thus, even under conditions of relative stability, any presently occupied sacred place is always understood as a lesser replica of one that is absent, a token of an encompassing type, and there are ritual techniques for linking the space of performances to other, hierarchically superior sacred spaces. For instance, symbolic contiguities might be asserted between a 'branch house' and its 'trunk house', which might be linked in turn, through oratorical and/or sacrificial practices, to a sacred mountain. During the occupation, conventional principles of substitution were enlisted to adapt to Indonesian policies that limited the scale of performances or precluded physical returns to origin places; Susana Barnes, for instance, notes that Nauete-speakers in Viqueque continued to stage 'simplified' harvest rituals and constructed makeshift storehouses for ancestral sacra. Through such means, people preserved the communication with their ancestors through which the unity of scattered house-groups is articulated.

Themes of origins, mobility, displacement and return resonate through the papers. Andrea Molnar's study of Atsabe Kemak communities in the uplands of Ermera accords analytical weight to the place of origins and mythical centres. Here the shifting histories of colonial politics, migration and dislocation have radically complicated social relations, but ideas of 'origin' and the various rhetorical strategies deployed to assert emplaced authority and relative status remain important narrative orientations for constituting and reconstituting the notion of community. Her chapter is explicitly comparative with Clamagirand's earlier ethnography of the mountain Kemak of Marobo (Renard-Clamagirand 1982), revealing in the process the contested nature of origin discourses and the shifting contours of political positioning that accompany all narrative histories.

Origins and mobility are also exemplified in Antoinette Schapper's linguistically inflected contribution exploring the historical expansion of Bunaq-language communities from their origins in the central highlands of Timor. The cultural landscapes of Bunaq, a non-Austronesian language, nevertheless illustrate their long-term engagement with proximate Austronesian speakers. Schapper highlights the complex historical processes of assimilation and adaptation that have accompanied expanding Bunaq settlement strategies in response to shifting political pressures and inducements.

Under Indonesian occupation, local authority structures organised on the basis of appeals to mythical origins held little sway in terms of land management and jurisdictional claims. Customary claims tended to be subsumed or marginalised by successive Indonesian Government regimes privileging their own political and developmentalist agendas. In post-occupation Timor-Leste, these older patterns of authority and mythical legitimacy are once again finding traction in the public domain. These ideas are well expressed in Lisa Palmer's contribution to the volume, which focuses not so much on land management as on water sources and the customary significance of water supplies that make life and livelihoods possible. In this case, her study explores cultural associations of groundwater flows in the karstic limestone country of Baucau including the town itself. The life-giving water that flows underground from the great origin spring of Uai Lia (water cave) feeds multiple subsidiary settlements downstream, enjoining them in complex mythical and sacrificial relationships of interdependency that have been partially obscured by state interventions to allocate flows.

For many, the liberation space of political independence offered an unprecedented opportunity for settlement return and the reclamation of ancestral entitlements and landed inheritance. Multiple households and close-knit communities have made this choice, reclaiming former settlement and garden areas in the emptied hinterlands of Timor-Leste and renewing their ties to their forebears by revisiting ancestral origin places and rebuilding sacred houses that had been neglected or destroyed. At the same time, decades of social engineering and control are not easily disentangled, particularly where customary protocols of settlement and resettlement were overridden by government authority or decree. For some communities, the desire to return is tempered by the advantages of proximity to services and the costs of starting anew. For others, the desire to remain is complicated by host-community resentments of their uninvited presence, even after many years of residence and the complications of intermarriage.

Susana Barnes discusses the social dynamics of what she calls a 'return to custom' in the south-eastern district of Viqueque. Her study reveals the complex adjustments and accommodations experienced by local Naueti communities in the process of reasserting cultural values and claims over defined ritual territories. They do so in a context marked by successive flows of in-migrants and outsiders settling on their lands and seeking livelihood spaces.

When the coercive resettlement policies of the Indonesian or the preceding Portuguese colonial regimes bypassed customary protocols and local authority structures, questions over the legitimacy of residence have frequently resulted in a variety of long-term protracted disputes. A sense of these patterns of negotiated mobility in Timor is illustrated in the contributing papers of the volume. Meitzner-Yoder's account of farming practices and relocation strategies in Oecussi highlights the creative persistence of customary arrangements, despite much reorganisation of village settlements in the enclave and the absence of any formal state recognition of local authority figures. The significance of historical mobility also features in Sandra Pannell's study, where she questions the common assumptions around seasonal farming and agrarian work as the principal historical livelihood strategy for Timorese rural communities. Arguing for the existence of more mobile practices of place making that allowed for adaptive adjustments to radical environmental uncertainty, Pannell considers the contribution of hunting and gathering to Timorese livelihoods, particularly in the low-population regions of eastern Timor, and argues that the diversity and flexibility of subsistence practices facilitated resistance to the Indonesian occupation. Nevertheless, the impact of Indonesian resettlement policies and political prescriptions based on idealised agrarian citizens continues to frame much government policy and planning and, according to Pannell, threatens to erase the multiple social interests and ancestral connections to forests and other non-cultivated spaces that have been emptied of their resident populations.

Ideas and claims extended to land and territory in Timor-Leste are inevitably expressions of landed authority and assertions of claim to a locally constituted legitimacy. These patterns are revealed in different ways among the contributing papers. Central to the process of asserting pre-eminence or political centrality is an appeal to continuities with ancestral foundations of settlement. The legitimacy of their claims and the political support they attract are based on narratives of ancestral itineraries and the lands on which the ancestors settled, farmed, fought over, died and were buried. It is also founded upon claims to a spiritual connection to ancestral lands, both in terms of direct sacrificial invocation to the ancestral presence and a commonly expressed cultural formulation of spiritual potency or agency, known as *lulik* (sacred, dangerous, taboo) and by the phrase *rai na'in* ('lord of the earth' in the lingua franca of Timor-Leste: Tetun), whose engagement or acquiescence confers legitimacy and landed authority to claimant groups.

Bovensiepen's study of Idaté-speaking farmers of highland Manatuto reaches similar conclusions. In their eventual return to ancestral lands following forced relocation to the regional town of Laclubar, Idaté households reflect on their experience of the *lulik* potency of the land that was mobilised discursively as a powerful weapon of resistance and warfare, and where the authority of narrative could transform *lulik* potentials into ruling power (*ukun*). As she notes, dis-empowering situations such as those suffered by Idaté during Indonesian occupation were inverted by attributing historical agency to the spiritual potency of the land. But while the *lulik* properties of the land remain a source of fertility and power, the long years of absence and neglect of reciprocal obligations to the land have engendered a degree of ambivalence and anxiety.

McWilliam's contribution, drawn from Fataluku ethnography, explores a related set of cultural ideas about emplaced authority and the spirit domain. Fataluku place-making strategies and claims are seen to reflect and refract broader Austronesian cultural themes of mobility, belonging and emplaced legitimacy. As among Idaté communities, Fataluku material wellbeing and prosperity are held to be dependent upon the spiritual and sacrificial dimensions of social life and the living landscapes from which they and their forebears have drawn sustenance. In meeting the challenges of colonial intervention, Austronesian binary metaphors for living remain powerful symbolic principles of authority and entitlement.

Timorese populations have experienced multiple periods of social and political upheaval in living memory. What is striking to the observer is their resilience in the face of personal or collective setbacks, and their capacity to reinstate customary practices while accommodating change in a radically altered world. Hannah Arendt (1958:176–8) described this sort of adaptive response as one of natality: 'the tendency for all human action not only to conserve the past, but to initiate new possibilities.' In the ethnographic case studies of customary land attachments presented in this collection, the possibilities and limits of Timorese natality are explored. The essays confirm the view that many of the cultural principles and practices that inform customary relationships to land remain intact in contemporary Timor-Leste. For all the disruption and reconfiguring of residential arrangements that have occurred in Timor-Leste, the social institutions of customary authority continue to provide a locally legitimate basis for organising emplaced social relations and asserting seniority and authority over defined jurisdictions. The point is reinforced in Jim Fox's own closing contribution to the volume which offers a range of comparative reflections on the collected papers and the continuing vitality of Timorese cultural articulations of traditional practice.

From Origin Land to Homeland: Changing cosmologies of place

Discourses of origin as customary modalities for asserting landed authority remain a dynamic arena for asserting and contesting claims to place in contemporary Timor-Leste, but it is also apparent that the impact of Indonesian military occupation and the long struggle for independence promoted new forms of imaginative connection to land and landscape, especially around the idea of the 'homeland': *Rai Timor*. The idea of a national homeland draws upon assorted origin discourses, but it also reconfigures them through an imaginative, though equally politicised, construction of nation and the nationalist struggle. The powerful rallying cry of resistance, 'the warriors of Maubere' (*Maubere asuwain*)—once a derogatory Portuguese label for peasant farmers—came to symbolise the unity of struggle for a cultural homeland and a national identity, one that transcended the particularities of local ancestral jurisdictions and created new cosmologies of place encompassing a unity of purpose.

But its stunning success notwithstanding, a grassroots nationalist resistance to Indonesian rule was not inevitable. Austronesian cultures, as we have noted, have rich symbolic resources for incorporating outsiders into local orders. On Timor, local political communities are traditionally represented as products of encounters between autochthonous or earlier inhabitants of the land and newcomers from the outside; the former surrender political power to the newcomers, while retaining ritual or spiritual authority, including the authority to legitimise political rulers. Versions of such diarchic arrangements are documented by Molnar, Bovensiepen, Traube, Barnes and McWilliam, who explicitly draw out their broader comparative context. With regard to the figure of the incorporated outsider or stranger king, McWilliam observes: 'The idea speaks to the historical processes of displacement in the Austronesian world of Timor whereby influential or powerful outsiders become chiefly rulers through distinctive cultural processes of incorporation.'

Despite prolonged if uneven local resistance to colonial rule, the Portuguese colonial administration overall became a beneficiary of these indigenous legitimising ideologies, even as the incorporation of ritual domains into colonial administrative systems tended to elevate local political chiefs over spiritual leaders (see Traube, Molnar, Barnes, and McWilliam, this volume). The Indonesian regime received no such dispensation. The extreme brutality of the invasion and of the protracted 'pacification' campaign that followed became seared in popular memory. The apparatus of state repression erected over the 1980s kept those memories alive, while the regime's efforts at persuasion also had the unintended effect of intensifying Timorese nationalism. The promotion of Indonesian literacy and the educational opportunities it enabled, while conducted with hegemonic intent, provided access to the world for a younger generation of East Timorese, who became central players in the resistance during the 1990s.[10] Even the regime's investments in material development tended to reinforce perceptions of its destructive character. A common theme is that the Indonesian presence had antagonised the spirit guardians of nature, prompting them to ally with the resistance, like the Idaté and Fataluku land spirits (Bovensiepen, McWilliam), or to rise up on their own, like the water spirits who, according to Baucau residents, subverted an Indonesian development project through quasi-guerrilla raids and are said to have celebrated the departure of the Indonesian forces (Palmer).

Elizabeth Traube's original encounter with Aileu Mambai in 1973 was mediated by local constructions of Portuguese overseas foreigners (*Malai*) as returning younger brothers who rightfully assumed political rule; in her chapter, she shows how Mambai excluded Indonesians from the category of *Malai* and from

---

10   As Benedict Anderson (1998:135) observes, fluency in Indonesian did for Timorese youth what fluency in Dutch had done to the young Indonesian nationalists 70 years earlier.

the stranger-king slot associated with it. She goes on to explore the ways in which traditional ideas of a landed spiritual authority have been reconfigured as 'the people' (*povu*)—a category that combines an ideology of obligation to givers of life with new notions of popular sovereignty. In Mambai conceptions, 'the people' brought the nation into being through their sacrifices: they 'purchased it' with their own lives, and the new nation-state owes them 'their livelihood' (*ro ni morin*) in return. Similar rhetoric of collective sacrifice and reciprocal obligation is widely used in post-independence Timor-Leste to make claims on the new nation-state. Of course, the association of shared suffering with national belonging is hardly limited to Timor-Leste and might be construed as a foreign importation. Taken together, however, the essays in this volume suggest a 'natalist' perspective on the imagery. Viewed as a new way of using the old idiom of origins to assert emplaced authority, the discourse of popular suffering appears as an Austronesian inflection of a national imaginary (Anderson 1983).

Timorese societies, as the case studies in this volume document, have traditionally maintained a strong sense of belonging to particular places. Descent groups of varying depth are referred to as 'houses' and their unity is materially embodied in named cult houses, located in settlements associated with ancestral founders. Ancestral settlements, in turn, were linked at a higher level into local political communities within which specific houses claim authority as original donors of land and of regalia of office. Models of community structure are articulated in ancestral narratives and, as the papers document, are subject to local contestation. But what needs emphasis here is the hierarchical nature of emplacement in these models. Regional origin narratives represent community formation as a top-down process wherein ancestral leaders establish asymmetrical alliances with other houses. In a recurrent motif, the ancestors order the community by distributing regalia of office that inspire sacred terror in the ruled; thus, Mambai say that flags, staffs and swords from overseas cause 'women and men to tremble and fear' (Traube, this volume), and Nauete ritual leaders claim to have delegated tasks by giving tokens to subsidiary houses 'so that those under their jurisdiction would have something to "believe in" or "fear"' (Barnes, this volume).

Rai Timor is not merely a more encompassing homeland than these local communities; it is imagined in a different way, as a territory shaped from below, collectively, by the ordeals of 'the people', who become the active originators of the nation. If the constitutive act of a subject in the traditional ideology of rule is to recognise and defer to authority vested in ritual and political leaders, the constitutive act of belonging to the nation is to suffer and sacrifice for it. Such investments establish an affective tie, a more personal and intimate sense of connection than, say, the feeling of respect for an origin mountain that

Molnar attributes to Atsabe Kemak. The mountain's represented tie, moreover, is to particular groups, whereas the nation is imagined as forged and sanctified through a struggle that mobilises the populace as a whole.

Ideas of shared struggle against the Indonesian regime thickened a sense of pan-ethnic 'Timorese' identity cultivated under common submission to Portuguese colonial rule and became the basis for asserting a horizontal solidarity of fellow sufferers. Even before formal independence, however, a counter-tendency was also evident to distinguish unequal degrees of suffering and equate them with unequal contributions to and even membership in the nation. The rumoured claim that 'easterners' (*loro sai*) had 'suffered more' than 'westerners' (*loro monu*) territorialised an emotionally charged symbol and animated what has been described as regionalism. Publicly, at least, the claim was invoked only to be repudiated by political elites and ordinary citizens alike as a divisive distortion of historical reality. The war, people rhetorically reminded one another, had been waged and won by 'the people as a whole', not by any one part or region, and consequently, any inequality in the division of rewards was unjust. This logic was explosively evoked by the so-called 'Petitioners'—soldiers in the new Timor-Leste Defence Force (Falintil-FDTL)—whose allegations that easterners within the military were discriminating against westerners precipitated the political 'crisis' (*crize*) of 2006.[11]

If distinctions within the category of 'the people' (*povu*) are formally rejected, it is a widely held premise that 'the people' as a whole have suffered more for the nation than have many leaders of the new nation-state, and this perceived inequity is a source of considerable bitterness. Differential suffering has become a potent idiom of populist protest, a way of criticising the national leadership and simultaneously making claims upon the state. What is at stake is never portrayed as purely economic. Rather, perceived inequalities of wealth and opportunity are interpreted in terms of popular concepts of justice. Whether it is a matter of local claims for reparations (often asserted against neighbours) or expressing more diffuse expectations of the state, demands for material and symbolic benefits are presented as moral transactions required to compensate parties who have suffered harm. In speaking as or for 'the people', individuals rhetorically appropriate the horizontally emplaced moral authority of those whose blood flowed into the homeland and demands restitution.

In the volatile post-independence milieu, the legitimacy of the nation-state is far from assured, nor can it be secured within any of the local origin places that

---

11   See McWilliam and Bexley (2008:67–8). In seeming to support the allegations of the Petitioners in a speech made in March 2006, Xanana Gusmão's rhetorical point was to reiterate the idealised unity of the wartime resistance community.

proliferate across Timor-Leste.[12] Rather, its stability will depend on persuading the rural majority and unemployed youth in Dili that the nation they fought for will sustain them and help them thrive. In this respect, all look to the national government and its ability to convert the benefits of burgeoning oil and gas revenues into tangible material improvements and opportunities on the ground.

As a regional contribution to comparative Austronesian studies, the present volume offers a sustained and selective focus on just one island region of the vast Austronesian-speaking world. This is a region where the vitality of Papuan or non-Austronesian societies reveals their cultural accommodation with Austronesian cultural ideas and forms. It is also a region where the complications of military rule precluded sustained ethnographic inquiry for decades, and meant that the vibrant cultural diversity of most Timorese language communities was generally excluded from comparative scholarly consideration. The present volume seeks to redress those shortcomings and in the process highlight something of the rich specificity of Timorese ideas and practice in the light of broader understandings.

References

Anderson, B. 1983, *Imagined Communities: Reflections on the origin and spread of nationalism*, Verso, London.

Anderson, B. 1998, *The Spectre of Comparisons: Nationalism, Southeast Asia, and the world*, Verso, London and New York.

Arendt, H. 1958, *The Human Condition*, University of Chicago Press, Chicago.

Barraud, C. and Platenkamp, J. D. M. (eds) 1989, 'Ritual and socio-cosmic order in eastern Indonesian societies', *Bijdragen tot de Taal-, Land- en Volkenkunde*, vol. 145, no. 4.

Bellwood, P. 1996, 'Hierarchy, founder ideology and Austronesian expansion', in James J. Fox and C. Sather (eds), *Origins, Ancestry and Alliance: Explorations in Austronesian ethnography*, Research School of Pacific and Asian Studies, The Australian National University, Canberra, pp. 18–40.

Budiardjo, Carmel and Liem, Soei Liong 1984, *The War Against East Timor*, Zed Books, London.

---

12   Although the charismatic appeal of Major Alfredo Reinado to westerners (especially Mambai) could be read as an index of deepening 'regional' division, it arguably owed more to a general lack of confidence in the state's commitment to justice, which Alfredo persuasively claimed to uphold.

Commission for Reception, Truth and Reconciliation in Timor-Leste (CAVR) 2005, *Chega!: The report of the Commission for Reception, Truth and Reconciliation in Timor-Leste—Executive summary*, Commission for Reception, Truth and Reconciliation in Timor-Leste, Dili.

Durand, F. 2002, *Catholicisme et protestantisme dans l'île de Timor: 1556–2003*, Editions Arkuiris, Toulouse and Bangkok.

Durand, F. 2009, *42 000 ans d'histoire de Timor-Est*, Editions Arkuiris, Toulouse.

Fitzpatrick, D. 2002, *Land Claims in East Timor*, Asia Pacific Press, Canberra.

Fox, J. J. 1980, *The Flow of Life: Essays on eastern Indonesia*, Harvard University Press, Cambridge, Mass.

Fox, J. J. 1989, 'Category and complement: binary ideologies and the organisation of dualism in eastern Indonesia', in D. Maybury Lewis and L. Almagor (eds), *The Attraction of Opposites: Thought and society in a dualistic mode*, University of Michigan Press, Ann Arbor, pp. 33–56.

Fox, J. J. (ed.) 1993, *Inside Austronesian Houses: Perspectives on domestic designs for living*, The Australian National University, Canberra.

Fox, J. J. 1995, 'Origin structures and systems of precedence in the comparative study of Austronesian societies', in P. J. K. Li, Cheng-hwa Tsang, Ying-kuei Huang, Dah-an Ho and Chiu-yu Tseng (eds), *Austronesian Studies Relating to Taiwan*, Symposium Series of the Institute of History and Philology: Academia Sinica 3, Taipei, pp. 27–57.

Fox, J. J. 1997, *The Poetic Power of Place: Comparative perspectives on Austronesian ideas of locality*, The Australian National University, Canberra.

Fox, J. J. 2000, 'Tracing the path, recounting the past', in J. J. Fox and D. B. Soares (eds), *Out of the Ashes: Destruction and reconstruction of East Timor*, Crawford House, Adelaide, pp. 1–29.

Fox, J. J. and Sather, C. (eds) 1996, *Origins, Ancestry and Alliance: Explorations in Austronesian ethnography*, Research School of Pacific and Asian Studies, The Australian National University, Canberra.

Geertz, C. 1996, 'Afterword', in Steven Feld and Keith H. Basso (eds), *Senses of Place*, School of American Research Press, Santa Fe, NM, pp. 259–62.

Gunn, G. C. 2001, 'The five hundred year Timorese funu', in Richard Tanter, Mark Selden and Stephen R. Shalom (eds), *Bitter Flowers, Sweet Flowers: East Timor, Indonesia and the world community*, Rowman & Littlefield, Lanham, Md, pp. 3–14.

Gunn, G. C. 2007, 'The state of East Timor studies after 1999', *Journal of Contemporary Asia*, vol. 37, no. 1, pp. 95–114.

Hicks, D. 1976, *Tetum Ghosts and Kin: Fieldwork in an Indonesian community*, Mayfield, Palo Alto, Calif.

Josselin de Jong, P. E. de (ed.) 1977, *Structural Anthropology in the Netherlands*, Martinus Nijhoff, The Hague.

Lameiras-Campagnolo, M. O. 1975, L'habitation des Fataluku de Lo'rehe (Timor Portugais), Thèse de doctorat de 3ème cycle, Université René Descartes, Sorbonne, Paris.

McWilliam, A. R. and Bexley, A. 2008, 'Performing politics: the 2007 parliamentary elections in Timor Leste', *Asia Pacific Journal of Anthropology*, vol. 9, no. 1, pp. 66–82.

Needham, R. 1978, *Counterpoints*, University of California Press, Berkeley.

Pélissier, R. 1996, *Timor en Guerra: le crocodile et les Portugais (1847–1913)*, Pélissier, Paris.

Philpott, S. 2000, *Rethinking Indonesia: Postcolonial Theory, Authoritarianism and Identity*, Macmillan, New York.

Renard-Clamagirand, B. 1982, *Marobo: une société ema de Timor*, SELAF, Paris.

Reuter, T. (ed.) 2006, *Sharing the Earth, Dividing the Land: Land and territory in the Austronesian world*, ANU E Press, Canberra.

Robinson, G. 2001, 'People's war: militias in East Timor and Indonesia', *South East Asia Research*, vol. 9, no. 3, pp. 271–318.

van Wouden, F. A. E. 1968, *Types of Social Structure in Eastern Indonesia*, R. Needham (trans.), Koningklijk Instituut voor Taal-, land- en Volkenkunde, Translations Series Vol. 11, Martinus Nijhoff, The Hague.

Vischer, M. (ed.) 2009, *Precedence: Processes of social differentiation in the Austronesian world*, ANU E Press, Canberra.

2. Origins, Precedence and Social Order in the Domain of *Ina Ama Beli Darlari*

Susana Barnes

Since 1999, communities across Timor-Leste have been engaged in what some observers have described as a 'resurgence of custom'[1] (Hicks 2007). This resurgence is most vividly associated with the rebuilding of sacred ancestral houses (Tetun: *uma lulik*), which were destroyed, abandoned or fell into disrepair during the course of the Indonesian military invasion and occupation. The reconstruction of these social and symbolic structures has occurred hand in hand with numerous other processes of restoration and renewal including: a return to settlements of 'origin' after years of displacement; the physical and/or symbolic laying to rest of the dead and disappeared at ancestral burial sites; and renewed participation in communal ceremonies and rituals associated with the agricultural calendar. The time, effort and resources entailed in these rituals of return and renewal suggest that such actions are more than a simple reaffirmation of self-esteem following centuries of foreign domination. They involve the rearticulation of distinct forms of sociality structured around networks of kinship and alliance, closely tied to specific claims to land and access to natural resources (Bovensiepen 2009; Fitzpatrick and Barnes 2010; McWilliam 2006, 2007, 2008; Meitzner Yoder 2005; Palmer 2007).

Underpinning the social and spatial relations invoked by rituals of restoration and renewal are distinct principles and practices that have displayed considerable adaptive capacity and resilience in the face of historical processes of encompassment such as Portuguese colonialism and the Indonesian military occupation (Babo-Soares 2004; Fitzpatrick and Barnes 2010; Fitzpatrick et al. 2008; Hohe 2002; Traube 2007). Key amongst these principles are those relating to 'origins' and 'precedence' (Fitzpatrick and Barnes 2010; Fitzpatrick et al. 2008; Hohe 2002; Molnar, this volume; Traube 2007). Precedence describes a concatenation of relationships where the relative status of a person or group is conceptualised and defined by reference to their proximity to a common point of derivation or 'origin' (Fox 1994; Lewis 1996; Vischer 2009). What constitutes a common point of derivation or origin might be the subject of considerable

---

1   There is some debate in Timor-Leste today regarding the nature and role of 'custom' or 'culture' in contemporary society. Certain customary practices have been criticised for being rooted in the past, for being patriarchal and unequitable, while others have been extolled as providing people with a sense of meaning, order and value. See, for example, McWilliam (2005); Trindade (2008); Brown (2009).

debate and is frequently contested, reversed or reordered. Claims to 'origin'-group status can be established by diverse means. Most commonly, these include oral histories recounting ancestral connections to the land, the possession of sacred artefacts connected to the ancestral past, and the presence of symbolic structures such as sacred houses or particular sites including ancestral burial groups and settlements of origin. Viewed in this light, the 'resurgence of custom' must be understood as part of a process of reaffirming ancestral connections to land and renegotiating relations of precedence following years of war and displacement, policies of resettlement and relocation, and restrictions on movement and cultural practice.

This chapter describes how claims to land and relations of precedence are currently being renegotiated in a predominantly Naueti-speaking locality in the south-eastern district of Viqueque. In particular, it explores discourses of origins and precedence from the perspective of one particular house-based group from the village of Babulo as it seeks to reassert its authority over subsidiary and in-migrant groups within a defined territory.

Background to *Suco* Babulo

The village (*suco*) of Babulo is located in Uatolari subdistrict, Viqueque district, on the south-eastern coast of Timor-Leste. The *suco* has a total population of 4136 (Direcção Nacional de Estatística 2004), the majority of whom are of the Naueti ethno-linguistic group.[2] A minority of inhabitants of Babulo are of Makassae origin and some individuals and families are of mixed ethno-linguistic descent. The majority of the population are subsistence farmers. Agriculture is based mainly on the swidden cultivation of maize, cassava, legumes and root crops. Irrigated rice is cultivated in the lowland areas close to the Bee Bui River and dry land (rain-fed) rice is also cultivated in the upland areas. Coconut and candlenut plantations provide many families and individuals with an important cash income. Hunting and fishing are also part of local subsistence strategies. While a limited number of families possess livestock such as water-buffalo (*karau-Timor*) and cows (*karau vaca*), many keep pigs, goats and chickens. Livestock is generally considered to be a valuable household asset and holds an important role in patterns of reciprocal exchange, which are at the heart of rural social relations.

---

2   Alternative spellings: Nauheti, Nauhete and Nauoti. According to census statistics (Direcção Nacional de Estatística 2004), the total number of Naueti speakers in Timor-Leste (over six years of age) is 11 361, of which 9832 reside in Viqueque district.

Prior to the Indonesian invasion, the people of Babulo lived in dispersed upland settlements or *baha*.[3] It was common for these settlements to comprise groups of agnatically related males, their in-married spouses and children. As a result of Indonesian strategies of control, the majority of the population is now settled along main roads or the administrative-post buildings in Uatolari Leten. Since independence, however, there has been a gradual trend towards re-establishing pre-1975 upland settlements. In particular, the older members of the community have chosen to return to these settlements while a younger generation continues to live in Indonesian-period villages. The choice to remain is often dictated by considerations regarding access to services such as education and health care.[4] Many people also maintain simple temporary shelters in their swidden gardens where they might stay during planting or harvesting season.

Administratively, Babulo is divided into eight hamlets called *aldeia*: Beli, Darlari, Aha Bu'u, Kotanisi, Roma, Liasidi, Abadere and Asamuta. All but one of these hamlets were established and named during the Portuguese period, and little was done during the Indonesian occupation or since independence to alter these administrative units other than change their name from *povação* (Portuguese) to *kampung* (Indonesian) and, most recently, to *aldeia* (Portuguese).[5]

The Portuguese authorities relied heavily on pre-existing social structures and hierarchies for territorial control, labour recruitment and revenue extraction. In Babulo, each hamlet continues to correspond broadly to a descent group along with their affines and dependants, sharing common ancestors and centred on a common *uma luli* (sacred house). Each descent group is subdivided into a number of lineages and sub-lineages (*uma kain*), each of which has its own 'branch' or subsidiary cult house. In the past, these subgroups formed the core of *baha* settlements and each subsidiary cult house was associated with a specific function and role within the ritual and social organisation of the broader descent group. Members of each branch of a common descent group are typically classified as *kaka* (older) and *wari* (younger) in relation to one another.[6] The members of 'older' houses are considered to be more closely related to the common ancestors of the group and therefore have authority over 'younger'

---

3   In Naueti, *baha* may mean both mountain and settlement.

4   Other considerations include the investment made in housing during the Indonesian period.

5   The *aldeia* of Roma was established after independence. The people of Roma are predominantly Makassae speakers.

6   Three broad social subcategories are found in Babulo and across Naueti-speaking communities. These are *liurai*, *reinu* and *ata*. The distinction between *liurai* and *reino* is similar to that of *wari* and *kaka*. *Reinu* (sometimes *povo* or people) groups are subordinate houses of each lineage or sub-lineage within a descent group. *Ata* (Naueti: slaves) groups are the lowest social category whose ancestors were former slaves or war captives. Intermarriage between these groups was traditionally forbidden.

houses. The senior male members of the 'eldest' house of each descent group are often referred to as *Na'i* (Tetun: master) or *Bu Dato* (Grandfather Lord), and are considered to be the direct descendants of the groups' ancestors.[7]

Complex dynamics of kinship, marriage and long-term alliance bind the principal descent groups around which the administrative units of *aldeia* are structured.[8] However, it is unclear how long these groups have considered themselves to form part of a larger unit such as a *suco*. The village headman (*liurai* or *chefe suco*) of Babulo is traditionally 'selected' from the hamlets of Aha Bu'u and Kotanisi.[9] These hamlets represent two lineages of the same descent group, originally called Burmeta.[10] Informants suggest that the ancestors of the Burmeta emerged as political leaders in the area by threat of force and through strategic marriage alliances with local house-based descent groups.[11]

Despite a history of considerable in-migration during the late colonial period, followed by massive displacement and forced relocation of the population from the upland areas surrounding Matebian Mountain during the Indonesian occupation, *aldeia* and *suco* composition based on group membership has remained unchanged. As a consequence, approximately 50 per cent of the population currently residing in Babulo is originally from the neighbouring *suco* of Afaloicai and remains under the jurisdiction of their own hamlet and village chiefs. Although many of the people from Afaloicai have long been settled in the area, they continue to maintain physical links with their ancestral lands and make a clear distinction when speaking about their place of residence and place of origin. By the same token, while there is a long history of social interaction between the people of Afaloicai and Babulo, in particular through marriage alliances, many local groups continue to view people from Afaloicai as in-migrants with limited and sometimes temporary rights to access land and other natural resources. This apparent administrative anomaly is not

---

7   Hamlet chiefs are usually drawn from the members of the 'eldest' house—usually, the son (or nephew) of one of the senior male members.

8   Traditionally, members of each descent group are exogamous and must seek marriage with members of other groups. Marriage establishes the basis for reciprocal relations between groups who become wife-givers (*uma ana*) and wife-takers (*oa sae*) in relation to one another. In practice, it seems that marriages do occur between members of lineages and sub-lineages although these are often frowned on. Members of *liurai* lineages may not marry their subordinates and must *buka liurai* (seek marriage with other *liurai* groups).

9   While 'democratic' elections for the positions of *chefe suco* and *chefe aldeia* were held in 2004–05, as in other parts of Timor-Leste, in Babulo, only members of the recognised lineage were permitted to nominate themselves as candidates. Local informants state that candidates had to be members of the *liurai* family of Aha Bu'u or Kotanisi (descendants of Burmeta), in accordance with the ancient *juramento* that existed between the Burmeta and Darlari.

10   The Darlari refer to the people of Aha Bu'u and Kotanisi as Burmeta. The people of Aha Bu'u and Kotanisi acknowledge a common ancestor called Boru Buti. According to one informant, the name Burmeta was used to refer to warriors who came from Matebian Mountain. In Makassae, Matebian Mountain is also called Bere Meta-Bere: (Big) Meta (Black).

11   This interpretation of events reflects Fox's variation on the theme of the stranger king whereby the powerful 'outsiders' are installed 'inside' as local chiefs through processes of incorporation (Fox 1995).

uncommon in Timor-Leste. In the case of Babulo, it reflects the way in which the administrative units of hamlet and village were established and fixed during the Portuguese period. And it calls attention to how attachments to land are linked to local discourses of origin and precedence that underpin these colonial structures.

The Darlari Domain

In Babulo, hamlet and village administrative units, and the concomitant offices of hamlet and village chief, are considered to be relatively 'new', foreign structures, associated with 'external' relations between the community and outsiders—in particular, the state. The underlying community of house-based groups, on the other hand, forms 'old', autochthonous structures dealing with the 'internal' management of collective social and ritual relations within and between house-based groups.

Within the traditional community, members recognise the authority of specific 'origin groups' over defined territories or domains. Origin-group status is predicated on interrelated notions of ancestry, attachment to place, histories of migration and settlement and networks of alliance. In Babulo, one such group is composed of the 'eldest' houses, or senior lineages, of the hamlets of Beli and Darlari.[12] These groups represent the lineages of two brothers who were the direct descendants of the mythical founders of an ancient kingdom called Bubulu.[13]

According to local *tete bo'ona* (Naueti, lit.: oldest stories), the sibling ancestors of Beli and Darlari lived together near Baha Liurai, the ritual centre of their land and burial site of their ancestors. Both were entrusted with the custodianship of their ancestors' sacred land (*rea luli*) and sacra (*sasan luli*). One season, when the time came for them to harvest their rice fields, the brothers agreed that one of them would go and harvest their portion of rice while the other guarded the sacred land and sacra at Baha Liurai.[14] The elder brother (Beli) went to the fields first, while the younger (Darlari) waited silently for his brother to return. When the elder brother arrived at the fields, he saw that his harvest was plentiful and

---

12   The origin names of the descent groups that comprise the hamlets of Beli and Darlari are deemed sacred and may not be spoken. In everyday exchange and even during communal rituals, these groups are referred to using their hamlet denominations. The principal cult houses of Darlari are commonly referred to as the Um Buti (white house) and Um Ita (black house). Beli, on the other hand, have a single principal cult house, referred to simply as Um Luli (sacred house). The 'real' names of these houses are linked to the descent-group genealogies seldom disclosed to outsiders.
13   In Darlari origin narratives, Babulu is presented as encompassing 'all the land over which the sun reigns'. The narrative of ancestral origin focuses on the exploits of the Mane Hitu (seven brothers), the offspring of a human female and a crocodile male, who reached Timor Island from the sea and took possession of the land.
14   These rice fields are called Lia Kakeu and continue to be farmed by Darlari.

he was happy. Once he had finished harvesting, he returned to Baha Liurai so that the younger brother could go and attend to his crop. While the younger brother was away, however, the elder brother did not keep silent vigil over the sacred land and sacra but started celebrating the success of his harvest with singing, drum playing and dancing. In the meantime, the younger brother reached the rice fields but he could not find any of his own crops. When he returned to Baha Liurai and found his elder brother revelling, he flew into a fit of rage and grabbed the drums and other instruments, breaking them.[15]

By neglecting his duties to the ancestors, the elder brother had caused the younger brother's harvest to disappear. The brothers fought and decided to separate. The elder brother was banished from the sacred land of his ancestors and had to settle on land belonging to his wife-givers (*uma ana*).

The transgression of the elder brother and his exile to the territory of his wife-givers serve to justify the reversal of common concepts of authority based on genealogical precedence. As a consequence of the actions of their ancestors, the *liurai* lineage of Beli forfeited their right to claim status as heirs to the domain of their mythical founder-settler ancestors. This privilege was bestowed and retained uniquely by the male-line descendants of the younger (Darlari) brother who remained at Baha Liurai. Members of the senior Beli and Darlari houses continue to acknowledge their sibling status through the use of the terms *kaka* and *wari* (elder and younger), while other groups living on their ancestral lands related through marriage or long-term alliance refer to them collectively as *Ina Ama Beli Darlari* (Mother Father, Beli Darlari).[16] In recognition of its senior status, the *liurai* lineage of Darlari is accorded the title of *rea bu'u* or 'lord of the land'.[17] This is also expressed as *rea mumu, rea uato* (rod of the land, rock of the land) in formal ritual speech. Today, the authority of the 'lord of the land' is embodied in the headman (*Bu Dato*) and former *chefe povação* of Darlari. He shares this responsibility with two other senior Darlari members, one of whom 'sits and watches' over the ancestral sacra placed in the main Darlari cult houses, the *um buti* and *um ita* (white house and black house).

---

15 To this day, it is generally forbidden to play music or dance at Baha Liurai; however, exceptions are sometimes made for young children and when the elders wish to listen to the radio.

16 Darlari and Beli elders presented two versions of this narrative to the author on separate occasions. Both original narratives conform to this summary. They differ only with regards to the significance of objects that the elder (Beli) brother took with him to his exile. In the Darlari version of events, the elder brother left with no ancestral sacra. In the Beli version, the elder brother took with him the drums and instruments that were the cause of his exile. With time, these objects have become sacralised in their own right.

17 The term *in bu'u(n)* in Naueti literally means 'lord' or 'owner'. It may, however, also be translated as 'grandfather', 'ancestor' and sometimes 'spirit'—understood as a non-human entity. *Rea bu'u* = owner of the land or lord of the land; *uai mata bu'u* = owner of the spring; *rea bu'u* = owner of the land; *kai bu'u* = owner of the forest, and so on.

As 'lord of the land', the Darlari elders are the chief stewards of their ancestral lands.[18] Darlari elders claim that the 'original' boundaries of their domain extend far beyond current *aldeia* or even *suco* boundaries. They argue that these boundaries were established long ago (before the arrival of the Portuguese), often as a result of conflict with neighbouring groups and agreed upon by means of sacred oaths, or *juramento*.[19] However, they also recognise that throughout the colonial period their land was slowly encroached upon as the colonial authorities extended their control over the territory, often favouring powerful neighbouring kingdoms.

To the north and north-east of their domain, the Darlari identify two groups referred to as *ki butana/ki itana* (people of the white children/people of the black children); these correspond roughly with the principal descent groups that make up the *aldeia* of Liasidi (*ki itana*) and Balabaciba, Vessoru (*ki butana*), which are related to the Darlari through marriage. To the northwest, Darlari recognise the kingdom of Builo against whom their ancestors fought a fierce battle to establish a border.[20] To the east and west of Darlari (and Beli) lands, along the coastal plain, the descendants of an in-migrant group from Luca now dominate. Darlari claim, however, that in the past their authority extended as far as present-day Lughasa, close to the border with Viqueque subdistrict.[21]

While the Darlari elders continue to contest the boundaries of their domain in private, they are reluctant to make these claims public, as they believe this might stir up unnecessary and perhaps even violent conflict with neighbouring groups. To legitimise their claims, they refer to ancestral histories and name specific sites where the ancestors are believed to have landed, settled, farmed, fought, died and were buried. These sites are marked by physical features such as rocks, springs and specific areas of old-growth forest as well as symbolic structures such as stone altars, ancestral graves and particular *uma luli* (sacred houses) where ancestral sacra are stored. The memory of these histories and the significance of these sites are preserved through local *tete bo'ona* (histories) and reinforced through specific rituals associated with place. Many of these sites are considered to be *luli* (sacred) and access is restricted, or must be mediated through communication with the ancestors and *bu'u* (spirits) that guard them.

---

18   In the past (and perhaps in the present), 'lord of the land' status also gave rights to demand labour and services from other kin-group members.

19   These *juramento* took the form of blood-oaths and are considered to be *luli* (sacred)—broken on pain of death or some other form of ancestral retribution.

20   Builo is a mountain located within the ancestral lands of the kingdom of Ossurua, which is a predominantly Makassae-speaking area. The author visited this area and heard similar stories of conflict with a kingdom to the east (Babulo). They also confirmed histories of the 'passage' of representatives from Luca on their way to the Uatolari plains.

21   Of interest is the distant connection with Naueti speakers in the Beasu area of Viqueque. This group appears to me an anomaly in the spatial distribution of Naueti language (cf. Hicks 2007:245). Informants from Babulo, however, claim that these are descended from war captives who were taken to the coastal area to be 'traded' for firearms.

Histories of Incorporation and Accommodation

Ancestral itineraries and histories serve not only to reinforce the emplaced nature of claims to authority, but also to reaffirm the order of arrival and settlement of various descent groups living within these territories. At the same time, these narratives provide a guide to understanding the dynamics and processes whereby subsidiary groups were formed and in-migrant groups were incorporated into the social order (Lewis 1996). Darlari elders offer two interrelated and recursive narratives to determine precedence and explain the nature of social relations within their territory. One is concerned with the history of land allocation and the other explains the delegation of tasks or duties to subsidiary houses and in-migrant groups.

The Darlari elders represent the highest ritual or spiritual authority within a domain, which incorporates numerous house-based descent groups. Although Darlari elders claim that in the past their ancestors held both ritual and jural power over the territory and people of their domain, they acknowledge that at some stage in their history, their forefathers began to 'retreat into darkness', delegating specific tasks to members of other house-based groups. Ostensibly, the elders state that this 'retreat into darkness' was a conscious decision in order to keep the secrets of their land from 'outsiders'—in particular, the colonial authorities (and the Catholic Church).[22] However, they also acknowledge that the delegation of tasks to other groups was a means of appeasing subsidiary lineage houses and in-migrant groups that represented a potential threat to their authority. Similarly, the allocation of land as part of 'traditional' contracts including *juramento* (solemn oaths) or intermarriage was (and continues to be) used as a means of incorporating in-migrant groups into local social and political structures.

Today, the Darlari elders claim that within their domain there remains no 'unused' or 'unallocated' land. They state that long ago their land was divided into five areas corresponding to the five main 'houses' of the Darlari descent group.[23] Members of these houses gain access to land by virtue of their genealogical relation to the common Darlari founder-settler ancestors. To continue to benefit from the land and natural resources, members of these houses are expected to

---

22 The *Makaer* (spokesperson) for the senior Darlari house explained that their forefathers delegated these tasks to other houses because they wanted to be 'above' the everyday matters of managing their 'kingdom'. Rather than a sign of weakness or loss of power, this 'retreat' into darkness becomes a source of strength. In the context of independence—having resisted 'outsiders' and maintained their identity—this has become a means to legitimise attempts of the Darlari elders to reimpose their authority.

23 Darlari informants state that these territorial divisions are well known and marked by physical features such as streams, hills and rocks. Nevertheless, these demarcations do not represent five distinct units but rather a patchwork of holdings scattered across the domain, reflecting traditional farming practices based on shifting cultivation.

fulfil their ritual and social obligations to members of superior houses and the ancestors. Failure to do so is believed to incur the wrath or displeasure of the ancestors and might result in some form of misfortune, illness or death.[24]

Darlari elders also state that their ancestors delegated the task to monitor the use of land and natural resources—*lai bosa, lai wai* (Naueti: guard the fields, guard the water)—to one of the sub-lineage houses (*um kain*) of Darlari called the *uma kabo*. Later, according to local histories, the main representative of the *uma kabo*, the *Kabo Rai*, asked the *Bu Dato* to grant his house a token of office so that those under its jurisdiction would have something to 'believe in' or 'fear'.[25] As a result, the Darlari elders state that a *Makaer Luli* (keeper of the sacra), a ritual specialist, was appointed to assist the *Kabo Rai* in his task.

The *Kabo Rai's* function is practical: to monitor land use and access to natural resources, including the application of seasonal prohibitions on the harvesting of various products, collecting tributes for collective ceremonies and/or exacting fines for the infringement of prohibitions.[26] They are assisted in these practical tasks by representatives of two other subsidiary houses of Darlari: *Asu Rati Reino* and *Asu Rati Liurai*.[27] The role of the *Makaer Luli* on the other hand is more spiritual: presiding over collective rituals, acting as an intermediary with the spirit world, and 'watching over' the sacra held in the *uma luli* at Burlalu.

One of the principal in-migrant groups comprises the descendants of Burmeta. Today, this group is divided into two lineages corresponding to the *aldeia* of Aha Bu'u and the other Kotanisi.[28] Darlari describe the descendants of Burmeta as *asuwain* (warriors) and claim they arrived in the area some eight generations ago. The origins of the Burmeta are contested. Some claim they are *liurai* who came from the east of Matebian Mountain in search of land while others claim they were banished from their ancestral lands. Darlari elders claim that the Burmeta stopped and camped on land close to Baha Liurai on their way to offer vassalage to the kingdom of Luca. Rather than let these warriors join forces with their strong neighbour, the Darlari ancestors offered the Burmeta some land on which to settle and in exchange asked them to protect the borders of their domain.

---

24   The obligation to participate in regular communal ritual is essential to the production and reproduction of discourses of origin on which the social organisation of the community is structured.

25   Although local informants insist this is an autochthonous title, *kabu* appears to be derived from the Portuguese military rank *cabo*. *Kabo Rai* is a Tetun term.

26   Although most claimed to be children at the time, a number of older informants remembered the practice of collecting tribute for the yearly rice harvest. Today, the *Kabo Rai* continues to inform the 'lord of the land' of activities affecting land and natural resources. For example, the author was present when the *Kabo Rai* informed the Bu Dato that a local in-migrant family from Afaloicai had asked to build a permanent, cement-block house on their land. In order to do so, the family was to present a large pig at the communal rice-harvest ceremony.

27   It seems likely that the term *Asu Rati* is a corruption of the Portuguese term *ajudante*, or assistant.

28   Sometimes Kotanisi is referred to by its Naueti name, Kaidu.

To the Burmeta, the Darlari ancestors gave the title of *ana bo'ona, ana tadana* (the eldest and wisest son). This group was designated the task to *lai reinu, lai rea* (guard the people, guard the land), to rule over the people and protect the borders of the domain. More specifically, this group became known as the gatekeepers (*ita mata, kai hene*: door and gate) between the traditional 'inner' community and 'outsiders'—in particular, the colonial authorities.

The Portuguese granted the title of *Tenente Coronel* to the head of the Burmeta clan, and traditionally, *chefe suco* (village headmen) are chosen from this group. Members of this group stress that they were granted authority to *ukun* (Tetun: rule or govern) over the people of Babulo *suco* when they received a *rota* (a staff often used as a symbol of office) from Viqueque.[29] They describe their role in terms of local governance in relation to the state. In the past, this entailed specific duties and responsibilities regarding the settlement of local disputes, the collection of taxes (for the colonial authorities) and the recruitment of labour for colonial or state projects. Today, they continue to consider the role of the *chefe do suco* as an intermediary between the local community and the state, or other 'external' parties such as national or international non-governmental organisations.

Often described as the right and left hands of the Bu Dato, the descendants of the Burmeta and the offices of the *Kabo Rai* and *Makaer Luli* have come to represent jural and ritual power respectively within the Darlari domain.[30] The delegation of authority to these groups and dualistic structures of authority created in the process reflect common patterns and themes observed throughout Austronesian societies (Fox and Sather 1996). Darlari elders are keen to point out that the power of these groups is always subordinate to the authority of the *rea mumu, rea uato* (lord of the land).[31]

---

29   During the eighteenth and nineteenth centuries, the Portuguese colonial authorities granted military titles to local potentates. The rank of *tenente coronel* was usually superseded by the *dom* (de Menezes 2006). On the coastal plain of Uatolari, the rulers of the kingdom of Vessoru/Uaitame were given the rank of *dom*. Local informants from Darlari, however, claim that this dom was in fact a descendant of the Luca Dom who had been sent to broker peace between Babulo and Builo. The history of the kingdom of Luca is fertile ground for further research.

30   Today, the Uma Buti and Uma Ita of the Darlari represent the centres of ritual power but are politically weak. They are often juxtaposed with the *um luli* of Bur (Boru) Lalu and Bor(u)laisoba, which are now politically powerful but ritually weak. See Trinidade (2007) for more details on dualist power structures.

31   As proof of their seniority, the Darlari elders explain how they gave the Burmeta and the *Kabu Rai/Makaerluli* a number of sacred objects believed to have belonged to the Beli/Darlari ancestors. The objects given to the Burmeta are stored in an *uma luli* at a place called Burosoba. To ensure that the political leaders of Burmeta did not try to usurp the ritual authority of the Bu Dato by trying to handle and harness the power of these sacred objects, a second *Makaerluli* was appointed to guard the objects and control access to this house. The sacred objects given to the *Kabu Rai* and the *Makaerluli* on the other hand were placed in an *uma luli* built at Burlalu. This site was chosen as it was believed to have been the first place the founding ancestors settled on their arrival in the area from the sea.

Another in-migrant group closely associated with the Burmeta lineages now makes up the majority of people of the *aldeia* of Roma. Many Darlari and Aha Bu'u informants refer to this group as 'the *aldeia* without land'. The *aldeia* of Roma was established after independence. The members of the Roma group— locally known as Laka Roma—represent a group of *ata* (slaves) originally from Quelicai who traditionally served the *liurai* lineages of Aha Bu'u and Kotanisi. According to one history of the origins of this group, the Laka Roma served a *liurai* of the Burmeta descent group who lived in exile near Quelicai. When the *liurai's* family eventually asked him to return to Babulu and become the chief *liurai*, he agreed on condition that he could bring 'his people', who were 'stuck' to him like the 'seeds of a long grass' called *laka roma* in Makassae.

The Laka Roma were not granted specific areas of land on which to farm or settle by the Darlari 'lord of the land', but were servants of the chiefly houses of Aha Bu'u, Kotanisi and Darlari. In the past, one of the main tasks of the Laka Roma was to watch over the buffalo of their masters. Local informants state that in time the Laka Roma started farming land near the animal enclosures or land where they regularly took the animals to pasture. Many members of this group now claim these areas of land as their own, based on long-term occupancy.

The third, most recent and largest group of in-migrants was originally from the neighbouring *suco* of Afaloicai. Locally, people broadly distinguish between three movements of people from Afaloicai to Babulo. The first group, mainly from the hamlets of Buibela and Lena, arrived sometime in the 1930s in search of land. The second group came during the post-war period, at first seasonally, to work in the rice fields that were being 'developed' on the Uatolari coastal plain, and later settled more permanently in the area. The third group was forcibly displaced from their villages of origin as a result of the Indonesian invasion and 'relocated' following the 'surrender' of civilians from the resistance stronghold at Matebian Mountain in 1979. The way in-migrants from Afaloicai gained access to land on which to farm and settle depended on the circumstances of their arrival and the level of engagement with the Darlari 'origin group', their kin and affines. In-migrants from Afaloicai, however, do not appear to have been incorporated into the local social order in the same way as the descendants of the Burmeta or the Roma. They were not 'installed on the inside' (cf. Fox 1995) by taking up a specific role or rank within the social hierarchy of the Darlari domain.[32] They remained organised according to their own house-based descent groups, hierarchically ranked and ordered in accordance with their own

---

32 One could speculate numerous reasons why the people of Afaloicai were not fully integrated into the local social order—for example: timing, as migration occurred after wars of pacification. The local power of the Darlari 'lord of the land' was waning and the Portuguese were firmly in control and installed in the *posto* at Uatolari. It is possible that an alliance was made between the rulers of Afaloicai and the descendants of the Burmenta. The leadership of these ruling groups was later embroiled in the 1959 rebellion against the Portuguese.

histories of origin and precedence. Their residence on Darlari lands is often viewed as temporary, and in the context of communal rituals the people of Afaloicai are often referred to as 'the people who use the land for farming and gardening'.

Some suggest that in-migration in the 1930s was triggered by constant conflict between petty-kings around the area of Matebian, which led to the fragmentation of Afaloicai into three distinct *suco* (Afaloicai-Baguia, Afaloicai-Uatolari and Afaloicai-Uatocarabau) and forced some people to leave their land.[33] Others believe that the newly appointed *chefe suco* of Afaloicai-Uatolari, who was not of the 'ruling' houses of Afaloicai, wanted to move closer to the Portuguese colonial authorities at the *posto* (subdistrict centre) that had recently transferred from Tualo on the coast to Uato-Lari near Babulo Mountain. Still other informants, such as the current *chefe suco* of Afaloicai, state that increased population pressure, poor soils and difficult farming conditions in the rocky foothills of Matebian all contributed to the decision to migrate towards Babulo and other locations near the coast.[34]

Local informants recall that *Liurai* Gregorio, originally from the hamlet of Lena, arrived some time before the arrival of the Japanese. The elders of *aldeia* Darlari claim that *Liurai* Gregorio and his people arrived with some fanfare—accompanied by drums and whistles—and set up camp on *rea luli* (sacred land) near Baha Liurai. However, it was not long before they started falling ill because they had not respected the prohibitions associated with this land. As a result, *Liurai* Gregorio approached the Darlari elders and asked them for some land on which to settle and farm. A marriage alliance was established between the two groups and as a son-in-law, Liurai Gregorio and his people were offered some land to farm and settle. They settled at a place called·*Tua Rae Laleo* (shelter of palm wine leaves) and were also given land on which to farm at a number of sites around present-day Uatolari Leten and Kampung Baru.

Access to this land is mediated and managed within the framework *oa-sae/uma ana* relations (marriage relations). Throughout Timor-Leste, marriage alliances establish a set of reciprocal social and moral obligations between families and groups. Through marriage into the Darlari 'origin group', *Liurai* Gregorio and his followers were integrated into the broader community by entering into local

---

33 Informants from Babulo and Afaloicai also suggest that the Portuguese colonial authorities and their allies from the kingdom of Luca purposefully divided the kingdom of Afaloicai in order to weaken it. The border between the *posto* of Afaloicai Baguia and Afaloicao Uatolari split the main *uma luli* of Buibela/Lena in two (Source: *chefe suco* Afaloicai; also see Gunter 2008).

34 Local informants also claim that during this prewar period, people from Afaloicai began to settle beyond the boundaries of *suco* Babulo. Some state that the *liurai* (*chefe do suco*) of Uaitame, Dom Umberto, and his successor, Gaspar from Sana, invited people from Afaloicai to come to work on their land around present-day Darabai and west of the Bee Bui River. Much of this land has been the subject of an ongoing dispute between individuals and groups from Afaloicai and the *suco* of Makadiki and Matahoi.

networks of alliance and exchange. As *oa-sae* (wife-takers), Gregorio and his followers were expected to contribute goods and services to their Darlari *uma ana* (wife-givers). In exchange, they were allocated specific plots of land on which they were permitted to farm and build their houses. Over time, other marriage alliances were formed between families from Afaloicai and the local houses of Babulo in general and Darlari in particular.[35] Darlari elders insist, however, that according to the original *juramento* (oath or agreement) with *Liurai* Gregorio, land was not (and could not) be transferred outright but rather remained under the ultimate control of the 'lord of the land'.

From the 1950s onwards, colonial policies aimed at 'developing' local agriculture led first to seasonal and later to more permanent migration from the upland communities around Matebian, including Afaloicai, to the lowlands. Local informants state that during the 1950s and 1960s, *chefe suco* and *chefe povação* from the entire subdistrict of Uatolari were ordered to organise work groups to 'open up' the coastal plain for rice cultivation. For many of those who arrived in Babulo during the post-war period, access to land was no longer necessarily mediated through marriage into local groups but rather through their relationship with other family members from Afaloicai previously settled in *suco* Babulo and neighbouring Vessoru-Uaitame. Many in-migrants during this period set up temporary housing while they worked on land allocated to them by the local authorities.

War, Displacement and Disruption of the Social Order

The capacity of the Darlari 'lord of the land' to negotiate or determine land allocation to in-migrants was severely diminished as a result of the Indonesian invasion and its aftermath. Indonesian troops are reported to have advanced towards Uatolari subdistrict from the port at Beasu in mid to late 1976. Local informants describe both erratic and systematic patterns of displacement between 1976 and 1979. Some informants report taking part in group movements or 'evacuations' organised by local Fretilin (Frente Revolucionária de Timor-Leste Independente) delegates to specific sites; in other cases, individuals and families state that they made their way over a period of two to three years towards the Matebian Range, either on their own or in groups with their *chefe aldeia* and

---

35   For example, land at place called Kai Oris was given to the *oasae* (wife-takers) from Afaloicai of the house of the Kabo Rea.

chefe suco. Sometimes people sheltered for a few days in a particular area while at other times they stayed for a few months, often building temporary housing and finding time to plant crops.[36]

Informants from *aldeia* Darlari describe how the area 'emptied'. People left even the more remote settlements, fleeing the Indonesian troops, and looking for shelter from the aerial bombardments. Most informants described reaching Matebian in mid to late 1979 and staying there until the Fretilin leadership 'ordered' the 'surrender' of the civilian population.[37] Conditions on Matebian Mountain were traumatic. Informants describe how they lived in fear of the aerial bombardments, taking shifts to sleep in cramped conditions with little food or water. Many informants attribute their survival during this period to the fact that the Darlari elders (and their sibling, Beli) did not abandon their ancestral sacra but carried them with them to Matebian.[38]

The 'surrender' and return of the civilian population to areas under the control of the Indonesian military began in late November 1979. As elsewhere in East Timor, the inhabitants of *suco* Babulo were ordered to report to internment and resettlement camps while the troops conducted military mop-up operations in the area (CAVR 2005). The main internment camp in Uatolari subdistrict was established at the old *posto* at Uatolari Leten. People from all six *suco* of Uatolari, as well as the subdistricts of Baguia and Quelicai, were 'contained' within a restricted area around the subdistrict centre. For the first few months, the Indonesian military and East Timorese collaborators surrounded the encampment and people were not permitted to leave unless accompanied by an East Timorese or Indonesian guard. Informants describe how during this time people had little or no shelter and they had to sleep, eat, wash and go to the toilet within the guarded perimeter. Food was scarce and they had restricted (and sometimes no) access to fields and gardens beyond a specified distance.

In the early 1980s the Indonesian military began relocating the population. Most of the population residing in the *suco* prior to the invasion was relocated from isolated upland settlements to linear settlements along the main road

---

36 Most informants claim that political violence within *suco* Babulo was contained as a result 'traditional' alliances and oaths. The perpetrators of violence were often described as 'outsiders' from groups who were displaced to Babulo as a result of the internal armed conflict between UDT (União Democrática Timorense, the Timorese Democratic Union) and Fretilin, and the Indonesian invasion. The *chefe suco* of Babulo was (and is) closely related to the *liurai* families of Afaloicai. In fact, descendants of the Burmeta refer to the rulers from Buibela/Lena in Afaloicai as their 'younger brother'. During the Indonesian occupation, certain 'ruling' house-based groups from Afaloicai rose to political and economic prominence at local and national levels. Gunter (2007) has described the way in which local groups have become trapped in a vicious cycle of 'victim and victimisation' based on changing political fortunes.
37 Generally, this is dated about 23 November 1976.
38 Both Beli and Darlari claim that few of their own people were killed during this period; however, this is generally refers to people who had died as a result of bombing or later executions, rather than deaths due to illness and hunger.

networks. Some informants claim that East Timorese who collaborated with the Indonesians had considerable influence over where people could be relocated.[39] Within the Darlari domain, some degree of homogeneity was retained as members of the same house-based groups were relocated together. Today, members of the principal houses of Darlari, Beli, Aha Bu'u and Kotanisi state that at the time the *chefe do suco* of Babulo consulted with the Darlari and Beli elders as to where groups should be relocated.[40] The majority of the population, however, appears to have remained close the *posto* at Uatolari Leten or moved to the new settlement of Kampung Baru. Continued restrictions on movement during the 1980s and early 1990s meant that fields and gardens in more remote upland locations remained 'off limits'. Some informants claim that these restrictions were 'self-imposed'—as people feared attacks by the armed resistance, or of being suspected of collaborating with Falintil.

Darlari elders claim that increased population pressure and limited access to land meant that people just went ahead and farmed whatever land was available in order to survive, circumventing any 'traditional' principles and processes of land allocation. The destruction of *um luli* structures and restrictions on movement prevented regular ritual communication with the ancestors and inhibited ceremonial life around which the social order of the Darlari domain was structured. Nevertheless, informants claim that the relocation of the population into more densely populated clusters according to *aldeia* membership helped to maintain a degree of continuity. For example, the Darlari elders continued to perform yearly harvest rituals, albeit in a 'simplified' form. They constructed small traditional houses in which to store the ancestral sacra and people continued to seek their advice and assistance.

Knowledge and the Sacred

The authority of Darlari elders as 'origin group' representatives rests in their position as legitimate heirs of the founder-ancestors and is sustained by their intimate knowledge of their land and its history. Local informants claim that only the Darlari elders have the full knowledge from 'trunk to tip' (*la'a-na, rae-na*) of the arrival and settlement of the founding ancestors, the establishment

---

39 Some (but not all) of the East Timorese collaborators in Uatolari had previously been involved—directly or indirectly—in the anti-colonial uprising of 1959; others had suffered at the hands of Fretilin during the internal conflict and saw their opportunity for revenge.

40 For example, although Beli and Darlari were not permitted to return to their upland settlements, they were relocated to Aliambata. Darlari elders argue that this site was chosen as it was close to a number of important common *luli* sites, including the offshore gas seep located some 100 m from the settlement. The *chefe do suco* from Aha Bu'u and his family also relocated to Aliambata. Some suggest that this was in order to control access to the Aliambata gas seep and ensure that 'outsiders' did not try to exploit these resources without consultation.

of local houses and the eventual arrival of in-migrant groups. They know the history of conflict, past treaties, alliances and *juramento* (oaths) within and between local and neighbouring groups. They know the history of land use, the boundaries of their domain and the way land was allocated to local and in-migrant houses. But most importantly, they know the names of the various spirit and ancestral guardians that control access to the forest, fields and water sources of their domain. Knowledge of this ancient and therefore sacred time is not accessible to all members of the community.

Knowledge is considered to form part of the legacy of the ancestors and is usually passed on from one generation to the next at the last possible moment. Even if the person chosen to inherit this knowledge is not considered to be bright or eloquent, people believe that they will be 'possessed' or 'filled' by the knowledge they receive. Darlari elders describe the knowledge bestowed on them by their ancestors as both a privilege and a burden. Only the elders 'may speak' and therefore pass judgment on what is considered to be *luli* and what is not.[41] Through this knowledge, they have become the privileged intermediaries between the 'light' and 'open' world of the living and the 'dark', 'hidden' world of the ancestors. This knowledge also means, however, that they are bound to 'service' regardless of whether or not they receive any support—material or otherwise—from the community.

Darlari elders are keen to point out that they do not worship *uato no kai* (rock and tree) but rather they insist that, even prior to the arrival of the first Catholic missionaries, they believed in a creator-god entity called Wula' Lara (Moon Sun).[42] According to the elders, Wula' Lara created the world and then placed certain people on earth to 'control' (*ei*) and 'tame' (*masi*) the land. Before the arrival of these 'chosen' people, the inhabitants of the earth lived like 'people with no rules and regulations' (*ikutame, garteme*). As the chosen people took control of the land, they established behavioural norms and practices that formed the basis of the social and moral order. As descendants of these 'chosen' people, the Darlari elders have a duty to ensure that the social and moral order is maintained through the continued application of these norms and practices.

Behavioural norms and practices have developed over time and as such they have also been shaped by interaction between individuals and groups. With time, some have gathered strength and others have weakened. Often presented as *luli* (sacred), these norms and practices regulate everyday ritual and social life.

---

41   The term *luli* has a range of meanings and applications. In Naueti, the term *ba'ina* is also used to describe what is prohibited or considered to be 'untamed' or out of control. Something that is *ba'ina* or *luli* may become *masi* (tame or sweet) through ritual transformation. The word *luli* is frequently used to denote all that is sacred but at the same time all that is dangerous or prohibited. There is a direct correlation between time and the sacred (*luli*) objects; names, places and norms increase in value or potency across multiple generations.
42   Also sometimes spelt *Ulu Lara*.

The most sacred/dangerous of these norms are those associated with the arrival and settlement of the founding ancestors. In settling the land, the ancestors were responsible for naming the physical landscape: hills, rocks, rivers, streams, springs, forests and fields. They also began to exercise control over nature. They cleared and burned the land to make way for fields and gardens; they used natural resources from the forests to build shelters and provide food and fuel; and they used water from various springs to wash, cook and cleanse themselves. It is believed that, in taking control of the land and its natural resources, the ancestors set the precedent for interaction with the *bu'u*—the original 'owners' or guardians who inhabited the earth.[43]

Among the population currently living on Darlari lands, there continues to be a strong belief, among both young and old, in the existence of an 'unseen' or 'hidden' dimension inhabited by various forms of *bu'u*. The most powerful *bu'u* are independent or untamed 'owners' (of the land or natural resources) who can take on human or animal form. In general, it is believed that *bu'u* have the power to control natural processes and influence the relationship between people and the land. Many believe that failure to respect the *luli* proscriptions governing interaction with the *bu'u* has negative consequences. It is therefore customary to 'follow in the footsteps' of the ancestors by performing specific rituals, invocations and offerings in order to placate the *bu'u* and gain safe access to the resources they guard.

A number of informants recounted stories of individuals who failed to respect prohibitions associated with specific locations, such as areas of forest or bodies of water, and either became gravely ill or, in some instances, died as a consequence. It is common for people to interpret accidents, illness or some form of personal tragedy as a sign that they, or a member of their family, have somehow done something *luli* or prohibited. Those who survive or are able to overcome their difficulties are able to do so because they seek to make amends by consulting the elders on how best to placate the angered *bu'u*.

Over time, the ancestors themselves have been 'spoken into' the landscape. Numerous places and locations across the Darlari domain where ancestral spirits are believed to congregate are deemed *luli*. Through their actions and deeds—sometimes involving great personal sacrifice and even death—various named ancestors are remembered for having provided the first harvest, securing the borders of the domain or protecting the land from natural disasters.[44] The principal of reciprocity underpins the relationship between those living on the

---

43 See Note 13.
44 Part of the Darlari 'origin' narrative that deals with the arrival of the ancestors and the trials and tribulations of the Mane Hitu deals with the personal sacrifice made to secure the 'first' harvest of the founder-ancestors.

land and the ancestors. The seasons are punctuated with communal and smaller house-based rituals during which invocations and offerings are made to the ancestors to ask for their continued protection and bounty.

Small groups perform one such ritual in their fields just before the corn ripens for harvest. This ceremony, called *masi eka rae rea ena* (literally: washing the corncob leaves), is performed in order to ask the 'owners' of the field (*rea bu'u*) to protect their harvest. During this ritual, the corn (*eka rae*) is transformed from *ba'ina* (still forbidden and sour) to *masi* (tamed, allowed to be eaten and sweet). It is believed that *rea bu'u* have the ability to transform themselves into mice, insects or some type of plant parasite or plague that might destroy the crop. During the course of the ceremony, a number of other ancestral *bu'u*—usually those who first farmed the land—are also invoked. A ritual offering of eggs, rice and some meat is prepared. Part of the food is distributed along the boundaries of the field, some is placed in the centre and the rest is shared among those present. The eggs and meat are first 'distributed' to the ancestors and *bu'u*.[45] An invocation remembering the life or deeds of each is made directly to each ancestor or *bu'u*, that they will continue to protect, preserve and provide bounty to the person who farmed the field. Sacrificial meat is offered to the youngest of the *Mane Hitu*, who sacrificed himself to provide the ancestors with the first harvest; then to the *Mak Lihat* who is believed to watch over all Darlari lands; followed by the *Aman Uma Luli*, the founder of the Darlari descent group, and the *Mak Sabar*, the spirit guardian of the harvest. Final offerings are made to the 'creator-god', Wula' Lara and to the earth, giver of life.

Behavioural norms and practices are not limited to interaction with the land and natural resources but extend to the nature of relations between male and female members of the community, preferred paths of alliance/marriage and social ranking within and between house-based descent groups. Critical to the production and reproduction of these norms and practices are historical narratives and regular ritual communication with the ancestors. Darlari elders lament the fact that today many people living on their land—including members of Darlari houses—do not perform the necessary rituals to ensure the continued fertility of their land and the prosperity of its people. They also claim that many people do not know the history of the land or the correct invocations to be made, and some 'outsiders' continue to invoke ancestors from their places of origin rather than the local emplaced *bu'u*. According to the elders, this 'chaotic' situation has been the cause of many trials and tribulations over the past 30 years.

---

45   Sometimes people will bring non-food items to the spirit/ancestors, such as clothes, tais, and so on. The spirit/ancestor is treated like a living person with the same needs.

Restoration

Since independence, the diverse house-based descent groups of *suco* Babulo have been engaged in the process of returning to their pre-1975 settlements (*baha*) and rebuilding their ancestral cult houses. Darlari elders, and members of the Darlari descent group in general, consider the return to their settlement of origin at Baha Liurai an important and necessary step in re-establishing their credentials as 'lords of the land'. The Baha Liurai is the most sacred of all sites in Darlari narratives of origin. It is considered to be the burial place of the *ina ama* (mother and father) of the *Mane Hitu*. Access to the summit is absolutely prohibited unless accompanied by ritual authorities. Symbolically, Baha Liurai not only serves to legitimate Darlari precedence in relation to other groups living in the area, but also confirms the emplaced nature of their authority. Informants reported that during discussions as to whether or not the settlement should be rebuilt on its original site, closer to the summit of the Baha Liurai, or on a more accessible site, the elders agreed that it should be moved closer to the main road (from Uatolari to Quelicai) so that people would be made aware that they were 'passing through sacred land'.[46]

As early as August 2000, work began on rebuilding the main Darlari ritual houses, the *uma buti* and *uma ita*. Elders describe the *ma buti* as the principal *uma luli*. It 'belongs' to the whole community—understood as all those living within the Darlari domain—but is 'owned' by the Darlari. More specifically, this structure symbolically represents the 'origin' house of the Darlari ancestors. The *uma ita*, on the other hand, is described as an *uma ukun* or ruling house where Darlari headmen traditionally stored symbols of political power called *rotan*, which they distributed to subsidiary houses and allied groups. Both structures retain sacred heirlooms believed to have belonged to the ancestors and passed down from generation to generation. It is believed that the essence of the ancestors continues to live through these objects and inhabits specific spaces within *uma luli*. During collective rituals, food offerings, water, *bua* and *malus* (areca nut and betel pepper leaf) are placed within these sacred spaces and emerge transformed to be redistributed to members of the community. Areca nut and betel pepper leaf stored in these houses are believed to have special protective qualities. They are used in collective rituals as a marker of membership of the group but also to protect visitors to the area or in healing rituals.[47]

Following the completion of the *uma buti and uma ita*, representatives of all the house-based descent groups living on Darlari lands and neighbouring allies (namely, the *ki itana* and *ki butana*) were invited to take part in a rare ceremony

---

46   Younger members of the family stated that they felt that the site should be moved closer to the road and to the water source given the age of those who would be returning to the settlement.

47   Unlike the *uma ita*, the *uma buti* is not used as a meeting house and is not permanently lived in.

of ritual sacrifice to the ancestors on the summit of Baha Liurai. The elders explain that the purpose of the ceremony is threefold: to visit the burial site of the ancestors and communicate within them; to thank the ancestors for watching over the people living on their sacred land; and to ask for their continued protection and generosity. This ceremony last took place immediately prior to the community's displacement towards Matebian in late 1976. Prior to 1976, the Darlari elders stated that the ceremony took place every five to ten years or 'when it was deemed necessary'. During the initial stages of the ceremony, there was considerable debate and negotiation regarding various aspects of the 'order of things'. In part, this was due to the fact that none of the elders who had directed the last ceremony is alive, but this contestation also forms an integral part of the nature of relations between the various house-based groups now living on Darlari lands.[48]

In essence, the ceremony is the re-enactment and representation of key discourses of origin and precedence that underpin the social organisation of house-based descent groups within the Darlari domain. During the course of the ceremony, key notions of ancestry, attachment to place, histories of migration and settlement and networks of alliance are all acknowledged within a single visual narrative.

From the Darlari perspective, the ceremony begins at the *uma buti* and the *uma ita*. During this first stage of the ceremony, the main sacrificial offerings—rice, areca nut and 'holy' water—are brought to or taken from inside the *um buti* and handed to the senior members of the diverse Darlari lineages, sub-lineages and their affines. The *Kabu Rai* then directs those participating in the ceremony to form into single file according to rank, with senior members of the 'elder' houses preceding the 'younger' house members. Once the group is assembled, they begin the procession to the summit of Baha Liurai.

Representatives of the sibling Beli and Darlari descent groups approach the Baha Liurai from their separate domains. At a location called *ita mata, kai hene* (door and gate), they are met by representatives from the Burmeta clan, who have made their way there from their principal cult house at Burosoba.[49] Together the group continues their 'pilgrimage' to the ancestral burial site on Baha Liurai. The *Makaer Luli* from Burlalu and the Darlari elders are responsible for 'opening the door' to the summit before all others may pass. The *Makaer Luli* carries with him sacra from the *uma luli* at Burlalu and acolytes from the houses of *Asu Rati Reino* and *Asu Rati Liurai* lead the way towards the summit of Baha

---

48 To a certain extent, the ceremony at Baha Liurai provides a space for a degree of 'theatre' where representatives of different groups attempt to redefine their role within the broader group. One such discussion involved the placing of the ex-*nurep* in relation to the former *chefe suco*. During the Indonesian occupation, the *nurep* represented a covert counterpart to the Indonesian-installed village leadership, *kepala desa*.

49 See previous note on the ritual name given to the Burmeta clan.

Liurai. They are followed by the *Bu Dato* of Beli and Darlari and the *liurai* of Aha Bu'u and Kotanisi. Other senior members of the community follow carrying animals and rice, which will be offered to the ancestors and shared amongst all those present. Sacred areca nut, betel pepper leaves and water drawn from one of the *we-mata luli* (sacred springs) are also carried.

An area of forest is cleared on the summit as preparations for the night-long vigil and communal feast begin. Two altars are prepared where food will be laid out for the *ina ama Beli Darlari* (mother, father Beli Darlari), the mythical 'original' couple. Once the food is prepared, it is laid out on the altars. According to custom, all those present are required to stay awake and alert throughout the night in solemn vigil, remembering the ancestors and members of the community who cannot be present. There are strict rules regarding behaviour throughout the ceremony. These include: no alcohol, no areca nut chewing, no smoking, no defecation and no swearing or inappropriate conduct between men and women. Throughout the night, representatives of the Darlari *uma kain* (sub-lineages) ensure that no-one falls asleep or breaks these prohibitions. Every so often, men from the houses of *Asu Rati Reino* and *Asu Rati Liurai* beat the sides of the altar with bamboo sticks to keep malignant *bu'u* away.

At sunrise, following the sharing of food that is distributed according to precedence, the spokesperson for the Darlari elders, supported by the *Kabo Rai*, reminds all those present of their social and moral obligations to the ancestors and the *rea mumu, rea uato* (lord of the land). This proclamation includes statements of behavioural norms and practices regarding social interaction between men and women as well as descent groups. It also reiterates any prohibitions regarding access to certain areas of land, forest or other natural resources and reminds those present of protocols pertaining to land use such as those determining the season for certain agricultural tasks such as clearing, burning, planting and harvesting. Once these rules—collectively known as *luli* or *bandu* (Tetun)—have been declared, all the participants prepare to leave the Baha Liurai in single file and in silence without turning back. The last to leave must be a Darlari ritual specialist who 'closes' the *ita mata* (door) through which they passed the day before.

The ceremony at Baha Liurai provides a vivid visual medium for understanding the role, function and status of each house-based group and the nature of the relationships that bind house-based groups within a single domain. Critically, the ceremony at Baha Liurai also constitutes a 'renewal' or 'reaffirmation' of the bond that exists between the ancestors and members of the different house-based groups. The ritual (re)connection with the founding ancestors was considered indispensable for the restoration of the 'proper order of things' after 24 years of war, occupation and displacement. The time, effort and resources invested in the ceremony at Baha Liurai suggest that the community is committed to maintaining the social and moral order within which the different house-based groups are situated, including the rights, duties and obligations that this implies (cf. McWilliam 2005). Since independence, communities throughout Timor-Leste have been engaged in processes of restoration and renewal similar to those described in this chapter. Many communities have felt a great degree of pride in the reconstruction of their ancestral cult houses and the revival of cultural performances.[50] Furthermore, for many rural communities, the (re)turn to custom has provided a sense of security and continuity as a counterpoint to the violence and disruption caused by the political turmoil centred on the nation's capital.[51] Beyond the interest of anthropologists and other scholars engaged in understanding the nature of social relations in a time of change, the 'resurgence', persistence or resilience of customary forms of constructed sociality provides a fertile field of study into understanding the strategies and struggles of communities as they seek to re-establish themselves after years of war and displacement.

Acknowledgments

Research for this chapter took place between 2004 and 2008. A major part of the research was conducted under the auspices of an Australian Research Council Discovery Grant for a joint legal–anthropological research project on customary land tenure in Timor-Leste at The Australian National University. My thanks to friends and advisors in Babulo—in particular, the elders of the Darlari descent group Senhores Carlos, Anacleto and Gaspar, the 'eldest sons' Miguel, Lorenzo, Zeferino, *liurai* Joaquim, Ama Bo'ot, Ama Ki'ik, Maria Alexandrina and Felismina. Also thanks to Andrew McWilliam for encouraging me to write and Josh Trindade for his constant support and advice on all things *Naueti*.

---

50 RTTL (Radio Telivisaun Timor-Leste) has been invited to film *uma lulik* inaugurations and other ceremonies in a number of locations across the country. Although few communities where these ceremonies have taken place are able to watch RTTL—there is no power, no television sets, no reception—many still feel great pride in the fact that their histories, houses and land are being viewed at the national level.

51 In 2006 and 2007, what began as a dispute within the armed forces led to a general breakdown of law and order and the displacement of tens of thousands of people. Most of the violence and displacement was centred on the capital, Dili.

References

Babo-Soares, D. 2004, 'Nahe Biti: the philosophy and process of grassroots reconciliation (and justice) in East Timor', *Asia Pacific Journal of Anthropology*, vol. 5, no. 1, p. 15.

Bovensiepen, J. 2009, 'Spiritual landscapes of life and death in the central highlands of East Timor', *Anthropological Forum: A journal of social anthropology and comparative sociology*, vol. 19, no. 3, pp. 323–38.

Brown, A. M. 2009, 'Security, development and the nation-building agenda— East Timor', *Conflict, Security and Development*, vol. 9, no. 2, pp. 141–64.

Commission for Reception, Truth and Reconciliation in Timor-Leste (CAVR) 2005, *Chega!: The report of the Commission for Reception, Truth and Reconciliation in Timor-Leste—Executive summary*, Commission for Reception, Truth and Reconciliation in Timor-Leste, Dili.

De Menezes, F. 2006 [1968], *Encontro de Culturas em Timor-Leste*, Crocodilo Azu, Dili.

Direcção Nacional de Estatística 2004, *Census of Population and Housing. D. N. d. Estatística*, Direcção Nacional de Estatística, Dili.

Fitzpatrick, D. and Barnes, S. 2010, 'The relative resilience of property: first possession and order without law in East Timor', *Law and Society Review*, vol. 45, no. 2.

Fitzpatrick, D., McWilliam, A. and Barnes, S. 2008, 'Policy notes on customary tenures in Timor Leste', *East Timor Law Journal*.

Fox, J. J. 1994, 'Reflections on hierarchy and "precedence"', *History and Anthropology: Special Issue*, vol. 7, nos 1–4, pp. 87–108.

Fox, J. J. 1995, 'Installing the 'outsider' inside: The exploration of an epistemic Austronesian cultural theme and its social significance'. *The First Conference of the European Association for Souteast Asian Studies: Local Transformation and Common Heritage in Southeast Asia*. Leiden University.

Fox, J. J. and Sather, C. A. (eds) 1996, *Origins, Ancestry and Alliance: Explorations in Austronesian ethnography*, Department of Anthropology, The Australian National University, Canberra.

Gunter, J. 2007, 'Communal Conflict in Viqueque and the 'Charged' History of '59'. *The Asia Pacific Journal of Anthropology,* vol 8, pp. 27 – 41

Gunter, J. 2008, Violence and 'being in history' in East Timor: local articulations of colonial rebellion, MA thesis, Department of Anthropology, Instituto Superior de Ciências do Trabalho e da Empresa, Lisbon.

Hicks, D. 2007, 'Community and nation-state in East Timor', *Anthropology Today*, vol. 23, no. 1, pp. 13–16.

Hohe, T. 2002, 'The clash of paradigms: international administration and local political legitimacy in East Timor', *Contemporary Southeast Asia*, vol. 24, no. 3, p. 21.

Lewis, E. D. 1996, 'Origin structures and precedence in the social orders of Tana 'Ai and Sikka', in J. J. Fox and C. A. Sather (eds), *Origins, Ancestry and Alliance: Explorations in Austronesian ethnography*, Department of Anthropology, The Australian National University, Canberra.

McWilliam, A. 2005, 'Houses of resistance in East Timor: structuring sociality in the new nation', *Anthropological Forum: A journal of social anthropology and comparative sociology*, vol. 15, no. 1, pp. 27–44.

McWilliam, A. 2006, 'Fataluku forest tenures and the Conis Santana National Park in East Timor', in T. Reuter (ed.), *Sharing the Earth, Dividing the Land: Land and territory in the Austronesian world*, ANU E Press, Canberra.

McWilliam, A. 2007, 'Harbouring traditions in East Timor: marginality in a lowland entrepot', *Modern Asian Studies*, vol. 41, no. 6, pp. 1113–43.

McWilliam, A. 2008, 'Fataluku healing and cultural resilience in East Timor', *Ethnos*, vol. 73, pp. 217–40.

Meitzner Yoder, L. S. 2005, Custom, codification, collaboration: integrating the legacies of land and forest authorities in Oecusse enclave, East Timor, PhD thesis, Yale University, New Haven, Conn., pp. xviii, 370.

Palmer, L. 2007, 'Developing Timor Leste: recognising the role of custom and tradition', in *Exploring the Tensions of Nation Building in East Timor*, University of Melbourne, Melbourne.

Traube, E. G. 2007, 'Unpaid wages: local narratives and the imagination of the nation', *Asia Pacific Journal of Anthropology*, vol. 8, pp. 9–25.

Trindade, J. 2008, 'Reconciling conflicting paradigms and East Timorese vision of the ideal state', in D. Mearns (ed.), *Democratic Governance in East Timor: Reconciling the local and the national*, Charles Darwin University Press, Darwin.

Vischer, M. P. 2009, *Precedence: Social differentiation in the Austronesian world*, ANU E Press, Canberra.

3. Opening and Closing the Land: Land and power in the Idaté highlands

Judith Bovensiepen

In 2006, Xanana Gusmão, the then President of Timor-Leste, launched a national program to 'return sharp and pointed materials/weapons' (Tetun: *halot meit ho kroat*). The aim of the program was to initiate a series of small ceremonies all over the country, in which weapons that had been taken up to fight the Indonesian military would be returned to their proper places (Trindade and Castro 2007:43). Conflicts broke out in Timor-Leste in April 2006 after a dispute within the East Timorese military erupted and turned into a more generalised conflict between different regional factions throughout the country. This internal conflict occurred just four years after Timor-Leste had gained independence following a long and violent period of occupation by Indonesia (1975–99). Gusmão's program was based on the premise that during the resistance struggle against Indonesia, weapons containing ancestral potency had been taken from people's ritual houses and they had not been returned. The failure to restore these weapons to their proper storing places was given as the reason conflicts erupted in the country in 2006. The ceremonies were aimed at returning these weapons to the ritual houses in order to create peace and stability in the country.

In the Laclubar subdistrict in the central highlands, a slightly different interpretation of these events was given, which more or less followed the same line of reasoning. Several of the people in Laclubar maintain that during the Indonesian occupation, the land was opened to fight the occupiers. Conflicts erupted in 2006 because of a failure to hold a ritual to 'close the land' (Idaté: *douk larek*). The *lulik* potency of the landscape is considered to be a powerful resource during warfare once it is properly mobilised by human beings who can 'open the land' (Idaté: *lo'e larek*). *Lulik* land always needs to be repaid, however, and people argue that conflicts erupted in 2006 because of a failure to do this.

In the Laclubar subdistrict, certain sites in the landscape, particular objects and houses are considered to be potent, or *lulik* (Idaté and Tetun). *Lulik* has commonly been translated as 'holy', 'sacred' and 'taboo' (Hull 2002:227). Borrowing directly from Durkheim, David Hicks (2004:25), who carried out research among the Tetun people of south-eastern Timor in the 1960s, maintains that *lulik* means sacred and that this is opposed to the category for the profane: *sau*. Similarly, Elizabeth Traube (1986:143), whose research in the 1970s focused on the Mambai people of central Timor, argues that *lulik* does not refer to an essence but is rather a relational category that 'signifies a *relation of distance*, a boundary between things'. Among Idaté speakers, *lulik* is used as an adjective, noun and verb and can designate an avoidance relationship, but also refers to a potent source of power, prosperity and danger, usually associated with the land and the ancestors.

This chapter focuses on Idaté narratives about the political significance of *lulik* land. It investigates how attachment to place is created through this narrative practice and how this in turn reinforces the central significance of the potency with which the ancestral land is invested. This will allow me to explore how people perceive the relationship between humans and their environment by concentrating on the way narratives mediate this relationship. In the first part of the chapter, I introduce the Laclubar subdistrict, its history and spiritual geography, focusing specifically on people's understanding of *lulik* potency in relation to ancestral activities. Subsequently, I draw out how people's claims to the potency of the land vis-a-vis outsiders are expressed in a narrative that concerns Laclubar's interactions with colonial powers and neighbouring domains. In the final part, I discuss the role of this narrative in the present, how it is used to interpret the current conflict as a failure to 'close the land', and explore how competing political perspectives are reflected in people's conflicting claims to have access to the land's potency.

Overview of Laclubar History and Spiritual Geography

Laclubar subdistrict is part of the district of Manatuto and is situated in the central mountain range of Timor-Leste, some 130 km by road from the capital city, Dili. With a population of about 8000 people (NDS 2006:67), the subdistrict is divided into six smaller administrative units or villages called *suco*, and is one of the most thinly populated areas of Timor-Leste (Arquitectura and GERTiL 2002:81). The language spoken in the region is Idaté, an Austronesian language closely related to the national language, Tetun.[1] Most of the inhabitants in this region are subsistence farmers and grow a variety of tubers, maize, citrus fruits and coffee, and there are some rice fields in the lowlands. The region is also known for its production of palm wine, which is traded during Sunday markets in Laclubar Town. There are also oil and gas resources in the area around Pualaka. Most hamlets outside Laclubar Town cannot be reached by car, and heavy rainfall frequently leads to some of the hamlets being entirely cut off from the main roads, health stations and markets. Laclubar Centre has a newly built hospital, a large church and several schools.

---

1   Idaté is spoken by approximately 10 000 people, mainly in the Laclubar subdistrict. The inhabitants of the area frequently mix Idaté and Tetun, which is why I use both languages in this chapter.

During the Indonesian occupation of East Timor, the inhabitants of the more remote hamlets and villages were forcibly resettled in Laclubar Town, and a large part of the population has returned to their ancestral lands since independence. A certain proportion of the population still lives in West Timor, to where they were voluntarily or forcibly moved during the post-referendum violence in 1999. In other regions of Timor-Leste, the inhabitants of Laclubar are sometimes considered to have been supporters of Indonesian occupation, since the East Timorese Governor during the Indonesian occupation, Abílio Osório Soares, was born in Laclubar. Political affiliation in the area varies widely, however, and in the 1970s there were supporters of all three main parties in Laclubar: Fretilin, UDT and Apodeti. During the internal conflict that broke out in the country in 2006—which was frequently expressed in terms of a conflict between easterners (Tetun: *lorosa'e*) and westerners (Tetun: *loromonu*)—many of Laclubar's inhabitants insisted they were 'neutral' arguing that they were 'the land of the middle' (Tetun: *rai klaran*).

Laclubar Town is situated in a small valley, surrounded by steep mountains that form around the town centre in the shape of a horseshoe. The landscape is characterised by rugged mountains and fertile stretches of forest interspersed with small springs. Certain conspicuous sites in the landscape, such as springs, stones, rivers, hilltops or holes in the ground, are considered to be potent (*lulik*) and must be avoided. Two important *lulik* sites near Laclubar Centre are called Susuk and Orlau. Susuk is a wide hole at the bottom of the mountains surrounding Laclubar Town. Orlau is a spring located in a forested area close to the main road leading to Laclubar Centre, in a lush and fertile area planted with fruit trees and coffee. Susuk and Orlau are two of the most important ritual sites for the inhabitants of Laclubar, because they are considered to be doorways (Idaté: *lalamatak*) to *lulik* potency. Rituals to mobilise this potency were carried out at these sites, including the ritual to 'close the land'.

During everyday activities, *lulik* sites must be avoided because they are considered dangerous, and walking too close to *lulik* sites is said to risk madness, confusion and death. *Lulik* is gendered female, even though I found no evidence to suggest that people identified the land with a specific female deity, as described by Hicks (2004:27) for the Tetun people of Caraubalo. Those I encountered during my fieldwork in Laclubar maintained that at *lulik* places one is likely to encounter land spirits (Idaté: *larek-nain*), which can appear in the form of pythons, eels or as human beings, such as a beautiful woman or a foreigner (Idaté and Tetun: *malae*) with white skin and red hair. The Idaté term *larek-nain* has multiple meanings: it can refer to land spirits who appear at *lulik* sites. The term also refers, however, to the earliest population of the area and their descendents, who are the 'people of the land' or landowners today (cf. Hicks 2004:30; McWilliam, this volume). Hence, the category of *larek-nain* is frequently merged with ancestors (Idaté: *luli'ain*). There is an ambiguity about the precise nature of the relationship between ancestors, *lulik* and land spirits. When asked directly, the people I spoke to said these categories are not the same, however, during ritual and everyday interactions with the land, these entities were often conflated. Thus, although they are conceptually separate, they are implicitly treated as transformations of each other and their combined presence in the land makes up its powerful potency.

Lulik is said to precede human ancestors. One of my respondents, named Ghuillermino, expressed this by saying: 'in the past, there was *lulik*, nothing else.' He went on to explain that before human beings came into existence, there was just potent *lulik* land in Laclubar. Subsequently, land spirits created human beings and raised animals. Some ancestors grew from the land and others came from stones. The land gave golden objects to people and they built houses for these objects. His narrative absorbs biblical notions of the human genesis by stating that God gave His blessing to this act of creation, but it was the land that created human beings. He concluded that 'everything comes from the land'. In this line of thinking, human beings are extensions of the land; they emerge directly from it. *Lulik* is thus closely linked to notions of autochthony in that the original inhabitants are said to have emerged from the potent landscape. The autochthonous origins of the original population are expressed in the narratives of different house groups, which recount the origins of the first ancestral siblings travelling through the landscape in order to find an appropriate place to settle. In several cases, the name of the house group refers to the place where the ancestors settled or emerged from the landscape, thus uniting the land, the house and its human members in a single entity. These origin narratives are frequently described through the recitation of place names, which the ancestors visited—a practice that Fox (1997a:8) has called 'topogeny'. The recitation of these narratives creates emplacement (cf. Scott 2007:33), continuously re-establishing attachment to the ancestral environment. The recounting of narratives is therefore an essential part of the way people make place.

Territorial place making, according to Feuchtwang (2004:10), is a way of centring and establishing focal points. People in Laclubar create a sense of centrality through various idioms. Some house groups express this through the common Austronesian botanical metaphor of likening their ancestral origin house to a banyan tree, whose ancestors are the 'trunk' or 'base' (Idaté: *uun*) and whose descendants are the tips or flowers of the tree (Idaté: *hunan*) (cf. Reuter 2006:25). The sense of centrality is also expressed through bodily metaphors according to which Laclubar is 'the navel of the land, the liver of the land' (*larek usar, larek nau*). The west of Timor-Leste represents the tail of the land (Idaté: *hiak)* and the east the head (Idaté: *ulun*). The navel land, called Balulin, refers to a hole in the ground, which is situated at the bottom of Mount Maubere near Laclubar Centre.

This *lulik* site represents the place where the original ancestors of Laclubar were buried and it is thought to be the entrance to the world of underground spirits. The claim to be the navel of the world is a way of expressing that Laclubar is the origin place of humanity (cf. Therik 2004:69–70), and people at times contend that the first ancestors were actually Adam and Eve (cf. Fox 1983). Thus, by identifying themselves as the centre of the world and the origin place of human history, Laclubar's inhabitants are creating a powerful focal point that anchors them firmly in the landscape.

Claims to centrality are also a way in which precedence (Fox 1997b:91) is established in relation to other incoming groups. The autochthonous inhabitants are the ritual guardians of the land. Hence the land cannot be alienated, or, as Ghuillermino said, 'the land does not want to be sold'. The potency of *lulik* sites makes them particularly 'hot' and thus dangerous. Claims to centrality are often accompanied by an emphasis on the potency of the land, which is at times expressed through the notion that *lulik* sites are places where gold is located under the earth. Moreover, as the following narrative illustrates, the land is said to have given golden objects to the original inhabitants, thus bestowing them with entitlement to political leadership.

The Narrative of the Golden Star

As in many other regions of South-East Asia (Errington 1990:47), in Laclubar, there is a distinction between ritual and political power. These two kinds of power are closely intertwined and essentially interdependent. *Lulik* potency may be a source of ruling power (Idaté and Tetun: *ukun*). This is illustrated through an important narrative that recounts the independence of Laclubar from the neighbouring domain, Samoro. The narrative concerns the story of an ancestor of Laclubar called Dom Geraldo who managed to gain independence from the neighbouring domain or 'kingdom' (Portuguese: *reino*), Samoro, through the help of *lulik* land. It is one of the most frequently told stories in this region and is part of a longer narrative that concerns the origins and journeys of the first ancestors. People were keen for me to record this account and it was told on many occasions during rituals and other public events. Nearly everyone in the region knows and recognises this story and people take great pleasure in telling it and listening to the narrative. There are several different versions of this narrative. Every narrator told the story in a slightly different way, occasionally changing the names of the main actors, adding or leaving out details or making different interpretations of the meaning of the story for the present-day situation. In this version, I summarise the most important elements that recur in most of the accounts in a way I believe most of the narrators would accept.[2]

> In the past, Laclubar had to listen to orders from the *reino* of Samoro. Then, good fortune was brought to one of the ancestors: the *lulik* land Susuk 'gave' good fortune to an ancestor called Dom Geraldo. During that time, palm wine was stolen from the field of Dom Geraldo, whose 'pagan name' is Kei Tu. This happened over and over again.[3] Dom Geraldo set out to catch the thief. [In some versions of the story, Dom Geraldo sends someone else to the field, called Bita Loin.] During the night, he sat under the palm trees and waited. But he became very tired and fell asleep. The next morning he woke up and saw that the palm wine was gone. The same event took place the next day and then again the following day. But Dom Geraldo never managed to stay awake to catch the thief who was stealing his palm wine.
>
> So one night, he cut open his finger and squeezed lemon juice into the wound. He did this all night and, because of the pain, he did not fall asleep. Suddenly he heard a noise. He jumped up and said, 'Oyye! Who is it? Who has been stealing my palm wine?' Once he uttered the words, a golden star appeared above him. The star said to the ancestor: 'I have been stealing your palm wine. What do you want from me to reimburse you for my theft?' Dom Geraldo answered, 'I don't want anything. I don't want any wealth or treasures. The only thing I want is independence [or self-rule; Tetun: *ukun-rasik-an*].' And that is what happened. The *lulik* land Susuk, where Dom Geraldo's palm trees were planted, 'gave good fortune' and independence to Laclubar's ancestor. The land bestowed the title 'Dom' to Geraldo 'Kei Tu', hence making him a local ruler or *liurai*.

This account is often followed by another short story, which is thought to be directly related to this earlier account and gives another perspective of the relationship between Laclubar and Samoro.

> The ruler of Samoro, Dom Felis, was not very happy about Laclubar's efforts to become independent. [The name of the *liurai* of Samoro differs in some versions.] Hence Dom Geraldo and Dom Felis were summoned to appear in front of the Governor in Dili in order to resolve the dispute

---

2   My own explanations are included in square brackets.
3   In Timor-Leste, palm wine (Idaté: *nau buti*) is often produced far away from home directly in the field. A bamboo container is attached to the palm tree, while the branches are beaten for several days with the wine slowly dripping into the bamboo container. Some people distil the product and make a stronger liquor (Idaté: *nau arak*).

[the Governor is referred to as the *Governador* or the *Administrador*]. It took Dom Felis three days to get to Dili, as he rode on horseback. But Dom Geraldo asked the *lulik* land for advice: 'Who do I ride?' he said. The *lulik* land told him to 'ride on brother wind' [Tetun: *sai kuda mau anin*]. He did this by entering a hole in the ground and by reappearing straight away in Dili at the Governor's house. When Dom Geraldo arrived, the Governor told him to wash and put on some clothes. Dom Geraldo put on the Governor's uniform and his hat and sat outside on the porch, waiting for Dom Felis. When Dom Felis finally arrived, he did not recognise Dom Geraldo, so he greeted him by saying 'Bondia, Senhor Governador.' [In some versions of the story, he greets him by saying 'Bondia, *liurai*.'] The Governor heard this and said to Dom Felis: 'You greeted Dom Geraldo. Now you shall both have a flag each and a drum each!' [The drum and the flag are symbols of rule.] This meant Laclubar had gained self-determination. Henceforth Dom Geraldo ruled over Laclubar and Dom Felis ruled over Samoro.[4]

The most important aspect of this story is indisputedly the fact that the *lulik* land 'gave' good fortune and independence to Laclubar. In the story, the golden star embodies the *lulik* land. People narrating the story use the two expressions interchangeably: 'the golden star brought good fortune to Dom Geraldo' or 'the [*lulik*] land gave good fortune to Dom Geraldo'. Through the intervention of the *lulik* land alone, the inhabitants of Laclubar obtained self-determination. The fact that Dom Geraldo was mistakenly addressed as *liurai* by the ruler of Samoro was due to the fact that the land had 'given good fortune' to Dom Geraldo.

According to this narrative, *lulik* legitimises the political position and authority of ancestral rulers and the current political order, because the descendants of Dom Geraldo are considered to be the righteous heirs of the position of the traditional ruler (*liurai*) today. People who tell this story claim that it is proof of the power and strength of the *lulik* land because the *lulik* land Susuk gave political independence to Dom Geraldo and by extension to the people of Laclubar. By continuously recounting this story at gatherings, rituals or public events, the strength and importance of the *lulik* are established and reinforced. Hence one might say that *lulik* land is partly so strong and powerful because of the narratives that are told about it. *Lulik* land and the narratives about it are mutually constitutive.

Moreover, the narrative illustrates several points I made about the nature of *lulik* potency earlier, such as the fact that it is considered to have agency of its own, by 'giving good fortune' and advice to Dom Geraldo. The idea of Dom Geraldo 'riding the wind' to Dili by climbing into a hole in the ground reinforces

---

4   Some people today refer to Laclubar as the 'little Samoro' (in Tetun: Samoro *kiik*).

my suggestion that *lulik* is associated with the underground. Moreover, some narrators claim that in return for giving independence to Laclubar, the *lulik* land took away Dom Geraldo's wife, because she died shortly after independence. They say the land 'wanted' his wife; she was the sacrifice for independence. Agency and motivation are attributed to *lulik*, which is potentially dangerous. While interactions with *lulik* land might be productive, they are also dangerous; for one human being to channel the potency of the underground, another human being must join it.

In Laclubar, several different individuals claim that they or their house group are the rightful descendants of Dom Geraldo in the present day and thus have the right to political power as the local ruler or *liurai*. The controversy over these claims is related to the content of the narrative. Some argue that Bita Loin, who in some versions of the narrative encountered the golden star instead of Dom Geraldo, is actually the legitimate ruler, but that he was forced to pass the sceptre—that is, political rule—to the house of Dom Geraldo. Opposed to this is the claim that the descendants of Dom Geraldo are the legitimate rulers and that Bita Loin was merely Dom Geraldo's servant. Moreover, there is controversy about which house groups descend from Bita Loin and from Dom Geraldo, because the houses split into different sub-houses and several people claim descent and the right to be in power. None of this, however, is expressed directly, but can be deduced from the way the story of the golden star is told and interpreted.

Narratives about ancestral interactions with the land and particular *lulik* sites establish long-lasting attachment between house groups and certain sites in the landscape. Attachment to land and claims to authority deduced from this are created discursively by emphasising the potent connections with the landscape. Despite the emphasis on these autochthonous connections, the narrative of the golden star also contains a number of references to the Portuguese interference in this relationship.

Colonial Evaluations of the Land

The people who recounted the narrative of the golden star tend to represent this story as a victory of the people of Laclubar over their neighbours in Samoro. They use the story to assert the fact that the people in Laclubar are independent and do not 'listen to orders from Samoro'. Interestingly though, the narrators rarely make explicit references to the Portuguese when telling this story. This is surprising considering the fact that there are several implicit references to the Portuguese in the narrative: the Portuguese title 'dom', the flag, Portuguese names and, most importantly, the 'Governador' in Dili. When asked specifically, most narrators concede that the Governor was probably a 'foreigner' (malae), but this is rarely mentioned when the story is recounted.

Considering that in the narrative Dom Geraldo and Dom Felis seek advice from the Governor in Dili, who decides that the two domains should be ruled separately, it is likely that this narrative refers to a change in the administrative boundaries undertaken by the Portuguese colonial government at the time. According to the Portuguese records, Laclubar was recognised as an independent domain only in 1868, by Governor Afonso de Castro (Corréa 1934:277). In 1896, Governor Celestino da Silva mentions Laclubar as one of those domains that was 'not yet subjugated' (Pélissier 1996:137), and in 1898 a military post was established in Laclubar (Pélissier 1996:180). It is possible that the story of the golden star refers to these events, which led to the recognition of Laclubar as an independent domain by the Portuguese. Moreover, when the military post was established, the Portuguese also appointed a local ruler of Laclubar by granting him the title of 'dom'. It is interesting to note that although the establishment of indirect rule in Laclubar probably meant a loss of independence through subjugation to an external colonial administration, it is recounted in the local narrative as a story of victory. The independence of Laclubar as an administrative unit that is separate from its neighbours is presented as a product of local circumstances, not as the outcome of external interference. What is clearly a colonial division of the region is recounted as the intervention of lulik land. The narrative thus represents a mythical justification of social and political relations via people's connection with the land.

Another reason for the increasing interest of the Portuguese in Laclubar at the end of the nineteenth century was that petroleum was discovered in the area (Pélissier 1996:241). There are reports from the 1890s onwards about German, British and Australian companies inspecting the area around Pualaca (near Laclubar) for petroleum deposits, and a British company established a more permanent presence by 1910 (Pélissier 1996: 118, 241, 244). When I carried out fieldwork, several people in Laclubar expressed fears that foreigners could come to the region to steal their gold. This concern could reflect an historical worry that foreigners might steal Laclubar's natural resources. Gold stands for the wealth of the natural environment, but also for lulik, as in the case of the golden star where the lulik land, in the shape of a golden star, gave political leadership to Dom Geraldo.

Although in the narrative the foreign governor agrees to Laclubar's independence, the real source of independence and political power is the lulik land. The story diverts authority away from the external colonial institution and projects it onto a local source. So on the one hand, people localise power by projecting it onto the lulik land. On the other hand, power is transferred from the realm of human agency onto the realm of subterranean potency. For the people of the Laclubar region, land is a vital resource of wealth and political power that can be gained through its *lulik* potency. There is, however, strong competition among the claimants for access to *lulik* sites and by extension to political leadership and authority. By recounting narratives of the potency of the land, people reassert their claims to political influence in the present. Another important connection to the land is its perceived capacity to protect local inhabitants from outsiders.

Raising Troops from the Ground

In the most commonly told version of the narrative about Dom Geraldo's encounter with the golden star, there is no mention of any fighting or war between Samoro and Laclubar. Nonetheless, a small group of narrators, belonging to the same origin house, recounted a particular addition to the narrative of Dom Geraldo that qualifies the case narrative.

> The people of Laclubar were obliged to deliver cotton and wax for candles to Samoro [a form of tribute]. As a sign of their protest, they decided to deliver only very small and poor-quality candles to Samoro. The *liurai* of Samoro, Dom Felis, was furious about this. So he gathered his best warriors, assembled troops from the neighbouring domains Same, Alas and Barique, and marched towards Laclubar.
>
> When the people of Laclubar heard that the warriors of the three neighbouring domains were approaching, they were scared. So the elders and ritual specialists gathered to ask the *lulik* land for help. They killed an animal to 'feed' the land and uttered words of ritual speech [Idaté: *sede*]. When the enemy troops were advancing, suddenly an army of spirits rose from the *lulik* land around Mount Maubere. The spirits were wearing weapons and they were everywhere. Their fighting screams echoed through the mountains and valleys. To the approaching troops, it looked as if Laclubar was swarming with people and warriors. But in reality, Laclubar was empty. There were no human beings around. Laclubar's inhabitants themselves could not see anyone. But to the troops from Samoro it looked as if an enormous army was waiting for them, prepared to fight. Struck by fear, Samoro's warriors fled. This is how Laclubar won the war over Samoro.

According to this story, Laclubar was saved from being destroyed by its neighbouring domains by raising spirit troops from the ground to frighten them. This kind of protection is referred to as 'opening the land'. The narrators of this story emphasise that just three elders managed to raise a whole army by carrying out a ritual at the *lulik* sites Susuk and Orlau. The spirit troops who were raised are the spirits guardians of Mount Maubere. They are the *larek na'in* or 'land spirits' that reside below the earth. It is for this reason that people refer to Mount Maubere as 'the warrior' (Idaté and Tetun: *asuwa'in*).

Narratives of this kind inform and set the context for accounts of more recent events. In 1999, after the referendum that led to East Timor's independence, East Timorese militias and Indonesian troops approached Laclubar. People say that when the Indonesians were coming up the road from Manatuto towards Laclubar they suddenly heard loud screams echoing through Laclubar. The town and surrounding mountains were filled with armed spirit troops. Thinking that members of Falintil—the East Timorese guerrillas—had come out from the forest to fight them, the Indonesians fled in panic. Yet, to the local inhabitants of Laclubar, the town looked empty. Again, it was the spirit troops from Mount Maubere who had saved them.

In 1999, Indonesian troops and local militias did enter Laclubar, destroying and burning parts of the town, and killing a number of people associated with the resistance. This fact seems of little relevance to those telling the story about the underground army, who insist that things would have been much worse otherwise. The main purpose of the account is not to explain why Laclubar was spared or not, but to stress the superiority of the potency of the land vis-a-vis external forces (cf. Traube 1986:55). The narrative inverts the historical and political relations of power. Similar to the threat posed by the Portuguese colonial government or the neighbouring domain Samoro, faced by an external intruder, the people of Laclubar say they can rely on its autochthonous potency to protect them. Faced by a dis-empowering situation, re-empowerment has to come from an internal other—the potent *lulik* land.

This is just one example of how narratives of the past are used to interpret what is happening in the present, emphasising the continuing power of *lulik* potency in people's daily lives. References to *lulik* land were also made in relation to the internal conflict in Timor-Leste from 2006 onwards, as I illustrated in the introduction. The program launched by Xanana Gusmão to return weapons to the ritual houses is based on the same line of reasoning as the idea that *lulik* must be returned to the land by 'closing' it. A closing ritual was held at the *lulik* site Susuk in order to close the land, because people argued that the reason for the conflict in 2006 was a failure to 'thank' the land for its help during the Indonesian occupation. By making an animal sacrifice to the land, harmful forces could be returned to the ground. Hence the relationship with the *lulik* land is a reciprocal one. And recent conflicts are seen as a failure of the inhabitants of this region to maintain their reciprocal obligations with it (cf. Traube 2007).

There are, however, different opinions as to which elders and political factions in the region were able to open or close the land. Many people thought the person who carried out the ritual as part of the national program did not actually possess the knowledge to close the land. Some claimed that the reason for this was that he was not a direct descendant of Dom Geraldo. Yet others were of the opinion that he had lived far away from Laclubar for too long and hence was not capable of carrying out the ritual correctly. People in Laclubar agree that land can be 'opened' to fight wars and has to be 'closed' in order to re-establish peace, but the narratives about *lulik* land also reflect competing claims to power and leadership.

Lulik land is considered to be invaluable for the protection of the local inhabitants. Nonetheless, there is competition over the access to *lulik* land. Several different factions in Laclubar claim that only they know how to open or close *lulik* land. This conflict is never expressed openly, but only through the way people interact with these sites during rituals and through the narratives they tell about the land. In order to continuously reaffirm one's connection with the land, in the face of intense competition, it is necessary to live close to the land to reassert one's own narrative account.

Conclusion

For the people of the Laclubar subdistrict, the inhabited environment is intersected with an invisible realm of *lulik* potency, ancestors and land spirits. This realm is a source of fertility, wealth and power, but it can also pose a threat to human beings when the reciprocal obligations towards the land are neglected. The potency of the land may be appropriated for protection during war by 'opening the land' and raising spirit troops from the ground. Once the land has helped its inhabitants, however, animal sacrifices need to be made to the land in order to 'close' it, thus establishing long-term peace and stability.

Narratives mediate between people and the land in three significant ways. First, they are practices through which people create attachment to the ancestral landscape. Second, they are a way in which claims to political leadership are asserted. Through oral narratives that create a connection between a house group and an important ancestor (Dom Geraldo), whose political position was established through a gift from the landscape, *lulik* potency is transformed into a source of ruling power (*ukun*). Competing accounts reveal rivalry and lingering conflicts about the legitimacy of the local ruler (*liurai*) of Laclubar in the present day. This competition is expressed not only in claims about the descendants of Dom Geraldo, but also in rival claims about who is entitled and knowledgeable to close or open the land.

A third way in which oral narratives mediate between people and place is that they allow people to invert and reframe historical experiences. The accounts

I discuss in this chapter give a local account of colonial and neo-colonial interventions by Portuguese and Indonesian powers, and the more recent internal conflict in 2006. In these narratives, people make sense of external decisions and changes in government that are beyond their immediate control. As a repository of autochthonous potency, the ancestral land localises external influences. In the narratives discussed here, dis-empowering situations are inverted by attributing historical agency to *lulik* land, which ultimately is considered to determine the course of events.

Acknowledgments

This chapter is based on fieldwork in Timor-Leste (2005–07) made possible by financial support from the Wenner-Gren Foundation for Anthropological Research, the Economics and Social Research Council (ESRC), and the German National Academic Foundation (Studienstiftung des deutschen Volkes). I would like to thank Andrew McWilliam, Elizabeth Traube, James Fox, Hercus do Santo and Lisa Palmer for their helpful comments. I would also like to thank the people of the Laclubar subdistrict for their valuable assistance during my fieldwork.

References

Arquitectura, F. d. and GERTiL 2002, *Atlas de Timor Leste*, GERTiL, Grupo de Estudos de Reconstrução de Timor Leste, Faculdade de Arquitectura Universidade Técnica de Lisboa, Lidel—edições técnicas, Ida, Lisboa, Porto, Coimbra.

Corréa, P. A. 1934, *Gentio de Timor*, Edicão do Autor, Lisboa.

Errington, S. 1990, 'Recasting sex, gender, and power: a theoretical and regional overview', in S. Errington and J. M. Atkinson (eds), *Power and Difference: Gender in island Southeast Asia*, Stanford University Press, Stanford, Calif., pp. 1–58.

Feuchtwang, S. 2004, 'Theorising place', in S. Feuchtwang (ed.), *Making Place: State projects, globalisation and local responses in China*, UCL Press, London and Portland, Ore., pp. 3–30.

Fox, J. J. 1983, 'Adam and Eve on the island of Roti: a conflation of oral and written traditions', *Indonesia*, vol. 36, pp. 15–23.

Fox, J. J. 1997a, 'Place and landscape in comparative Austronesian perspective', in *Poetic Power of Place: Comparative perspectives on Austronesian ideas of locality*, Department of Anthropology, Published in association with the Comparative Austronesian Project, Research School of Pacific and Asian Studies, The Australian National University, Canberra, pp. 1–21.

Fox, J. J. 1997b, *Poetic Power of Place: Comparative perspectives on Austronesian ideas of locality*, Department of Anthropology, Published in association with the Comparative Austronesian Project, Research School of Pacific and Asian Studies, The Australian National University, Canberra.

Hicks, D. 2004, *Tetum Ghosts & Kin: Fertility and gender in East Timor*, [Second edn], Waveland, Long Grove, Ill.

Hull, G. 2002, *Standard Tetum–English Dictionary*, [Third edn], Sebastiao Aparicio da Silva Project, in Association with Instituto Nacional de Linguistica, Timor-Leste, Winston Hills, NSW.

National Directorate of Statistics (NDS) 2006, *Timor-Leste Census of Population and Housing 2004*, National Directorate of Statistics, United Nations Population Fund, Dili.

Pélissier, R. 1996, *Timor en guerre: le crocodile et les Portugais, 1847–1913*, R. Pélissier, Orgeval, France.

Reuter, T. 2006, 'Land and territory in the Austronesian world', in T. Reuter (ed.), *Sharing the Earth, Dividing the Land: Land and Territory in the Austronesian world*, ANU E Press, Canberra, pp. 11–38.

Scott, M. W. 2007, *The Severed Snake: Matrilineages, making place, and a Melanesian Christianity in southeast Solomon Islands*, Carolina Academic Press, Durham, NC.

Therik, T. 2004, *Wehali: The female land—traditions of a Timorese ritual centre*, Department of Anthropology, Research School of Pacific and Asian Studies, The Australian National University in association with Pandanus Books, Canberra.

Traube, E. 1986, *Cosmology and Social Life: Ritual exchange among the Mambai of East Timor*, University of Chicago Press, Chicago.

Traube, E. 2007, 'Unpaid wages: local narratives and the imagination of the nation', *Asia Pacific Journal of Anthropology*, vol. 8, no. 1, pp. 9–25.

Trindade, J. J. and Castro, B. 2007, *Rethinking Timorese Identity as a Peacebuilding Strategy: The Lorosa'e–Loromonu conflict from a traditional perspective*, European Union Rapid Reaction Mechanism Programme, Technical Assistance to the National Dialogue Process in Timor-Leste, Funded by the European Union, Implemented by Deutsche Gesellschaft für Technische Zusammenarbeit, Dili.

4. Fataluku Living Landscapes

Andrew McWilliam

For each of us is one of the ancestors. And that in itself is a value to be preserved. (Cardoso 2000:21)

Introduction

In his magico-realist depictions of life and times in East Timor during the 1960s, Luís Cardoso writes about sharks as transmuted forms of ancestors: 'No one from the island was ever lost. Sometimes they lived in the sea, sometimes on the land. These cycles demanded their due if they were to continue' (2000:21). In a variety of evocative encounters, Cardoso draws attention to certain Timorese cultural notions of attachment and agency in relation to land and its living forms that are constituted in terms of spiritual and moral authority. Reminiscing about his own father's connection to revered freedom fighter Xanana Gusmão, for example, Cardoso writes:

> My father never mentioned his name. He was afraid that saying it might break the charm. This was what he had always done. When he traversed rivers, he did not call out the name of the creature that lived there, the crocodile. When he crossed the sea, he never invoked the name of the master of the coral-rich waters, the shark. He thought he was still in the middle of a long crossing, that men needed a rai-nain or *lord of the earth* to watch over their paths. (2000:148; my emphasis)

Across Timor, engagement with the emplaced 'spirit' realm is an enduring cultural value. It forms an important component of customary landownership and connections to land among the dispersed rural populations who rely on the blessings and providence of the natural environment to secure their livelihoods. Cardoso's reference to the *rai nain*—the 'lord of the earth'—speaks to this cultural orientation and provides a starting point for understanding the nature of Timorese customary land relationships.

In the lingua franca of Timor-Leste, Tetun, the phrase *rai na'in* and its regional linguistic counterparts have a double aspect, distinguished in terms of visible and less visible forms. In its material and more mundane characterisation, the 'lord of the earth' or the 'land lord' refers to senior local clan groups and their leaders who assert a historically constituted possession of specific tracts of land

and its constituent living forms. Typically, the status of 'lord of the land' is one founded on narrative claims of mythical precedence as first settlers or pre-eminence as warrior usurpers over defined localities.

All villages across Timor-Leste reflect complex histories of engagement and alliance between *rai na'in* groups. These clans make up indigenous political communities and order their affairs around a composite collective local authority. Typically too, senior *rai na'in* clans of local political domains are represented in the public sphere by spokespeople known as *lian na'in* (lord of the words): accomplished ritual speakers who serve as authorities over land matters within their respective jurisdictions and adjudicators of moral behaviour (for example, Meitzner Yoder 2003:19–20).

The authority and entitlement of *rai na'in* clans and their constituent agnatic membership, however, rest on a second order of relationship to land that is constituted in spiritual form. Assertions of ownership of customary lands are simultaneously statements of claim about particular relationships and obligations towards the 'spirit' community that resides and is believed to enliven the land. It is this understanding that accords the idea of the *rai na'in* a double aspect—namely, a human and visible form embodied in the living senior representative of the clan community of owners, and a second mostly invisible realm that comprises autochthonous emplaced 'spirit' entities of the land itself together with the collective ancestral shades of the living owners.

In this cultural construct, the living community of landowners together with their affinal allies who are granted land entitlements through marriage alliances maintain a continuing relationship of sacrificial commensality with their living domain. In exchange for placating and feeding emplaced 'spirits' of the land, the living community ensures access to its abundant blessings and protection—a relationship I have previously described as one of consubstantiation where living and 'spirit' forms are mutually constituted and strongly interdependent (McWilliam 2007b).

It is within this relationship of mutuality between the visible and invisible worlds that the continuing local legitimacy of the *rai na'in*—the 'lord of the land'—might be said to reside. Characteristically, the relationship is described in classificatory terms as hot (*manas*) with 'sacred' and dangerous properties—a term glossed in Tetun as *lulik*, and one that evokes a complex range of attitudes from fear and awe to familiarity and comfort (see Forbes 1989; McWilliam 2001; Pannell 2006).[1]

---

1 British Naturalist Henry Forbes, who visited Timor in 1882, described the *luli* in terms of a sacred institution, a taboo practice (1989:442), something awesome and protective in times of war (p. 446) and something that invoked fear of its vengeance if transgressed (p. 443).

In this chapter, I explore something of the distinctive shape and character of this doubly constituted notion of the 'lord of the land', which arguably reflects a deep orientation to binary classification and the ontological basis of diarchy as a characteristic of Austronesian ritual polities. While it finds broad application across the range of ethno-linguistic communities of Timor (see Bovensiepen, this volume; McWilliam 1999, 2002:103) and the Austronesian cultural sphere more generally, here I wish to focus on the concept as it informs contemporary practice among Fataluku communities in far eastern Timor. For Fataluku, local concepts of cultural sovereignty and natural resource entitlements are necessarily mediated and actively reproduced through the indeterminate agency of the spiritual realm. The association has retained its vitality and importance in Fataluku society during the long years of colonial rule and into the post-independence period. If personal beliefs in the spiritual realm are held unevenly among the population, and the influences of Catholicism and modernity have been at work here, they nevertheless form an integral legacy of the cultural domain across Fataluku living landscapes.

As a final introductory comment, I note that my use of the terms 'spirit' and 'spiritual' in this chapter is intended to refer to the complex range of largely invisible or only temporarily embodied entities in the landscape with which people engage and through ritual means enjoin, placate or invoke blessings. Use of the term 'spirit' has been criticised variously for its allusion to outmoded explanations of animism, for its tendency to mask or diminish the nature of the very complex it seeks to reveal, its religious implications as something disembodied, non-material or transcendental (see Harvey 2006), and as an inappropriate application of Western body/spirit dualism (Bird-David 1999). In the absence of a succinct and satisfactory alternative, however, I find it a useful gloss for describing the kind of elusive yet tangible phenomena discussed in this chapter. I find its replacement with forms of non-human 'persons' (Harvey 2006) or 'superperson' (Bird-David 1999) unsatisfactory and confusing. My concession is to use the term 'spirit' in inverted commas to denote that it glosses the nature and reality of a broader set of relationships that living human society maintains with other forms of being, whether other-than-human or ancestral in nature. The argument is partly semantic: if animism can be rehabilitated in new and productive ways, so can the definition and concept of spirit (see Peterson 2006 for a critique of these notions).

Land and Life in Lautem

Fataluku society forms the main ethno-linguistic community of Lautem[2] district in far eastern Timor-Leste (sometimes referred to as *Ponta Leste*), with an estimated population of about 40 000 people (National Census 2004).[3] A Papuan-language-speaking peoples, Fataluku society nevertheless shares many cultural features with their Austronesian-speaking neighbours (McWilliam 2007a). The majority of residents are farmers and pursue forms of near-subsistence swidden agriculture combining seasonal maize and secondary food-crop cultivation with smallholder livestock production. Buffalo (*arapou*) and pigs (*pai*) hold important and reciprocal roles in local livelihoods, especially in the complex ceremonial exchanges that mark life-cycle transitions and the making and remaking of social alliances.

Hamlet settlements are dispersed and these days cluster along access roads or around administrative centres—a legacy of Indonesian times when tight security policies prevailed. Many people also maintain simple houses in their swidden gardens following the pattern of earlier times when forest settlements (known as *otu*)[4] tended to be scattered and more mobile. Extensive use is also made of fallowed forest areas and coastal shorelines foraging for wild foods and other livelihood resources (see Pannell, this volume).

In the years since the withdrawal of the Indonesian Government from Timor-Leste in 1999 and the subsequent attainment of national independence, Fataluku communities have been busy with the task of rebuilding their lives. The loss of Indonesian subsidies and services along with the collapse of the formal market economy have fostered a renewed community focus on self-reliance and the restoration of a range of customary relationships that was previously curtailed and constrained under Indonesian military rule. These practices include the revitalisation of ceremonial exchange economies, a return to indigenous religion and a renewed interest in customary land tenure and assertions of landed authority at a time when formal systems of land administration have yet to be promulgated through national legislation.

---

2   A corruption of the phrase *Lau tein(u)*: 'sacred' woven cloth.

3   The main population area of Fataluku speakers lives in the subdistricts of Lautem, Tutuala and Fuiloro. In Luro and Iliomar subdistricts, the main population groups are Sa'ané (a dialect of Makassae) and Makalero speakers respectively.

4   The term *Otu* refers to a settlement site with a varying number of constituent households usually comprising a core group of agnatic kin and their affines.

Fataluku Lords of the Land: The visible realm

> Lautém terrified intruders. It was a land of proud, passionate men, all
> speakers of Fataluko. They guarded their honour with swords which
> they always carried with them and were quick to use. There were tales
> of vendettas dating back hundreds of years. (Cardoso 2000:46)

A fundamental social institution that informs the organisation of Fataluku
society is the *ratu*—a term I define as a dispersed, exogamous, paternal 'house
of origin'. *Ratu* membership typically includes male agnates, their in-married
spouses and children. The unity of the group is articulated through affiliation
to common male ancestors,[5] narrative myths of settlement and mobility, along
with shared ritual obligations and access to inherited common property in
clearly defined localities. Social and personal identities of people are intimately
connected and reproduced through the discursive frames of *ratu* ritual practice
and relation. These markers of affiliation and differentiation are expressed
through inherited names, ritual knowledge and commensality, especially of
sacrificial meat (*leura tei*), as well as food proscriptions, textile designs and
various clan-specific heirlooms and ancestral regalia. Periodically, members of
the *ratu* gather in ritual commensality to celebrate their common origins at sites
of mythical significance.

The settled landscape of Lautem proliferates in named resident *ratu* groups and
their scattered constituent households.[6] Their frequently contested histories
of segmentation, dispute and dispersal across the landscape provide the basis
for varying degrees of alliance and cooperation. Normative social relationships
beyond closely related agnatic households are formulated around continuing and
complex systems of exchange and marriage between the exogamous *ratu*. For
this reason, all Fataluku settlements in Lautem form composite communities of
intermarrying *ratu* households whose relationships are structured around shared
narrative histories of mutual assistance and interdependency.[7] This feature is

---

5   Female ancestors of the *ratu* may hold a significant place in the oral histories of the group but the general
emphasis remains on the continuity of the paternal progeny.

6   There are dozens of named *ratu* in Lautem (with names such as Cailoro *Ratu*, Latuloho *Ratu*, Naja *Ratu*,
Lavera *Ratu* and so on), and while clearly finite in number, precise enumeration is complicated by contested
views over the status and standing of different groups. I have recorded at least 60 named clans, many of which
have split off from other 'sibling' *ratu* in the distant past. Historically, when a number of households separated
from the main clan group and settled elsewhere, they sometimes took on the name of the locality in which they
settled for their *ratu*. Many groups also veil or mask the 'real' names of their origins.

7   *Ratu* clans form the most senior and highest status of three broad categories or castes of person in
Fataluku society, distinguished by the terms *ratu*, *paca* and *akanu*. The term *paca* represents a subordinate but
complementary 'younger sibling' (*noko*) grouping who maintain a close relationship and long-term alliance
with their *ratu* counterparts. The origins of the *ratu* and *paca* divisions are obscure and much debated. Here, I
would simply note that *paca* groups typically maintain long-term alliances with their classificatory *ratu* elder
siblings (*kaka*). A third category or caste of person and the lowest in social status is *akanu* or slaves whose
ancestors were former war captives or who were bankrupted into slavery in Portuguese times. Conventionally,

even more pronounced today as a result of the population-concentration policies initiated under Portuguese colonialism following Japanese occupation during World War II and intensified under Indonesian rule (see McWilliam 2007b). But for every existing or former settlement area across the Fataluku culture-scape, there is typically one *ratu* group that is accorded the senior status of *mua ocawa* or 'lord of the land'. This title acknowledges the authority and relationship of the principal landowning *ratu* to a defined landed jurisdiction and honours their precedence or mythical 'first-settler' status in the area. As elsewhere in Timor, here, the Fataluku title *mua ocawa* also contains a double aspect that differentiates the living members of the senior landowning group from their invisible 'spirit' counterparts—sometimes distinguished by the extended form *mua hocavaru* (land and lord).[8]

More specifically, in Fataluku ritual speech, the formal title of the senior landowning *ratu* is expressed by the phrase

Mua caovele ocawa   Land head skin lord

Horo caovele ocawa   Gravel head skin lord

The term *horo* in this binary representation refers to the widespread distribution of coralline rubble across the region—a feature of the karstic limestone character of the landscape and a material commonly used to construct sturdy stone fences that mark food-garden boundaries. Collectively, the reference speaks to the Fataluku distinction between the 'body' of the earth and its covering 'skin' (*vele*). By inference, people may cultivate the skin (*vele*) of the land for food crops or hunting, but only the 'lord of the land', the *mua ocawa*, asserts a pre-eminent authority over the whole of the land in question. This is an enduring relationship reaffirmed through social consensus and a sustained sacrificial engagement. It also means that in a general sense all land across Lautem is held as forms of common property by the collective members of various discrete *ratu* groups who share 'one blood, one serum' (*vehe ukani, ahi ukani*). Their territory is said to form part of the 'sacred land and the sacred garden' (*mua teinu ho pala teinu*) of the *ratu*—a phrase that links contemporary living members to the earliest settlements of their ancestors and the long history of cultivation and food production that has provided life and sustenance to the clan and its allies over generations (McWilliam 2007b).

---

intermarriage between these levels is proscribed, and although modernist pressures over recent decades have challenged the legitimacy of these cultural categories, they continue to inform social and political relations both within and between community settlements. Publicly identifying someone's caste status is considered bad form and these days most people will assert a more generic membership of a *ratu* group while denying connection to *paca* or *akanu* status.

8   In this chapter, as an orthographic convention for Fataluku words, the letter 'c' is pronounced 'ch'. The pervasive use of ritualised parallel speech is a common linguistic feature of the language.

The particular pattern of *ratu* landownership and the comparative size of their respective territories derive[9] from the mythical origins of settlement and the inherited entitlements of ancestral spatial practices. Adjustments and modifications reflecting complex and mobile histories of inter-group warfare and shifting political alliances have also informed boundary-making processes over time. Today, the limits of these ancestral common-property lands are more or less fixed, their meandering edges marked variously by sacrificial alter posts (*ete uruha'a*), ridge lines or prominent marker stones, as well as by crumbling stone walls of fallowed garden sites, creek lines and other topographic traces. The knowledge of boundaries (*varuk ho fetil*)[10] is retained as part of the heritage of the *ratu* agnatic community, especially the senior male affiliates and customary leadership of the group (referred to as *laficaru* or, in their role as ritual speakers, by the parallel phrase *hoponocawa :: luku-lukunocawa* [master of chants, master of words]).[11]

With established dominion over the land, founder groups assert a temporal and political precedence in relation to subsequent settlers whose subsidiary claims are framed in relation to the established 'lord of the land' (*mua ocawa*). These later arrivals—groups seeking refuge from inter-clan warfare or banishment from other lands—ally themselves to the resident owners and gain access to favourable marriage arrangements, settlement sites and arable land. One way Fataluku describe the protective, nurturing role of the *mua ocawa* is to refer to them metaphorically as the *nalu lafae*, the great mother, who, in the marriage of their daughters to immigrant husbands, provide the *susu ho ami*[12] (white sap and milk) that enables their households to prosper and grow. In a real sense, wife-givers 'give life' (*lauhana mina*) to their in-marrying affines. In Fataluku marriage terminology, this relationship is expressed as one between the progenitors, *ara ho pata* (base and post, trunk and stem), and their progeny, *tupurmoko* (little women), which establishes lifelong asymmetrical alliances of mutual obligation and exchange.

As in-marrying affines, and cultivators of the skin (*vele*) of the land, they are said to enjoy the *mina ho vai'a* (oil and fat) of the land—a distinction expressed in formal speech as:

---

9   A definitive survey of *ratu* land boundaries, although still feasible, has never been undertaken.

10   A parallel speech form that combines the idea of a boundary and visible border markers.

11   A further title is that of 'he who sits in front of the sacrificial hearth' (*acakaka emer miré*). Conventionally, all *ratu* recognise an internal differentiation based on the birth order of sibling lineages. Namely, first born (*moco kaka*), who take priority and political precedence, middle born (*moco ulu penu*) and last born (*moco vehula*). *Ratu* leadership may emerge from any of the sibling groups, but conventionally the first-born lineage (*moco kaka*) is accorded seniority.

12   *Ami* is the Fataluku word for breast milk while *susu* is the name given to the white sap of the forest fig tree (*hama*) that grows in abundance in the lowland forests and is often the site of ritual veneration (somewhat ironically given that *susu* [*susubeen*] is the Malay/Tetun term for milk).

Vaian a i mina i vai'a una   The brother-in-law eats the oil and fat

i ara ia mua ocawa i hini varini   The trunk/base continues to own (the land)[13]

The relationship is also conveyed in the Fataluku botanical trope between those who are 'rooted' in place (*ara ho pata*) and those who receive the flowers and fruit of the land (*icipi imana*) and build on the base established by the *mua ocawa*.[14] But the precise arrangements over access and use are dependent upon specific histories of negotiated agreement and alliance. There are numerous narratives that describe the multiple circumstances under which wandering groups have sought and found refuge with landowning clans.[15] In generations past, for demographic reasons as much as any other, migrant male settlers could be granted permanent or nested ownership rights in land by the resident *mua ocawa*. In the process, they become 'lords or masters of their own garden areas' (*pala ocawa*) and permanent resident allies, able to bequeath land to their children and fully participate in the community exchange economy. Collectively, the subsidiary allied households that reside with the *mua ocawa* group may be referred to as *i namaunu: i tara maunu* (those who come later: those who have recently arrived) or *olo comaunu: aca comaunu* (literally: 'birds' coming from afar). This category includes both allied *ratu* households with longstanding relationships of marriage exchange and newcomers with shallow histories of engagement.[16] But, ever conscious of transgressing cultural sensitivities and the fines that may accompany them, by convention, they are referred to variously as 'sisters and children' (*leren ho moco*), 'affines and friends' (*vaian ho paienu :: lan[u] ho tava*)—a relationship that may not be arbitrarily severed without retributive consequences. Conversely, the subsidiary houses remain conscious of the need to respect the authority of the *mua ocawa* and to inform and consult them on significant matters dealing with the land.

If the local 'lord of the land' (*mua ocawa*) is positioned at the apex of a residential complex of subsidiary households and affinal segments of in-marrying origin groups, their capacity to sustain this pre-eminent position is only in part founded on their political authority and settlement precedence. It is also constituted through an enduring bond and ritual engagement with the inspirited landscapes to which their ancestors negotiated, through ritual sacrifice with other-than-human forms, into an enduring sovereignty over the land.

---

13   The reference also alludes to the obligatory gifts of food offered by wife-givers (*omara*) to their affines known as *ore fai*—portions of cooked pork for which they reciprocate with buffalo meat, known as *leura*.

14   *A'a lalune* (to make the base), *a'a ca'unu* (to layer or stack on top).

15   For illustrative purposes, I was given the example of the person who builds a house and when visitors come they are allocated a room, but if they then want to extend or change the structural arrangements they need to consult with the house owner.

16   In more recent times, the practice of allocating more or less permanent land entitlements to in-marrying affines is now less common as land availability has declined with population growth.

Inspirited Landscapes: The invisible realm

For most Fataluku, the experience of the 'spirit' domain is part of the lived reality of social life. They refer to this ever-present though largely invisible presence by the generic term *tei* (sacred, taboo, prohibition) or *teinu* (pl.)—a concept that combines moral authority and protective familiarity with elements of dangerous uncertainty and retribution. That which is *tei* or accorded the properties of *tei* must be treated with caution, respect and ritual restraint.[17]

The concept of *tei* extends to a wide range of spiritually charged locations across the land, to certain forms of behaviour, the consumption of sacrificial meat (*leura tei, ipilu tei*), forms of avoidance relationships (*nita tana tei*),[18] the sanctioned names of origin ancestors and *ratu*-specific knowledge of healing spells, sorcery (*vetiku, hupia, kori*) and protective invocations (*lukun teinu: hopon teinu*). As Pannell and O'Connor (2004:2) have argued, 'the notion of *tei* is positioned in the centre of a discourse which explores the often perilous limits of sociality', where the idea of the sacred or of sacrality expresses the inherent ambiguity of power and lies in the indeterminate space between blessings and threats, malevolence and benevolence.

Within a broadly Catholic framework under God (*uruvacu*: moonsun), Fataluku make a distinction between two broad classes of *tei*—namely, between a set of autochthonous beings of the land that is conceived of as predating human settlement; and *tei* that are created or emplaced by human action including ancestral shades and places in the landscape that memorialise ancestral spatial histories.[19] This distinction also informs the idea of an inspirited landscape that combines a notion of engaging pre-existing and emplaced 'spirit' forms along with active processes of inspiriting as a means of religious transformation of the landscape. The latter point includes legitimating processes of clearing and cultivating the soil, hunting and utilising its resources, being born and dying in the land, all of which contribute to the conversion of the country from the strange to the familiar, from 'other lands' to 'our lands'.[20]

---

17   People often carry with them small bundles of charms (*ete lari*: tree root) that are designed to protect them from unwanted threats or spiritual attack from witches (*acaru*) or other dangerous influences.

18   This phrase might be glossed as 'our hands are *tei*' and refers to a situation where two groups engaged in past feuding in which members were killed and who have not undertaken subsequent ritual peacemaking. For this reason, they avoid situations of sharing food and other forms of sociality because of the risk of severe spiritual sanction associated with the blood curse.

19   There is a degree of transformational blurring and indeterminacy in this division. Some *ratu* recognise their ancestral origins to derive from animals or creatures that inhabit the region—sharks, crocodiles, dolphins and so on—which take on some of the attributes of totemic significance and association.

20   I have adapted the term 'inspiriting' from the anthropologist Basil Sansom, speaking on the nature of Australian Aboriginal land connections and migrations (1993:29). The idea supports Pannell's observation that 'the foreign is rendered familiar through the presence and experience of *tei*' (2006:8).

For Fataluku, over generations of interaction and engagement, of ritually feeding (*fané*) and placating the wild, unrestrained nature of *tei*, the senior landowning group, the *mua ocawa*, confirms their entitlement and authority over the land in question. As a Fataluku colleague described this relationship, 'the *mua ocawa tei* is wild, jealous and dangerous and only the [human] *mua ocawa* has the authority and right to manage it'. There is, some say, little distinction between the living *mua ocawa* and their invisible counterpart. The latter form is at times able to take on the visible appearance and substance of their living counterparts. They are mutually constituted, consubstantiated or, as one Fataluku colleague put it, 'there is no clear boundary between the *mua ocawa* that can be seen and the one that can't'. That is why people honour and respect the 'lord of the land' and seek their permission to reside on the land and utilise the abundant resources of which they are custodians.[21]

In a similar fashion, Pannell has described the autochthonous being who inhabits the cliff site of Ili Keri Keri in Tutuala as one 'which, like all other beings [who] occupy pre-existent *tei* places within the Fataluku landscape, has a ritual name considered hot and dangerous and known only by (the generic term) "lord of the land" from Tutuala Ratu (*mua caoveli hocawa*)' (Pannell 2006:11).

The presence of the spiritual 'lord of the land' might manifest itself in a variety of living forms including pythons (*nana*), green tree snakes (*cuale'u::pelikafu*) or the mythical *aka*, which can appear as part-human–part-snake (see King 1963:151). Crocodiles (*lavei*), dogs (*iparu*), species of birds (*olo*) or even insects (bees: *wani*, and a species of cricket: *napa*) might also be recognised. In any specific bounded jurisdiction, one or two of the native fauna might be construed as the senior 'lord of the land', the *tei ocawa* (lord of the *tei*) over the living forms in its domain.

It is said the wild *tei* of the land (*mua cupenu*) are calmed or 'tamed' (*tei ma'a varin pai*) through the actions of their human counterparts. Sacrificial offerings of blood, offal, rice and palm liquor with appropriate invocations (*lukunu tei*) render them amenable to the control of the living lords of the land.[22] The formulaic words and language of address to the *tei* are the property of the senior landowning group, which secures the protection of those who legitimately reside within their lands. But the nature of the invisible *mua ocawa* is capricious and demanding, and they might turn on their living custodians when neglected or addressed incorrectly. As ever, there is a high degree of indeterminacy in

---

21 When farmers open new food gardens (*pala miri*), they perform a small divination known as *minin fai*, which is undertaken to ensure there are no issues that might hinder the growth and harvest success of the gardening activity. The ritual is simultaneously an acknowledgment of their permission to do so.

22 Hicks' argument about 'snagging divinity' and the dynamic interdependency, even parity, between the realm of humanity and the divine is relevant here (see Hicks 2007:51). He cites with approval the early position of Hubert and Mauss (1964:91) that 'not only is it in sacrifice that some gods are born, it is by sacrifice that all sustain their existence'.

relation to engagement with the *tei*. The middle of the day, when the sun is hot and strong, is considered a dangerous time when *tei* beings appear and move about. People are encouraged to be alert to signs of their presence or action—unusual noises, movements or bodily sensations—and to avoid places where malevolent entities are said to reside. The occasion of a whirly-whirly (*refutu*), for example, might signal the presence of the tutelary 'spirit' (*mua hocawaru*), and one should step aside and let it pass. As a Fataluku interlocutor has put it, 'nature still has authority over us', and this attitude facilitates a range of cultural practices designed to placate that which is potentially malevolent and to invoke its assistance in times of need (*i tei lira fai*: to invoke the *tei*). As the custodians of an abiding relationship with the living environment, the senior representatives of the living lords of the land have the inherited responsibility of managing this relationship on behalf of their co-resident affines and allies.

In this chapter, I do not intend to explore the ontological foundations of Fataluku cultural ideas about the nature of the living world, except to comment that, in my view at least, inspirited landscapes of Lautem are inhabited, not conscious. The land and its topographical features—its rocks and trees, flora and fauna—are not sentient, as has been argued of some other indigenous traditions (for example, Poirier 2005; Viveiros de Castro 1998).[23] Rather, I would argue for a living realm that is construed in symbolic and metonymic forms and which serves as a medium for addressing the uncertainties and contingencies of social life. Fataluku relationships to land are complex and inflected with high levels of sentiment and inscriptions of meaning—'analogous identification', in Pederson's terms (2001:416). As forms of externalised moral authority, the inspirited landscape is understood to be inhabited by an indeterminate set of other-than-human and formerly human identities that might be recognised and manipulated through processes of discovery. These processes of recognition are learned reactions and responses to cultural expectations and Fataluku society has developed an elaborate complex of divinatory diagnostic techniques to interpret sources of affliction and resolve otherwise unexplained events. In this context, people often turn to trusted diviners and healers (in formal speech, known as *i na haran :: i na lolon navarana*) to interpret and identify remedial strategies for addressing and resolving the arcane and often deleterious impact of inspirited forms on their lives.[24]

The living world of *tei* includes a second corpus of potent shades constituted in ancestral form. In ritual speech, the ancestors are called the *umun ho upenu*

---

23   The issue, however, remains open to interpretation and the whole matter is somewhat ambiguous as Fataluku sometimes appear to impute agency and awareness to the land itself.

24   An example offered to me was people who might have participated in the murder or death of others during the Indonesian period of oppression, but who did not divulge their complicity or sin. In time, they might be 'caught' by the shade of the victim seeking revenge, possibly appearing in the sudden death of children or an economic disaster for the household.

(those who are deceased and those who are no longer), and there is a high value placed on the memorialisation and sustained ritual engagement with clan ancestors, conventionally addressed as *calu ho papu*.[25] Through prayer, invocation and sacrificial feeding (*fané*), the ancestors are urged to provide blessings and protection[26] for their descendants, to ward off illness and heal the sick, to bring abundant harvests and healthy babies, to restore reputations and alleviate suffering. Even in times of economic hardship, Fataluku households put substantial resources towards commemorating the death of relatives and the construction of large, elaborately decorated concrete graves.

The majority of Fataluku communities locate their ancestral origins in the long-range sailing exploits of their forebears who made landfall on the coast of Lautem in their oceangoing *perahu* (F: *loiasu*), leaving mythologised inscriptions of their settlements across the forested landscape. These marks and signs of ancestral activity are variably expressed, but typically include the following elements: carved sacrificial alter posts (*ia mari tulia*, ancestral footprints) located around the coastal fringe, which identify places where mythical ancestors made landfall and established their first settlements;[27] specific ancestral 'stone boats of origin' (*loiasu mataru*) that beached on Timor and became lodged in the landscape, now manifest as fossilised limestone outcrops;[28] and numerous overgrown former hilltop settlements (*lata paru* and *lata irinu*) or stone-walled forts (*pamakolo* and *laca*), often containing massive stone graves (*calu lutur*[u]) with spaces for ceremonial enactment (*sepu*). Collectively, these sites mark the historical and spatial imprint of *ratu* ancestral activity across the landscape. Each might provide a focal point for ritual invocation in the hope that blood sacrifice and prayer can resolve grave misfortunes afflicting members of the living origin group, or celebrate the blessings of their abundance. These early and old sites of ancestral presence are reputed to be the most powerful in terms of their restorative or influential effects. Their seniority, it is said, gives them the authority to 'assemble' a wider group of ancestral shades.[29] Powerful ancestral sites are also, however, fraught with risk where errors in ritual performance and narrative forms of address carry heavy sanctions such as illness and even death

---

25 The phrase is a collective reference to the corpus of ancestors of the *ratu*. It refers specifically to the names of the second and third ascending generations of male ancestors (grandfather, great-grandfather).

26 The protective agency of the ancestors is expressed in the phrase *ufur*(*o*) *ho namu utupé*, to protect (our) body and person.

27 The statement elides a complex variety of mythical knowledge and belief. Some of the founding ancestors (known generically as *Cal*[*u*] *arafura*) are said to have arrived in the guise of sea creatures: crocodiles, dolphins, sharks or stingrays. Others rode on their backs or walked along the seabed. Each group has its own narrative myths of origin and arrival.

28 Carved wooden alter posts and naturalistic figurines (known generically as *ete uruha'a* or *sikua*) that represent ancestral figures or sites for sacrificial invocation to ancestors.

29 In death, the shades of the newly deceased are enjoined, through forms of ritual chanting known as *sau* and *nololo*, to travel back to the origin settlements and join the collective ancestry of the *ratu* community. As Campagnolo (1975:75) has observed, Fataluku might sometimes say of the death of someone that 'they have gone to plant coconuts in the land of the first village'.

for practitioners. For that reason, Fataluku generally rely on the knowledge and ritual skills of their leaders (*laficaru, luku-lukunocawa*) to determine and conduct the necessary invocations at the more potent origin sites of veneration. At other times in the absence of good reason, people tend to avoid approaching iconic ancestral sites or do so with caution and care, especially those associated with other clans.[30]

For spiritual comfort, most Fataluku households rely on prayer and invocation to their immediate household ancestors through the medium of ritual hearths (*acakaka* or *lafuru tei*). There structures of invocation are maintained within the domestic house itself. Culturally, it is expected that a newly married couple will install an *acakaka*, the initial burning embers of which are brought from the hearth of a senior agnatic relative in a process that symbolically links all members of the agnatic group to their common ancestral origin hearth.[31] The *acakaka* provides the principal site for all sacrificial activities associated with the life-cycle events of the household and the maintenance of its health and wellbeing.[32] At these times, kinsmen gather to provide sacrificial offerings (*leura tei, ipilu tei*) to group ancestors who are invited to attend the sacred hearth (*acakaka na cuaré*; to assemble at the hearth) within the house and participate in commensal union. For these events, portions of the sacrificial food might also be fixed to the outside perimeter of the house. The food is designed to feed ancestral shades reputed to be more threatening or unpredictable and who are said to stand outside and listen:

(*Tava*) *koco pu na nehere* (They) stand outside the walls,

Le upu na nehere   behind and outside the house.

Their reported role is to ensure that only those who are entitled to participate in the ritual consumption of the sacrificial meat enter the house. Interlopers or strangers would be immediately identified and struck down.[33]

The primary relationship of an agnatic community with its ancestors is fundamentally mutually protective and interdependent (Schefold 2001). Just as people depend on ancestral blessings for their own health and wellbeing,

---

30   The converse of this idea is that sacrifices should be undertaken only at sites with direct ancestral connection to the clan members concerned.

31   These days, younger people, especially those living in Dili or Los Palos, might rely on the ritual hearths of their fathers or grandfathers for sacrificial blessing.

32   Households will also often fix a small forked stick (*saka*) above the entrance to the house, which they bless or 'feed' with a raw egg—leaving the upturned shell on one of the forks of the *saka*. These objects (*leo'o utunatana*) activate an ancestrally sourced protective perimeter around the house, which is said to ward off sickness and untoward malevolent influences. Food offerings to ancestors mirror social feasting practices and typically comprise a cooked and uncooked portion, the latter intended to be taken 'home' to feed those who were not able to attend (*i camé la'a, tor apu una*: a portion to take [home], for the many to eat together).

33   I have also heard the explanation that only the senior ancestors are invited into the house; those who have died more recently are thought to assemble outside and listen.

so ancestors cannot exist without the continued ministrations of sacrificial offerings and the attention of their living descendants.[34] The mutually implicated obligatory nature of this relationship provides at least one of the motivations for the continued enactment of sacrificial invocations within contemporary society. In a real sense, the survival of the *ratu* as a living, embodied group is dependent upon continued attention to its ancestors.

At the margins of the ancestral domain lie other inhabitants of the living environment that are considered inimical to healthy life and threaten the wellbeing of the household and family. These categories of being lie outside the ancestral realm proper but are nevertheless associated with or derived from the world of society and community. Their nature is more unpredictable and potentially harmful—an example being the shades of persons who suffer sudden and untimely deaths, who are murdered or commit suicide (*ulao ucanu*). Bad deaths such as these are highly inauspicious and the shades of the victims might be lost to the community of ancestors, becoming wild or threatening to the living (*huma'ara kaparana*: evil shades) (for comparison, see Fox 1973). Their presence might be signalled through dreams (*ufarana*)[35] or upon hearing unusual sounds or movements in the dead of night (*ula mosiku*). They are thought to cause illness and sudden death when confronted.

In the same fashion, the unrestrained shades of miscarried foetuses might be associated with misfortune, injury or death among family members. These issues arise when a women miscarries or spontaneously aborts a foetus, which are referred to as 'fallen children' (*moco i fan*). If this event occurs early in a pregnancy when a mother might not have been aware of her condition, the living being of the child (*i hutu*) is released into the world as an uncontrolled 'spirit' agent (*huma'ara*), causing accidents, slips or sudden deaths from falling among family members.

In response to the multiple possibilities and categorical ambiguities of the spiritual realm,[36] Fataluku farming communities rely heavily on the mediating role of diviners and ritual leaders knowledgeable in the cultural techniques who can identify, direct and engage the complex elements of the living landscape that frame and influence embodied social life. All households and the extended family networks of which they are a part undertake a variety of domestic ritual performances and sacrificial engagements to facilitate and protect their own wellbeing. Collectively, however, they reside under the emplaced authority

---

34 Commenting on neighbouring Makassae practice, Lazarowitz noted that '[i]f one fulfils all the responsibilities owed to the ancestral spirits, life will follow a true and even course' (1980:181).
35 Fataluku contrast the 'spirit' (*huma'ara*) of the deceased with that of the living (*ihutu*). A person's *ihutu* living 'spirit' is said to be active and moving about when they dream.
36 I have not included discussion here of a further class of malevolent agents at work in Fataluku society, known as *acaru* (*acare*): witches and shape-changers who present as living human beings but are inherently dangerous and thought to cause illness and debilitating body disorders.

of their respective 'lords of the land' whose cultural intimacy and enduring engagement with the living landscape, its cycles of life, death and renewal reaffirm the abiding connection of landowning clans and their co-dependent resident affinal allies. The moral authority of the autochthonous *tei* of place, combined over successive generations with a growing collectivity of human ancestral shades, merges into the composite and diarchic authoritative figure of the *mua ocawa: mua hocawaru*, the lord of the land.

Landscapes of 'Spirit' Allies

> His hair was long and dishevelled, his beard thick and white, like that of a be'e na'in or spirit of the water. (Cardoso 2000:149)

Lautem is a diverse and heavily forested district,[37] and this feature, along with the fringing coastal reefs and waters, provides an abundant array of foodstuffs and other resources that help sustain the domestic economy of Fataluku households. Local residents draw on a whole range of plant species—apart from firewood, timber and other building materials (bamboos, rotans and thatch for roofing)—for fibres, ropes, baskets, gums and vegetable supplements such as tubers, wild beans, leaf vegetables, resins, honey and forest fruits. An extensive pharmacopoeia is also recognised and drawn upon from the plant world (see Collins et al. 2007),[38] while hunting is a popular activity throughout the year, and the use of various poisons, traps, spears and dogs provides a regular supply of game meat and seafood.[39]

A key principle of Fataluku landed authority is the protocol of seeking permission from the *mua ocawa* to access or engage in these various forms of resource extraction. The notion of permission here applies explicitly to outsiders, but the idea is inferred through interaction and consultation between affines and co-residents. Once again, the notion of permission extends to both the living human and the 'spirit' resident owners of the land in question.

37　In June 2007, as one of the final legislative actions of the former Fretilin Government, acting Prime Minister, Estanislau da Silva, was able to secure the legal establishment of the first national park in Timor-Leste, which honours the memory of former Fataluku and Falintil resistence leader (1993–98) Nino Konis Santana, and creates an extensive multipurpose conservation reserve in Lautem (see McWilliam 2007b).

38　The forests of Lautem, particularly the mountainous Pai Cao region, provided a long-term sanctuary to armed Falintil guerillas, who benefited from a committed clandestine support network of Fataluku families.

39　This diversity of harvestable food includes fish (*api*), clams (*saka*), sea turtles (*ipitu*), sea eels (*suanu*), crabs (*capuku*) and sea urchins (*tiri*), as well as freshwater shrimp (*asi*) and turtles (*veu*), bats (*maca*), monkeys (*lua*), civet cats (*loh*), cuscus possums (*acuru*), deer (*vaka*), feral pigs (*pai hoto*) and birds (*olo*). Reef gleaning (*meti fai, tono fai*) for shellfish, seaweed and other edible marine creatures is practised along the foreshore during low tide (see Pannell, this volume).

Fataluku describe the process of ritual invocation and divination directed to the invisible realm of *teinu* with the term *ucuté*, meaning to 'request something'. This is usually paired in formal Fataluku speech with the phrase *lisé parité*, to request agreement in the sense of obtaining permission. The phrase speaks to the relationship between customary landowners and the collective resident living forms in the land and its topographical features. The idea of requesting permission incorporates the related notion that generations of ancestors who preceded the living landowners have resided, worked and sweated in the landscape, and are now buried in the former settlements (*lata paru*) and abandoned garden sites (*pala cenu*) that are scattered around the clan country and its fallowed forests.

One example of acknowledgment is the casual practice of apportioning small offerings of food as gifts during meal breaks in the forest—a generic offering to unseen recipients as a sign of respect. More specific invocations might also be undertaken to enhance prospects for hunting or gathering wild foods at sites known to be inhabited by *tei* beings such as large trees (*ete lafai*), springs (*iraina*), caves (*veraka ho acacapak*) or other prominent topographical features. Active engagement with the indeterminate 'spirit' realm might be especially indicated when Fataluku pursue hunting or foraging activities beyond the settlements where forest 'spirits' (*cat[u] catu*)[40] have the potential to befuddle or confuse the hunter, making game invisible or elusive, and where inspirited springs and watercourses (*ira tei*) can withhold their food resources (shrimp, crab, fish) from the fishers' gaze or net.

As a generic form of invocation or prayer for blessing, which can be used for securing forest game and other wild foods including marine resources, the following speech segment expresses this sense of humility and benefit. The reference is to wild bean but its application is broad:

e una pore'e naci'e,	This food satisfies and fills,
et fo fon koron lari koron	raw bean and raw legume
unum ini ina inat la'an	a food portion given to us to take away
le mara em ete asa taru asa	to take (to our house) as leaf and vegetable
le meset zeu ho moco,	(sweetening) the house of my wife and children
horu una, em nia tana polu pai	eating together, our hands and feet replete.

---

40 Fataluku recognise a range of different *cat catu* spirit forms including those in large forest trees (*cat catuserelai*), spirits of the mountains (*ili cata cat[u]*) and those associated with the ocean (*tahi cat cat[u]*).

Another expression of the intimate and mutually sustaining relationship between living community and 'spirit' realm expressed in the formal phrase 'lord of the land' (*mua caoveli ocawa*) is illustrated in the Fataluku cultural concept of *curé*, which I would gloss as a process of 'arising' or 'standing up'. The performative modality of *curé* might be mobilised in circumstances of dire threat or immanent danger to members of the ritual community. In the process—usually undertaken secretly at night—sacrificial invocations are enacted by senior clan members of the living 'land lords' to engage the collective living agency of the land and confront an enemy or threat. Only they have the authority and capacity to enact this process. The ritual words are designed to call the power of *tei* into action and to bring the silent living forces of the land into a state of defensive alertness:

Mua caoveli cure	The land arises
Horo cao veli cure	The ground arises
Tua o cure pala o cure	Sugar palms and food gardens arise
Ete o cure taru o cure	Trees and vines arise
Ete pata eni.	Trees and branches as well.
Ili moko eni	Rocky outcrops too.

By this ritual invocation of the taboo sphere (*tei*), the world becomes hot (*timiné*) and dangerous (*malaru*)[41] for both the ritual community and the aggressors or opposing group. The former will receive the protection of the land from the *mua hocawaru* as long as they follow attendant moral codes including proper behaviour, abstaining from sexual intercourse[42] and following relevant food proscriptions. Conversely, the intruding enemy will find themselves befuddled in the landscape as it turns against them. They will be unable to see their targets, spiked on thorns, bitten by insects, bruised by falling rocks, and their weapons also become ineffective:

| *Pata mucu elevé* | The gun becomes cold |
| *kanu mucu elevé* | the gun stock becomes cold. |

In this way, the invocation of the *tei* of the land is activated through ritual speech to resist or attack (*nacula*) enemies of the resident landowning community.

---

41   The literal translation of *malaru* is 'bitter', but it carries the sense of danger and threat. The ancestors, *calu ho papu*, for example, are also said to be 'bitter'. This concept is one that might also have cultural associations with the healing power of indigenous medicines (*larinete asa*: literally, tree leaves) that are often bitter to taste, their efficacy deriving in part from the humoral association of bitterness and ancestral blessing.
42   Sexual relations are symbolically connected to fertility and ritual coolness—inimical to the heated state of warfare or violence in what might be considered a typical Austronesian cultural symbolic operator (Fox 1989:45). Breaking this injunction might cause the magical protection of the ritual form to fail.

Em neré naté	Directed to engage (the targets)
Em horopé em aporé	told to shadow and pursue.

The manipulation of the retributive potential of the *mua hocavaru* allows for a range of applications. The process was reportedly invoked by 'all the *ratu*' during the 1975 military occupation of East Timor by Indonesian armed forces, and allowed the resistance fighters to hold out for years against prodigious odds. Pannell and O'Connor (2004) also discuss the ritual release of the 'president' *tei* at Titiru, Tutuala, during the violence and destruction that accompanied the popular referendum around independence in 1999. Following a request from then resistance leader, Xanana Gusmão, the local 'lord of the land' (Tutuala *Ratu*) sacrificed a pig at the stone *tei* and invoked the spirit to emerge from its hole to take action against the Indonesians (Pannell and O'Connor 2004:14).

There are also possibilities for mobilising the properties of the invisible *mua hocavaru* during the course of local hostilities or, for example, in longstanding disputes over unpaid bride-wealth (*fai inu*), thefts of buffalo or matters where group honour has been seriously impugned. The key idea is that the invisible world of *tei* may be invoked and directed by its living counterparts to consume or infuse (*me a laku*) the offending group or site with its poisonous intent. Each *ratu* has clan-specific *tei* connections that may be mobilised ritually to seek out and punish enemies.

When the task of the avenging *mua ocawa* is deemed complete, when justice has been meted out, a further sacrificial invocation is enacted to dispel the magical protective state, to close down its malevolent intent (*nere pa'i*) and return it to a condition of calm, life-giving coolness (*fulehe pa'i*). Similarly, as Pannell and O'Connor (2004:14) note: 'when the Indonesians left [Timor-Leste] the lord of the land returned to Titiru and sacrificed another pig to calm the *tei* down and entice it to enter its hole once again, satiated with food and drink, and the blood and flesh of the enemy.' In formal Fataluku speech, this ritual invocation may be expressed in the following way, accompanied with appropriate offerings and blood sacrifice:

Em uraceru	Ordered to return
em uraneru	called back
ma'u hin halivana nai	coming to the place of origin
hin hulutu'a nai	to the permanent resting place.

Landed Authority in a Binary Idiom

In Lautem, as elsewhere in Timor-Leste, the initial euphoria of victory in the independence struggle has given way to a more subdued acceptance that economic hardship is not about to be alleviated any time soon. Under these circumstances, Fataluku communities are once again called upon to demonstrate their well-tested capacity for self-reliance and resilience. In that process, the cultural ideas and practices that draw upon the protection of the inspirited landscape continue to inform social life in multiple ways. They remain what they have always been: strategies and symbolic action designed to account for uncertainties in a world where any event might be significant and nothing can be left to chance (Pannell 2006:15).

These ideas are not, however, universally held in Fataluku society. The significant conversions to Catholicism,[43] and the opportunities created by modernist secular education over more than two decades of Indonesian rule, have modified the degree of adherence to animistic ontologies. Many young people, in particular, who have forsaken the over-familiar confines of settlement life for wider opportunities in Dili and further afield, feel less constrained by ancestral conventions. Nevertheless, as one Fataluku colleague, a senior civil servant in Dili, commented to me: 'whether you believe or not doesn't really matter, but you shouldn't half believe because this can have serious consequences.' He then proceeded to tell me the apocryphal story of a man from Lorehe who decided to give up ancestral beliefs and practices by becoming Catholic and threw out his *acakaka* (sacrificial hearth). Not long after, his family began to suffer, his parents died suddenly, then his wife and his siblings, until he was the only one left, and people remonstrated with him, saying, 'Look what you have done by ignoring the *calu ho papu*'. He is then reported to have replied, 'Well, that is my sacrifice for God, but I will not return to those practices'—and then he died. The story is a lesson that confirms the self-fulfilling idea that if you forget your past and the names of the ancestors and discontinue your connection with them then you leave yourself unprotected from their blessings and are destined for oblivion.

The Fataluku living landscapes that I have outlined in this chapter and the relationship between the visible living 'lord of the land' and their autochthonous invisible counterpart (*mua hocawaru*) are ones that resonate with complementary concepts of land attachment and 'spirit' domains both in other areas of Timor,

---

43   Catholicism is estimated to have had just 17 per cent of the population of East Timor as adherents to the faith at the time of Indonesian occupation in 1975, but this had increased to upwards of 90 per cent by the late 1990s (Boyce 1995:79). This dramatic increase was in part driven by government insistence that Timorese follow the state-sanctioned moral philosophy of Pancasila, which required all Indonesians to follow an approved theistic religion, and the fact that the Catholic Church was also perceived as an institution of refuge against Indonesian military pro-independence repression.

as noted in the Tetun concept of *rai na'in*, and widely across the Indonesian archipelago and the Austronesian-speaking world more generally (for example, Forth 1998; Molnar 2000). By way of comparison, I would cite Hicks' (2004:36) comments on the *rai na'in* among Tetun-speaking communities in Vikeke, where he notes that '[b]oth spirits of the land and…water exercise a strong measure of control over the lives and aspirations of human beings', and where encounters can bring great good fortune (wealth, physical prowess or invulnerability) but equally the prospect of infertility, sickness, insanity and death. In a similar fashion but with more historical depth, van Wouden, writing on northern Tetun populations and following Grijzen's earlier 1904 report, makes the observation that

> the term 'lord of the land' also occurs among the forms of address applied to a ruler. These are: *nai lulik*, sacred lord; *rai na'in*, lord of the land; and *ata na'in*, lord the people. *Rai na'in* are also earth-spirits, whose worship occupies such an important place in religious life. (1968:49)

A similar set of ideas extends well beyond Timor. Wessing, for example, has described a comparable complex on Java in remarkably similar terms. He notes that Javanese speak of 'the spirits of place as *penguasa*, the ones who are in authority or control', and he interprets the status of the 'lord of the soil' (*tuan tanah* in Indonesian) as the divinisation of the energies that produce the fruits of nature by which the resident community is sustained in its locality (Wessing 2006:18). In these terms, the blessings that derive from this divinisation are also extended to the living counterpart of the tutelary spiritual 'lord of the land', which adds to and reproduces their status and authority.

More than this, Wessing has interpreted the relationship between living, human settlers and their spiritual counterparts as one that 'socializes the symbolically wild realm of nature spirits' and renders it conducive to human settlement. Through ritual offerings and invocations, the spirits acquiesce to the occupation of their land by human beings and become the objects of cult celebration. 'Ensnared by sacrifice, they are then bound to render assistance' (Wessing 2006:34). He concludes that the person who controls the spirit is usually the one who opens the area, the founder of the village or their descendants. Their demonstration of spiritual authority and control of the 'spirits' of the land place these figures and their inheritors in leadership positions of their communities.

This doubly constituted notion of the lord of the land is also strongly suggestive of two further possibilities or interrelationships that have long been recognised as foundational concepts for Austronesian ritual polities. The first of these connections is the widespread theme of diarchy and diarchic models of politico-ritual leadership (see Cunningham 1965; Fox 1989). Across the island of Timor itself, the historical pattern of indigenous governance was one composed of a double ruling centre usually distinguished by gendered symbolism. Leadership of the domain was commonly shared between a ritual and political ruler (Schulte Nordholt 1971) in which landed spiritual authority and executive political power were constituted asymmetrically and diarchically. In these realms, a symbolically female, ritual lord, on receipt of harvest gifts and other tribute from the land, reciprocated with ritual blessings that ensured continued fertility and abundance for the people. The symbolically masculine counterpart was responsible for executive political leadership, the organisation of the people living within the domain and the defence of the realm itself. Over centuries of Portuguese and Dutch colonial attempts to manipulate and control Timorese political life, much of the delicate and dynamic balance of these diarchic patterns of authority has been disrupted and undermined, but they remain informally evident in many areas of Timor where customary protocols require their explicit articulation within clan organisation or in the rhetorical narrative structures that frame and support contemporary village (*suco*) authority (see Freidberg 1989; Traube 1986).

The diarchic mode of leadership is similarly expressed in that other pervasive theme of landed authority in Austronesian societies: the mythology of the stranger king. This cultural motif and its narrative variants[44] typically revolve around an original transfer of power to an immigrant prince signified by the surrender, usually in marriage, of a native or autochthonous woman of rank (Sahlins 1985:87). The concept is one eminently compatible with, for example, the prehistoric maritime expansion of Austronesian settler communities across insular Asia and the Pacific (Bellwood 1996; Siikala 1996), as it is with contemporary Austronesian claims to legitimacy and contested cultural sovereignty over local jurisdictions (for example, Graham 1996). In a variation on the theme of the stranger king, Fox has explored the complex recursive patterns expressed by the process of 'installing the outsider inside'. The idea speaks to the historical processes of displacement in the Austronesian world of Timor whereby influential or powerful outsiders become chiefly rulers through distinctive cultural processes of incorporation (Fox 1995).[45]

These three foundational mythologies of emplaced authority—the lord of the land, the diarchic polity and the stranger king—are cultural themes that ramify across Timor and the Austronesian world. In their rich and diverse local renditions, they each appear to represent reflections or refractions of the same guiding principle—namely, the discourse of origins expressed as contested

---

44   A variant of this mythology is that of the returning younger brother who is accorded political power over his 'elder siblings' who have remained in place at the centre of the world tending to their ritual responsibilities (see, for example, Traube 1986).

45   Similarly, Sahlins has recently argued that the elemental relationship between affines is the archetype for stranger-king politics: 'the affinal relationship is the experiential ground cum social enactment of people's dependence for their own existence on external sources they do not control' (2008:195, 196).

precedence (Vischer 2009), whereby the spiritual or autochthonous element is temporally prior, but submits—literally gives ground—to a subsequent political authority, thus forming a complementary and composite unity. The diarchic principle of authority is one that signifies and celebrates the negotiated and recursive patterns of accommodation between emplaced autochthonous communities and settler immigrants that have informed the dynamic histories of island societies for generations (for comparison, see Forth 1989; Freidberg 1989). The finding is consistent with Fox's exploratory study of Austronesian ideas of rule and of the dialectic relationship of political power and spiritual authority to the categories of 'inside' and 'outside'. In comparative Austronesian terms, political orders are never constructed entirely from 'within' but are constituted from both internal and external origins (Fox 1995:18). For Fataluku society, the ritually mediated and sustained landed authority of the composite lord of the land—the *mua ocawa*—provides one cultural version of this fundamental and life-affirming understanding.

Acknowledgments

Research for this chapter has been pursued intermittently over the period 2002–09 under the auspices and support of The Australian National University. Funding has also been provided by an Australian Research Council Discovery Grant (2005-2008), entitled, Waiting for Law: Land, custom and legal regulation in East Timor. My thanks extend to many patient Fataluku ethnographic advisers, especially Anita Ximenes, Almeida Fernandes Xavier, Fernando Santana, Sidonio da Cruz, Mario dos Santos Loyola, Amando Lopes (dec), Rikardo Lopes, Francisco Valela, Edmundo da Cruz, Robella Mendez, Carmeneza Dos Santos Monteiro and Justino Valentim. Thanks also to reviewers for comments and suggestions.

References

Bellwood, P. 1996, 'Hierarchy, founder ideology and Austronesian expansion', in James J. Fox and Clifford Sather (eds), *Origins, Ancestry and Alliance: Explorations in Austronesian ethnography*, Research School of Pacific and Asian Studies, The Australian National University, Canberra, pp. 18–40.

Bird-David, N. 1999, '"Animism" revisited: personhood, environment and relational epistemology', *Current Anthropology*, vol. 40, pp. 67–91.

Boyce, D. (compiler) 1995, Timor: where the sun rises over the crocodile's tail: a collection of environmental, historical and cultural notes, Unpublished manuscript, Dili.

Campagnolo, M. L. O. 1975, L'habilitation des Fataluku de Lorehe (Timor Portugais), Thèse de Doctorat de 3ème cycle, Academie de Paris, Ecole Pratique des Haute Etudes, Université René Descartes, Paris.

Cardoso, L. 2000, *The Crossing: A story of East Timor*, Granta Books, London and New York.

Collins, S., Martins, X., Mitchell, A., Teshome, A. and Arnason, T. 2007, 'Fataluku medicinal ethnobotany and the East Timorese military resistance', *Journal of Ethnobiology and Ethnomedicine*, vol. 3, no. 5, Published online 22 January.

Cunningham, C. E. 1965, 'Order and change in an Atoni diarchy', *Southwestern Journal of Anthropology*, vol. 21, pp. 359–82.

Forbes, H. O. 1989 (1885), *A Naturalist's Wanderings in the Eastern Archipelago*, Oxford University Press, Singapore.

Forth, G. 1989, 'The Pa Sése festival of the Nagé of Bo'a wae (central Flores)', in C. Barraud and J. D. M. Platenkamp (eds), 'Ritual and socio-cosmic order in eastern Indonesian societies', *Bijdragen tot de Taal-, Land- en Volkenkunde*, vol. 145, no. 4, pp. 502–19.

Forth, G. 1998, *Beneath the Volcano: Religion, cosmology and spirit classification among the Nage of Eastern Indonesia*, KITLV Press, Leiden, Netherlands.

Fox, J. J. 1973, 'On bad death and the left hand: a study of Rotinese symbolic inversions', in R. Needham (ed.), *Right andLeft: Essays on dual symbolic classification*, University of Chicago Press, London and Chicago.

Fox, J. J. 1989, 'Category and complement: binary ideologies and the organization of dualism in eastern Indonesia', in David Maybury-Lewis and Uri Almagor (eds), *The Attraction of Opposites: Thought and society in a dualistc mode*, University of Michigan Press, Ann Arbor, pp. 33–56.

Fox, J. J. 1995, Installing the outsider inside: the exploration of an epistemic Austronesian cultural theme and its social significance, [Revised draft], Paper presented at the first Conference of the European Association for Southeast Asian Studies: Local Transformations and Common Heritage in Southeast Asia, 29 June – 1 July, Leiden University, Netherlands.

Freidberg, C. 1989, 'Social relations of territorial management in light of Bunaq farming rituals', in C. Barraud and J. D. M. Platenkamp (eds), 'Ritual and socio-cosmic order in eastern Indonesian societies', *Bijdragen tot de Taal-, Land- en Volkenkunde*, vol. 145, no. 4, pp. 548–62.

Graham, P. 1996, 'Enacting sovereignty: sacrifice and the power of outsiders in Lewolema, Flores', in S. Howell (ed.), *For the Sake of Our Future: Sacrificing in eastern Indonesia*, Research School CNWS, Leiden, pp. 148–75.

Harvey, G. 2006, *Animism: Respecting the living world*, Columbia University Press, New York.

Hicks, D. 2004, *Tetum Ghosts and Kin: Fertility and gender in East Timor*, [Second edn], Waveland, Long Grove, Ill.

Hicks, D. 2007, 'Younger brother and fishing hook on Timor: reassessing Mauss on hierarchy and divinity', *Journal of the Royal Anthropological Institute*, vol. 13, pp. 39–56.

Hubert, H. and Mauss, M. 1964 [1888], *Sacrifice: Its nature and function*, W. D. Halls (trans.), Chicago University Press and Cohen and West Ltd, Chicago and London.

King, M. 1963, *Eden to Paradise*, Hodder & Stoughton, London.

Lazarowitz, T. F. 1980, The Makassai: complementary dualism in Timor, PhD thesis, State University of New York, New York.

McWilliam, A. R. 1999, 'From lord of the earth to village head: adapting to the nation state in West Timor', *Bijdragen tot de Taal-, Land- en Volkenkunde*, vol. 155, no. 1, pp. 121–44.

McWilliam, A. R. 2001, 'Prospects for the sacred grove: valuing *lulic* forests on Timor', *Asia Pacific Journal of Anthropology*, vol. 2, pp. 89–113.

McWilliam, A. R. 2002, *Paths of Origin, Gates of Life: A study of place and precedence in southwest Timor*, KITLV Press, Leiden, Netherlands.

McWilliam, A. R. 2007a, 'Austronesians in linguistic disguise: Fataluku cultural fusion in East Timor', *Journal of Southeast Asian Studies*, vol. 38, no. 2, pp. 355–75.

McWilliam, A. R. 2007b, 'Customary claims and the public interest: on Fataluku resource entitlements in Lautem', in Damien Kingsbury and Michael Leach (eds), *East Timor: Beyond independence*, Monash Asia Institute Press, Melbourne, pp. 165–78.

Meitzner Yoder, L. 2003, *Custom and conflict: the uses and limitations of traditional systems in addressing rural land disputes in East Timor*, Discussion Paper prepared for a regional workshop on Land Policy and Administration for Pro-Poor Rural Growth, Dili.

Molnar, A. K. 2000, *Grandchildren of the Ga'e Ancestors: Social organisation and cosmology among the Sara Hoga of Flores*, KITLV, Leiden, Netherlands.

National Census of Population and Housing in Timor-Leste 2004, Direcção Nacional de Estatística, Dili, Timor-Leste.

O'Connor, S. and Pannell, S. 2006, Cultural heritage in the Nino Conis Santana National Park, Timor Leste: a preliminary assessment, Unpublished report.

Pannell, S. 2006, 'Welcome to the Hotel Tutuala: Fataluku accounts of going places in an immobile world', *Asia Pacific Journal of Anthropology*, vol. 7, no. 3, pp. 203–19.

Pannell, S. and O'Connor, S. 2004, Where the wild things are: an exploration of sacrality, danger and violence in confined spaces, Paper presented at the Society for American Archaeology Sixty-Ninth Annual Meeting, Montreal, pp. 1–19.

Pederson, M. A. 2001, 'Totemism, animism and North Asian indigenous ontologies', *Journal of the Royal Anthropological Institute*, vol. 7, no. 3, pp. 411–27.

Peterson, N. 2006, A sentient landscape? Animism, metaphor and symbolic action in Australia, Paper presented at the American Anthropological Association Conference.

Poirier, S. 2005, *A World of Relationships: Itineraries, dreams and events in the Australian Western Desert*, Toronto University Press, Toronto.

Sahlins, M. 1985, *Islands of History*, University of Chicago Press, Chicago.

Sahlins, M. 2008, 'The stranger-king or, elementary forms of the politics of life', *Indonesia and the Malay World*, vol. 36, no. 105, pp. 177–99.

Sansom, B. 1993, *The Warai people and the Wagait land dispute: an anthropological report to the Northern Land Council*, Darwin.

Schefold, R. 2001, 'Three sources of ritual blessing in traditional Indonesian societies', *Bijdragen tot de Taal-, Land- en Volkenkunde*, vol. 157, no. 2, pp. 359–81.

Schulte Nordholt, H.G. 1971 *The Political System of the Atoni of Timor,* Nijhoff, The Hague.

Siikala, J. 1996, 'The elder and the younger—foreign and autochthonous origin and hierarchy in the Cook Islands', in James J. Fox and Clifford Sather (eds), *Origins, Ancestry and Alliance: Explorations in Austronesian ethnography*, Department of Anthropology, Comparative Austronesian Project, Research School of Pacific and Asian Studies, The Australian National University, Canberra, pp. 41–54.

Traube, E. G. 1986, *Cosmology and Social Life: Ritual exchange among the Mambai of East Timor*, University of Chicago Press, Chicago.

van Wouden, F. A. E. 1968, *Types of Social Structure in Eastern Indonesia*, Nijhoff, The Hague.

Vischer, M. P. (ed.) 2009, *Precedence: Social differentiation in the Austronesian world*, ANU E Press, Canberra.

Viveiros de Castro, E. 1998, 'Cosmological deixis and Amerindian perspectivism', *Journal of the Royal Anthropological Institute*, vol. 4, no. 3, pp. 469–88.

Wessing, R. 2006, 'A community of spirits: people, ancestors and nature spirits in Java', *Crossroads*, vol. 18, no. 1, pp. 11–111.

5. Darlau: Origins and their significance for Atsabe Kemak identity

Andrea K. Molnar

Introduction

Membership in the former Atsabe domain is not separate from Atsabe Kemak identity. But in order to understand this identity relation, it is important to appreciate the Atsabe Kemak's relation to land and particularly to places of origin. Darlau Mountain is one such focus, one origin place, and the question of who is a 'true' Kemak with a legitimate Kemak identity is enmeshed with this particular place of origin. In this chapter, I discuss the centrality of the great mountain of Darlau in Atsabe Kemak discourse on Kemak origins and identity.

Within the former Atsabe domain, Darlau is the tallest mountain (about 2400 m). Atsabe Kemak represent Darlau as the cosmic origin place where sky and earth were connected in the beginning of time when differentiation had not yet taken place. Darlau Mountain, as a place of origin, is often paired with or discussed in opposition to Atsabe Lau or Ramelau Mountain. Kemak people associate Ramelau with the dead, with funerary rites and the invisible villages of the ancestors, while they associate Darlau with living human descendants.[1]

According to myth, Darlau is the mountain where the origin village, Lemia, was founded by the first Kemak ancestors. Even the later invader who subjugated local related chiefdoms and amalgamated them into the larger Atsabe domain is legitimised through a connection to Darlau and the origin village there. The dispersal of settlements and the former small chiefdoms that emerged from these settlements, and thus made up the Atsabe domain, are elaborated upon by the Atsabe Kemak in relation to Darlau.

Darlau is also claimed as the site of origin for all sacred trees that, ordinarily, were not allowed to be cut down. In the ceremonial context of building origin houses, however, these trees are specifically utilised: *ua*, *ora*, *taha buci* and *goru* trees. In the myth of the origin of fire, the ancestor brings fire from the top of Darlau with a *taha* branch. Identification with Darlau is thus a significant aspect of Atsabe Kemak identity and a means by which they distinguish themselves in relation to other groups. Old origin villages that made up the Lemia chiefdom

---

1 See Molnar (2006) for discussion of the local concepts related to funerary rites and ancestors.

were located on Darlau and are still visited once a year by descendants to clean the graves of the ancestors and to place offerings. Through origin stories, I will highlight each of these significant elements of Darlau for the Atsabe Kemak, particularly in relation to notions of authority, precedence and subordination (cf. Fox 1995, 1999). The argument reinforces Reuter's (2006a:13) point that 'in a traditional cultural context, Austronesian-speaking societies have constructed their sense of identity and legitimised their territorial claims to land and other resources by reference to local and sometimes regional origin narratives'.

Various ANU-based anthropologists have developed the concept of precedence for the comparative study of Austronesian societies.[2] This group of anthropologists has suggested that a fruitful comparative study of Austronesian societies needs to focus on indigenous conceptions of origins. Fox (1988:15, 1995:214–28) labelled the different configurations in which this preoccupation appears as 'origin structures'. He proposed that the studies of 'origin structures' and of the systems of precedence they generate are useful forms of comparison across Austronesian societies.[3] Two major issues in the study of precedence concern 'what validates precedence and what it confirms'. The study of origins in these societies sheds light on what precedence confirms, since it is only in relation to the past that precedence is justified (Fox 1994:106). Furthermore, 'it is necessary for participants in systems of precedence to be able to trace relations to prior events, structures and persons' (Fox 1994:106). 'Context is paramount in the application of precedence…It is multivalued…[and] precedence can be used to create hierarchies, to dispute them, or simply undermine their creation' (Fox 1994:106). Relations of precedence among the smaller chiefdoms encompassed by the former Atsabe domain are expressed in origin myths in relation to specific places of origin and the dissemination of settlements from such places of earlier origin. One way the Kemak define their cultural identity is through their relation to the Darlau, particularly to the first origin village, Lemia, and the first chiefdom that coalesced there. Origin stories are significant among the Atsabe Kemak in narrating the past in relation to the local topography and landscape, and indeed in connection with the ordering of social relations within the former Atsabe domain in relation to specific places within their locality (cf. Fox 1997). The origin village and Darlau Mountain serve as significant metaphors for 'Kemakness'. While origin houses serve as the pivotal nexus of all marriage alliances that weave together the larger social fabric of a former domain, hierarchical relations among the component chiefdoms (the current main villages) are expressed in relation to origins from Lemia and Darlau. A relation to this mountain and to other significant places in the landscape is

---

2   See, for example, Fox (1988, 1989, 1994); Graham (1991); Grimes (1990); Lewis (1988); McWilliam (1989); Vischer (1992).
3   The concepts of hierarchy and precedence are discussed by Fox in a number of publications. See, for example, Fox (1993, 1994:1–22, 1996a, 1996b).

central in the narratives and local discourse on identity and intra-group relations and thus social reproduction. Various previous studies (for example, Fox 1997; Reuter 2006b) have highlighted the ways Austronesian cultures relate to place and the landscape in encoding their memories of place as an 'origin' structure, a 'metaphor for living' (cf. Fox 1980a:333).

Before proceeding to a background discussion on the Kemak of Atsabe, I wish to clarify the ways I will use the terms domain, and chiefdom and domain. Chiefdom and domain refer to a hierarchical, centralised political organisation of varying size with a formal leader: a chief or ruler. Domain refers to the extent of the territory over which a ruler or chief had authority. The heads of these various domains had different titles. The ruler of the Atsabe domain held the title of *koronel bote*; other lesser domains were headed by figures that held the ranked titles of *nai*, *dato* and *rati*.

While kin relations were recognised among the various chiefdoms that derived from the original Lemia chiefdom on Darlau, they were completely autonomous in their authority over their chiefdoms' territorial domains and internal affairs. Once these chiefdoms coalesced into the Atsabe domain, the degree of autonomy of each chiefdom was affected—the authority of that chief had to be legitimised and confirmed by the rulers and the chiefs had to fulfil various obligations towards the ruler and the domain. Furthermore, the individual chiefdoms ceased to be territorially expansionist. The Atsabe domain, however, engaged in the expansion of its territorial domain that brought under its authority other groups, some of which were not Kemak. I shall elaborate further on the hierarchical organisation of the Atsabe domain in a later part of this chapter.

The Kemak of Atsabe

The Kemak-speaking group of Timor-Leste is found in the Bobonaro, Ermera and Ainaro districts. Very few professional anthropological studies existed on the Kemak[4] (Barnes 1985; Clamagirand 1971, 1972, 1975, 1980, 1982; Hicks 1986) until a few years ago. Before I discuss the Atsabe Kemak, I acknowledge what remains the classic study of East Timorese Kemak culture, focusing on the Marobo Kemak. Clamagirand produced one superb monograph and four articles, based on her fieldwork undertaken between 1966 and 1970. Clamagirand's work is the basis for other comparative analysis of Kemak social practice (for example, Barnes 1985; Fox 1996b; Hicks 1986). The Marobo Kemak community members as described by Clamagirand (1982) are swidden cultivators with a

---

4   In the literature, various spellings have been used for the designation of this ethno-linguistic group, including Kema, Kemak, Ema and Quemaq. Molnar (2004, 2006) produced recent articles on the Atsabe Kemak based on ethnographic field research since 2002.

social organisation that can be characterised as a 'house society' (see Fox 1993, 1996a). The house (*uma*) is the basic social unit and the focus of Marobo Kemak social organisation and relationships. The *uma* has a pivotal role in private and collective domains as well as in social organisation, ritual, myth and the indigenous belief system. The house defines an individual's place in the social hierarchy according to his or her house's place in the order of precedence (cf. Fox 1988, 1993a, 1993b, 1995, 1996b:130–53). Generalised exchange characterises Marobo marriage alliances that are contracted between and among houses. Clamagirand argues for a cyclical four-partner model of alliance. Houses are also arranged hierarchically around chiefdoms, thus having a significant role in local political organisation. Individual houses are also the focus of life-cycle rituals and private rites with the presence of both wife-takers and wife-givers, while collective rituals involve the entire community. Aside from the monograph produced on the Kemak, Clamagirand authored a number of articles, one of which focuses entirely on Kemak social organisation, and another on the house, both as a physical and as a social structure (her other articles focus on ritual and traditional weaving, respectively). While Clamagirand does not explicitly speak of local social organisation in terms of 'orders of precedence', her data appear to indicate the analytical significance and utility of this concept. Her ethnography, however, does not situate the Marobo in relation to other Kemak, such as the Atsabe Kemak, nor does she mention marriage alliances with major origin houses in Obulu and Boboe villages. The ethnography gives the impression that the Marobo are a 'self-contained unit' whose most enduring social relations are constructed within the Marobo community itself.

I encountered a similar attitude among the Atsabe Kemak towards the Marobo Kemak. There was very little emphasis on how Marobo fits into their Atsabe-centrist view in which all Kemak originate from Darlau. In their view, the Marobo ancestors were the first to leave the origin village of Lemia and Darlau Mountain a very long time ago when the early Kemak people still lived on Darlau and had not yet dispersed and differentiated into various villages or chiefdoms. I did encounter a few comments that suggested negative attitudes towards the Marobo, depicting them in derogatory terms as rather backwards. Boboe and Obulo villages, however, never expressed any negative sentiments about the Marobo with whom they have close marriage alliances. They simply portrayed them as 'not true Kemak' since the Marobo tend to marry more within their own group and even more intensively with their Bunaq neighbours. The Marobo were viewed as marginal due to their lack of greater integration into the social fabric of component units of the former Atsabe domain. When I interviewed some Marobo people who were visiting their in-laws in Atsabe, they also tended to emphasise how they differed in customs and dialect from the Atsabe people. Atsabe Kemak recognise Marobo as the place of origin for weaving *tais*. Marobo people are viewed as the first people to plant cotton and to give cotton seeds to other regions. The Marobo are also considered to be among the first to make pottery for storage. Atsabe Kemak talk about them as 'different Kemak, since they are more like the Bunaq with whom they intermarried. Even their language [they mean dialect] is mixed with Bunaq words.' Obulo village of Atsabe subdistrict is considered to be Marobo since most of the named houses of Obulo are said to have derived from Marobo.

Clamagirand's ethnography does not situate the Marobo in the larger universe of East Timorese Kemak people in the sense of inter and intra-group relations with the populations outside Marobo. While I was unable to find references in Clamagirand's ethnography to the represented place of origin of the Marobo Kemak, or reference to the origin village of Lemia, the names of the main origin houses engaged in marriage alliance within Marobo provide clear indication of being branch houses (or 'descendant houses',[5] as the Atsabe Kemak put it) of some of the oldest origin houses of Lemia. For example, *uma* Goru Ubu is the genitor house to a number of houses with *ubu* in their name. More importantly, the oldest source house on Darlau, *uma* Tali Meta of Lemia, is a wife-giver to a multitude of Kemak source houses in many villages and is thus regarded by these source houses as their *ai mea* ('red tree or red trunk')—referring to the first marriage alliance established between two houses and the repetition of this marriage over generations. *Uma* Tali Meta has a branch house by the same name in Marobo, *uma* Talite (a dialectical variant of the name) (Clamagirand 1982:23).[6] This can occur only if this house was founded by a family who were members of the original Tali Meta house of Lemia.

Atsabe Kemak Origins

The Atsabe subdistrict in Ermera district is the centre of the former Atsabe domain. There are 12 main villages, as has been indicated in the historical records of Portuguese colonial writing, with a new, thirteenth village that recently emerged as an official village in 2002. Some of the village names have changed over time, or rather the original village name is now retained only in the name of a hamlet.

---

5 'Descendant house' was expressed in terms of the relationship that exists between the source house (*uma pun*) and a house derived from it: 'child house' (*uma ana*).

6 This is not the place to go into naming 'origin houses', however, I do want to point out that a branched house will bear a part of the parent-house names—such as Goru Ubu of Lemia giving rise to Lulu Ubu; or Ilat Lara giving rise to Ilat Laun; or Soi Leki giving rise to Soi Lesu; Mali Ubu of Lemia giving rise to Mali Ubun Uma Dolen, and so on. I deliberately show the connection here between the oldest origin houses in Lemia and some of the main origin houses in Marobo (Clamagirand 1982:72).

Atsabe contains the following villages

- Lemia Leten (upper Lemia), the origin village of all Kemak; Lemia Craic (lower Lemia) is now in a different administrative district—namely, Ainaro

- Laclo, one of the first to branch from the founding origin village of the Kemak from Lemia

- Boboe Leten and Boboe Craic (formerly one village, Boboe)

- Tiar Lelo (Ciar Lelo), which is central given its status as the village of the *koronel bote*, or the *liurai* of Atsabe

- Malabe (Atu Dame or Acu Dame in old writings)

- Obulo, whose population is related to the Marobo group and also heavily intermarried with Bunaq

- Paramin, with a mixed Kemak and Mambai population due to intermarriages

- Laçao

- Lau Buno

- Batu Manu

- Estado

- Atara

- Mali Mea, the new, thirteenth village, which branched off from Atara.

After Lemia on Darlau, the villages of Laclo, Tiar Lelo, Boboe and Malabe (Atu Dame) are viewed by the Atsabe Kemak as central given that all other villages are considered to be 'satellites' or offshoots of these four[7] central villages (and former chiefdoms) with the same named houses present in the satellite villages. It must be pointed out, however, that Laclo, Atu Dame, Tiar Lelo and Boboe are considered to be branch settlements of Lemia with many of the same origin houses having a branch presence in these villages. It was also repeatedly stated that for major ritual occasions the populations of the 'satellite' villages convene at these four central villages. Along with Lemia, the four villages are also the nexus of the marriage and political alliances of the former domain of Atsabe.

Place, origin villages and named houses are the basic structuring units of groups, although in a couple of cases, such as those of Tiar Lelo and Boboe (Craic) villages, the first house's name (the house of the founder ancestor) is used in the same way as a clan or group name. Often this house encompasses the main source houses, each of which gives rise to, or encompasses, other named branch houses. Usually the first main house is the *uma luli* (sacred house, the repository of ancestral heirlooms as well as the focus for the rituals of the whole group). Named houses are the basic units of marriage exchanges and thus

---

7   Four central villages are Laclo, Tiar Lelo, Boboe and Atu Dame, thus not counting Lemia, the ultimate source village of all Kemak. The four focal villages made up the core of the Atsabe domain.

anchor the highly complex nexus of alliances. There is a great emphasis on the founding village, the founding ancestor and the ordering of houses and social relationships in terms of both place and ancestor. There are many named houses but people tend to list the main source houses in the first instance since all other named houses derive from these main source houses.[8]

Topographically, most of the subdistrict is spread out on steep mountainous terrain with a few valleys. The great, rapidly flowing Kumubia River creates a border with the Letefoho subdistrict and features a beautiful waterfall (Bendera). The mountains of Atsabelau, Darlau and Ramelau are the most significant borders of the territorial domain[9] and figure significantly in the ancestral belief system as well as origin stories. The great mountain of Darlau is considered to be the place of origin of all Kemak people.

In terms of local social organisation, the Kemak place great emphasis on founding villages and their associated founding ancestors. The hierarchical ordering of named source houses and social relationships is oriented to both place and ancestors. They extend out to the Mambai in Ailieu, the Bunaq and Tetun groups in the western part of Timor-Leste as well as in the Atambua region of Indonesian Timor. These alliances are still strongly maintained, particularly those within the sphere of power of the former domain of Atsabe. While most historical documents of the Portuguese era refer to regions within the current Atsabe subdistrict (Atsabe, Boboe, Obulo and Tiar Lelo) as separate domains (see, for example, Felgas 1956; Sherlock 1983), local constructions of social relations view the Atsabe domain as the all-encompassing unit whose authority subsumed that of Boboe and Obulo. With its centre at Tiar Lelo, it provided the line of the Atsabe rulers. Furthermore, there existed a specific order of precedence among these four domains. The authority of the Atsabe domain extended over all Kemak-speaking populations of Timor-Leste, covering a geographical distribution that, according to the Kemak, included not only the region of Atsabe in Ermera, but also most of northern Bobonaro, northern Ainaro and the Suai regions of Kova Lima. These assertions are based on migration and expansion through marriage and thus the foundation of new source houses.[10]

---

8   I did not start to find out about other named houses of the group until collecting genealogies and data on the marriage alliances.

9   Here the boundaries of the territorial domain of the original Atsabe domain are meant and not the much later expanded boundaries of the domain as claimed by the Atsabe Kemak.

10   In addition, I also recorded claims that the authority of the Atsabe domain was broadened through territorial expansion, and indeed, the domain had authority over the territorial domains of these other regions.

Contending Versions of Origin

Atsabe Origin Myths: Landscape and social relations—a connected earth and the sky

Cuha is the vine that connected the earth and sky in the past. Earth and sky were connected by a huge, thick vine [*cuha*], and that way the people of the two realms could visit one another and God could talk directly to the people. The voices of the female sun and the male sun [*Lelo Hine* and *LeloMane*] were close in those days. The earth and the sky were linked on top of Darlau Mountain.

One day a man sent his wife to the top of Darlau to get fire, while he looked after the children. When the woman got to the top of the mountain, she heard beautiful music coming from the sky realm. The people in the sky were playing (pinging on) brass spiral armbands [*lu'u*]. The woman was so mesmerised by the music that she climbed up on the vine to the sky realm. It was already late at night and she still did not return. The children were crying as they were hungry. The husband was getting angrier and angrier and was very jealous. In anger, he started to sharpen a sacred heirloom sword. He was going to kill her. He sharpened and sharpened and tested it on his hand so that it was sharp enough. He then went up to the top of Darlau and in anger severed the vine connecting earth and sky. The sky flew up and up. That is why God's voice is too far away for us to hear and Lelo Hine, Lelo Mane no longer talk to us directly. Lelo Hine, Lelo Mane used to tell us what to do and how to do it if we had problems, like when we were sick. The sacred *suri* is still present. A chunk from the edge of the blade is missing. It broke off when the huge vine was chopped. The sacred sword that cut the vine is called *siaka daka tai*; it belongs to the *luli* [sacred] objects of Uma Mali Ubu[11] in Lemia Leten village.

In this mythical representation of primeval times, the earliest Kemak ancestors lived together in the origin village of Lemia on Darlau, before sky and earth were separated and when humans and gods/spirits were not yet fully differentiated. The object that brings about the differentiation becomes a sacra (*luli*) of one of the oldest origin houses of the Atsabe Kemak in Lemia. The reference to Lelo Hine, Lelo Mane was further elaborated as follows.

Maromak created the ancestors and would visit with them. In ancient times, people could still see God. Maromak gave customs [*lia hu'u*] to

---

11   See house by same name in Marobo (Clamagirand 1982).

the people and gave them sacred prayer beads [*loi ana*] so that during a funeral when praying with the *loi ana*, the soul of the deceased [*sera mara*] can be transferred into the *loi ana* and thus transmitted to God through prayer. Maromak also gave the people the *aitos* [a carved post with a tip shaped like a human head], which we continue to 'plant'. The *aitos* represents the early link with God and His domain in the sky; the *aitos* connected the earth and sky.[12] Only earlier we did not refer to God as Maromak, but as *Lelo Hine, Lelo Mane*.

Dispersal from Lemia and the Emergence of the Atsabe Chiefdoms

The oral histories, which are rather Atsabe centric, suggest that the first settlement to branch off from Lemia centre and become an independent chiefdom was Laclo,[13] followed by Tiar Lelo and Atu Dame, and finally Boboe. Laclo distinguishes itself in that it faithfully adheres to Kemak traditions and the performance of all rituals in the ritual cycle, even the ones that appear to have disappeared from most of the 13 villages (victims of the Catholic Church's

---

12 I recorded two main explanations for the significance of *aitos*. One explanation—the secret meaning of the post—was told only in hushed tones by the sacred men of the village. The other explanation is the most public form, which connects the *aitos* to the Christian God. According to this explanation, God (Maromak) came down from heaven to look at the first human beings (including ancestors of the Kemak) and divide land among them. The *aitos* represents His walking staff (*rota*) on which He rested against a stone. *Aitos* in its secret (and indeed sacred) meaning represents the founding ancestor (or first ancestor born of the union of Lelo Hine and Lelo Mane), therefore the top of the post is carved with the representation of a human head. The *aitos* must be made of a special wood from the *ai dagha* tree. A small *menaka* (stone platform) and the accompanying *aitos* must be present at all source houses not just the *uma luli*. The *aitos* of all source houses represents the founder of that house. Also according to these more secretive meanings attributed to the *aitos*, the post carved to resemble a human head must be embedded in a stone platform since the first ancestors arose from the earth and stones, from earthly caverns. Before the *uma luli* (or other source houses) is built, the axes and swords (*ta no suri*) that will be used in acquiring wood from the forest are placed at the feet of the *aitos* for blessing so that the implements will cut only the wood and not the hands or cause other injuries to the men. *Aitos* is also said to represent Lelo Hine Lelo Mane and Rae Hine Rae Mane (female earth male earth), and this united divinity is present in the *aitos*. When the *ai dagha* tree is acquired for the *aitos*, the eldest member of the *uma luli* will assume the role of Lelo Mane, who will call to the spirit of this tree to follow the ceremonial procession that is transporting the tree into the village, and to make the wood less heavy and easier to lift and carry. The elder representing Lelo Mane must lead the procession. The spirit within the *aid dagha* tree is that of Rae Hine and the *aitos* is the united presence of sky and earth as they united in primordial times (I was asked not to mention this meaning to the priest or others who might accuse the storytellers of being pagans).
13 As pointed out earlier, Atsabe people recognise that people of Marobo left Lemia first while all other people who were to found the various constituent chiefdoms of Atsabe domain still lived together in Lemia. Given the local perceptions that the Marobo are not as intimately interconnected with the various houses and former chiefdoms of Atsabe as those who make up the Atsabe domain, in oral histories the Marobo rarely if ever get a mention. It is through direct questioning about how the Marobo 'fit' with the rest of the Kemak that one is told that they were the ones to differentiate first from the ancient foundation site of Lemia and that Obulo arose as a settlement through the differentiation of source houses from Marobo.

interference). Laclo's closest marriage ties are with Boboe, Lemia (Lemia Leten and Lemia Craic) and Tiar Lelo, specifically with the branch houses from the origin village of Lemia.[14]

The foundation narratives of Tiar Lelo village and chiefdom—the second to differentiate from Lemia—are interesting and not just from the perspective that they make copious references to places in the local landscape, including Darlau Mountain. In one version it is made clear that the territory under question belongs to the Lemia founders. This version also places the Boboe and Tiar Lelo chiefdoms in an elder/younger sibling relationship; Boboe is senior to Tiar Lelo based on their founders and the level of seniority of their origin houses in the origin village of Lemia. The narrative also asserts a common origin for Tiar Lelo and Boboe. The story also recognises a hierarchical relationship between the two groups. This, however, is explained from the perspective of the current state of affairs, which takes the political hierarchies within Atsabe domain as a reference point for the hierarchical relation between Tiar Lelo and Boboe.

Version 1: The founding of Tiar Lelo (Ciar Lelo) village

There were two founding ancestors; they were brothers. The elder founded Boboe, and the younger founded Tiar Lelo. As the two brothers were descending from the top of Darlau Mountain after obtaining fire there, the younger asked the elder: 'What is that place?', pointing. The elder answered: 'That is Ai Rei.' Then the younger pointed to another place and asked again. The elder answered: 'Lesu Mau.' Next the younger cut a *hulo* bamboo and sharpened the tip into a spear and he threw it towards the sun. The elder chewed on betel and spat far away [*lota aba*]. They did not know where the spear and the spittle landed. They kept descending the mountain and looked for where the spear and spittle had landed. When they arrived at a place that was level and was wet with spittle they named the place Aba Rema [*aba*: saliva, spittle; *rema*: level]. This name now designates the territorial domain of Tiar Lelo. When they got to the place where the bamboo spear was standing in the ground on the level surface, the spot was called Hulo Rema [*hulo*: bamboo type; *rema*: level]. That is the place where the village was built, the village of Tiar Lelo. Darlau Mountain belongs to the people of Lemia; it was their origin village that was on the top of Darlau. The name of the village Tiar Lelo comes from the act of throwing the bamboo spear towards the sun [*tiar* or *ciar*: to throw far away; *lelo*: sun].

---

14 Lemia Leten (upper Lemia) is considered the origin village, while Lemia Craic (lower Lemia) represents the expansion of the named houses and branch houses into a new settlement, which currently is located in the Ainaro administrative district.

The original Tiar Lelo village was established in the place of Aba Rema.[15] The first origin house was Uma Lulu Ubu within the territory of Lemia Leten. The two ancestors who founded Tiar Lelo were Aba Rema and Hulo Rema. Both ancestors spat betel spittle. Where Hulo Rema's spittle landed became the territory of Tiar Lelo. Where Aba Rema's spittle fell became the Kumubia River in Lemia. Uma Mali Ubu in Lemia was the origin house of the ancestral brothers.

Version 2: The foundation of Tiar Lelo as a chiefdom

At first there was only one domain and Laclo was a part of this domain but was a separate chiefdom that descended from Lemia. The one domain was Lemia, the place of true origin of all Kemak on Darlau Mountain. Tiar Lelo split off first (and then Boboe split off from Tiar Lelo). The Boboe people, the Tiar Lelo people and the Lemia people are descendants of three founding brothers: Lemia and Laclo people from the eldest brother, Boboe people from the second brother, and Tiar Lelo people from the youngest brother. The split of Tiar Lelo from Lemia occurred over an insult and ensuing warfare over it. The story of how the split occurred is as follows: an elder named Sur Talo was the *dato* of the Tiar Lelo settlement within the domain of Lemia. He was also a relative of the senior house of Lemia. One day when Sur Talo was taking off his sword, the tip accidentally pointed towards the son of the ruler of Lemia. This was perceived as a grave affront and Sur Talo was put to death. This precipitated warfare between Tiar Lelo and Lemia and brought about the establishment of Tiar Lelo as a separate chiefdom.

Another version comes from the family of the *koronel bote* or *liurai* family who controlled the Atsabe domain from Tiar Lelo at its centre. This alternative version of the foundation narrative attempts to incorporate the line of the outsider/usurper of power—namely, the line of the *koronel bote*—as it attempts to justify the presence of Uma Kase ('the house of the foreigner/outsider') as part of the Tiar Lelo social structure. Through the narrative, the myth's tellers seek to legitimise the authority of the group that will unite the various related chiefdoms that derived from Lemia on Darlau into the Atsabe domain. Also, while other narratives I will discuss below emphasise that Tiar Lelo separates first in terms of establishing its own settlement and chiefdom, and only thereafter does Boboe achieve its own independent status, this origin story clearly suggests

---

15 'When the last *koronel bote* opened up rice fields there, they were all washed away by landslides—the lesson was that agricultural fields must not be opened on a sacred site. The last *koronel bote* is descendant from Koko Lia who was an outsider and conquered all the people originating from Lemia.' This was part of the original telling of the variant of foundation. It is included here as a convenience, so it does not disrupt the flow.

that when Tiar Lelo was first established, the distinction in terms of separate chiefdoms was not yet present. According to this version, two origin houses of Lemia branched out to establish their settlement in Tiar Lelo. The claimed seniority of Tiar Lelo over Boboe is a legitimisation device employed by the myth's tellers who are descendants of the invaders and outsiders who became integrated into the social structure of the original Tiar Lelo group and who, in effect, usurped the authority of the original Kemak settlers of Tiar Lelo.

The Story of Conquest (Recounted by descendants of the koronel bote who claim direct descent from Koko Lio)

Koko Lio first lived in Ainaro, Hatubuilico. Next he went travelling and his journey took him across Ramelau. He decided to settle in Genu Mera in the Lemia domain/chiefdom[16] where he left behind his authority in the form of the first *Acu Boso* [a stone platform called *menaka* by all other groups of Atsabe, except those in Tiar Lelo] and Aitos.[17] These served not only as a sign that he once settled there but also that he had the authority over the place and he was the ruler. He possessed a sacred tablet, the size of a cassette,[18] which he could order to make a loud sound that would gather all the people together. When the people came to see what the noise was, he announced to them that he was the ruler and he had authority over the place. Next he travelled to Soru Aci in Laclo. The ruler there bowed to Koko Lia and submitted to his authority, and that domain was also integrated into the growing domain of Koko Lia. The various chiefs submitted to Koko Lia and were integrated into his domain, because he possessed three *luli* (sacred) objects: the tablet, a rattan staff that could change into a snake and a special weapon—a gun from which lightning emitted. He could also travel with superhuman speed and glowed like the sun. After Soru Aci, Koko Lia went to Ai Lea (now a town of Atsabe in the centre of the subdistrict); then he continued to travel back up to Darlau Mountain and also brought the ruler of Lemia into submission. The ruler was Lei Mia. When Lei Mia and Koko Lia were descending from Darlau Mountain, Lei Mia spat betel spittle upwards and it landed close by the Kumubia River [a river in the territory of the present-day Lemia Leten people].[19] When Koko Lia spat, his betel spittle landed very far away—at Abu Rema. There is a spring there called Lias Tete, which originated from his spittle. The

---

16   The storytellers used the Indonesian term *kerajaan* (domain).

17   In Tiar Lelo, the origin houses are also not round architecturally but rectangular.

18   This was an interesting comparison with a modern object, especially since I was using a digital recorder and not a tape recorder.

19   In the myths of all other people of Atsabe, this story is told as the founding ancestor whose origins are in Lemia on Darlau. Koko Lia's story is narrated much later in the accounts of oral history when his conquering of the Atsabe people is emphasised.

ruler of that region, the ruler of Lias Tete (Tiar Lelo), also submitted to the authority of Koko Lia, at Atsabelau Mountain. The ruler of Lias Tete was Loko Ubu. So, the entire domain of the Atsabe was built by Koko Lia as all the local chiefs and rulers submitted to his authority and sacred power. Koko Lia's domain and authority extended over a wide territory, with borders to Atabae, Bobonaro, Hatubuilico and Aileu at Orna Mau Siga. One of his wives came from Atabae, and Koko Lia gave his *umamane* [wife-giving house] the right to govern Atabae. The domain of Atsabe remained the same until the time of Dom Siprianu [a ruler of Atsabe] prior to the Japanese invasion. Dom Siprianu then extended the territory of the Atsabe domain into Suai. Koko Lia sent his younger brother to acquire and govern the territory of West Timor. His brother was called Nai Loko and he was to govern the Wehali domain, but the people there did not accept him and rebelled against his rule. He returned to report this to his brother, Koko Lia, in Atsabe. So, Koko Lia sent his youngest brother, Nai Saur, who became ruler of Wehali. Koko Lia possessed sacred power so strong that all his wives were killed by it. Only the wife he took from Uma Kai Si Ubu in Obulo survived because before he took her as wife, he transferred his sacred power into a gong [*ko*]. This gong is now a sacred heirloom protected by the *uma luli*. Koko Lia's staff and tablet—the other sacred objects—were taken by Mortago, a Portuguese stationed in Hatolia, to the museum in Lisbon. The gong will sound by itself as a warning and omen that a member of the house will die.

The Sacred History of Atsabe[20]

This origin story attempts a grand synthesis of the historical experiences of the Kemak people from primeval times, Timor's relations with other islands, relations among the different groups within Timor from the time of the first founding human ancestors, and the hierarchical nature of relations among Kemak groups. A version of the myth below demonstrates the significance of place and local geographic features in the formulations of group identity as well as in narrating complex histories of human migration and group relations. From the Kemak perspective, Ramelau Mountain is considered the place of origin of all Timorese people. This is consistent with the Atsabe Kemak conception that

---

20 I recorded variants of this origin narrative from Boboe, Laclo, Lemia and Obulo. There was a defiant and challenging tone to the introduction of this narrative by all the 'sacred men'—challenging the authority of Tiar Lelo, or rather, the authority of the line of the king of Atsabe. Some of these Kemak consultants also revealed that the long 'historical' narrative could be pictorially represented and that particular sacred parts of the story are often drawn while recounted in a very low (almost mumbled) voice. Curiously, the pictographs resembled motifs of tattoos, textiles and even some of the carvings on *uma luli*. When I mentioned the resemblance to tattoos, one of the elders recounting the narrative pulled up his sleeve with a gentle smile to reveal a tattoo that looked like the drawing he had just made while explaining the pictographs.

considers it the current place for the villages of ancestors. This myth also gives an example of Kemak topogeny (cf. Fox 1997), which establishes discursive links between groups of people and localities through the recitation of a sequence of place names (see also Reuter 2006a:19).

> The earliest ancestors emerged from the earth. The very first ones were Loa Lae and Mau Lae. They emerged but continued to live deep within the earth, lime and earthen cave. The first ancestors were giants. When they emerged from the earth, they emerged with a white textile [*taisbuci*] that was so long that when the ancestor took it up to the Ramelau Mountain it covered the mountain's slope. Bu Leki was the wife of Loa Lae Mau Lae. They have rights over all of Timor; his and her descendants have rights to all of Timor. They had two children: Suri Mola and As Mola. Their founding house was called Acula Mundu. Their descendants spread to populate Ambon, Alor, Kisar and also Flores. These early ancestors were living on Ramelau Mountain. They were digging for salt. Then a flood [*tasi beno*] came, the sea covered the land right up to the Ramelau Mountain. So they had to build their homes on the top of Ramelau. When the sea receded there were no more trees left on the lower lands, everything was swept clean. Land was still very small at that time. So the ancestors came down from the top of Ramelau and went to the earth cave of the first giant ancestors (they were still alive after many, many generations). They looked down inside the giant cave of the first ones. They asked for trees and vines to replant the earth. From below they were given a sacred basket [*taka luli*] filled with 20 vines [*tali hua*] and fruit trees [*ai hua*]: five male and female pairs of *ai mamar, ai ta buci, ai ora, ai ili goru, ai taha buci* [all different local trees] and five male and female pairs of vines: *tali si meta, ga tala, tali sogha, tali nena, tali oho gatal bote*. Two ancestors, Mau Hui and Loko Hui, made a *menaka* in Boboe. At that time the land was still very small so they threw fruits and vines [*sali tali hua*] in different directions and in each direction, the land expanded so the world grew larger.

> Four ancestors, Loe Mau, Dada Mau, Pi Kali Mau and Kali Mau, went on a trip [Loe Mau and Dada Mau each founded a source house; Pi kali Mau and Kali Mau together founded one house]. They were heading to Liu Rai Tasi Balu, but only got as far as Lis Tete Bu Rema. It was very dark and they could not see the path. So they went to Loa Lae and Mau Lae to ask for a big male disc [*cumara*] and used this to light the path [*pilo sala*]. On the way they went down to the River Luro and then went up

to Boboe. With their spear [*belaki*], they made a hole in the earth after stabbing the earth. They looked inside and saw Bu Leki weaving. They threw down a very sweet orange. The giant ancestress was surprised as the orange fell on the *tais*. She called up to them: 'Speak Mambai' [as an aside, the teller explains, 'the first language of Timor was Mambai']. Then she said: 'Not bad!' ['*mika ba kode*'].[21] Then the ancestors pulled up from that earth cave the sacred sword and spear and the sacred axe [*belaki luli, suri luli, ta luli*]. Then the ancestors went to cut down some sacred trees [*ai mamar, ai ta buci, ai ora, ai ili goru* and *ai taha buci*]. There are no more sacred trees inside the earth, in the ancestral earth cave; they are all on top of the earth now. They cut down the trees to build houses but the sacred trees were so heavy, they could not lift them. So they piled the trees on the sacred spears and then they could easily lift them to take back to the village. First they made rectangular houses with no roof. Then they remembered and made long houses [*lobor*] with rooms for each family. But still they did not build a roof. When the big rains came, they were always wet. They observed that their dog was always dry. So one day they tied the lime container with a piece of cloth to the dog's neck and followed the chalk line. When it rained, the dog hid inside the high grass [*lei*: Imperata cylindrica] and was dry. So they collected this *lei*-grass [*dut mau lei*] and covered their houses. But with heavy rains they still got wet so they went to get a central post and two supporting posts and made a round roof that they thatched with *lei*-grass. Now that is how we make our *uma lulik*.

When they first wanted to make houses and the village, whenever they cut a tree or dug into the earth, the earth and trees screamed. So the ancestors climbed down into the earth cave of the first giant ancestors and asked what to do. The ancestors gave them a small plaited basket and betel/areca [*taka ana* with *da'a no bo*] and prayer beads [*loi ana*]. The four ancestors made a *menaka* from four stones and on top of the platform they placed their offering with the sacred beads [*loi ana*]. After the offering, the earth and the trees did not scream when wounded and it is still like that today.

Next came another great flood [*tasi beno*] where the sea level rose and flooded the land. The ancestors went to war with the lord of the sea. Lelo Rae[22] went to war with Kuku Ratu Tasi Ratu. Lelo Rae asked the

---

21   *Mika ba kode* was translated by the teller as 'the orange is sweet'. I would like to thank the reviewer of this chapter who is knowledgeable in the Mambai language, who pointed out that *mika* means 'not' and *ba kode* means 'bad'; thus, a literal translation would be 'not bad'.

22   Lelo Rae, which literally means 'sun earth', is a collective name that subsumes the first original ancestral brothers, Loa Lae and Mau Lae. Thus, taking the literal meaning, the first ancestral brothers represent the sun or sky and the earth, alluding to the union between the sun and earth that produced the first ancestral progeny.

four ancestors to return the sacred swords and spears, and they did that. Lelo Rae chased the lord of the sea with the sacred spear [*belaki luli*]— chased him as far as Ba Tata. Lelo Rae speared Kuku Ratu Tasi Ratu until his tongue hung out. In Boboe Leten, Uma Tali Meta stored the tongue as its sacred heirloom. The name of the spear is Bere Bada Mau Lai; another spear used is called Cima Mo Lako. (Now it is the heirloom of Uma Bere Heu.) So at Ba Tata, the lord of the sea was killed. The spear Liu Rai La Gora was thrown forward and landed by the rivers of Gora Racu and Gora Ai. The lord of the sea started to revive so at these rivers the ancestors cut the lord of the sea into pieces with the sacred sword. He kept hacking with the sword at the lord of the sea but the pieces kept reviving. But his wife, Abo Hine [title of the first ancestress], came to help and with one hack, cut off the head; so the lord of the sea finally died. While the rest of the body was washed out to the sea as finally the sea retreated, the head stayed behind. It was so heavy that it could not be lifted. The head stayed by the rivers and was going to revive if not disposed of and then the sea would return and there would be a flood. So the ancestor called up from inside the earth Manu Napa Tasi and he came. The ancestors (Lelo Rae and the four) told him that the head of the lord of the sea could not be lifted and could Manu Napa Tasi help? What payment should they give? Manu Napa Tasi said no payment was required but in the morning he would come and take chickens, pigs, dogs and goats. So Manu Napa Tasi lifted the head and carried it to Adi, a place on Ramelau. The spears and swords used to kill the lord of the sea lost their edge; they are now dull.

Next the ancestors built a dam from *mi kase* and *ai tasi* wood as a boundary for the sea. But this was not strong enough to hold the sea. So they looked for *aka diru* to reinforce the woods from which the dam was built. So now there are no more *aka diru* here; all are down on the coast. When the sea rumbles, these vines also make noises like when the winds make the reeds creak.

Next the ancestors went to look for good land and found it in Loes [now in Bobonaro district]. They made their houses in Loes. There were eight straight paths in Loes that led to the houses. The founding house in Loes was Uma Acu La Mundu. Houses were made like large granaries [*lako bote*]. Loes was a very wealthy region, everything was in plenty: animals and wealth inside the house. The ancestors Laku Mau Mese Mau went to look for Krisi Mau Talo Mau of the house Acu La Mundu and asked him to look for the feet of the lord of the sea so that the sea would not rise again and the lord of the sea would not revive. They searched for seven years; on the coast they finally found the feet and speared them with the sacred spears and twisted the spears in a counterclockwise direction so that the feet ran back to the sea.

By the time they returned to Loes, they found that all the animals and sacred cumara [*cumara mia*] were divided among the people of Timor—Loro Sa'e, Alas, Betanu, Tutuala, Kupang, Liquiça and Maubara. The four ancestors (Loe Mau, Dada Mau, Pi Kali Mau and Kali Mau) were disappointed that in Loes they did not wait for them and they divided everything already.

The ancestors were called Kole Bau and Mau Bau. Their sons were called Rai Sa and Kelo Hale, respectively. Kole Bau Mau Bau gave the four ancestors a huge boulder called *usi luli* to place on top of the *menaka* in order to repair it and strengthen it since the sea had eroded (damaged) it.

Next they made a multicoloured sacred mortar [*nesu luli*]. They also raised eight wooden posts that they brought from Loes. These posts were for hanging the meat of sacrificial animals [*ri pun*: 'source posts']. Mau Bau was the elder brother and Kole Bau was the younger brother. They brought a large earthenware water jug with a narrow neck [*cu'u bot*].[23] The two ancestors took the water jug and the sacred mortar to get seawater. Kole Bau told Mau Bau to get inside the *nesu luli*, and then dipped it into the sea. Then Kole Bau got inside the *cu'u bote* and he also dipped his jug into the sea. These containers were then taken to the village. As they sat inside the containers, the people gathered around the eight posts with meat hanging from them.[24] At night the four ancestors called the dog and the dog accidentally knocked over the containers, which broke into pieces and the seawater ran out. As the seawater returned to the sea, it washed some people away while others ran and escaped. Seven ancestors ran to Ai Ede (near Lemia)—a place of origin of the ancestors of Atsabe Kemak. The first ancestor, Loa Lae Mau Lae, also died at Ramelau and is buried there. The children of this giant first ancestor are Me Tasu and Bole Asu.

Others who escaped the seawater are the ones who populated Timor Loro Sa'e. The path they followed is as follows: to Maubara, Liquiça, Curi Leu, Rae Pu, Tibar, Bila Verde, Be Ai Kua. In Bila Verde they found an egg and took it with them. The place where this egg hatched they named Manututu. The ancestors, whose chicken that was, were called

---

23 Vessels of this kind are still used in Marobo.
24 After ritual sacrifice, the meat of the sacrificial animal is first hung on posts after the butchering process, ready to be cooked for a communal feast or divided among the participants. This passage seems to allude to some ritual undertaking in the village.

Me Tasu and Bole Tasu. They gave the name to the land of Manututu at La Lia, where the egg hatched. As they went on, the place where the chick made a sweet sound they named Be Masi. The ancestors had many children and their descendants now populate the eastern part of East Timor.

Those ancestors who were washed out to sea became the ancestors of other people, but they are all descendants from Timor. Two ancestors whose names are not known were washed away by the sea as far as Angola. Their father was from Loes. One day when this ancestor was sitting in the morning, his *tais* slipped down so his butt was showing. His children saw this and were laughing at him. So the father said to them 'one day when you have children their skin will be black and their hair will be crinkly'. So that is why the Angolan Timorese are black with crinkly hair.

Other ancestors who were washed out by the sea landed on West Timor, Alor, Flores, Kisar and Ambon. These people are descendants of Flores. When the first giant ancestor was dying, he divided the languages as well. His language was Mambai, the first language of Timor; he divided Kemak, Makassai, Tetun, Galoli, Bunaq—all the languages of Timor Island, even those of West Timor.

Oral History Legitimising Power Relations

It is interesting to note some of the differences in emphasis between the two previous narratives. In the version of the foundation of Atsabe that was told by family members of the Atsabe ruler, the emphasis was placed on the hierarchical power relations both within and outside the domain. The myth extended to a discussion of Atsabe's perceived circle of power, even claiming conquest of the influential domain of Wehali and the installation of a ruler there who derived from the family of the Atsabe ruler. Therefore, the myth also aimed at explaining the basis of the power relations between Atsabe and other domains of the western region of Timor-Leste and the eastern part of present-day Indonesian Timor. The sacred history of Atsabe, on the other hand, stressed cooperation and emphasised relations of connectedness among the various groups of Timor including groups outside Timor with virtually no emphasis on power inequalities. Other striking differences between the two myths are the different ways of alluding to legitimacy—namely, utilising the sky in place of the earth metaphor for legitimacy. In the first myth told by the descendants of the Atsabe ruler and ultimately by descendants of an outsider conqueror, power and legitimacy derive through an association with the sky. In the second myth, on the other hand, legitimacy derives from the sacred connection with the earth. In Kemak conceptualisations of the dual pair of sky and earth, the sky is the superior category to that of the earth. This categorical superiority of the sky is not, however, an uncontested notion, particularly by Kemak ritual leaders (the 'sacred men' of the group)[25] who derive from Lemia and not from the line of the rulers of the Atsabe domain. Without exception, in my interviews with the 'sacred' men and ritual leaders of groups that derive from Lemia, there was a strong objection to and even criticism of the Tiar Lelo version. They claimed that even the telling of Kemak origin narratives was changed by the Atsabe ruler/conqueror line in giving priority to the sky and to Lelo Hine and Lelo Mane over the 'real' origins of all Kemak human beings—the ancient human ancestors who emerged from the earth and the first sacred giant ancestors who lived in the caves in the bowels of the earth whom the Kemak venerated, and from whom they learned and derived all things of human need. These 'sacred' men and ritual leaders also emphasised that the version of the origin myth that gives superiority to the sky and a sky god was strengthened after Catholicism was established. The family of the Atsabe ruler was indeed a strong supporter of the Church and of the spread of Catholicism and some of their claims to power were indeed strengthened by the Catholic Church.

While there were some variations as each of the four main groups tried to stress their own importance or 'priority' or 'seniority' in terms of justifying rights to power and authority, there was general agreement that the place of origin for all Kemak was Lemia on Darlau. Here the first Kemak ancestors occupied the sacred mountain slope where the sky and earth were connected by a vine and from where fire originated. As to how Tiar Lelo became the ultimate authority over the Atsabe Domain, there are various versions.

According to oral histories, the establishment of settlements that later expanded and had autonomous authority over their territorial domains (talked of mainly in terms of founder-house names) is viewed as the first branch of satellites from the Lemia domain. There is much emphasis on the story of the establishment of Tiar Lelo and Boboe's settlement. Laclo has its own stories of the foundation of its settlements and territory, which its population insists occurred before that of Tiar Lelo or Boboe. At least one informant pointed out that Obulo's foundation (like Marobo's) is contemporaneous with Laclo's in the mythical chronology. Chronologically, the establishment of Atu Dame (Malabe) is closely linked with that of Tiar Lelo. While these branched settlements grew into independent

---

25   See Molnar (2006) for a fuller discussion of the notion of '*luli*' and the secular and ritual personages that are imbued with spiritual potency that makes them 'sacred'. Here I would only note that a ritual leader (*gase ubu*) of a group derives his power and legitimacy through descent from founders and through ritual knowledge, particularly through his role as the guardian of sacred history and lore. His domain of authority is in the ritual realm.

chiefdoms, all acknowledged the overarching sacred authority of Lemia. These small chiefdoms were, however, autonomous in terms of political power and territory.

The various claims made by these origin myths are interesting in terms of current relationships between the groups and especially in terms of the use of varied sources to claim legitimacy for power and authority, as often these claims hark back to the oral histories. There are elaborate versions of how Tiar Lelo became the dominant political authority in the region and united the politically and territorially autonomous smaller chiefdoms that derived from Lemia into the Atsabe domain. This unification was accomplished by a supernatural ancestor from the sky, Koko Lia. He first conquered Laclo, then Ai Mea, which was a hamlet of Tiar Lelo and thus part of the original Tiar Lelo people's settlement. Next Lemia was conquered and then the ruler, Loko Ubu of Lias Tete, a settlement within the territory of Atu Dame. Then the conquest continued and spread out to Obulo as well as Atabae. The conquering ancestor intermarried with the main house of Tiar Lelo and also established marriages with the main source houses of each of the conquered chiefdoms. Lemia and Obulo were acknowledged as major chiefdoms that had authority over matters within the territory of their own chiefdoms and were essentially in a tributary relationship with Tiar Lelo. On the other hand, the Laclo and Atu Dame chiefdoms were completely swallowed and incorporated into Tiar Lelo and were completely under its authority. Thus, Laclo and Atu Dame had no autonomy and they were integrated into the Tiar Lelo chiefdom, which was the centre of authority for the whole Atsabe domain. The Atsabe domain was established via expansionist conquest.

Tiar Lelo of Atsabe domain then reigned unchallenged and it was not until a serious uprising in the former Atsabe domain, which the Portuguese tried to quell, that Boboe split and founded its own chiefdom. This split was in response to the fact that most of the Boboe group was almost wiped out during the uprising. Boboe was, however, still part of the larger Atsabe domain with the same status as Lemia and Obulo chiefdoms within the larger Atsabe domain. The various oral histories describe the situation as a large ruler having dominion over smaller chiefdoms. The ultimate authority resided within the Atsabe ruler with its leadership coming from the Tiar Lelo group. Lemia's authority as the place of origin encompassed that of Obulo, Laclo and Lias Tete (Atu Dame) as these chiefdoms derived from Darlau Mountain as well. Tiar Lelo and Boboe were just settlements within Lemia chiefdom's domain.

The nature of the relationship between chiefdoms within the former Atsabe ruler can be summarised as follows.

- The Tiar Lelo chiefdom had the highest political authority as the centre of power of the entire Atsabe ruler and as such had precedence over Lemia,

Obulo and Boboe. The *koronel bote*, the ruler, to whom all other chiefs were subordinate, was based in Tiar Lelo. Atu Dame was considered a part of both Tiar Lelo and Boboe. Thus, in the political hierarchy, Tiar Lelo chiefdom had superiority—the place where an outsider had gained control of local power and established itself through marriage within the most senior house of Tiar Lelo.

- Relations with the origin place of the Kemak, the Lemia chiefdom, were described in marriage terms: Lemia is wife-taker to Tiar Lelo (*nai hine nai mane*).

- Relations with Obulo were also described in marriage terms: Obulo (and Marobo) are wife-givers to Tiar Lelo.

- The Obulo chiefdom appears peripheral in most Atsabe accounts, but always had excellent and close relations with the former chiefdom of Boboe. The relationship is described as that of mutual alliance, friendship and defence (an elder–younger relationship: *ka'ara–aliri*) that always supported Boboe in any dispute or war. It is interesting to note that Obulo has some source houses that are wife-givers to Tiar Lelo and specifically to the house of the *koronel bote* and its junior-branch named houses, the group with which Boboe has had the most disputes and conflict. The Obulo chiefdom, while considered a part of the Atsabe ruler, is nevertheless viewed as a part of Marobo, and the Obulo people are considered Marobo (a fact inconsistent with the Marobo chiefdom granting independent chiefdom status to Obulo).

- Relations with Boboe Craic[26] were described as a friendship alliance, *ka'ara–aliri* relationship, with Boboe Leten as a marriage ally: Boboe Leten is wife-giver to the main source houses of Tiar Lelo.

- Atu Dame's closest relations are with Boboe (as a former chiefdom) given that their connection is described as an elder sibling/younger sibling relationship. Atu Dame and Boboe are descendants of the same ancestor but Atu Dame are from the first wife of the ancestor and Boboe are from the second wife of the ancestor. This is also reflected in the very close marriage-alliance ties that exist between the two villages and also in the fact that Boboe has some of its branch houses located in Atu Dame. According to the oral narratives about the first ancestral pair to leave Lemia, Tiar Lelo is the descendant of the younger brother and Boboe of the elder brother.

---

26   Boboe Craic as a settlement/chiefdom is within the territorial domain of the former Boboe chiefdom. This settlement is, however, considered to be the most recent, established only after the Manufahi war, with a foreigner (a Manututo man) marrying a woman from Boboe chiefdom and thus founding Boboe Craic. The descendants of Boboe Craic are viewed as outsiders, not 'true Kemak'. Therefore, the nature of the relationship with Boboe Craic is not conceptualised in terms of the complex dynamic networks of marital alliances but simply in terms of an ally.

Tiar Lelo Settlement	Boboe Settlement	Lemia Chiefdom
Laclo Chiefdom	Obulo Chiefdom	Lias Tete (Atu Dame) Chiefdom

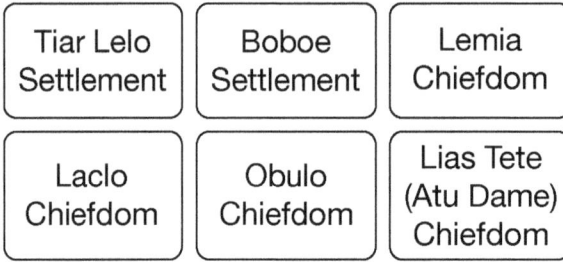

Figure 5.1 Diagrammatic representation of authority over domains prior to the establishment of the Atsabe ruler

In Figure 5.1, the chiefdoms are independent of each other in terms of authority over their respective domains. Boboe and Tiar Lelo are satellite settlements from Lemia and not yet at chiefdom status.

TIAR LELO CHIEFDOM

Tiar Lelo Settlement	Boboe Settlement
Laclo Chiefdom	Atu Dame Chiefdom

OBULO CHIEFDOM	LEMIA CHIEFDOM

Figure 5.2 Diagrammatic representation of authority over domains with the centralisation of authority by Tiar Lelo chiefdom vis-a-vis the outsider conqueror 'installing himself within'

Figure 5.2 represents the distribution of authority after the conquest and unification of the chiefdoms by an outsider. Tiar Lelo settlement, where the conqueror installed himself through marriage, became the centre of authority for the Tiar Lelo chiefdom after Boboe settlement, Laclo and Obulo chiefdoms were conquered and integrated into the sphere of authority of Tiar Lelo. Laclo and Atu Dame become sub-chiefdoms under the authority of Tiar Lelo. Lemia and Obulo retained their autonomy within their respective domains through a tributary relationship with Tiar Lelo chiefdom.

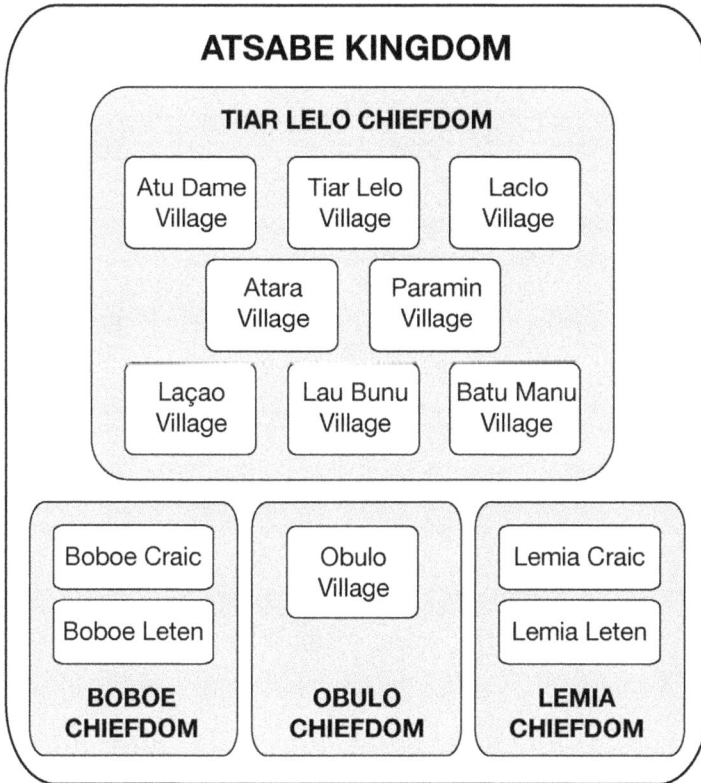

Figure 5.3 Diagrammatic representation of authority and territorial domain of the Atsabe ruler

Figure 5.3 illustrates how at the height of the Atsabe ruler, Atu Dame and Laclo no longer had chiefdom status but were village settlements within the Tiar Lelo chiefdom. As the figure shows, several other villages arose through group differentiation. Boboe attained its chiefdom status and, along with Obulo and Lemia chiefdoms, possessed semi-autonomy over its own domain.

Rulers, Chiefs and Village Heads

Political leadership of the various levels of territorial domains in the former ruler of Atsabe resided with the *koronel bote*, *nai*, *dato* and *rati*. The Atsabe ruler was referred to as the *koronel bote*. The heads of former chiefdoms (chiefs) were called the *dato*. The chiefs of the chiefdoms of Obulo and Lemia, however, had the title of *nai*, which is higher in status than that of *dato*. This higher status reflected the seniority and autonomy of their chiefdoms compared with that of other chiefdoms. While both Laclo and Atu Dame were incorporated into the Tiar Lelo chiefdom and both lost their autonomy, the leaders of these former chiefdoms were nevertheless called *dato*. The heads of villages enjoyed the title of *rati*. In terms of hierarchy of authority, the *nai*, *dato* and *rai* were answerable to the *koronel bote*. The *nai* and *dato*, however, did appear to enjoy a certain degree of autonomy and had authority to deal with the affairs of their chiefdoms, particularly when settling internal disputes and matters of inheritance and land issues. They also had authority to organise the inhabitants of their chiefdom for common undertakings, whether this involved communal work or ritual undertakings. The *rati* enjoyed similar autonomy when dealing with the internal affairs of their own village. Prior to Portuguese colonial presence in Atsabe, the domain was governed by the *koronel bote* in consultation with a council of elders (*bei*), which comprised the chiefs and village heads. Informants likened this council (*bei*) to a parliament. In addition, the *koronel bote* appointed a war leader, *eru ubu ahi nipa*.[27] This was necessary since there were many wars in the past with other groups and indeed many uprisings against the Portuguese. The war leader and the warriors came from Uma Mane Itu, an origin house in the Tiar Lelo group that was a wife-taker of the house of Lulu Ubu (founding house of the Tiar Lelo group). During the time of war, the war leader's authority superseded all other authority (except that of the *koronel bote* to whom the war leader was directly answerable). Uma Mane Itu remains to this day the 'hereditary army' of the descendants of the *koronel bote*'s family.

Conclusion

The Atsabe Kemak, like other Austronesians, have a preoccupation with origins. The origin stories discussed in this chapter provide the Atsabe Kemak with sources of authority when asserting their legitimacy and rightful place in hierarchical social relations within the former Atsabe domain. They are also invoked when challenging such hierarchies as people and groups negotiate their power and rights to authority. These origin stories of the past provide the Atsabe Kemak with the precedent and patterns for ordering their current social relations (cf. Fox 1996a:5, 2000:1–29). As Fox (1996a:5) points out, 'indigenous ideas of origin involve a complex array of notions. Conceptions of ancestry are invariably important but rarely is ancestry alone a sufficient and exclusive criterion for defining origins. Recourse to the notion of place is also critical in identifying persons and groups, and thus in tracing origins.'

Atsabe Kemak stories have shown that place is a significant metaphor for discourse on history, social relations in terms of inter and intra-group relations of precedence, on the organisation of the former Atsabe domain, and on

---

27 *Eru* means 'monkey', *ubu* is 'lord' or 'owner', *ahi* refers to 'pig' and *nipa* means 'teeth'. Thus, the expression literally means the monkey lord and owner of pigs' teeth.

legitimising the authority—and the sphere of influence of this authority—of the Atsabe ruling house. There is a great emphasis on the founding village, the founding ancestor and the ordering of houses and social relationships in terms of both place and ancestor. As Clamagirand (1980:140) points out—and this is also true for the Atsabe Kemak—there is no Kemak term used for village. Settlements are, however, named after their location in relation to the land and often in association with a particular action taken by a founding ancestor. Aba Rema, for example, was named for the plain where mythical ancestral spittle landed. McWilliam (1997:106) also draws attention to the importance among the Meto of West Timor of 'associating the group's name with specific places and named localities', thus affiliation extends spatially across the landscape.

For the Atsabe Kemak place, origin villages and named houses are basic structuring units. The name of the settlement is generally used to talk about a group, although the first house's name (the house of the founder ancestor) may also be used in a similar manner. Often this core source house encompasses the other main source houses that, in turn, have other named house branches. Usually the first main house is the *uma luli* (sacred house). Named houses are the basic units of marriage exchange and thus the basic anchor of a highly complex nexus of alliances. There are many named houses but people tend to cite the main source houses in the first instance since all other named houses derive from these main source houses (cf. Clamagirand 1980).

Indigenous authority (in ritual, land and governance matters) is conceptualised as the main right of Lemia, the founding settlement and the origin of all Kemak people.[28] The Kemak explain this right with reference to a number of key factors—namely

- with reference to the origin stories
- with reference to Darlau being a sacred mountain where earth and sky were joined and ancient ancestors had immediate relations with god and ancestors
- this connection with the sacred place imbued the people of the founding settlement of Lemia with 'sacred power/spiritual potency' (*luli*)
- Lemia people gave rise to all other Kemak through the dispersal of the population via the branching of the key source houses and the subsequent complex, interwoven affinal relations between core source houses and subsidiary named house branches.

The authority of Tiar Lelo is intimately tied up with the power of outsiders who subjugated the local population through conquest and then intermarried

---

28   I have mentioned in passing the issue of challenging local hierarchies and rights to power within the former domain of Atsabe. These are more complex matters that I will have to address in another venue. Here I only wish to point out the basic principles and reasoning provided by the Kemak Atsabe for understanding the founders' struggle for authority.

with emplaced source houses (see McWilliam, this volume). Their power is conceptualised mainly in terms of political governance and is grudgingly accepted. In local discourse, Tiar Lelo and the line of the *koronel bote* (the descendant of the outsider conqueror Koko Lio) are intimately connected to other sources of external power over the Kemak, including that of the Portuguese, the Catholic Church, the former Indonesian Government, and even the current national government.[29] Authority in these terms is conceptually linked with the power of coercive force and that of outsiders. Given this way of thinking, the legitimacy of this form of authority and the groups linked with it has always been contested, challenged and questioned in Atsabe.

Every Atsabe group—aside from Tiar Lelo—vehemently denies the legitimacy of Tiar Lelo when discussing the political history of the Atsabe domain. In these discussions, the concept of *luli* was consistently raised, as were Atsabe conceptions about the degree and amount of sacred power that groups and people possess, particularly in relation to sources of *luli*[30] and their personal connections with ancient ancestors, founders, Lemia and other sacred places and objects. Framing these distinctions in terms of earth and sky received consistent attention. Koko Lia's *luli* is legitimised through the claimed connection to the sky through the origin myths. Given that the objects that were imbued with this sacred power are, however, no longer in Tiar Lelo's possession, in popular discourse this opens the possibility for questioning the legitimacy of the ruling family (and Tiar Lelo) while the sacred power emanating from Lemia and its rightful descendants is re-emphasised.[31] Darlau continues to have a prominent presence in the lives and social relationships of the Atsabe Kemak. It is not just a real topographic place but serves as a metaphorical nexus for a wide range of Atsabe Kemak conceptions of origins and inter and intra-group relations.

References

Barnes, R. H. 1985, 'Tanebar-Evav and Ema: variation within the eastern Indonesian field of study', *Journal of the Anthropological Society of Oxford*, vol. 16, pp. 162–71.

---

29 From the former ruling family of Atsabe, a number of people received government jobs, whether as subdistrict administrators, members of the new East Timorese police force or parliamentary representatives for one of the political parties.

30 For further discussion on '*luli*', see Molnar (2005, 2006, 2009).

31 In Molnar (2004), I discuss the religious aspect of the Kolimau 2000 movement, which harked back to these indigenous notions of 'sacred potency', and Lemia on Darlau featured prominently in Kolimau presence in Atsabe. As a millenarian movement, it possessed features that questioned the rights and authority of both the Catholic Church and the new national government (the two being viewed as political bedfellows intimately linked with outsiders).

Clamagirand, B. 1971, 'Rapport de Mission au Timor Portugais', *Asie du Sud-Est & Monde Indonesien*, vol. 2, no. 2, pp. 22–9.

Clamagirand, B. 1972, 'Le Travail Du Cotton Les Ema De Timor Portugais', *Etudes interdisciplinaires sur le monde insulindien. Archipel 3*, vol. 3, pp. 55–80.

Clamagirand, B. 1975, 'La Maison Ema (Timor Portugais)', *Asie du Sud-est Monde Insulindien*, vol. 6, pp. 35–60.

Clamagirand, B. 1980, 'The Social organization of the Ema of Timor', in J. J. Fox (ed.), *The Flow of Life: Essays on eastern Indonesia*, Harvard University Press, Cambridge, Mass., pp. 231–47.

Clamagirand, B. 1982, *Marobo: Une société ema de Timor*, Langues et Civilisation de L'Asie du Sud-Est et du Monde Insulindien 12, SELAF, Paris.

Felgas, Hélio A. Esteves 1956, *Timor Português*, Agência Geral do Ultramar, Divisâo de Publicações e Biblioteca, Lisboa.

Fox, J. J. 1980a, 'Models and metaphors: comparative research in eastern Indonesia', in J. J. Fox (ed.), *The Flow of Life: Essays on eastern Indonesia*, Harvard University Press, Cambridge, Mass., pp. 327–33.

Fox, J. J. (ed.) 1980b, *The Flow of Life: Essays on eastern Indonesia*, Harvard University Press, Cambridge, Mass.

Fox, J. J. 1988, Origin, descent and precedence in the study of Austronesian societies, Public lecture in connection with De Wisselleerstoel Indonesische Studien, 17 March, Leiden University, Netherlands.

Fox, J. J. 1989, 'Category and complement; Binary ideologies and the organization of dualism in eastern Indonesia', in D. Maybury-Lewis and U. Almagor (eds), *The attraction of opposites; Thought and society in the dualistic mode*, University of Michigan Press, Ann Arbor, pp.33-56.

Fox, J. J. (ed.) 1993a, *Inside Austronesian Houses: Perspectives on domestic designs for living*, The Australian National University, Canberra.

Fox, J. J. 1993b, 'Comparative perspectives on Austronesian houses; an introductory essay', in J. J. Fox (ed.), *Inside Austronesian Houses: Perspectives on domestic designs for living*, Research School of Pacific Studies, The Australian National University, Canberra, pp. 1–23.

Fox, J. J. 1994, 'Origin structures and systems of precedence in the comparative study of Austronesian societies', in P. J. K. Li, Cheng-hwa Tsang, Ying-kui

Huang, Dah-an Ho and Chiu-yu Tseng (eds), *Austronesian Studies Relating to Taiwan*, Symposium Series of the Institute of History and Philology, Academia Sinica 3, Taipei, pp. 27–57.

Fox, J. J. 1995, 'Austronesian societies and their transformations', in P. Bellwood, J. J. Fox and D. Tyron (eds), *The Austronesians: Historical and comparative perspectives*, Department of Anthropology, Research School of Pacific and Asian Studies, The Australian National University, Canberra, pp. 214–28.

Fox, J. J. 1996a, 'Introduction', in James J. Fox and Clifford Sather (eds), *Origins, Ancestry and Alliance: Explorations in Austronesian ethnography*, Department of Anthropology, Comparative Austronesian Project, Research School of Pacific and Asian Studies, The Australian National University, Canberra, pp. 1–17.

Fox, J. J. 1996b, 'The transformation of progenitor lines of origin: patterns of precedence in eastern Indonesia', in James J. Fox and Clifford Sather (eds), *Origins, Ancestry and Alliance: Explorations in Austronesian ethnography*, Department of Anthropology, Comparative Austronesian Project, Research School of Pacific and Asian Studies, The Australian National University, Canberra, pp. 130–53.

Fox, J. J. (ed.) 1997, *The Poetic Power of Place: Comparative perspectives on Austronesian ideas of locality*, Department of Anthropology, Comparative Austronesian Project, Research School of Pacific and Asian Studies, The Australian National University, Canberra.

Fox, J. J. (ed.) 1999, 'Precedence in [ractice among the Atoni Pah Meto of Timor', in L. V. Aragon and S. Russell (eds), *Structuralism's Transformations: Order and revisions in Indonesia and Malaysia*, Center for Southeast Asian Studies, Arizona State University, Tucson, pp. 1–36.

Fox, J. J. 2000, 'Tracing the path, recounting the past: historical perspectives on Timor', in *Out of the Ashes: Destruction and reconstruction of East Timor*, Crawford House, Adelaide, pp. 1–29.

Fox, J. J. and Sather, C. (eds) 1996, *Origins, Ancestry and Alliance: Explorations in Austronesian ethnography*, The Australian National University, Canberra.

Graham, P. 1991, To follow the blood: the path of life in a domain of eastern Indonesia, PhD thesis, The Australian National University, Canberra.

Grimes, B. 1990, The return of the bride: affiliation and alliance in Buru, Master thesis, The Australian National University, Canberra.

Hicks, D. 1986, 'The relationship terminology of the Ema', *Sociologus*, vol. 36, pp. 162–71.

Lewis, E. D. 1988, *People of the Source: The social and ceremonial oder fo Tana Wai Brama on Flores,* Verhandelingen 135, KITLV, Dordrecht, The Netherlands.

McWilliam, A. 1989, Narrating the path and the gate: place and precedence in southwest Timor, PhD thesis, The Australian National University, Canberra.

McWilliam, A. 1997, 'Mapping with metaphor: cultural topographies in West Timor', in James J. Fox (ed.), *The Poetic Power of Place: Comparative perspectives on Austronesian ideas of locality,* Department of Anthropology, Comparative Austronesian Project, Research School of Pacific and Asian Studies, The Australian National University, Canberra, pp. 103–15.

Molnar, A. K. 2004, 'An anthropological study of Atsabe perceptions of Kolimau 2000: a new East Timorese religious cult or internal security problem', *Anthropos*, vol. 99, pp. 365–79.

Molnar, A. K. 2005, 'East Timor religions', in Thomas Riggs (ed.), *Worldmark Encyclopedia of Religious Practices*, The Gale Group, Montana.

Molnar, A. K. 2006, 'Died in the service of Portugal: legitimacy of authority and dynamics of group identity among the Atsabe Kemak in East Timor', *Journal of Southeast Asian Studies*, vol. 37, no. 2, pp. 335–55.

Molnar, A. K. 2009, *Timor Leste: Politics, history, and culture,* Contemporary Southeast Asia Series, Routledge, London and New York.

Reuter, T. A. 2006a, 'Land and territory in the Austronesian world', in Thomas A. Reuter (ed.), *Sharing the Earth, Dividing the Land: Land and territory in the Austronesian world*, ANU E Press, Canberra, pp. 11–38.

Reuter, T. A. (ed.) 2006b, *Sharing the Earth, Dividing the Land: Land and territory in the Austronesian world*, ANU E Press, Canberra.

Sherlock, K. 1983, East Timor: liurais and chefes de suco—indigenous authorities in 1952, Unpublished manuscript, Darwin.

Vischer, M. P. 1992, Children of the black Patola stone: origin structures in a domain on Palu'e Island, eastern Indonesia, PhD thesis, The Australian National University, Canberra.

Vischer, M. P. (ed.) 2009, *Precedence: Social differentiation in the Austronesian world*, ANU E Press, Canberra.

6. Planting the Flag

Elizabeth G. Traube

If the [national] flag came from the sea, it would be as if foreigners still ruled us.

Introduction

The Austronesian mythology of the stranger king links political order to an encounter between an indigenous presence and a newcomer from somewhere beyond the borders of the realm, often from overseas. Typically, their encounter involves a transfer of power whereby the newcomer takes over functions formerly vested in the indigenous authorities and is installed as ruler of the realm. Origin narratives of this general type are commonly associated with diarchic systems of leadership, in which political power over humankind and ritual authority over the cosmos are vested in complementary offices. The narrative patterning of diarchic divisions varies. In some narratives, the stranger king becomes the political ruler while the original lords retain ritual authority over the land; in others, the newcomer usurps ritual authority and subsequently delegates his executive duties to still other outsider figures. The content of such narratives as well as the claims to precedence they are used to support also vary according to whether the story is told from the perspective of the newcomers or of the original inhabitants of the land. What such accounts share, James J. Fox (1995b) has argued, is an Austronesian 'epistemology of origins' that makes the categorical distinction between 'inside' and 'outside' into a signifier of status distinctions.

With the historical expansion of the Austronesian peoples as its original matrix (Bellwood 1996), the stranger-king mythology could be used to incorporate foreign newcomers as chiefly rulers (Fox 1995b; McWilliam, this volume) and to symbolically distinguish indigenous chiefs from their subjects (Henley 2002; Sahlins 1985). The mythology is also compatible with colonialism and has been used to legitimise the rule of 'real' stranger kings from Europe (Henley 2002; Traube 1986, 1995). Its relevance for nationalist imaginaries is less obvious. In cases where nationhood is secured through a negotiated decolonisation process, nationalist leaders might model themselves on the outgoing colonial rulers to prove their fitness to rule (Li Puma and Meltzoff 1990:79) and claim a form of outsider status. Anti-colonial nationalist movements, however, would seem less hospitable to narratives about outsider rulers. Leaders of protracted anti-colonial liberation struggles that mobilise the subaltern population as 'the people' tend to seek legitimacy by claiming 'insider' status. Subaltern participation in such struggles, moreover, is a transformative experience that both reflects and shapes new practices of political imagination.

For many contemporary theorists, however, subaltern perspectives are secondary or marginal to nationalism, which, especially outside the core capitalist nations, has come to be viewed in largely negative terms, as an elite, top-down process. According to Neil Lazarus (1999:73:72), the hostility towards nationalism that characterises recent thinking reflects a persistent neglect of the specificity of particular nations, nationalisms and national movements. Lazarus is especially critical of a tendency to either stigmatise or deny nationalism's 'popular' dimensions. Thus, subaltern classes figure in current theorising either as a potentially violent 'primordial' force manipulated from above or, in post-colonial versions, as an appropriated voice ventriloquised by nationalist elites—a discursive effect that has no intrinsic connection to actual subaltern desires. What is missing from these models is close, located exploration of actual processes of mass mobilisation. Lazarus (1999:117) turns to Ranajit Guha, among other scholars, for his emphasis on elucidating the 'investment of the masses of the colonized historically in various kinds of nationalist struggle'.

Although some scholars have aligned Guha with their own critiques of nationalism as an elitist (Spivak 1988) or derivative (Kelly and Kaplan 2001) discourse, Guha in fact criticises liberal historiography because it 'fails to acknowledge, far less interpret, the contribution made by the people *on their own*, that is, *independently of the elite* to the making and development of this nationalism' (1982:3, emphasis in original). In the 'braiding together' of elite and subaltern politics, Guha (1982:6) saw an 'explosive' potential—as often blocked as realised—for the masses to 'break away' and transform elite-initiated nationalist campaigns into vehicles more expressive of their own aspirations. Guha stressed the role of inherited cultural resources in such transformative appropriations; in reworking nationalist movements from below, he observed, subalterns enlist cultural forms with roots in pre-colonial times that have been adjusted to colonial conditions.[1]

In 1974, when leaders of the Fretilin nationalist party in what was then Portuguese Timor devised the symbol of the 'Maubere people', there was more than a little ventriloquising involved. Fretilin was founded in the wake of the overthrow of the Caetano regime, by educated Timorese elites in the coastal capital of Dili, many of them recently returned from university study abroad. The Maubere symbol coded the leadership's claim to speak on behalf of the masses of poor, uneducated rural folk who inhabited the mountainous central

---

1   For example, Guha elsewhere (1997:60) called attention to the persistence of the dharmic idiom in Indian forms of subaltern resistance.

interior of Timor. The term was derived from an ethnic stereotype and had a mild anti-colonial tone. Maubere or Mau Bere is a common masculine personal name among Mambai people who occupy the mountains of central Timor-Leste. During the colonial period, the Mambai had acquired a reputation as the most 'backward' (*atrasado*) ethnic group in the province, and 'Maubere' was used (primarily by Portuguese and Chinese) as a condescending term of reference and address. In taking the Mambai as archetypes of the masses they sought to mobilise, Fretilin leaders claimed insider status by valorizing what the colonial rulers had denigrated.

From early 1973 through to November 1974, I resided in the Mambai district of Aileu, in the mountains 32 km south of Dili. I witnessed the early stages of decolonisation from the vantage point of people who represented themselves as archetypal 'insiders' and who were initially wary of the political process under way in Dili. Many Mambai viewed the abruptly initiated decolonisation process with apprehension, as a project orchestrated by and for local elites—Timorese who had 'put on trousers' (*tam kalsa*) and knew little about the people in whose name they claimed to speak.

But the process of 'producing the people' does not end with elite formulations. Over the course of the leadership's efforts to mobilise the masses, official nationalist discourses have been appropriated and reworked from below. I have written elsewhere about the resonance the 'Mau Bere' symbol acquired in Aileu, where it became entangled with a narrative tradition about a martyred prophet (Traube 2007). In this chapter, my focus is on mythical narratives of the origins of rule as they were used before, during and after the Indonesian occupation. From such discourse, I argue, a hybrid notion of popular sovereignty has emerged that blends inherited cultural categories with newer political sensibilities. Viewed from the perspective of an indigenous epistemology of origins, the category of *povu*—'the people'—reconfigures an orientation to the inside that was traditionally associated with the cosmic powers of the land and with the ritual authorities who watched over them. Suffering is the primary linkage. Like the beings traditionally associated with the inside, 'the people' undergo an agonistic but productive ordeal that requires compensation. Imagined as the product of the suffering and sacrifices of 'the people', the nation becomes a site from which local people make claims upon the new national-state.

Colonialism, Decolonisation and Stranger Kings

When I arrived in Aileu in early 1973, the local administrator arranged for me to live in the household of a village (*suco*) chief. That summer, at the annual census, I was introduced to several men who resided in the *suco* but whose clan origin houses were located in the mountains to the south, in an origin village known as Raimaus. I subsequently visited Raimaus accompanied by one of these men, Mau Balen, and we returned there for the opening stages of the annual agricultural rites. Then we 'crossed over' (*fak*) to Hohul, another village due south of Raimaus, which is represented as its younger brother. To explain the sibling tie, people often invoked a story about two brothers who lived together in Raimaus. One day, the story goes, the elder brother performed an agricultural ceremony while his younger brother was away. When the younger brother returned, he was so angry over this slight that he gathered up all the ancestral sacra in the house—the metal disks, coral necklaces drums and gongs—and set off southward to Hohul, where he founded a new house that stands as younger brother to the Raimaus house. The two villages are also represented as one house, oriented, as Mambai cult houses are, on a north/south axis. In this model, Raimaus is the northern 'door' (*damatan*), while Hohul represents the innermost, southern section of a house, the *umolun*, where the house altar post stands and where house sacra are laid out for rituals. That Hohul priests regularly officiate at Raimaus rituals is consistent with this metaphor. Etiquette also prescribes that newcomers enter Hohul by way of Raimaus (a sequence I have endeavoured to follow ever since).[2] At a lengthy house-building ceremony in Hohul, I met a young Hohul man named Mau Bere, the son of a minor Hohul priest, who agreed to join Mau Balen and I. Over the remaining six months of my fieldwork, the three of us visited many origin villages, and I became lastingly associated with Hohul and Raimaus.

My relationship to Mambai ritual centres was widely represented in binary terms. People contrasted my 'book and pen' (*libru nor labis*) with 'rock and tree' (*hauta nor aia*)—the ubiquitous icons of indigenous ritual life—as tropes of our respective ethnic identities. The technology of literacy marked me as a Malaia, a white overseas foreigner, while rock and tree in this context stood for all the indigenous peoples of the land, represented as 'Timorese'. Much emphasis was placed on my status as a 'returning outsider'. It was common knowledge among Mambai that Timorese and Malaia were kin, descended from 'one mother and one father' (*inan id nor aman id*), whom they always designated with the inclusive first-person plural possessive pronoun. In Hohul and Raimaus, people also preserved more esoteric origin narratives about the creation and peopling of the world, referred to as the 'walk of the earth' (*raia ni lolain*). Accounts of the origin of rule were embedded in this discourse on world creation. Here I simply note its central themes.

---

2   I suspect the reliance on Hohul personnel was conditioned by contingent differences in manpower. Leik Mau, who until his death in the late 1970s was universally acknowledged as the 'owner of Hohul' (*Hohul ni ubun*), had many sons, all of whom had followed their father and become priests. In Raimaus, his counterpart had died leaving only two sons, one of whom was often away serving in the Second Line; they both emphasised that their father had died when they were 'still little' and had passed on 'only a few words' to them.

Mambai are deeply invested in a mythology of common origins.[3] Not only all humankind, but all of nature—including animals, plants, rocks, as well as the earth itself—are ultimately descended (in the case of humans, by branching lines too complex to trace) from Mother Earth and Father Heaven (themselves, according to the few who claim to know such things, the divided halves of a still earlier unity). Mount Ramelau in the central interior, which Mambai call Tat Mai Lau, is identified as the first dry land. Originally surrounded by 'water and sea', the mountain centres the cosmos, and there at the centre Mother Earth brings forth the diverse inhabitants of the land. Her firstborn are the non-human phenomena of nature, who stand collectively to human beings as 'elder siblings' (*kaka*) to 'younger siblings' (*ali*). At first, Mambai say, their elder siblings were animated, and the trees and grasses screamed when people tried to cut them to build their houses. Then Father Heaven imposed what tellers called the 'ban of the interior' (*badu hoha nin*), removing the power of speech from his elder children, so that the younger ones could use them for their own livelihoods. Human beings, henceforth distinguished as 'speaking mouths' (*kuku kasen*), are authorised to exploit the 'silent mouths' (*kuku molun*), but they are also expected to show them respect. According to an ethic of reciprocity, the 'speaking mouths' offer ritual restitution for the suffering they inflict upon their silent elder kin.[4] As Mambai say of these obligations: 'We must repay them for their fatigue' (*Aim ten de seul ro ni kolen*).

The human ancestors are internally differentiated by the patrimony they receive from Father Heaven. To Au Sa, the firstborn or 'head man' (*maen-ulun*), went the 'nail and hammer, the bellows and forge' (*karifi nor maknuta, toh-matan nor rai-inun*); he wandered off to the west, taking with him his blacksmithing skills, and he played little part in the stories I was told. These centred on 'middle man' (*maen fusun*), Ki Sa, claimed as founding ancestor by houses in Hohul and Raimaus, and the lastborn or 'tail-man' (*maen-ion*), Loer Sa, from whom we Malaia descend. On Ki Sa Father Heaven bestows mystical powers, referred to as his 'luck and fortune' (*ubdaida nor fortuna*). Meanwhile, the youngest, Loer Sa, draws water from a white spring and 'rinses white, bathes clean' (*luk buti, riu mo*), seizes the entire patrimonial collection of regalia of office, and disappears across the northern sea.[5]

I am, it should be noted, splicing together what were far more fragmentary narratives. I have written elsewhere (Traube 1986, 1989) about the tension in Mambai discourse between an aesthetic ideology of narrative plenitude and

---

3 In this respect, Mambai cosmology is reminiscent of Maori creation myths; in contrast, many other Austronesian peoples assume a multiplicity of origins (Fox 1996:231).
4 I find persuasive Graham Harvey's (2006) usage of 'animism' to designate codes of respectful behaviour towards non-human persons.
5 In some accounts, Loer Sa crosses the sea by way of the 'door of the interior' on Tat Mai Lau, taking the 'path of the spirits of the dead' (*maeta ni dan*).

the partial character of narrative performances. I am more reluctant than ever to over-systematise the narratives of rule I transcribed during my original research, for I believe that what I took to be their (only partially coherent) sequential ordering was in great part the product of my persistent requests for temporal sequence. Indeed, it is the incoherence of myths of rule that most strikes me today—the proliferation of radically diverse, conflicting accounts preserved from different social positions. Nevertheless, while the ordering of mythical events was no doubt always contested, many Mambai insisted that they were part of a single story that could and should be told 'from trunk to tip'. In Hohul and Raimaus, storytellers absorbed Portuguese colonial rule into the story of world creation and wove it together with narratives about the subsequent ordering of the realm.

In the latter, Ki Sa engages with other mythical ancestors in a contest for precedence, which he wins through cunning use of his mystical powers.[6] Accounts of the contest climax with reiterations of Ki Sa's status as *res-res, lau-lau*—literally, 'most-most, top-top'. But despite his supremacy, 'the rule is not heavy, the ban is not weighty' (*ukun ba rihu, badun ba mdeda*). Loer Sa's theft has left Ki Sa 'with only rock and tree' (*nor si hauta nor aia*)—the silent tokens of ritual authority. When he displays them to the realm:

Women do not tremble, men do not [show] fear   *Hina ba rih, maena ba tmau*

They stab one another and slay one another   *Ro sa ro, ro tar ro.*

In search of a way out of this anarchic and violent state, Ki Sa uses his 'luck and fortune' to cross the seas and confront his younger Malai brother. On being informed of the situation in the homeland, Loer Sa hands over assorted regalia of sovereign power: named staffs, swords, drums and a flagpole and flag. He pledges to send representatives to Timor later on. Ki Sa returns home, where 'women and men tremble and fear' when he displays the new tokens. Tellers conclude: 'Then the rule was heavy and the ban was weighty' (*Ukun rihu sois, badun dmeda sois*).

In other versions of the quest narrative, Ki Sa's descendants are the ones who make the journey overseas. By some accounts, there are two separate visits, the first to obtain the regalia, and then, when peace is again disturbed, a subsequent visit to ask the Malaia to return in person. Such doubling is not without precedent—for example, a Balinese tradition describes two successive delegations to Majapahit to receive regalia from the ruler (Fox 1995b). Still, it always seemed to me that Hohul and Raimaus tellers were labouring to subsume

---

6 The contest for precedence is a widespread Austronesian theme; in many traditions, the trickster is an outsider or latecomer who defeats an established indigenous ruler (Fox 1995b), but in Hohul and Raimaus versions, the contest takes place in an open field of insiders.

within a single overarching story two different narrative bases for their villages' claims to precedence: the claim that Hohul and Raimaus ancestors had brought the Malaia back to Timor as supreme political rulers and the claim that their ancestors were the first settlers and original lords of the land who had later 'turned over the rule' (*sra ukun*) to indigenous newcomers from outside the realm.

The second claim, which relates to local diarchic arrangements, was asserted repeatedly, with considerable passion, and continues to be invoked today. Yet especially in contrast with the epic story about the Malaia, narrative accounts of these local events seemed thin. Hohul and Raimaus people depict their surrender of rule as a voluntary act, rather than the outcome of a contest or defeat. Once having ordered the realm, their ancestors simply grow old and weary; they 'sit down to look after the rock and watch over the tree', retaining their ritual function, while they 'hand over the rule' (*sra ukun*)—embodied in named drums and flags from overseas—to later arrivals to the realm: the leaders of an origin village known as Bandeira Fun ('base of the flag'), who become the rulers of the kingdom known as Aileun. Bandeira Fun, by all accounts, is originally the home of one Bau Meta, who later 'surrenders the rule' to in-marrying strangers from the house of Bar Tai. Although Bau Meta's line has no descendants, his house is maintained in Bandeira Fun, next to Bar Tai. After his death, his head turns into a twisted tree (*ai-leun*), from which the kingdom of Aileun takes its name; the name of the kingdom was in turn extended to the colonially created administrative district of Aileu.[7]

Bau Meta is also the protagonist in a well-known tradition that shares motifs and themes with tales told by other ethnic groups (see Bovensiepen, this volume). In this tradition, he owes the title of 'Dom' to certain spirits of the land whom Mambai call *rai ubun*—owners or masters of the earth. The term is equivalent to the Tetun *rai nain*, but unlike many other Timorese peoples (see McWilliam, this volume), Mambai never apply it to human beings. To my knowledge, it is used solely to designate a class of spirits associated with 'wild' (*hui*), uninhabited spaces; their counterparts are the 'sacred objects' (*saun lulin*) that are kept sequestered inside clan origin houses and which Mambai distinguish in this context as 'tame' (*maus*).

Bau Meta, the story goes, went out one morning to tap his palm trees; by afternoon, the buckets were filling with palm wine, but when he came back the next morning, they were empty. After the same thing happened several times, he hid himself near the trees to observe. Late at night, two young girls appeared and drained the buckets. Bau Meta demanded to know who they were and

---

7 'Ai-leun', Mambai are fond of observing, 'is not in Aileu [the district capital], but in Bandeira Fun'. I use 'Aileun' to designate the kingdom and 'Aileu' for the administrative district and its capital town.

why they had been stealing his wine. Their mother and father, they told him, had ordered them to do so, and they took him home to meet their parents, who were spirit 'owners of the land' (*rai ubun*). They instructed him to go to Dili, where they said the Malaia would soon arrive from overseas and would make him a great ruler. Bau Meta did as the spirits instructed and was recognised by the Malaia. They presented him with a book that conferred on him the status of 'Dom', making him superior to the Mambai ruler of the coastal kingdom of Motain.[8] But later on, Bau Meta went to visit the Motain ruler and was seduced by his wife, who stole the book while he slept and gave it to her husband. As a result, the order of precedence was reversed and Motain became superior to Aileun.

I have heard this story many times, from many people; it is common knowledge, a genuinely popular tale, usually told in prose rather than poetic ritual language. Bau Meta's misadventure in the denouement—typically narrated in a tone of comic self-deprecation—expresses an ethnic stereotype of Aileu Mambai as foolish 'maubere' highlanders, easily outwitted by cleverer coastal folk. In many accounts, the episode motivates Bau Meta's subsequent abdication to his Bar Tai wife-takers, having proved himself unfit to rule through his stupidity.

Hohul and Raimaus people also tell the Bau Meta tale, which they refer to as 'recent' (*fnoir*). In their accounts, the Koronel Aileun are politically subordinated to both Motain and the Malaia, and are also obligated to show deference to Hohul and Raimaus (the 'old mother/old father'), who are the original sources of rule. Formerly, people said, Aileun's deference included bringing gifts of salt and livestock from Motain on the northern coast (*taisa*) to Hohul and Raimaus in the southern interior (*hoha*), in return for harvest gifts that Hohul and Raimaus collected from outlying villages and sent to the coast. Indigenous tribute systems of this type linking coastal and highland chiefs had been replaced at the end of the nineteenth century with the colonial head tax; the replacement was deeply resented in Hohul and Raimaus, where the Aileun rulers rather than the Malaia were held accountable. Nevertheless, Aileun remained obligated to bring water buffalo to Hohul and Raimaus house ceremonies, and that obligation was a source of great pride in the ritual centres.

At least as viewed from the ritual plane, installed outsiders (whether the Malaia or Aileun) do not come to represent the inside, as occurs in some other diarchic systems (Fox 1995b). Mambai ritual authorities who claim precedence as the original sovereigns are categorically associated with the inside, the sphere of rock and tree, while political executives are associated with the outside, the

---

8   Fernando, Mau Bere's younger brother, offered a particularly clever explanation of the doubled-donor function. In his account (narrated in 2001), the spirits tell Bau Meta that they cannot give the book to him directly because he is illiterate and thus no-one will believe he is its rightful owner. In order for the book to command respect, the spirits explain, it must be publicly bestowed on him by the Malaia.

sphere of women and men. The situation is complex, as distinctions between inside/outside are replicated at multiple levels within both diarchic poles: in Bandeira Fun, Bau Meta's empty house is maintained as the passive sacred, inner counterpart to the active ruling house of Bar Tai, while within both Hohul and Raimaus distinctions are made between particular houses and functionaries oriented to the inside and others, which represent the villages to the outside world. It is nevertheless possible to portray the diarchic relationship in terms of a distinction between what I will call 'interiority' and 'exteriority'. Ritual or spiritual authority—defined as an orientation to the inner realm of silent, life-giving, non-human persons—immobilises the subject, while political rule entails an orientation to the outside, the volatile sphere of human affairs, and requires continuous mobility. This distinction can be represented as a gendered contrast between female and male, and Mambai would sometimes directly compare their ritual authorities with housebound women, as many other Timorese peoples do (Cunningham 1965; Fox 1995b; McWilliam 2002; Therik 2004). Ritual leaders also participate in the darkness attributed to Mother Earth, whereas political rulers have symbolic associations with Father Heaven. I have argued elsewhere (Traube 1986:104–5), however, that age is emphasised over gender in Mambai discourse, and the point is consequential. As 'old mother/old father', ritual leaders evoke the cosmic couple, whose union they ritually secure, while their relative age also evokes the silent rocks and trees, whose immobility and fixity they share. They are the encompassing part that stands for the whole, and the ritual gatherings they preside over symbolically recreate the totality before division (Valeri 1989).

Confined to a perpetual vigil over the cosmic beings, sacral leaders are ignorant of worldly affairs. They represent themselves as 'stupid and dense' (*beik nor bodu*), literally closed off to external stimuli, with 'heads that are still whole, ears that are still full' (*ulun hi tema, kikan hi benu*), like a newborn child. But where Bau Meta's stupidity is laughable and disqualifies him as supreme political ruler, the perceptual closure attributed to ritual authorities entails a deeper wisdom—a knowledge of origins that is implemented in ritual. Political chiefs, in contrast, are depicted as sharp-sensed, vigilant and mobile, 'dog-nosed and bird-eyed' (*inun ausa, matan mauna*) sentries, whose portion of ritual sacrifices is the leg ('in order to walk'). Where spiritual wisdom involves a condition of closure, political rulers are perceptually open, attuned to the volatile outside world that they oversee.

The oppositional symbolism of diarchic functions is widely shared, but its narrative ordering is contested. Aileun recognises the ritual authority of Hohul and Raimaus, but not—at least as far as I could ever ascertain—their claim to precedence as original donors of political rule. Yet in Hohul and Raimaus, people believed that their status as founders of the realm made them vulnerable to accusations of usurpation; they insisted that Aileun rulers suspected them of a desire to 'seize the rule' (*hau ukun*) and take back that which they had once 'handed over' (*sra*). A story that Mau Bere's younger brother Fernando told me in 2001 conveys the ambiguities, as seen in Hohul, and I repeat it here.[9]

Some years before my first visit, Fernando recounted, Hohul was rebuilding its sacred houses. As is customary, they also planned to replace the flagpole—the token of their ancestor's quest overseas—and they had cut down a tree for this purpose. But the Aileun rulers grew suspicious: 'Hohul is not Koronel', they said, 'that office belongs to us', and they ordered Hohul to transport the fallen tree to their village, Bandeira Fun (which literally means 'base of the flag'). But when the people tried to obey, the tree turned into a snake and glided back towards Hohul, where it turned back into a tree. They tried once more to remove it, but it grew too heavy to lift, so they left it where it was and continued rebuilding their houses. When the houses were ready, the tree became light, so they brought it into the village, carved it, and erected it in its customary place.

In this story, the tree-pole knows its proper place, both literally and metaphorically. Its Hohul guardians refer to it as the 'trunk' or 'base of rule' (*uku-fun*), which it is their task to 'hold' (*fail tu*) and 'keep steady' (*tid*). The category *fu*—'trunk, base, source, origin, cause'—is a botanical origin category that links the idea of temporal origins to the image of the trunk or stem of a tree (Fox 1995a:5–8). Represented as the 'trunk' of rule, the flagpole encodes a claim to precedence. During my first research, Hohul and Raimaus people had frequent recourse to this botanical origin discourse. They would contrast their position as holders of the trunk of rule with that of political executives: the Aileun chiefs and above them the Malaia, who 'held the tip of rule' (*fail tu uku-laun*)—that is, the flag. The vertical imagery of rule could be inflected in numerous ways: the flagpole was likened to the digging stick, and thus to the ritually ensured fertility of the earth, while the flag was compared with a shade tree or an umbrella that protects the realm from excessive heat. Another, and arguably primary, implication of the botanical metaphor is that rule might have many 'tips' but it has a single trunk. To Hohul and Raimaus people, their status as original founders and guardians of the trunk of rule entailed the right to legitimise any new successors to office.

This discourse took on heightened significance after April 1974, when the new Portuguese Government embarked on a program of rapid decolonisation. In Dili, three political parties were rapidly formed: Fretilin, UDT (União Democrática Timorense, the Timorese Democratic Union) and Apodeti, their programs based respectively on national independence, federation with Portugal, and integration into Indonesia. Both Fretilin and UDT sought support in the countryside, and

---

9   Mau Bere died two years before my first return visit.

a lively debate was soon under way. At the Raimaus house-building ceremony I was attending, people framed the political situation as a problem of succession. Their 'younger brothers', people said, had 'grown old and weary' and would have to 'surrender the rule' to younger, fleeter heirs. Many people voiced fears of a return to the anarchic past; Hohul and Raimaus people warned that such fears would be realised unless all the parties assembled at their villages, for the guardians of the trunk to legitimise a chosen successor.

When I left Timor in November 1974, the Aileun rulers had already declared their support for Fretilin, but it seemed that many people remained uncertain. A year later, however, when a UDT coup disrupted the decolonisation process, Fretilin mobilised the district of Aileu. Aileu Town, the seat of the district, was the site of a Portuguese training centre; Fretilin forces seized its arsenal and distributed the weapons to the local populace, to meet a UDT force advancing from neighbouring Ermera.[10] The Portuguese colonial administration abandoned the island during the fighting and refused to return when it ended, despite repeated requests from the Fretilin victors. Fretilin leaders, as much as Mambai sacral authorities, had wanted a formal transmission of rule in which they would have ceremonially succeeded the outgoing colonisers. But under the escalating threat of an Indonesian invasion, Fretilin unilaterally declared independence on 3 December 1975. Over the years that followed, Mambai learned that the national flag was unlike other tokens of office; it could not be bestowed by old leaders on new ones, but would have to be won through the suffering and sacrifice of 'the people'.

Under the Rule of the Eldest

At the time of the invasion, Indonesian authorities forced UDT leaders to sign a letter (the so-called 'Balibo Declaration') calling on Indonesia to restore order. The 'invitation' might well have been designed at some level to legitimise the occupation to the East Timorese populace, as well as to the international community, but at least to the former, its coerced character was evident.[11] The Indonesian regime received no ideological benefit from the instability its agents had helped to create. The scale and force of the invasion undercut any effort to frame it as the arrival of peace-bringing stranger kings.

---

10   The Carrascalao brothers who founded UDT were major landholders in Ermera, which became the party's base. To what extent the Aileu resistance to the Ermera force was motivated by nationalism or localism is difficult to say.
11   Dated 30 November 1975, the text had actually been prepared in Bali during August by the Indonesian secret service and Timorese collaborators. The text demanded the integration of the territory into Indonesia and asked for help from the Government to this end; many leaders, including those responsible for the UDT coup, were forced to sign in order to be allowed to return to East Timor (Durand 2001:109).

Although Portuguese colonialism had certainly involved violence, Portuguese rule had been gradually extended and, moreover, offered certain advantages to local rulers as well as to their subjects. Over the course of the colonial 'pacification' campaigns, local rulers repeatedly allied with the Europeans against traditional rivals (Pélissier 1996).[12] For their subjects, the possibility of appealing to impartial European outsiders had its attractions (Henley 2002); whereas local rule was experienced as unjust, even the fantasy of such appeals enabled people to preserve expectations of justice from the higher and more remote colonial authority.

But the Indonesians confronted a nationalist movement that radicalised the political situation, even if it had not instilled a uniform nationalist consciousness. Aileu district had become known as a Fretilin stronghold during the civil fighting, and this reputation put the population at high risk; the majority abandoned their homes and gardens and retreated into the mountains behind Fretilin's armed wing, Falantil. For the next three years, people led an unsettled existence in what they represent as 'the forest' (*ai laran*), moving between Fretilin base camps, homes of relatives and their ancestral origin villages. In 1978 the Indonesian armed forces began a new advance, based on a combined strategy of saturation bombing and encirclement of the population within a given area (Dunn 2003; Taylor 1999). Unable to protect the civilian population, Falantil encouraged them to surrender and transformed itself into a guerrilla force.

People told me in 2001 that when they surrendered to Indonesian authorities, they would represent themselves as *povu*, which here means civilians, as opposed to military or *forsa*, and would claim to have fled out of fear rather than political commitment. Prior loyalties to the resistance were tactically disavowed, as anyone even suspected of Fretilin sympathy was likely to be killed. Yet nationalist loyalty at this point does not appear to have been irreversible. People repeatedly assured me that if the Indonesians had treated them well, they could have come to accept their rule in time. Indonesia's contributions to Timor's material development were readily acknowledged and contrasted with the chronic neglect of the colony on the part of the Portuguese rulers. Indeed, the Indonesians were determined to outdo their colonial predecessors, and they invested heavily in roads and schools, largely but not only for purposes of control (Anderson 1998:134–5). What precluded accommodation was the regime's murderous hostility towards the indigenous population. Civilians who surrendered continued to be subjected to diverse forms of state terror, including arbitrary arrests, torture, disappearances and intensive, continual surveillance. The Indonesian occupiers behaved not as irredentist nationalists towards fellow

---

12   The kingdom of Aileun was in fact one of the 'loyal allies' of the Portuguese Crown and had participated in both the campaigns against the Manufahi rebels.

countrymen but as colonisers towards what they regarded as a 'backward' and peculiarly 'ungrateful' population, who in turn perceived the regime as bent on their annihilation. As one Mambai friend put it to me: 'We saw that they wanted the land, but not its people.'

On one occasion in 2001, I asked my old friend Mau Balen and my 'sister' Fatima if they considered Indonesians to be 'Malaia'. The query elicited heated denials. At once and in unison they declared that Indonesians could not be Malaia because they are 'black like us [exclusive]' (*meta man aim*). When I observed that they referred to Africans as 'black Malaia' (*Malai metan*), Fatima countered that Africans came from overseas, like other Malaia, whereas Indonesians had come 'by land'.[13] But Indonesia, I protested, comprised many islands and was at least technically 'overseas'. Fatima grudgingly conceded the point, but even so, she maintained, they referred to other islanders by their particular provenance, as 'Javanese' or 'Balinese' and so on, not as Malaia.[14] When I continued to look quizzical, they shifted to behavioural distinctions. Indonesians were not Malaia, they said, because they had brought war rather than peace to the land. Mau Balen pointed out that the invaders' claim to have come as helpers was immediately belied by the sheer force of their arrival, with ships, planes and guns that could fire from Dili to Aileu. Fatima, still pondering the sea/land distinction, added that they referred to the continuing stream of immigrants by the Indonesian term *pendatang* ('settlers'), which she glossed as uninvited guests—people who 'just come' (*ma lea*) and who travel by land (*lolai raia).*

Various other people with whom I repeated the exercise gave similar responses, excluding the Indonesians from the category of Malaia and from the stranger-king slot affiliated with it. Another way that people set the Indonesians apart was by representing them as descended from Au Sa, the blacksmith eldest brother of the mythical ancestors, Ki Sa and Loer Sa. I suspect that this lineage was already established in the 1970s, though I do not recall having heard it, but in 2001, it seemed to be common knowledge. Like the Malaia, Au Sa's descendants are 'returning outsiders', but they lack the qualifications of a ruler (which can be logically expressed as coming 'by land' rather than from overseas). Au Sa, of course, is also black, like the peoples of the land. Even before the invasion, Mambai frequently rejected Apodeti's integrationist program on the grounds that 'black ruling black is no good'. Such assertions, I think, have less to do with internalised racism than with the old ideology of rule, which posits difference (between exteriority and interiority) as the condition of order. Moreover, as I have noted, historical experience had also provided a pragmatic basis for subaltern preferences for European over indigenous rulers.

---

13   In fact, the marked term 'black Malaia' indicates that whiteness is the unmarked form of the category.
14   Fatima, who is high school educated, was certainly familiar with the geography of the region; Mau Balen is illiterate and, I suspect, the primary referent of 'Indonesia' for him might be western Timor.

Ideological legitimation of Portuguese colonial rule never precluded criticism of colonial attitudes and policies. Indeed, it was always possible to construe particular individuals, acts and policies as deviations from the idealised rule of stranger kings, and discourse on such represented lapses amounted to what I have called a 'critique of the rightful rulers' (Traube 1995). But the identification of the Indonesian occupiers with an ancestor who was black, older and of the land neatly amplified their categorical unfitness for political rule and provided symbolic resources for a particularly bitter critique. On the one hand, with its systematic corruption and propensity for extreme state-sponsored violence, the Indonesian regime demonstrated its lack of the 'exteriority' ideally expected of a ruler, who should be an open, perceptive, impartial arbitrator of disputes. On the other hand, in place of the 'interiority' of a properly immobilised ritual leader, Indonesians displayed negative forms of inwardness that showed their intellectual and moral limitations. Fernando, who had a knack for constructing homely analogies, once compared the Indonesians with a provincial elder brother who stays at home and does not develop himself, while his younger sibling leaves home to improve himself through study. A poetic representation of Au Sa portrays the ancestor as reclusive and inhospitable: he 'fears the whinny of the horse, fears the jangle of the bridle' (*tmau kud-kiin, tmau freu-hahan*). Instead of welcoming guests with generous gifts, he withdraws into himself, refusing the spirit of reciprocity that organises Mambai social life—and so it was with his Indonesian descendants.[15] In principle, Au Sa's identification as blacksmith eldest brother could have come to signify development and modernisation, but under the brutal conditions of the occupation it conveyed a combination of material power and moral inferiority that many people saw in the Indonesian authorities.

Such symbolic practices both reflected and reinforced experiences of the regime as fundamentally antagonistic to the population; they helped to deflect official efforts to instil a spirit of Indonesian nationalism—which were admittedly weak at best—at the same time as they strengthened an oppositional nationalist identity that might otherwise have been diffused. Mambai constructions of the occupiers belong to the 'arts of resistance' (Scott 1990)—cultural forms through which the dominant are portrayed not as they wish to be seen, but in ways that reaffirm the moral superiority of the dominated. Under the Indonesian occupation, such locally constructed moral communities came to imagine themselves as part of a wider national community of Timorese who were linked by their shared suffering and by their renewed aspiration to political self-determination. In the next and final section, I focus on the cultural construction of a distinctive mode of popular sovereignty grounded in ideas of moral obligation. In contrast with

15   In a somewhat lighter vein, people claimed to have been offended by the Javanese practice of packing up food presented at ceremonies and taking it home to consume in private.

the liberal rights-bearing subject, 'the people' in Mambai political imagination are those who claim consideration on the basis of what they have suffered for the nation.

The Suffering People

Although Mambai are familiar with the Portuguese-derived term *nasaun*, they use it infrequently. Particularised in songs as *rai Timor*, the nation is most commonly evoked through the metonymy of the 'national flag' (*bandeira nasional*), which is intimately associated with the idea of *povu* ('the people'). It is a commonplace that the flag 'was not purchased with silver or gold, but with the blood of the people' (*ba los nor os-butin nor os-meran fe al, mas nor povo ni laran*).

During the transition to formal independence, the flag referenced in such statements was the flag of the Democratic Republic of East Timor (RDTL), the nation declared by Fretilin in 1975. Although the 'national' status of the 1975 flag was uncertain during the transition, it retained a considerable affective charge. The Fretilin party flag, on which it had been closely modelled, was distinguished from it as the 'political flag', representative of a particular party (albeit still a uniquely prestigious one in early 2001), whereas the 1975 flag was associated with the people as a whole and evoked the ideal unity of the nation. In Aileu, many people expressed concern that the political process under way during the transitional period was dividing the nation instead of uniting it. Sixteen parties, including Fretilin, had been recognised by the United Nations Transitional Administration in East Timor (UNTAET) and authorised to compete in the upcoming constitutional election.[16] Many Mambai professed to see not democratic freedom in their proliferation, but a troubling and potentially dangerous disunity. People were quick to point out that the formation of parties in 1975 had led to violent conflict, and there was no guarantee that the past would not be repeated. Fuelling that anxiety was a deep suspicion of the new crop of political elites. A widely held and frequently voiced assumption was that the party leaders or 'big people' (*tun ro*) were pursuing position or status rather than the collective good; literally, they were 'looking for their chairs' (*klai kadeira*), and had formed parties for that purpose. In this rhetorical vein, speakers often asserted that 'the people' had not suffered and sacrificed for parties but for the national flag.

---

16   To UN 'nation builders', a multiparty system is both a sign and an instrument of democratisation, and many East Timorese elites also believed that unless new parties were encouraged, Fretilin, with its immense cachet, would unduly dominate the political process, but popular opinion remained largely antagonistic to party division. I would argue that the subsequent popularity of the ASDT in Aileu was due in part to local perceptions of it as the 'trunk' or 'source' (*fun*) of Fretilin, not a new party but the totality before division.

Mau Balen once offered a splendid commentary on the distinction. He began by comparing 'political flags' with 'white blood' or semen—a substance that, as he and Mau Bere had once laboured to explain to me, is productive only when it is combined with female menstrual blood, *lar maten* (literally, 'dead blood' or 'spilled blood'). So, too, he explained, 'political flags' are 'just talk'—the weightless discourse of party elites who, in 2001, as in 1975, droned on and on about their programs and promises. Like white blood, he said, such discourse was unproductive by itself. It had required the blood shed by the people in the war to produce the flag of the nation.

Mau Balen offered this analogy in the context of a narrative account of the origins of the national flag, which he often recited. Like many nationalist intellectuals, Mau Balen had invented a primordial origin for the nation, projecting it back onto the mythical past. He represented the national flag as Ki Sa's flag—'the flag of the interior' (*bandeira hoha nin*)—which he said the ancestor had left behind on Nama Rau (a poetic name for Tat Mai Lau or Ramelau).[17] This purely indigenous power token was the counterpart to the colonial 'flag of the sea', which the Malaia had taken away and brought back. The interiority of the national flag also figured in Mau Balen's account of the day it was first raised in Aileu, in December 1975. According to Mau Balen, the Hohul priest who had been designated to perform the chant for the flag had represented it as originating overseas. At this, he said, the Aileun rulers had intervened and declared the chant to be incorrect. Mau Balen said he eventually stepped in himself and in a brief chant traced the flag's descent from Nama Rau into the hands of Xavier (do Amaral) and (Nikolau) Lobato.

Mau Balen was not always a reliable narrator, and several people challenged his account of his own role in the flag ceremony (see Traube 2007). But the considerable force of the traditional association of political rule with the sea could indeed generate ambiguities of the sort he described. I once asked a group of Dai Lor ritual leaders where the national flag had originated. Their formulaic response—'from the water and sea'—prompted Fernando's objection, cited at the beginning of this chapter, that this would be as if foreigners still ruled. Fernando, who is a schoolteacher, did not invent a mythical origin for the national flag. He did, however, on my request, subsequently retell the myth of the colonial flag. He had clearly learned the story from his elder brother Mau Bere, but there was one innovation, which I suspect was his own. In the versions Mau Bere and Mau Balen had recounted for me, the realm's non-response to sacred symbols motivates the quest for the flag, but Fernando amplified the theme of pre-political anarchy and gave it a Hobbesian twist. Before the return of the

---

17   Fretilin leaders showed their appreciation for the cultural significance of the mountain in selecting the poem *Foho Ramelau* as the anthem of the nationalist movement. After independence, however, other parties argued that this song was too associated with Fretilin to serve as the national anthem.

Malaia, he said, everyone had guns, and people would resort to armed violence at the slightest provocation—a situation he described as a negative form of 'self-rule' (*uku-lolo*). When the Portuguese arrived and took stock of this situation, their first act as sovereign was to compel the Timorese to surrender their arms to the state. 'The guns', Fernando said, 'had to be turned over and stored together, in one place. In the event of a war, they would be redistributed to the forces, to meet the attack.' In this way order was restored, and the Portuguese ruled for 450 years. Nando represented the Portuguese as staying on to give a protracted course in civic education that should have concluded in 1975, when 'the Portuguese gave us liberty'—a reference to the official launching of the decolonisation policy.[18] But just as people were beginning to understand the different party programs, UDT had 'spoiled' (*estraka*) things by launching the coup.

It was clear from the context that the motif of the armed and disarmed population refracted recent political events. Earlier in the same conversation, Nando had described Fretilin's seizure of the Aileu arsenal in 1975 and its distribution of the weapons. The more recent arming of anti-independence militias by the TNI (Tentara Nasional Indonesia, the Indonesian military) in August 1999 was also never far out of mind—a reminder of the fragility of civil society. By implicitly incorporating experiences of local armed violence into a mythical narrative, Fernando articulated a shift that was under way in political subjectivity. In the versions of the flag myth that I had recorded in 1973–74, order comes from the cosmic ruler and his human representatives. The subjects of the realm are not called *povu* but 'women and men', and in the narrative they function not as sources of sovereignty but as obstacles to it. They are negative actors, characterised by their failure to 'tremble and fear', rather than by any innate capacity for citizenship. When they finally recognise and defer to the ruler, they are motivated by the sacred terror that the regalia from overseas inspire.

To return to the pre-political state as represented in the earlier version of the myth would be to relapse into a state of chaos, where people indiscriminately 'stab and slay one another' (a prospect that Mambai often rhetorically evoked, not without cause, as a potential danger). Nando, however, constructed a pre-political state that allows for a partial, productive return in times of emergency. Much like social-contract theorists, he projected a version of 'the people' onto a mythical 'state of nature' in the form of essentially rational subjects who voluntarily surrender their arms to the colonial state. They are, moreover,

---

18   The Portuguese Government officially recognised the right of the East Timorese to independence (Durand 2001:107) for the first time on 2 May 1975. Like Fernando, a group of Bar Tai people I met with also reconfigured colonial rule as a kind of protracted decolonisation; they said that the Portuguese had come to offer instruction and would have stayed only a short time. But when their appointed representative, Bau Meta, died, they ended up staying for 400 years.

citizens, or citizens-in-training, who can be legitimately rearmed in a national crisis. He adapted the traditional origin narrative and made it consistent with and expressive of a modern political subjectivity.

Not everyone is a storyteller, and most constructions of 'the people' did not take narrative form. The category was continually articulated in everyday discourse, most often in opposition to an imagined elite 'other'. Claims to speak as 'the people' as well as for them took on a populist edge that has persisted and intensified in the post-independence era. In this discourse, suffering is constitutive of national belonging and provides an idiom for challenging the commitments of particular individuals and groups. People in Aileu were well aware and deeply resentful of the claim that easterners had suffered more than westerners during the resistance struggle; in the most generous interpretation, they attributed such views to the easterners' lack of understanding of the early history of the war. Mambai themselves used the idiom of differential suffering to mark the boundaries of 'the people'. Recently returned diasporans were especially vulnerable to exclusion. That some exiles had been active in the resistance and had fled to save their lives was accepted, but the *capacity* to leave distinguished them. Mobility—in the form of access to planes, boats and passports—was often framed as an index of privilege, while 'the people' had no such resources and remained behind, as much out of necessity as inclination. In the calculus of those who remained behind, whatever suffering homesick exiles might have endured abroad could not come close to their own. Nor was the charge that so-and-so had not truly suffered with the people reserved for returned diasporans; it could be directed against any leader a speaker disapproved of, mistrusted or opposed. In Aileu, José Ramos-Horta remained the privileged exile who was held to have selflessly represented Timor's plight to the world, and Xanana Gusmão was a genuinely popular leader who had shared the people's ordeal, suffering with them in 'the forest' and for them in an Indonesian prison. In contrast, party leaders as a category were suspected of 'using the people's name' (*oid povu ni kalan*) without having participated in their suffering.

Speakers who identified or affiliated with 'the people' would often represent them as 'stupid' (*beik*) in contrast with educated (*matenek*) elites. Used literally, the attribution of stupidity referred to the widespread illiteracy among the rural masses and could be described as a social problem that needed to be overcome. Some individuals also portrayed their personal lack of formal educational qualifications as an index of their prior commitment to the resistance, on the dual grounds that resistance activities had taken time and energy away from schoolwork, and that the regime had rewarded collaborators with educational opportunities, while penalising families suspected of supporting the resistance. In figurative usage, the represented stupidity of the people took on positive connotations; it signified a form of popular wisdom or commonsense, while formal learning was characterised as a mode of stupidity. A Tetun proverb that Mambai often recite captures the popular mood: 'We stupid folk procure education; the educated ones return, and they are stupid like us' (*Ami beik-teen sosa matenek; matenek mai fail, beik tuir ami*).

The most egregious forms of elite stupidity, according to popular opinion, were evidenced in the competitive disunity that characterised *politika* (politics)—a term that was commonly used in the sense of manoeuvring for power and advantage. Critics pointed to the squabbling and bickering among party leaders as symptomatic of the discord and division that resulted from the political pursuit of self-interest. In contrast, 'the people' were said to understand the need for inclusive unity and to be already unified in their demands; what they expected from the state was assistance in securing 'their livelihood' (*ro ni morin*). The primary demand made in the name of the people on the state was to promote collective welfare by investing in the agricultural economy.

Conclusion

Since Timor-Leste's formal independence in 2002, and especially since the breakdown of civil order and security during the political 'crisis' (*crize*) of April–May 2006, much has happened in Aileu; yet, on the basis of several short return visits, I believe that the themes I have sketched remain salient in popular discourse. I conclude by suggesting that the discourse of 'the people' has tapped and reconfigured older notions of ritual authority.

Both categories embody forms of 'interiority'—a condition that binds subjects to the land and imposes on them a 'stupidity' that is also a form of wisdom. Like the sacral authorities of the indigenous polity, the people are symbolically associated with fixity, immobility and constancy. Although they lack formal knowledge, they have a practical understanding of national needs, especially the need for unity. The people (*povu*) also understand that agricultural productivity—traditionally associated with ritual leaders—is the precondition of a vibrant nation. Where the agricultural rites staged by ritual leaders symbolically reunite the realm as a whole, the unified nation is constructed by the people in the liberation struggle. Above all, the people resemble ritual authorities through their productive suffering. Their agonistic 'purchase' of the national flag resonates with the Christian economy of salvation, but it also evokes the ideology of animist rituals, wherein those who suffer to bring something forth must be repaid for their 'fatigue' (*kolen*). Traditionally, the position of a suffering source belonged to status superiors—the cosmic beings themselves and the ritual leaders who were their human counterparts and guardians.

Today, it also belongs to the mass of ordinary, rural folk, most of them poor and illiterate, who sacrificed themselves for the nation and now demand that the state repay them for their 'fatigue'.

A post-colonial state that ignores aspirations nurtured during an anti-colonial national liberation struggle puts its legitimacy at risk (Davidson 1992:214–15). In Timor-Leste, the post-independence years have seen a breakdown of trust in the national leadership, which the 2007 parliamentary elections failed to overcome (McWilliam and Bexley 2008: 79). When I visited Aileu briefly after the elections, Fretilin was the main target of popular grievances and faith in a new coalition government led by the CNRT (Conselho Nacional de Reconstrução do Timor, the National Congress for Timorese Reconstruction) was cautiously voiced. But I had the sense that people were already bracing themselves for further disappointment from the new national leadership. Indeed, East Timorese political leaders, whatever their party affiliations, face an ideological dilemma: whereas indigenous political culture once legitimised outsider rulers, legitimacy now depends on claims to insider status that very few individuals can authenticate.

Xavier do Amaral is a partial exception. In 2001, Xavier had founded a party he named ASDT (Associacao Social Democratica Timorense, the Timorese Social Democratic Association), which was the original name of Fretilin. In Aileu, ASDT was received as Fretilin's original 'trunk' or 'source', and it has won substantial majorities in every election.[19] Xavier is a Mambai from the district of Ainaro, and his ethnicity as well as his matrimonial connections with important Aileu families have contributed to his popularity, but his greatest asset is the aura of interiority he projects. Xavier has consistently aligned himself with the 'inner' pole of the political plane, as the elder, peace-oriented chief who 'cools' the land after war.[20] While his supporters do not seem to expect much from him in the way of policy, he is widely praised (even by members of other parties) as a unifying counterforce to the perceived egoism and divisiveness of most state elites, a wise 'grandfather' (*tata*) who puts the welfare of the people before all else. Such esteem for Xavier was itself symptomatic of frustration with politics as usual. A still more telling index of popular mistrust of the state was the

---

19   Much was also made of Xavier's role as *fundador*, ('founder') of Fretilin; although the term is derived from Portuguese, I have always suspected that for many Mambai it evokes their botanical origin category *fu*.
20   After the Indonesian invasion, Nikolau Lobato oversaw military operations for the resistance, while Xavier confined himself to political matters; Xavier's growing lack of confidence in a military solution and his pursuit of a negotiated settlement led to his being deposed and charged with treason by Fretilin. He was later captured by the Indonesians. During the UN-administered transition, many people anticipated the day when Xavier would preside over a ceremony to 'put away the sharp and pointed things'.

considerable regard for another Mambai, the renegade Major Alfredo Reinado, whom many of my friends proudly described in July 2007 as a 'defender of the people'.[21]

Such disillusionment with the national-state is indicative of the strength rather than the weakness of popular nationalism. The nation is the discursive site for a critique of the state that draws on pre-national traditions. From the vantage point of the imagined nation, the state is obligated to provide for the welfare of the people; its perceived failure to do so leaves the people in the position of the donor and defines their suffering as an unreciprocated gift. The situation is in some ways comparable with that of Hohul and Raimaus, where the self-defined founders of the realm continued to claim respect from Aileun chiefs who neglected and allegedly abused them; when the chiefs (by some accounts) sent the militias to burn their 'old mother/old father' in 1999, their legitimacy came into question (Traube 2007). Today, the legitimacy of the national-state depends on its willingness and ability to recognise and repay its founders.

Acknowledgments

This chapter is based on research pursued between 1973 and 1974 (supported by grants from the National Science Foundation and the National Institute of Health) and since 2000. I first returned to Aileu in October 2000 for approximately nine months of fieldwork; this work was supported by grants from the Wenner Gren Foundation and Wesleyan University. I returned again for two months in 2002, with the help of a summer research grant from the National Endowment for the Humanities, and in July 2007, I visited several Mambai districts, including Aileu, as an election observer for the Carter Center. A short version of this paper was published as Traube, E., 2011, "Producing the People", in Kathleen M. Adams and Kathleen A. Gillogly (eds), *Everyday Life in Southeast Asia*, Indiana University Press, Bloomington, pp .247-57.

---

21   I suspect, although I cannot pursue the point here, that Alfredo might have evoked at some level the sentinels who traditionally surrounded and guarded sacral centres.

References

Anderson, B. 1998, 'Gravel in Jakarta's shoes', in *The Spectre of Comparisons: Nationalism, Southeast Asia and the world*, Verso, London and New York, pp. 131–8.

Bellwood, P. 1996, 'Hierachy, founder ideology and Austronesian expansion', in James, J. Fox and Clifford Sather (eds), *Origins, Ancestry and Alliance: Explorations in Austronesian ethnography*, Research School of Pacific and Asian Studies, The Australian National University, Canberra, pp. 18–40.

Cunningham, C. E. 1965, 'Order and change in an Atoni diarchy', *Southwestern Journal of Anthropology*, vol. 21, pp. 359–82.

Davidson, B. 1992, *The Black Man's Burden: Africa and the curse of the nation-state*, Times Books, New York.

Dunn, J. 2003, *East Timor: A rough passage to independence*, Longueville Books, Double Bay, NSW.

Durand, F. 2001, 'Timor Lorosa'e 1930–2001: Partis politiques et processus électoraux à hauts risques', *Aséanie*, vol. 8, pp. 103–26.

Fox, J. J. 1995a, 'Austronesian societies and their transformations', in Peter Bellwood, James J. Fox and Darrell Tryon (eds), *The Austronesians: Historical and comparative perspectives*, Department of Anthropology, Comparative Austronesian Project, Research School of Pacific Studies, The Australian National University, Canberra, pp. 229–43.

Fox, J. J. 1995b, Installing the outsider inside: the exploration of an epistemic Austronesian cultural theme and its social significance, [Revised draft], Paper presented at the first Conference of the European Association for Southeast Asian Studies: Local Transformations and Common Heritage in Southeast Asia, 29 June – 1 July, Leiden University, Netherlands.

Fox, J. J. 1996, 'Introduction', in James J. Fox and Clifford Sather (eds), *Origins, Ancestry and Alliance: Explorations in Austronesian ethnography*, Department of Anthropology, Comparative Austronesian Project, Research School of Pacific and Asian Studies, The Australian National University, Canberra, pp. 1–17.

Guha, R. 1982, 'On some aspects of the historiography of colonial India', in Ranajit Guha Delhi (ed.), *Subaltern Studies I: Writings on South Asian history and society*, Oxford University Press, Oxford and New York, pp. 1–8.

Guha, R. 1997, *Dominance Without Hegemony: History and power in colonial India*, Harvard University Press, Cambridge, Mass., and London.

Harvey, G. 2006, *Animism: Respecting the living world*, Columbia University Press, New York.

Henley, D. 2002, *Jealousy and Justice: The indigenous roots of colonial rule in northern Sulawesi*, VU University Press, Amsterdam.

Kelly, J. D. and Kaplan, M. 2001, *Represented Communities: Fiji and world decolonization*, University of Chicago Press, Chicago.

Lazarus, N. 1999, *Nationalism and Cultural Practice in the Postcolonial World*, Cambridge University Press, Cambridge and New York.

Li Puma, E. and Meltzoff, S. 1990, 'Ceremonies of independence and public culture in the Solomon Islands', *Public Culture*, vol. 3, no. 1, pp. 77–92.

McWilliam, A. 2002, *Paths of Origin, Gates of Life: A study of place and precedence in southwest Timor*, KITLV Press, Leiden, Netherlands.

McWilliam, A. and Bexley, A. 2008, 'Performing politics: the 2007 parliamentary elections in Timor Leste', *Asia Pacific Journal of Anthropology*, vol. 9, no. 1, pp. 66–82.

Pélissier, R. 1996, *Timor en Guerre, Le Crocodile at les Portugais (1847–1913)*, Pélissier, Orgeval, France.

Sahlins, M. 1985, *Islands of History*, University of Chicago Press, Chicago.

Scott, J. C. 1990, *Domination and the Arts of Resistance: Hidden transcripts*, Yale University Press, New Haven, Conn.

Spivak, G. C. 1988, 'Can the subaltern speak?', in Cary Nelson and Lawrence Grossberg (eds), *Marxism and the Interpretation of Culture*, University of Illinois Press, Urbana, pp. 271–313.

Taylor, J. 1999, *East Timor: The price of freedom*, Zed Books, London and New York.

Therik, T. 2004, *Wehali, The Female Land: Traditions of a Timorese ritual centre*, Department of Anthropology, Research School of Pacific and Asian Studies, The Australian National University, in association with Pandanus Books, Canberra.

Traube, E. G. 1986, *Cosmology and Social Life: Ritual exchange among the Mambai of East Timor*, University of Chicago Press, Chicago.

Traube, E. G. 1989, 'Obligations to the source', in David Maybury-Lewis and Uri Almagor (eds), *The Attraction of Opposites: Thought and society in a dualistc mode*, University of Michigan Press, Ann Arbor, pp. 321–44.

Traube, E. G. 1995, 'Mambai perspectives on colonialism and decolonization', in P. Carey and G. Carter Bentley (eds), *East Timor at the Crossroads: The forging of a nation*, Social Science Research Council, London, pp. 42–55.

Traube, E. G. 2007, 'Unpaid wages: local narratives and the imagination of the nation', *Asia Pacific Journal of Anthropology*, vol. 8, no. 1, pp. 9–25.

Valeri, V. 1989, 'Reciprocal centers: the Siwa-Lima system in the cCentral Moluccas', in David Maybury-Lewis and Uri Almagor (eds), *The Attraction of Opposites: Thought and society in a dualistic mode*, University of Michigan Press, Ann Arbor, pp. 117–41.

7. Water Relations: Customary systems and the management of Baucau City's water[1]

Lisa Palmer

Introduction

In post-independence Timor-Leste people are seeking to rebuild the local and regional social and economic ties that were repressed under the violent 25 years of Indonesian military occupation (McWilliam 2005; Ospina and Hohe 2001; Palmer 2007a; Palmer and Carvalho 2008). Since the intervention in 1999 there has been a flood of aid and development-sector money into Timor-Leste, much of this directed to the water and sanitation sectors (ADB 2007: Schoeffel 2006). While customary practices are often explicitly acknowledged in the official governmental and donor discourses in Timor-Leste (Grenfell 2009), in the arena of water and sanitation the locally dynamic flows of water resources, customary rights and interests that 'sustain clan identity, maintain rights to land, redistribute income, and cultivate community' (Gibson-Graham 2004:415; cf. Langton et al. 2006) are largely invisible. The failure to address issues of resource ownership and control and to engage the strengths and importance of local customary institutions are having serious ramifications for the successful implementation of Timor-Leste's national water objectives in the city of Baucau and elsewhere in the country.

This chapter investigates the ritual ecology of water in Baucau and the ways in which diverse local water-management institutions coexist in management of the underground water resources that supply the city. I argue that in Baucau's distinctive karst (limestone bedrock) topography the local management of water, and the springs from which it emerges, is deeply embedded in the most important organising principles of Timorese (and Austronesian) social life: the wife-giver–wife-taker (*umane–fetosaun*) and older sibling–younger sibling (*maun–alin*) traditions. These foundational principles, which are consistently highlighted in local spring myth narratives, ensure that the norm of water management is one

---

1 The local cultural terms glossed in the national language of Tetum in this chapter are, depending on the speaker and context, referred to locally in either the Makassae or Waima'a languages. Because of this spatial and temporal ambiguity, here language translations for key cultural concepts are in all but two cases provided in Tetum (in two places, local Makassae terms are used and are identified by the placement of an 'M:' prior to the English translation).

of interdependence between water-sharing communities who are bound within relationships of obligation and reciprocity in relation to both water resources and a full spectrum of ceremonial life-cycle and livelihood activities. Grounded in an analysis of Baucau's complex diverse economy, this chapter asks how alternative social and economic practices might be meaningfully acknowledged and embraced by the state and the development sector in the negotiation and management of rural and urban water resources.

This research builds on the diverse-economy work of Gibson-Graham (2006), and demonstrates its relevance for environmental governance (Lemos and Agrawal 2006). Mapping the stories and customary institutions and exchanges that continue to circulate through Baucau's urban landscape in relation to water, it explores what importance these narratives and practices have for Baucau's ongoing development. By marrying together notions of environmental governance with those of a diverse-economy framework, it begins to analyse the varieties of knowledge (explicit and implicit), and ethical (who is obligated to whom) and aesthetic (what water to use and how) practices that come together in the everyday materiality of Baucau's water-management regimes. The chapter is based on fieldwork (interviews and participant observation) carried out by the author in Baucau between April 2004 and May 2009 (totaling eight months).

Why Water?

There are no published accounts of local people's customary management of karst hydrological systems—despite their existence throughout the world—which are distinguished from other groundwater aquifers by their unique open underground conduits developed in the limestone bedrock. Moreover, in Timor-Leste, while much academic and increasingly governmental focus has been placed on customary land-tenure issues (ARD 2008; Fitzpatrick 2008; Fitzpatrick and McWilliam 2005) and land-based resource management practices (D'Andrea et al. 2003; McWilliam 2003; McWilliam and Fitzpatrick 2005; Meitzner Yoder 2005), customary practices in relation to the governance of aquatic environments have attracted relatively little attention (see Jennaway 2008; McWilliam 2002; Palmer and Carvalho 2008 ; Costin and Powell 2006: 67-73). This chapter begins the task of undertaking a close and nuanced reading of a place-based instance of community water management and provides a critical counter to the enclosure and separation of water and the imposition of apolitical notions of 'community' common in 'community-based water-management models' currently deemed best practice around the globe (see Schoffel 2006). Nation-states and development practitioners have identified the water sector as an area of high priority (AusAID 2008; WaterAid and World Vision 2007), yet to date there is little research on the social and cultural complexity and effect/ impact of local indigenous life worlds and claims to water on the implementation of water policies (Altman 2008; Lansing 2007; Strang and Toussaint 2008).

In this way, the chapter is both an ethnography of a significant and never previously documented instance of environmental governance and a contribution to an opening up of an important site of politics in relation to the management of water in Timor-Leste. It demonstrates that ritual and ceremonial activities in relation to water must be taken seriously as performative practices that also 'bring forth, define, and empower social relationships' (Lansing 2007:15; cf. Palmer 2007c). Furthermore, it examines the ways in which effective collective decision making over resources is tied to a broader socio-cultural understanding of interdependence at the social, economic and environmental levels. Recognising and legitimising such interdependencies—which are deeply embedded in the life worlds of kin-based economic exchange and ethical decision making— could, I argue, be a potential catalyst for the engagement of community and the recognition of new regimes for natural resource management.

Baucau's Customary Water Governance

Jennaway (2008:28) has written in a review of the Timorese ethnographic literature that the '[c]ultural constructions of space, kinship affinities and social identity encoded in water and articulated in myth and ritual enactments constitute evidence of profound local affinities with water sources in the fluid social and cosmogonic economy of East Timor' (cf. McWilliam 2002). Hicks (1976:21–4) wrote about the karst formations in Baucau's neighbouring Viqueque region as being important conduits between the sacred and secular worlds, leading in local understandings down into the earth's womb. Ritual offerings must be made to ensure the harmonious relations between these two separate domains. In the Baucau region, local myth narratives demonstrate as well a complex understanding of the karst hydrology of the region and signal complex arrangements for inter-village cooperation across a wide area. Drawing together what some might see as the region's natural and social capital, these independencies give rise to governance processes grounded in collective decision making. This is perhaps both in spite of and because of the fact that conflict, even inter-regional wars, over water are said to have also historically featured in the governance landscape (Spillett 1999:270). The norms and nuances of local and regional governance interactions have, however, been disrupted through the colonial period and into the interdependence era by state regimes of water management that base their management of the city's water on their own configurations of knowledge, and ethical and aesthetic practices.

Today, water supply and management are issues with major development implications for the city of Baucau (population 16 000; elevation: 300 m). The Government's water and sanitation department operates on an inadequate budget, lacking resources to address the myriad water-management and supply issues that the city faces. In addition to an inadequate water supply and large-scale infrastructure limitations, the department also struggles to deal with smaller-scale issues such as leaks and illegal connections by city residents. To date there have been no hydrological surveys to better understand the region's water resource flows—although it is widely believed that the source spring for much of the region's water resources is located some 20 km away near the village of Darasula on the Baucau Plateau (elevation: 500 m; see Figure 7.1).[2]

In contrast with the lack of scientific knowledge of this complex system, many local people associated with locally significant springs possess relatively detailed knowledge of these underground conduits (see Figure 7.1). It is widely believed, for example, that the Darasula spring (known in one local language, Makassae, as Wai Lia Bere [the great Wai Lia] and in another, Waima'a, as Wai Lia Oli) is a gateway for water flowing to many other springs in the region connecting springs lower down, on and off the plateau. While local myth narratives about these springs and their connections might vary (depending on who is telling the story, where they are from, and the purpose of their telling), all emphasise the interconnections between this 'parent' spring and other springs and peoples in other areas. It is also believed that the water from Darasula on the Baucau Plateau channels off through underground cave systems in four directions (an area of roughly 20 sq km): one to the western edge of the escarpment to the village of Bucoli, one to the eastern edge of the escarpment to the village of Wailili, one to Wai Lia spring in Baucau and a vertically parallel one directly to the coastal springs of Wotabo below Baucau City (see Figure 7.1). An underwater spring in the ocean off the coast from Wotabo is believed to be the final exit for much of the spring water that channels through the Wai Lia and Wotabo conduits. This ocean spring, like other sites along the Baucau coast, is considered sacred (*lulik*) by local peoples. Many people and boats are said to have disappeared along this stretch of coast, particularly near the spring, which is said to be guarded by water spirits or the owners of the sea (*tasi na'in*).

It is asserted by those from places lower down from the Darasula spring that elders known as *bee na'in* ('the owners/custodians of the water') from the parent spring have specific knowledge that enables them to ritually direct or divert water (*hamuluk*) and on occasions even to enter these underground conduits and manipulate the water flow to particular areas using woven palm matting, or,

---

2   At the time of writing, a hydro-geologist employed with the newly established Timorese Department of Water Resources had begun a dye-tracing experiment to try to understand underground water pathways and flows.

more commonly today, corrugated-iron sheeting. Local elders of one Baucau City village asserted that Baucau's water-supply problems are caused by diversions of water away from the underground conduit leading to the city's main spring to springs and agricultural communities elsewhere on the Baucau Plateau. Such actions were explained as 'sanctions' imposed by the source spring *bee na'in* for the failure of Baucau City's residents, government and businesses to properly acknowledge the interdependencies between the springs, and to carry out the requisite ceremonial activities.

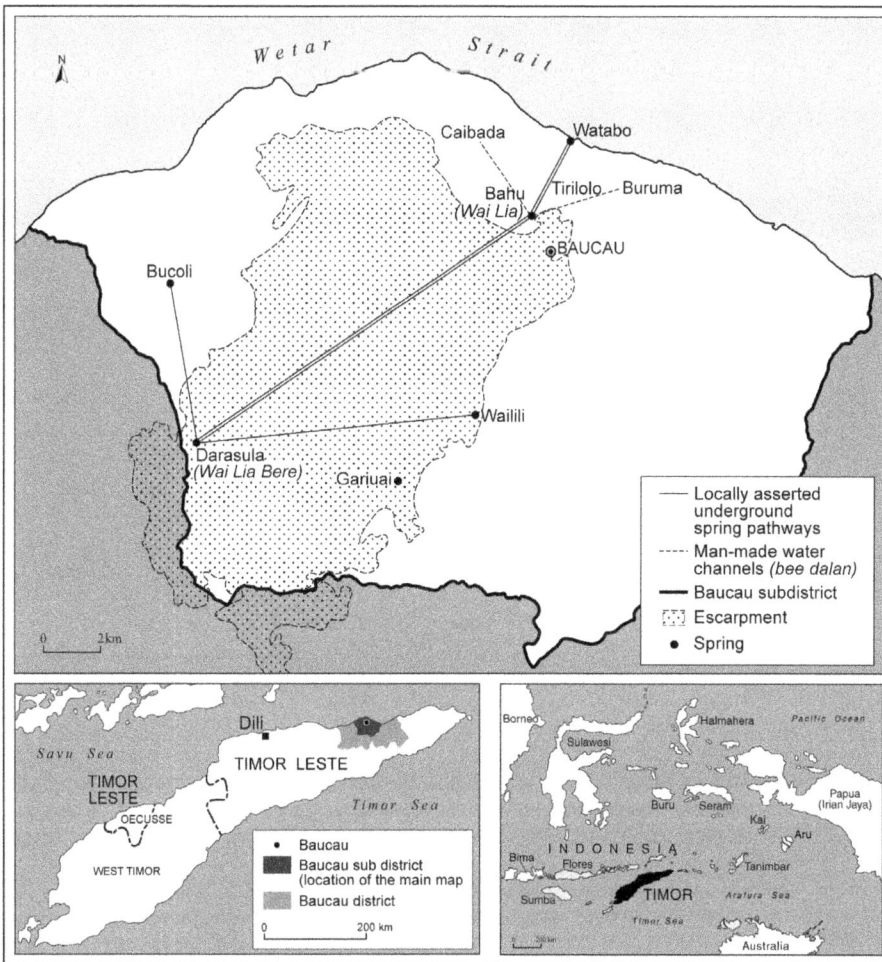

Figure 7.1 Locally asserted underground spring pathways

This capacity to actively divert water is, however, denied by the *bee na'in* of the Darasula spring. While they concede that the water flowing from Wai Lia Bere to other areas can be highly variable (and in the case of water flowing to Wai Lia in Baucau, counterintuitive, as the flow is weak in the wet season and stronger in the dry season), they maintain that this is a 'natural' process. By 'natural' they mean that nature or the water itself is responding to the presence or absence of the annual requisite gift giving and ceremonial activity of those lower down the water chain. The agents of this water-flow control are asserted to be the spirits of the underworld themselves—the true *bee na'in*.

To demonstrate these interdependencies, I relate here the story of the Wai Lia spring—Baucau City's main water source—told to me by a senior ritual leader (*lianain*) of one of Baucau's indigenous polities.

The Story of Wai Lia

Wai Lia spring has its *fuu* [M: trunk, origin] near a place called Darasula. In the beginning there were two brothers there tending buffaloes. One day they were hungry so they decided to dig, cook and eat some yams. But then they were very thirsty. While they were sitting down wondering where they could get water they remembered the day when their dogs went missing and came back all wet. They wanted to know where the dogs got this water. So they made a plan. They cooked some more yams to give to the dogs, but before they gave them to the dogs they made a bamboo collar—tied with string—for one of the dog's necks. Inside the hollow piece of bamboo they placed ash from the fire and made a small hole in the bamboo. Then they gave the yams to the dogs to eat. The dogs were thirsty and headed off. In about one hour they returned all wet. Now the brothers had a way to find the water. They followed the ash that had trickled from the bamboo collar until they came to a big cave with water inside. They both went down into the cave and drew water, which they carried back out of the cave to drink. After this they were still thirsty so the younger brother then went down again to draw water. Inside the cave there were two places to draw water. On one side was a big cave; on the other side was a small cave. From the large opening he could hear the water flowing very loudly. He went in to have a look at what was making such a loud noise. Suddenly someone came out of the water and pulled him down into it. He was underwater a long time until eventually he emerged in the still water of another cave—Wai Lia spring in Baucau. He was now naked, as he had lost his clothes in the water, so he decided to stay there beneath the surface and wait.

Then to the spring came two women, the daughters of a woman from Bahu. The sisters had come to draw water. The older sister entered the cave and drew water from what was a very clean spring. The man from Darasula was crouching beneath the surface and saw this woman drawing water but decided not to do anything. Then the younger sister came down to draw water, but when she got back up to the surface she saw that in contrast to her older sister the water she had drawn was dirty. So she threw it away and went to draw water again. Again it was dirty. Next her older sister went down and drew water again, and again her water was clear. The younger sister went down again and drew water for the third time. It was still dirty. 'What is making my water dirty', she thought with frustration? She looked down into the water and beneath it she made out a naked man. The older sister came down to join her and the younger sister demanded to know where this naked man was from that he thought he could make her water dirty. The naked man explained: 'I am from Darasula; I was tending buffalo there when I was thirsty and went down into a cave to draw water. Then I somehow ended up here.' 'But what do you want?' asked the women. 'Could you go and ask your brothers to bring me some clothes to wear?' asked the man from Darasula. So the women went to ask their older brothers to take the man a *tais* [woven cloth] to wear. They did this and he got dressed in the water.

When he came out of the water the two sisters and their older brother who had brought the *tais* were still there. It was decided that the younger sister would now marry this man. So they got married and lived together at the woman's home and they had a child together. And then the woman said, 'Now it is time for us to go to try to find your place so I can see where you come from. Do you still have family there, I wonder?' So they set off to look for this place, telling his story along the way and asking people if they knew of his brother and if he was still alive. Eventually they found some of his possessions hanging in a tree: his carry basket, cotton spinning stick, spear and digging stick. 'This is the place where I was tending buffaloes the day I became lost', he said. He got down his possessions and they kept walking.

They kept asking people they met about his brother and finally one man responded: 'Yes, it is me, I am your older brother. I thought you were lost forever.' The two hugged each other and cried together. The older explained 'I am your older brother and you are my younger brother. You went down into the water and got lost, I thought you were dead. I waited seven days and seven nights but you didn't appear. I went down to look for you in the water but I didn't find you. I thought you were dead but now you have come back. In the past we looked after buffalo together and now you have come back. I am still here and you have come back.' The older brother explained that now as the younger brother had returned to his *fuu* [M: trunk/origin] he needed to make a traditional house here at this place by the water at Darasula. The house was needed so that offerings could be made to the water and the story would not be forgotten. 'When the time comes for us to make offerings to give thanks to the water which we both found together, the people from Bahu, Caibada, Buruma, Tirilolo [the four villages in Baucau that receive water from Wai Lia] must also come together to kill goats, buffalo, pigs and chickens and then bring them here for us to make our offerings at Darasula.' 'You must also make a traditional house at Wai Lia,' said the older brother. This was so the four villages could also make the same collective offerings at Wai Lia spring in Baucau.

After the older brother explained all of this, the younger brother was also reunited with the dog who had led them to the cave and who had since had many puppies. He explained to the dog that he had married a woman from Bahu and had also had children. He hugged the dog and cried. He hugged his brother and cried. After this they made the traditional houses in both places so they could remember this story and give thanks to the water. Each year the local population would carry out ceremonies so that the two springs would never be dry. This meant that they could make fields and plant rice and have plenty to eat.

However, eventually the people from the four villages sharing the water from Wai Lia forgot to make their sacrifices. The water stopped flowing and many animals, crops and trees began to die. The people from Baucau went to the owners of the water in Darasula and asked, 'Why is our water dry?' The Darasula people explained the reason: 'You have not been making the sacrifices and you need to start doing this again.' So the people in Baucau started to make the required sacrifices again and after this their rice could grow again.

What this narrative highlights is the way in which the management of the Wai Lia water source is intimately embedded in the most important organising principle of Timorese social life: the wife-giver–wife-taker (*umane–fetosaun*) and older sibling–younger sibling (*maun–alin*) traditions. A man from the parent spring on the plateau marries a woman from the subsidiary spring lower in Baucau, creating an ongoing asymmetrical ritual and exchange relationship between the peoples from the two areas, linking together themselves and their water resources. In order to ensure the ongoing gift of life giving (a plentiful supply of water, crops, animals and children), ceremonies must be carried out at both springs. The people of the four Baucau villages must provide these sacrifices (and as we will see later, annual tribute) to their water's *hun* (trunk, origin) and the *bee na'in* at Darasula, and must also come together to carry out their own ceremonies at Wai Lia. The broader Wai lia complex in Baucau City is made up of seven sequential springs and each of these springs is the responsibility of one of the neighbouring villages. Coming together in a sibling relationship, they must organise the ceremonies required to properly manage the springs in the complex.

These sacrificial processes—known in Tetun as '*fo han*' (feeding)—involve small-scale annual sacrifices and larger seven-yearly collective ceremonies (*tinan hitu dala ida*), which involve people from all the water-sharing communities over a period of seven days and seven nights. During this time, there is much singing and dancing (*tebe*) and elders call forth and commune with the sacred eels that inhabit the springs (the eels are also a manifestation of the owners/custodians of the water or *bee na'in*). The ceremonies also mediate relations between humans and ancestral ghosts, metaphysical relations between the sacred and the secular, and geographical relations between the secular world and the sacred world (cf. Hicks 1976:108).

Yet while the knowledge of these underground water connections has remained vibrant, at the Wai Lia spring the customary ritual processes involved in activating these connections are just re-emerging. In the town's Portuguese era (effectively from the 1920s), the rice fields in the immediate vicinity of the Wai Lia spring slowly disappeared, making way for shops, markets and roads. Post World War II, elders were hampered in their efforts to carry out the requisite sacrifices by a colonial tax placed on the slaughter of animals and in the 1960s a water pumping station was built around the Wai Lia spring complex. Meanwhile, on the escarpment where the location of the Wai Lia Bere cave and underground spring had erstwhile been a closely guarded secret, in the 1960s a Chinese Timorese market gardener from Baucau town arrived in the area and attempted (unsuccessfully) to harness the underground water supply (see Palmer 2010). This was followed by an incident at a market cockfight in Baucau when an altercation broke out between members of the Darasula community and others from Baucau. Following this incident, the water at the Wai Lia spring complex ran dry, leading people to speculate that the Darasula *bee na'in* had intervened (either physically or spiritually) to shut off the town's water supply. It is said that the Portuguese administrator at the time was so incensed he sent an armed convoy of cars to Darasula to arrest those suspected of such acts. A group from Darasula was brought down and detained in Baucau until one of the elders descended and convinced the administrator that as he was not God, he was not in control of the water supply.

Following the above events, the water supply at Wai Lia remained intermittent at best and in the late Indonesian era it dried up again completely. In panic, the Indonesian administrators conferred with the village heads and money (and Indonesian Government permission) was provided to enable the organisation of a *tinan hitu dala ida* ceremony. The respective ritual leaders of the four villages were called together and an approach was made to the *bee na'in* in Darasula. The ceremony was eventually carried out in August 1999 and the water flowed again soon after. Following the Indonesian withdrawal from Timor-Leste in late 1999, however, the traditional political ruler (*liurai*) of Bahu village, where Wai Lia is located, fled across the border to West Timor, adding yet another obstacle to the customary governance of the spring, and, at the time of writing, water flow continues to be intermittent. As discussed below, the surface water at the main Wai Lia spring in Baucau City was completely dry in April 2008. While water from other springs in the Wai Lia complex is still available to be pumped uphill to supply the storage reservoirs feeding the domestic water supply of the ever-growing 'new town' (above the 'old town' where the pumping station is located), the intermittent nature of the overall flow can have serious ramifications for the water available to other areas. The gravitational system piping domestic water to the villages below Wai Lia, as well as the flows through the pumping station to the man-made water channels (*bee dalan*) beneath it are particularly susceptible at these times. The water flow to these two major *bee dalan* is essential to the productivity of the irrigated rice fields below and disruptions to this supply lead to disgruntlement, and some say sabotage, on the part of the rice farmers.

Given the history of disruption yet ongoing rich complexity of the customary governance of these springs, there is a clear need for more research to fully understand their impact on Baucau's present day water supply and the materiality of water use. It is necessary also to map local karst spring pathways and the associated socio-cultural formations, including the complexity of the springs' interconnected ritual ecology. This requires detailed mapping of springs, underground channels, water infrastructure, irrigation flows and relevant sacred house (*uma lulik*) locations. A full map would establish water flows, allocations and the interlocking ritual cycles from relevant locations across the plateau. By researching the practices, contexts and scales through which negotiations and decision making over water occur, what would become clear is the range of market, state and non-state/non-market economic practices at work in the management of local water resources. Identifying precisely what individuals and households associated with the interconnected springs know—in both an explicit and a tacit sense—about water in the region and how they access it is critical to a better understanding of the customary governance process.

Custom and Nation Building

The *bee na'in* (of both the secular and the sacred worlds) at Darasula have not, it appears, taken kindly to the absence of ritual processes at Wai Lia, whatever the constraints on the local community. Baucau City is reportedly perceived by the upstream *bee na'in* and water users to be resource rich with access to markets, government and international aid money. Water users in Baucau are seen as expecting to receive water without returning anything to the upstream water owners. The Government takes the water for civic needs, some people illegally tap into this supply, and some even collect water in trucks and profit from its sale.[3] The *bee na'in* (temporal and spiritual) of the water at Wai Lia Bere see such activities as violating the foundational principles of interconnection, obligation and reciprocity related in local spring myth narratives. City people are not unsympathetic to this sentiment and many agree that something needs to be done. A traditional political leader of one of the city villages (himself a local businessman) explained that the Government and the non-governmental organisation (NGO) sector 'just take water, they don't know how to make it. They pick the fruit, but they don't know how to grow it. They have no interest in *lulik* [the sacred]' (Personal communication, May 2006). As this person understands it, the Government and the NGO sector do not help in the management of such resources, rather they exploit them and at the same time by providing these resources for free they put up disincentives for active community engagement in their management.

While the government officers are not unaware of the customary water-management system and its hold over issues of water supply at Wai Lia, the extent to which such sensitive issues are openly discussed in communications between the national and regional offices is difficult to gauge. Such issues are very sensitive and both government officers and customary leaders are generally reticent to discuss the matter outside formal processes. Moreover, conducting the requisite ceremonies and engaging in customary processes are complicated matters that must be properly negotiated by the ritual authorities across all of the water-sharing villages and this takes an immense investment of time, community coordination and money. Community members must also take the initiative to coordinate the preparation activities and collect the money. With money scarce in a testing post-independence economic environment, it is difficult for most households to contribute to such an undertaking. Moreover, for those in the population who are not engaged in rice farming and who are not dependent on significant water resources for their livelihoods, there is less incentive to give money to conduct rituals or pay tribute to customary owners. This is especially the case when they are today getting water largely for free from the Government or aid organisations.

Despite a healthy wet season in 2007–08, which should in a karst-fed spring system result in good water flows, the Wai Lia spring was still not flowing well. A local elder from Baucau City explained that this was due to water being actively diverted from the Wai Lia conduit to increase supply to rice fields in other areas. By February 2008, despairing at the lack of water available for his village rice fields, this senior ritual leader organised amongst his kinsfolk to take 26 bags of unhulled rice to the *bee na'in* in Darasula (under the exchange relationship between the two areas, such gifts are expected to be made annually

---

3 In 2009 the *bee na'in* for the spring where the water trucks now fill their tanks charged truck owners a levy of 50 cents per tank (a tank of water sells for US$20).

to the Darasula *bee na'in* by the irrigation collectives sharing Wai Lia water). Following these activities, the water supply returned to Wai Lia in May 2008. The Baucau *lia na'in* was careful to point out that this timing coincided with the ripening and harvest of rice crops in areas elsewhere on the plateau that already had water. Although too late for the season's rice crop in the rice fields below Baucau, the increased flow was nevertheless seen to be a valuable source of water for the next season's corn crop in areas downstream from Wai Lia.

While the efficacy of these rituals and associated practices in addressing the actual water flows might be mystifying to outsiders, for local people, they are an essential means through which the community is engaged and compelled to take seriously their obligations and responsibilities to a water commons. It is asserted by some that if the Timorese Government and the aid sector were serious about fixing the water problem in Baucau, they would come together and formally talk with the ritual authorities and discuss the need for the requisite customary ceremonies and gift-giving practices to begin again. Until the population is actively involved in the management of water in this way, nothing will be resolved or properly implemented. The Darasula *bee na'in*, they assert, will continue to intervene with the water supply and city people will continue to abuse what is today a 'common property' resource alienated from its community of commons. Such a process needs to engage elders in formal agreement making about water-supply issues and management processes, and would require (at a minimum) the involvement of the Baucau water-sharing villages and the Wai Lia Bere *bee na'in* as well as the engagement and financial support of the national and district governments.

While the details of such agreement making remain to be negotiated, what is clear is that the process would potentially open up important sites of politics for the management of water in Baucau—constituting 'a place of encounter' between those in control of the formal system and those who normally have no part in that system (Dikeç 2004). Yet it is also possible that such engagements could be little more than a means of demarcating and controlling the customary economy. Zerner (1994:1107) has written of the risks for customary systems elsewhere in the region of becoming beholden to external regulatory control whereby 'the complicated ritual nexus in which these practices are embedded has been reduced to a sparse, functional system'. Lansing (1987) made a similar point in relation to the recognition of the role of religious institutions in the inter-village management of water in Bali. Furthermore, in Indonesian times while such ceremonies might have been carried out with the assistance of grants of money, the local Indonesian-appointed authorities (such as the village head) are said to have chosen inappropriate people to lead the rituals. This resulted in both a de-sacralisation of the process and ineffective, if not dangerous, ritual practices (see Carvalho et al. 2008). In the independence era, it is expected that financial support for ceremonial activities would be ongoing rather than event based and that the Government would recognise that locally autonomous processes are what need to be fully engaged with if they are to achieve their aims: mutually harmonious relations.

The Power of the Diverse Economy

In recognising the existence of a customary water economy in Baucau, one is struck by the pervasive insistence on local autonomy embedded in the narratives and practices. Despite the post-independence rhetoric of economic development, most people in Baucau have little surplus wealth to reallocate. Yet local economic-exchange principles maintain such a hold over resource allocation and use as to pose a serious challenge to conventional understandings of economic development (cf. Yang 2000). These exchanges are based on understandings of power and of the world that enliven and connect both place and people. It is, in short, a socialised landscape where ritual performances constitute 'serious world making work' (Verran and Christie 2007: 219).

As noted at the outset of this chapter, the violence and control of the Indonesian era saw widespread suppression of locally autonomous rule. In the independence era, there is currently a revitalisation of indigenous custom and tradition where across villages and subdistricts the communal management of natural resources (fields, forests, fisheries) is being enhanced by the reinstatement of ritual prohibition and/or harvest ceremonies (Carvalho and Haburas Foundation n.d.; D'Andrea et al. 2003; McWilliam 2003; Meitzner Yoder 2005; Palmer 2007a; Palmer and Carvalho 2008). The reconstruction of sacred houses (*uma lulik*) is another example of this revitalisation process, although these 'houses' were also of great symbolic and functional importance in the organisation of the Timorese resistance during the Indonesian occupation (see McWilliam 2005). Since 2001–02, dozens of sacred houses have been constructed each year in the Baucau district, replacing many of the houses burnt down in Indonesian times (da Costa et al. 2006). Reconstruction of these houses involves a major undertaking of economic resources—money, building materials, time (dependent on the size and status of the house)—and there are prescriptive offerings that must be made by those associated with the house both during its construction and at the feast to consecrate the house. It is also a process that brings family (and their economic resources) back together from locations around the country. A further reason for this flurry of reconstruction is the pressing need to provide a place to rest for all the souls who passed away without a proper burial in Indonesian times—those who are still hovering around and causing trouble for the living (cf. da Costa et al. 2006; Hicks 1976, 2008; McWilliam 2008).

It is also important to note that such an economy is not without its negative aspects. For example, particularly in urban landscapes brimming with aspirational modernity, some feel customary obligations are a burden. People will often state that *lulik*—the sacred animist realm—is too greedy and excessive (see also Ospina and Hohe 2001:175). For city dwellers and wage labourers in particular, life-cycle and intergenerational customary exchanges between wife-giver and wife-taker (*umane* and *fetosaun*) groups (of things such as buffaloes, pigs, horses, goats, swords, necklaces and woven cloth) are made not by drawing on family livestock resources but via monetary payments (which are either pooled and used in the exchange directly or used to purchase the livestock and goods to be exchanged). In local critiques of the excesses of the ritual economy, however, not only is the replacement or phasing out of customary processes with capitalist approaches being suggested, there are also initiatives emerging from within the customary repertoire that draw on the power of communal ritual processes to impose a reduction in the size of customary payments (see Palmer 2007a). Such cases further demonstrate the need for engaging with the full range of practices embedded in the customary economy. It is unclear whether this resurgence of the customary or community economy will remain a permanent feature of Baucau's diverse economy.

Where to Now?

It is critical that further information be sought on this spring ritual ecology—namely, the enduring cultural beliefs that shape individual and social action and the role of particular ritual processes, springs, sacred houses and associated material objects in water management. Also important to understand is the degree to which water ritual exchanges are organised around political and linguistic boundaries. For example, it appears that the human representatives (the *bee na'in*) of the sacred houses primarily associated with the various springs are not possessory owners of the water but custodians, messengers between the secular world and the sacred world of the water ancestral spirits (also known as *bee na'in*). In the case of Darasula, it is said by those who assert that the practice of closing the underground water channels occurs, that detailed knowledge of the cave and gating system is highly secretive and sacred, and is prohibited from being passed outside the lineage through fear of spiritual retribution such as sickness, infertility or death. For this reason, they say that any changes to water flows within the cave systems require the *bee na'in* to first carry out ceremonies and seek permission for their activities from the ancestors. These are not trivial matters and research must proceed with caution, bringing to the public arena only those aspects of knowledge and practice that can be properly shared. To enter into serious discussions about the ritual management of water is to embark on a process that demands proper protocols be observed.[4] Adding to the complexity of researching the importance of water rituals in village and regional formal governance arrangements is the fact that, following the Manufahi uprisings against the Portuguese colonial powers (c. 1895–1915), the Portuguese administration ensured that ritual power was formally emasculated at the sub-village level and above, and vice versa in relation to political power at the *knua* or hamlet level (Personal communication, Antonio Vicente, May 2006).

Recognising the above issues, mapping must also be concerned to document the range of relevant practices for water management, the consequences of different water flows and allocation processes and quarrels over water, the timing of ceremonial and gift exchanges, links with agricultural rites, and the impact of modernising agricultural practices (cf. Lansing 2007). Furthermore, questions must be asked about how the city is being incorporated into customary exchange process and the range of uses of the city water supply that is claimed to be 'illegal' in either a formal or a customary sense. Also important to assess are state practices of legibility—what narratives about water does the state tell? What are the intersecting dynamics of the full range of state, market and non-state/non-market uses and practices in relation to water and the relationship with wider social, political and economic issues?

Attention, too, needs to be paid to the agency ascribed to water in customary configurations and the ways in which wider societal relationships to water are potentially reconfigured through notions of the 'land as citizen', or environmental citizenship (Borrows 2002:138–58). In local understandings, recognising the materiality and agency of water constitutes recognition of a 'sentient' environment wherein water is an essential partner in community negotiations, not an entity separated from land and people and readily available to be traded through virtual abstractions such as water quotas. Examples of this pervade anecdotal accounts of water management in the region. It is widely reported that immediately after the Indonesian departure in 1999, the Wai Lia spring began suddenly gushing water—the spirits expressing their pleasure at this turn of events. Likewise, spirit-world actions can also be frequently disruptive of events that transgress orderly relations between the sacred and the secular; it is said that attempts in the Indonesian era to put in place a large-scale water facility and infrastructure at the Darasula spring triggered a large explosion and the project was abandoned after very little water was able to be extracted. It is unclear whether such occurrences are attributable only to specific spirit actions or whether in some cases people hold to a more generalised

---

4 Following my interview with the senior ritual leader who offered the Wai Lia narrative, a chicken had to be sacrificed to *taka naran* (literally, 'close the name' of the ancestral beings who were spoken about) to properly close a discussion of such ritually important matters. Failure to close proceedings in this way could lead to serious ramifications including sickness or other misfortune.

notion of the landscape as a subjective entity, alive and in communication with its inhabitants through the agency of the spirit world (cf. Bovensiepen 2009; McWilliam, this volume).

Negotiating Water

The customary domain's desire for the Timorese Government to engage with kin-based ethical decision making and the ritual domain in the formal management of Wai Lia is not a call to codify structured sets of relationships, but rather is asking them to embrace performative practice and to reframe the state's normative expectations of social relationships. Such a process would need to recognise the considerable slippage and overlap that today exist within local community notions of water as a public good provided by the state, as a community commons and as a commodity available for private sale. Local water users find no logical reason to delineate secular or sacred water-management practices, and notions of ownership and possession are (if relevant at all) subservient to the recognition and performance of interdependence. In such agreement-making proposals there are considerable tensions already between the customary political realm's acknowledgment and involvement in always in-process customary practices and the need of the state and the market sector for both 'legibility' (Scott 1999) and certainty through 'definitive valid representations' (Verran and Christie 2007:225). As Verran and Christie have argued in an extra-regional context, indigenous 'knowledge work does not produce effective representations of an external world; rather it produces effective worlds in place as performance' (2007:219).

Situated in the heart of a region long engaged in trade and alliance making (Gunn 1999; Van Engelenhoven and Hajek 2000), Timorese people have a history of engagement in both capitalist and customary economic exchanges. For example, as well as engaging in intra-island trade and alliances, the people of Baucau forged longstanding traditional alliances and exchanges with the nearby island population of Kisar until the beginning of the twentieth century (Correa 1944). Local oral histories also recount trade (of cloth, alcohol, foodstuffs), marriage and ritual relationships with the nearby island of Wetar as well as intermittent trade and ritual exchange with visitors from islands beyond. Hence, (extra-) customary notions of agreement making and alliance building are nothing new—and these are processes and practices that 'politically' marginalised people in the region have long employed to respond to and influence the various regimes of governance they have encountered. These are processes in which tradition and custom are always responding to and embracing something more than the local and are embedded in a long history of regional and more recently nation-state level influences and dialogues (see Palmer and Carvalho

2008; cf. Tsing 1993; Zerner 1994). What is needed is for these practices to be made credible in a development landscape where they are rendered largely non-credible, if not invisible. It needs to be recognised that the dynamic flow of commodities, customary rights and interests constitutes a unique and finely nuanced form of economic—including property—relations. Such economic relations 'are markedly distinct from, yet not incommensurate with, the normative conception of economic relations' (Langton et al. 2006:307) in the modern marketplace. Hence, a reformulation of ideas about economic life is necessary for the recognition of both diverse indigenous economic institutions and the negotiation of integrated and sustainable natural-resource management regimes.

Conclusion

In Baucau's water-management and supply sector, a customary economy is actively undermining a weak capitalist/development sector. It would seem, however, that foregrounding and engaging with the foundational customary economy under whose auspices local water politics play out could be one potential catalyst for 'new economic becomings' in Baucau, opening up 'a politics of possibility' (Gibson-Graham 2006) for economic development and the recognition of the legitimacy of custom in resource management in the city.

The Wai Lia myth recounted in this chapter constitutes poetic politics—an insight into the workings of Baucau's customary economy and the relationships and social institutions through which at least some water resources in the region are managed and controlled. In these customary practices, people are not passive recipients of projects and programs but active players in their own life worlds and as such are critical participants in the pursuit of 'development'.[5] My account is not meant to imply idealised traditional communities capable of managing their resources if only the state and/or the development sector would butt out. Rather, recognising that ecological resources are embedded in complicated socio-historical contexts is also to recognise 'tangled threads, difficult to unpick' (Mosse 2003), especially in a country as culturally diverse as Timor-Leste. Moreover, the story recounted is not an unfamiliar story of water politics, replete with jealousies over resource use and access (see Mosse 2003). There was, as even the myth makes clear, never a 'golden age' of harmonious cooperation; rather there were and are always varying degrees of 'uncertainties, disharmony and disruption' (Mosse 2003:4) as well as cooperation in the ongoing processes of social and political negotiation that address the changing

---

5   Although as Mosse (2003:308; see also Batterbury 2005) notes, the opposite can also be the case with development interventions of all kinds offering 'material and symbolic resources for use in the ongoing renegotiation of social relations (within villages and with the state)'.

economic circumstances of water-resource use. In the new nation of Timor-Leste, institutional changes and pressures in relation to water management have created circumstances where more than ever before the institutions of the 'state', 'international development' and of 'community' intermingle in the practices of statecraft (cf. Mosse 2003, 2005; Tsing 1993, 2005). Critical to their role in such processes will be the ability of local-level leaders to draw outsiders into their own ritual ecology of water-resource management while at the same time finding ways into the conversations of state and non-state development interests around water (see Tsing 2005).

To recognise the persistence of customary models in a post-development context is to acknowledge the embeddedness of Timorese organising principles, their binaries and symbolic operators, and to take them seriously. Yet, the power and opacity of customary law, practices and strong kin-based allegiances are not things that can be easily accepted by liberal-democratic capitalist values. Such processes are threatening to other entities whether they are the state, the church or the rational economic and community development planning of many national and international development agencies. Yet recognising that full engagement with a diverse economy is enabled when local people are able to draw on and activate their own understandings of power based in customary processes opens up political spaces for the negotiation of local economic development and resource management (Gibson-Graham 2006). In the customary economy of Baucau, local people's understandings of the intricate power relations at work between relational spheres are the substance of everyday life—something in which all can engage. Yet currently this economic reality is elided in official discourses in favour of a dominant model of development that has a tendency to alienate or disengage the very people it is supposed to benefit. Unless the customary economy is given a place in the development economy, it will continue to be a dangerous and powerful undertow—sweeping out to sea the unsuspecting.

Acknowledgments

Fieldwork for this chapter was carried out with the assistance of an Australian Research Council Grant (LP0561857). I would like to thank all the Baucau families and individuals who hosted me and contributed in many variable ways to the insights and understandings that form the basis of this chapter. Particular thanks go to those elders (*lia na'in*) in the region who shared with me elements of their knowledge of the regional waterscape; in particular, thank you to Antonio da Costa Gusmao. Louisa Freitas and Quintiliano Mok provided invaluable assistance as interpreters of the Makassae language. Also thank you to Katherine Gibson, Brian Finlayson, Andrew McWilliam, Pyone Myat Thu, David Hicks and Simon Batterbury for their comments on earlier drafts of the chapter. All errors and omissions are mine.

References

Altman, J. 2008, *Fresh Water in the Maningrida Region's Hybrid Economy: Intercultural contestation over values and property rights*, Centre for Aboriginal Economic Policy Research, The Australian National University, Canberra.

Asian Development Bank (ADB) 2007, Proposed ADB Fund Grant RDTL: Dili Urban Water Supply Sector Project, Asian Development Bank, Dili.

Associates in Rural Development (ARD) 2008, Strengthening Property Rights in Timor-Leste Project (Ita Nia Rai), ARD/USAID, Burlington, Vt, and Washington, DC.

Australian Agency for International Development (AusAID) 2008, *Water and sanitation initiative*, Draft for Public Comment, November, AusAID, Canberra.

Batterbury, S. 2005, 'Development, planning, and agricultural knowledge on the central plateau of Burkina Faso', in R. Cline-Cole and E. Robson (eds), *West African Worlds: Paths through socio-economic change, livelihoods and development*, Pearson Education, Essex, pp. 259–80.

Borrows, J. 2002, *Recovering Canada: The resurgence of indigenous law*, University of Toronto Press, Toronto.

Bovensiepen, J. 2009, 'Spiritual landscapes of life and death in the central highlands of East Timor', *Anthropological Forum*, vol. 19, no. 3, pp. 323–38.

Carvalho, D., Palmer, L., Delimas, A. and noVieira, P. 2008, *Koserva Natureza Liu Husi Tara Bandu*, Draft report prepared for Concern, Dili.

Carvalho, D. and Haburas Foundation (in preparation), *Tara Bandu Sebagari Salah Satu Kearifan Ecologi Timor Leste*.

Correa, A. P. 1944, *Timor De Lés a Lés*, Agencia geral das colonias, Lisboa.

Costin, G. and Powell, B. 2006, *Situation analysis report for Timor-Leste*, Australian Water Research Facility, Brisbane.

da Costa, C., da Costa Guterres, A. and Lopes, J. 2006, *Exploring Makassae Culture*, Instituto Catolico para Formacao de Professores Baucau, Publicacoes Matebian-Grafica Diocesana Baucau, Baucau, Timor-Leste.

D'Andrea, C., da Silva, O. and Meitzner Yoder, L. 2003, *The Customary Use and Management of Natural Resources in Timor Leste*, Oxfam, GTZ & DTP, TL, London.

Dikeç, M. 2004, 'Space, politics and the political', *Environment and Planning D*, vol. 23, pp. 171–88.

Fitzpatrick, D. and McWilliam, A. 2005, 'Waiting for law: land custom and regulation in Timor-Leste', *Development Bulletin*, vol. 68, pp. 58–61.

Fitzpatrick, D. 2008, 'Mediating land conflict in East Timor', in *Making Land Work. Volume 2*, AusAID, Canberra, pp. 175–98.

Gibson-Graham, J. K. 2004, 'Area studies after poststructuralism', *EPA*, vol. 36, pp. 405–19.

Gibson-Graham, J. K. 2006, *A Postcapitalist Politics*, University of Minnesota Press, Minneapolis.

Grenfell, L. 2009, 'Harnessing local law in the post-conflict state: the case of Timor-Leste', in W. Binchy (ed.), *Timor-Leste: Challenges for justice and human rights in the shadow of the past*, Clarus Press, Dublin, Ch. 2.

Gunn, G. 1999, *Timor Loro Sae: 500 years*, Livros do Oriente, Macau.

Hicks, D. 1976, *Tetum Ghosts and Kin*, Mayfield, Palo Alto, Calif.

Hicks, D. 2008, 'Glimpses of alternatives—the Uma Lulik of East Timor', *Social Analysis*, vol. 52, no. 1, pp. 166–88.

Jennaway, M. 2008, 'Aquatic identities, fluid economies: water affinities and authenticating narratives of belonging in East Timorese myth and ritual', *Oceania*, vol. 78, pp. 17–29.

Langton, M., Mazel, O. and Palmer, L. 2006, 'The spirit of the thing: the boundaries of Aboriginal economic relations at Australian common law', *Australian Journal of Anthropology*, vol. 17, no. 3, pp. 307–21.

Lansing, S. 1987, 'Balinese "water temples" and the management of irrigation', *American Anthropologist*, vol. 89, no. 2, pp. 326–41.

Lansing, S. 2007, *Priests and Programmers: Technologies of power in the engineered landscape of Bali*, [Revised second edn], Princeton University Press, Princeton, NJ, and Oxford.

Lemos, M. and Agrawal, A. 2006, 'Environmental governance', *Annual Review of Environment and Resources*, vol. 31, pp. 297–325.

McWilliam, A. 2002, 'Timorese seascapes: perspectives on customary marine tenures in Timor Leste', *Asia Pacific Journal of Anthropology*, vol. 3, no. 2, pp. 6–32.

McWilliam, A. 2003, 'New beginnings in East Timorese forest management', *Journal of Southeast Asian Studies*, vol. 34, pp. 307–27.

McWilliam, A. 2005, 'Houses of resistance in East Timor: structuring sociality in the new nation', *Anthropological Forum*, vol. 15, no. 1, pp. 27–44.

McWilliam, A. 2008, 'Fataluku healing and cultural resilience in East Timor', *Ethnos*, vol. 73, no. 2, pp. 217–40.

Meitzner Yoder, L. 2005, Custom, codification, collaboration: integrating the legacies of land and forest authorities in Oecusse enclave, East Timor, PhD thesis, Yale University, New Haven, Conn.

Mosse, D. 2003, *The Rule of Water: Statecraft, ecology, and collective action in south India*, Oxford University Press, Oxford.

Mosse, D. 2005, *Cultivating Development: An ethnography of aid policy and practice*, Pluto Press, Ann Arbor, Mich., and London.

Ospina, S. and Hohe, T. 2001, *Traditional power structures and the community empowerment and local governance structures*, Project Final Report, The World Bank, Dili.

Palmer, L. 2007a, 'Developing Timor Leste: recognising the role of custom and tradition', in L. Palmer, S. Niner and L. Kent (eds), *Exploring the tensions of nation building in Timor Leste: proceedings from the forum, 15 September 2006*, SSEE Research Paper No. 1, <http://www.pasi.unimelb.edu.au/research/papers/SSEE-papers/rp-01-Timor-Leste.pdf>

Palmer, L. 2007b, 'Interpreting nature: the politics of engaging with Kakadu as an Aboriginal place', *Cultural Geographies*, vol. 14, pp. 1–19.

Palmer, L. 2007c, 'Negotiating the ritual and social order through spectacle: the (re) production on Macassan/Yolngu histories', *Anthropological Forum*, vol. 17, no. 1, pp. 1–20.

Palmer, L. and Carvalho, D. A. 2008, 'Nation building and resource management: the politics of "nature" in Timor Leste', *Geoforum*, vol. 39, no. 3, pp. 1321–32.

Palmer, L. 2010, 'Enlivening development: water management in the post conflict Baucau city, Timor Leste', *Singapore Journal of Tropical Geography*, vol. 31, pp. 357–70.

Schoffel, P. 2006, *Community-Managed Water Supply and Sanitation: A case study from the 2004 Project Performance Audit Report for Water Supply and Sanitation Rehabilitation Project Phase I and Phase II, Timor Leste*, Asian Development Bank, Manila.

Scott, J. C. 1999, *Seeing Like A State: How certain schemes to improve the human condition have failed*, Yale University Press, New Haven, Conn.

Spillet, P. 1999, The pre-colonial history of the island of Timor together with some notes on the Makassan influence in the island, Unpublished manuscript, Museum and Art Gallery of the Northern Territory, Darwin.

Strang, V. and Toussaint, S. (eds) 2008, 'Water ways: competition and communality in the use and management of water', *Oceania: Special Issue*, vol. 78, no. 1 (March).

Tsing, A. L. 1993, *In the Realm of the Diamond Queen: Marginality in an out-of-the-way place*, Princeton University Press, Princeton, NJ.

Tsing, A. L. 2005, *Friction*, Princeton University Press, Princeton, NJ, and Oxford.

Van Engelenhoven, T. and Hajek, J. 2000, 'East Timor and the southwest Moluccas: language, time and connections', in *Studies in Languages and Cultures of East Timor. Volume 3*, University of Western Sydney, Sydney, pp. 107–24.

Verran, H. and Christie, M. 2007, 'Using/designing digital technologies of representation in Aboriginal Australian knowledge practices', *Human Technology*, vol. 3, no. 2, pp. 214–27.

WaterAid and World Vision 2007, *Getting the Basics Right: Water and sanitation in South East Asia and the Pacific*, WaterAid and World Vision Australia.

Yang, M. 2000, 'Putting global capitalism in its place: economic hybridity, Bataille, and ritual expenditure', *Current Anthropology*, vol. 41, no. 4, pp. 477–509.

Zerner, C. 1994, 'Through a green lens: the construction of customary environmental law and community in Indonesia's Maluku Islands', *Law & Society Review*, vol. 28, no. 5, pp. 1079–122.

8. Finding Bunaq: The homeland and expansion of the Bunaq in central Timor

Antoinette Schapper

Introduction

The Bunaq people occupy a large area of central Timor, straddling both sides of the modern border. Whilst the Bunaq of Lamaknen in West Timor have been the focus of detailed ethnographic research by Louis Berthe and Claudine Friedberg, there is no broader work on the Bunaq in other parts of East and West Timor. This chapter aims to contribute to a better understanding of the region of central Timor by exploring the history of the Bunaq-speaking area as a whole.

The Bunaq are linguistically and socially isolated in central Timor. Bunaq is a Papuan or non-Austronesian language, spoken by approximately 80 000 people. They are surrounded on all sides by Austronesian languages: Kemak to the north, Mambai to the east and Tetun to the south and west. The other Papuan languages of Timor—Fataluku, Makasai and Makalero—are located in a contiguous coastal area on the island's eastern tip.[1] The Bunaq language is widely recognised by the Bunaq and their Austronesian neighbours as 'different', and, while Bunaq is rarely learnt by non-Bunaq, almost all Bunaq are fluent in at least one Austronesian language.

In addition, the Bunaq are typically regarded by their neighbours with disdain, frequently being characterised as a coarse and aggressive people. This view has ensured that the Bunaq have remained somewhat apart from them. What is more, this external perception of their nature has fed into the Bunaq's own traditions, such as the concluding moral of the folk story of two brothers, Asa Paran and Mau Paran: *En Emaq g-epal legul. En Bunaq g-epal gol* ('The Kemak people have

---

1 More distant relatives are found on the islands of Alor and Pantar to the north of Timor. Together, the Papuan languages of Timor–Alor–Pantar (TAP) form a language family that broke up and dispersed some time before the Austronesian arrival in the region some 3000 years ago. The wider genetic relations of the TAP language family to other Papuan languages of the New Guinea mainland, such as the Trans-New Guinea family, remain highly speculative.

long ears. The Bunaq people have small ears.') The metaphor of short versus long ears refers to the contrasting temperaments of the Bunaq (short-tempered and impatient) and the Kemak (quiet and uncomplaining).

These factors of linguistic non-conformity and social isolation have set them apart to some degree. But they have also led to an inclusive cultural attitude on the part of the Bunaq, involving widespread borrowing and adaptation from Austronesian language and society, such that Berthe (1963) was compelled to describe the Bunaq as having a mixed Austronesian–Papuan descent.

This chapter documents the processes of Bunaq expansion, using evidence from oral histories, placenames and data from the dialects of the Bunaq language. A subsidiary aim of this chapter is to illustrate how linguistic materials can be used to supplement and improve the picture of the past presented in oral histories. The data discussed here were collected during field trips in 2006, 2007 and 2009 surveying the Bunaq area.

After a brief outline of the basic principles of dialectology and how they apply to Bunaq in section two, I explore the history of the individual Bunaq areas in section three, showing where and how the Bunaq have expanded into new areas, mingled and partly taken over from groups of Austronesian speakers. Finally, in section four, I discuss the position of the Bunaq in central Timor in light of the traditional Papuan–Austronesian dichotomy. I suggest that, whilst the Bunaq have taken over Austronesian lands, they did not arrive after the Austronesians, but have incorporated many Austronesian features through sustained contact—a form of cultural 'metatypy' (Ross 2006).

Bunaq Geography and Dialectology

Today the Bunaq-speaking area (Map 8.1) extends in the north from Maliana down to portions of the southern coast of Timor-Leste; it stretches east from the eastern edges of southern Belu regency in West Timor into the western edge of Manufahi subdistrict in Timor-Leste.

Across the wide geographical area in which Bunaq is spoken, there are several different dialects. Dialects are geographical variants of a single language and dialectology is the study of this variation. Dialects are distinguished from one another by the distinct phonological (sounds) and lexical (words) features they display. Features varying between dialects are treated as instances of diachronic divergence from a common ancestor. That is, dialect differences arise when a population of speakers of a single variation-free language in one area replaces an original feature, X, with innovative feature Y, while speakers in another area innovate feature Z for feature X, while those in still another area retain feature X as X, and so on.

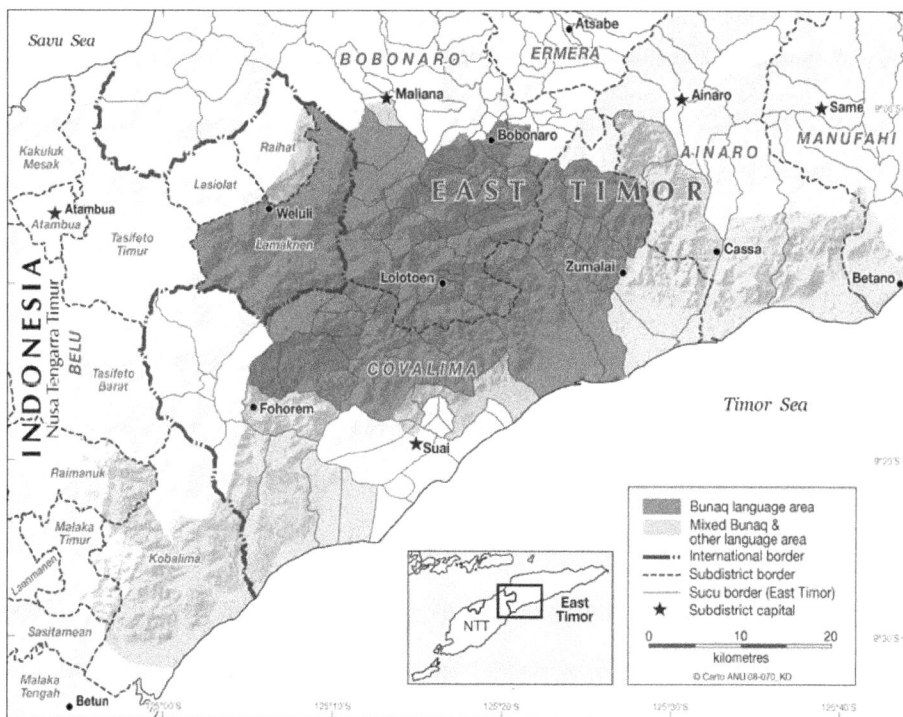

Map 8.1 The extent of the Bunaq language area

Phonological differences between dialects arise out of sound change across the lexicon—that is, in all words with the sound in question. The most common types of sound change involve replacing one sound with another or the complete loss of a sound. Sound changes are often environmentally conditioned. That is, a change in question may occur only in a defined environment, such as the middle of a word or before another sound of a particular kind, while the same sound remains unaffected in other environments. For example, the medial /t/ in words such as 'water' has come to be pronounced as /d/ in some dialects of English, but never an initial /t/ as in the word 'tap'.

Lexical differences between dialects arise in several different ways. A new word may be borrowed from another language with which the speakers in one area are in contact or are influenced by. A lexical item might be innovated—that is, a group of speakers may develop an entirely new word for an object or concept. A lexical innovation may also involve a semantic shift, whereby one word changes its meaning, thus replacing the original word with that meaning.

So, while lexical differences are the result of a new lexical item taking the place of an original lexical item with that meaning, phonological differences involve sounds changing in lexical items that are related to each other. A word can be assumed to be part of the proto-language—the single undifferentiated form of the language from which the individual dialects descend—when it is attested across the dialects and shows regularity of sound change. Words that do not show the expected sound changes characteristic of the dialects can typically be explained as borrowings or lexical innovations that have been taken after a sound change has applied in the dialect. The important point here is that sound changes are limited in the space to which and time in which they are active, and so can tell us about the relative chronology of dialect break-ups and thus people movements.

Based on phonological and lexical divisions, the Bunaq language area can be broken up into five major dialects: the South-West dialect, the Lamaknen dialect, the North-East dialect, the Ainaro dialect and the Manufahi dialect. The area covered by each of the dialects is represented in Map 8.3. These dialect regions represent only the major divisions between geographical varieties of Bunaq. It should be borne in mind that each of these dialect regions encompasses a great deal of variation, often with differences being found from one village to the next.

A few examples illustrating the dialect divisions on phonological grounds are provided in Table 8.1. We see that the South-West and Manufahi dialects preserve original *d and *t in all environments. Lamaknen is most radical in having *d changing to r both initially and medially, unlike the North-East where r is only an (optional) realisation of d medially. The North-East affricates *t before the vowels i and u; Lamaknen and Ainaro show some limited change of *t to ʧ (a sound represented in English orthography with {ch} as in 'church') before i word-initially, with Lamaknen further merging ʧ with s. Loss of *w and development of final *r into ʧ together characterise the three eastern dialects, with the subsequent loss of ʧ in Ainaro and Manufahi. Sporadic loss of initial *h is found in the North-East and Ainaro dialects.

A sample of the many lexical features illustrating the dialect divisions is provided in Table 8.2. The maximal differentiation pattern is illustrated by 'big' with each of the dialect areas having a distinct lexeme. The South-West is distinct from all other dialects in having two inalienable nouns, -ip 'wife' and -enen 'husband'; the remaining areas simply use pana 'woman' and mone 'man' for these concepts. For 'sleep', the North-East and Ainaro dialects have innovative malat, while the South-West, Lamaknen and Manufahi reflect proto-Bunaq *tier (cognate with, for example, Oirata taja and Makasai taʔe 'sleep'). In contrast, for 'stand', the South-West and Lamaknen have innovative duʔat, while modern net 'stand' in the other dialects has widespread cognates in related Papuan languages (for example, Oirata and Abui nate 'stand'). Ainaro and Manufahi share the borrowing boi 'not want' from Mambai, while only the Ainaro dialect has borrowed au 'I' from Mambai. Both the Ainaro and Manufahi dialects have innovated items for 'not exist', the former from *hazi?* 'disappear', the latter from *muel* 'be thin'. Finally, Manufahi is distinct from all other dialects in its item for 'exist'.

Table 8.1 Phonological Characteristics of Bunaq Dialects

Bunaq	South-West	Lamaknen	North-East	Ainaro	Manufahi
*d >	d	d ~ r / #_ r / elsewhere	d / #_ r / elsewhere	d / #_ d ~ r/ elsewhere	d
eg.	*doe* 'this' *adu?* 'hair'	*doe ~ roe* *aru?*	*doe* *aru?*	*doe* *adu ~ aru*	*doe* *adu*
*r >	r	d ~ r / #_ r / elsewhere	ʧ / _# l / elsewhere	l / _# l / elsewhere	l / _# l / elsewhere
eg.	*mar* 'farm' *rama* 'spear'	*mar* *dama ~ rama*	*maʃ* *lama*	*ma* *lama*	*ma* *lama*
q >	?	?	?	Ø	Ø
eg.	*ba?a* 'that'	*ba?a*	*ba?a*	*ba*	*ba*
*h >	h	h	h ~ Ø / #_	h ~ Ø / #_	h
eg.	*hati* 'is' *hobel* 'is not'	*hati* *hobel*	*aʧi* *hobel*	*aʧi* *hobel*	--
*t >	t	ʧ ~ s / #_i t / elsewhere	ʧ / _i & _u t / elsewhere	ʧ ~ t / #_i t / elsewhere	t
eg.	*tie* 'chicken' *gutu* 'with' *tol* 'break'	*ʧie ~ sie* *gutu* *tol*	*ʧie* *guʧu* *tol*	*tier ~ ʧie* *gutu* *tol*	*tie* *gutu* *tol*
*w >	w	w	Ø ~ u / #_ Ø ~ b/ elsewhere	Ø ~ u / #_ Ø ~ b/ elsewhere	Ø ~ u / #_ Ø ~ b/ elsewhere
eg.	*wil* 'dig' *sawe* 'comb'	*wil* *sawe*	*uil* *sabe*	*uil* *sabe*	*uil* *sabe*

Table 8.2 Lexical Characteristics of Bunaq Dialects

	South-West	Lamaknen	North-East	Ainaro	Manufahi
'BIG'	*bo?al*	*masak*	*tina*	*gemel*	*kaman*
'WIFE'	*-ip*	*pana*	*pana*	*pana*	*pana*
'HUSBAND'	*-enen*	*mone*	*mone*	*mone*	*mone*
'SLEEP'	*tier*	*ʧier*	*malat*	*malat*	*tier*
'STAND'	*du?at*	*du?at*	*net*	*net*	*net*
'PLAY'	*buku?*	*buku?*	*kisa?*	*buku*	*neun*
'NOT WANT'	*tia?*	*ʧia?*	*pia?*	*boi*	*boi*
'I'	*neto*	*neto*	*neto*	*au*	*neto*
'NOT EXIST'	*hobel*	*hobel*	*hobel*	*hazi*	*muel*
'EXIST'	*hati*	*hati*	*aʧi*	*hati*	*hono*

In the following section, we will see how such dialect data can be applied along with other forms of information to understanding and interpreting the history of the Bunaq in central Timor.

The Bunaq Dispersal

We see from Map 8.1 that, far from only having interaction with other peoples on the fringes of their area, the Bunaq also occupy vast tracts of land in which other Austronesian peoples are also settled. As suggested above, the modern dispersal of Bunaq speakers reflects a long history of migration and expansion into new territory. Excessive pressure on land caused by growing populations and the depletion of soil due to the nature of shifting agriculture have forced the Bunaq to look for new farming land over a period of centuries.

Political factors and governmental ventures have also affected modern Bunaq settlement patterns. Ongoing political turmoil and upheaval from the early Portuguese era until today have caused significant population displacements and in particular brought about successive waves of refugees from East Timor into West Timor. Isolated communities have been both drawn by convenience and compelled by successive administrations seeking greater access to the populace into the region of newly constructed roads or as part of agricultural development projects. In what follows, I will look at the evidence of the Bunaq dispersal region by region.

The Bunaq Homeland: Central-eastern Bobonaro and north-eastern Covalima

In the central-eastern area of Bobonaro and north-eastern Covalima subdistricts (defined by black line on Map 8.4), we find placenames with exclusively Bunaq etymologies, such as Odelgomo (< *odel* 'monkey', *gomo* 'owner'), Mapelai (< *mape* 'eagle', *lai* 'set') and Zoilpo? (< *zoil* 'k.o. tree', *po?* 'holy'/'sacred').

Outside this core area, we find Bunaq villages with Bunaq placenames alongside Bunaq villages with Austronesian placenames (area defined by grey line on Map 8.3). Bunaq placenames increasingly give way to non-Bunaq ones until all Bunaq villages have non-Bunaq names (grey shaded area). This dispersal of placenames strongly points to the 'homeland' of the Bunaq as being in central-eastern Bobonaro and north-eastern Covalima—the geographical centre of the modern Bunaq-speaking area. If the Bunaq were immigrants to the core area, we would expect to find traces of the previous populations left behind in placenames, as we do outside the core.

Further linguistic evidence for this region being the Bunaq homeland comes from the presence of lexical items in Bunaq dialects that have their origin in the Austronesian languages Kemak and to a lesser extent Mambai. Table 8.3 presents a sample of the items in Bunaq and their source in Kemak and/or Mambai. We can see that these items are borrowed from Austronesian into

Bunaq, since they can be reconstructed to higher levels of the Austronesian family. That is, they are historically known to be Austronesian words and to have cognates in other Austronesian languages. This directionality of borrowing seems anthropologically more likely since among the items in question are words encoding concepts associated with Austronesian culture—for instance, kin terms such as elder brother/sister, which show the kind of concern for precedence and rank typical of Austronesian society (McWilliam 2007). More recent influence of the Kemak in the north-east of the Bunaq area can be seen in the adoption of an exogenous name. In this region, the Bunaq refer to themselves and their language as *Gaiq* or *Gaeq*—a term not used elsewhere and very likely from *Mgai*, the Kemak name for the Bunaq.

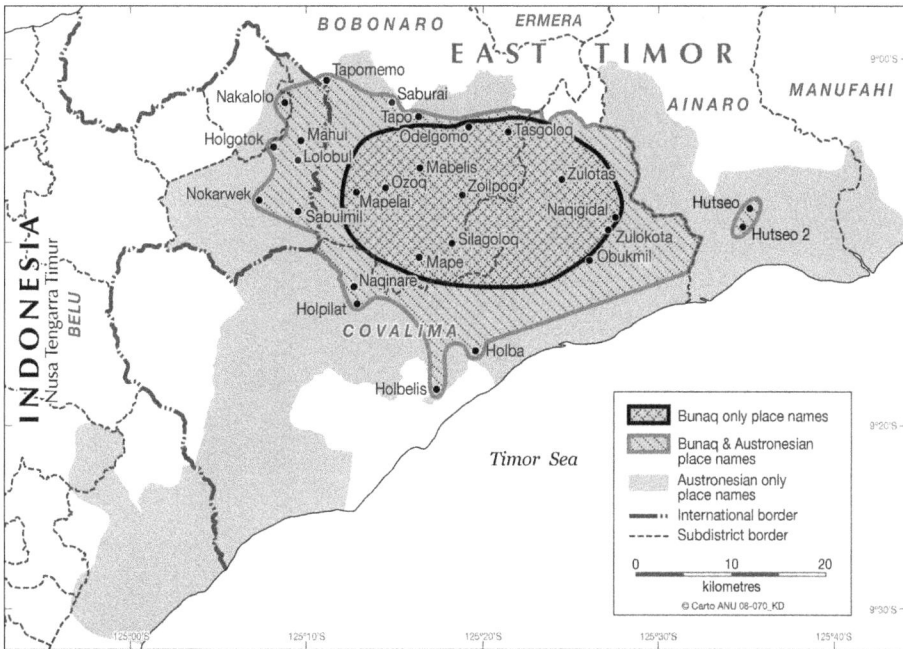

Map 8.2 The relative dispersal of Bunaq and Austronesian placenames

That these items are found across all Bunaq dialects points to their being present in the proto-language—in other words, present in the Bunaq language before dialect differentiation took place. This means that proto-Bunaq would have had to be spoken in an area that had intense contact with speakers of Kemak and Mambai, or at least where people were speaking the forerunners of these modern languages. The central-eastern area of Bobonaro and north-eastern Covalima subdistricts fit precisely this profile, with Kemak and Mambai both close by. Furthermore, the Bunaq of the north-east recognise themselves as historically having been part of the large Likosaen kingdom, which was centred on the Kemak–Tokodede region directly west of Dili (see Spillet 1999:242 ff.).

The significant influence of this kingdom could explain the apparent ready adoption of Austronesian terms and the concomitant cultural categories by early Bunaq speakers.

Table 8.3 Pan-Bunaq Borrowings from Kemak/Mambai

Bunaq			Source	
kaʔa	'older brother'	<	Kmk *kaʔa-r*	'older brother'
nana	'older sister'	<	Kmk *nana-r*	'older sister (of male)'
tata	'ancestor'	<	Kmk *tata-r*	'grandparent, ancestor'
lihur	'thousand'	<	Kmk *rihur*	'thousand'
tahoʔ	'low cloud'	<	Kmk *tahoʔ*	'cloud, mist'
huan	'heart'	<	Kmk *huan*	'heart'
hul	'moon'	<	Mam. *hul*	'moon'
si	'meat'	<	Mam. *si ~ sis*, Kmk *si*	'meat'
le	'light'	<	Mam. *le ~ lel*	'sun'
to	'year'	<	Mam. *to ~ ton*, Kmk *to*	'year'
loi	'good'	<	Kmk/Mam. *mloi*	'good'
hui	'wild'	<	Kmk/Mam. *hui*	'wild'

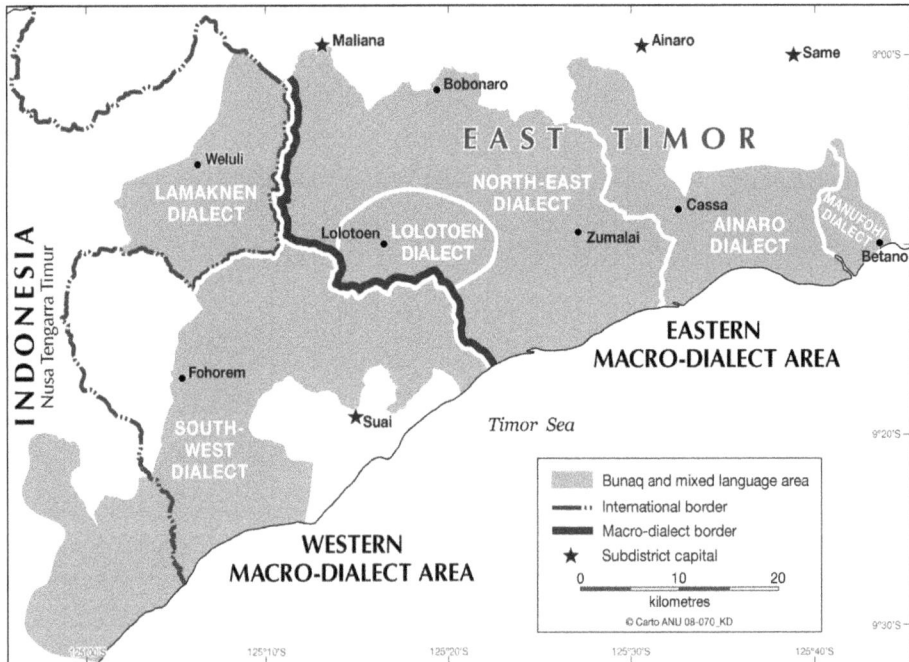

Map 8.3 The major Bunaq dialects

The North-West Bunaq Area

The north-west Bunaq area encompasses the lands south of Maliana in Timor-Leste and in the Lamaknen subdistrict and a small neighbouring area of Raihat subdistrict in the Belu regency of Indonesian West Timor (Map 8.4).

According to their own oral histories, the Bunaq in Lamaknen came to the area from the east. When they arrived they found either Tetun or Dawan people, depending on the particular account, with whom they freely mixed. This view of the past is supported by the many village names in Lamaknen and Raihat that have at least partial Austronesian etymologies—for example: Duarato > Tet. *dua dato* 'two kings', Aitoun > Tet./Daw. *ai* 'tree' *toun* '?'. The area is also home to many placenames with Bunaq etymologies—for example: in West Timor, Nakalolo > *naka* 'mud' and *lolo* 'mountain', and in Timor-Leste, Sabulai > *sabul* 'citrus' and *lai* 'put'. The significant admixture of Austronesian placenames and the absence of Austronesian speakers in this area point to the Bunaq having been established in this region before the beginning of the historical period.

The dialectal evidence suggests that Lamaknen has been the crossroads for movements of Bunaq people from the North-East and South-West dialect regions. The Lamaknen dialect is intermediate between these two. The linguistic feature best illustrating this split is the postposition 'at'. In the South-West, the postposition is realised as *ni*, while in the North-East it is *no*. In Lamaknen, speakers use *no* and *ni* interchangeably. Lexically, Lamaknen shares most in common with the South-West, retaining items in common with them, such as *buku'* 'play', *duat* 'stand' and *tier* 'sleep', but patterns with the North-East in using terms such as *taho* 'cloud' and in using *mone* 'man' and *pana* 'woman' only for 'husband' and 'wife', respectively. Phonologically, Lamaknen shows the influence of the North-East with the development of ʧ from *t and r from *d, but has taken its own direction with these sound changes. That is, in Lamaknen *t became ʧ and then s only before the vowel i, whereas in the North-East the change was only to ʧ, but applied in more environments, before the vowels i and u. Similarly, in Lamaknen *d became r not only word-medially but also initially, whereas in the North-East the change was limited to the medial position. The point here is that, whilst obviously being influenced by linguistic developments through contact with the North-East, their presence in Lamaknen Bunaq is limited, with conservative features of the South-West dominating.

The divided linguistic features of Bunaq Lamaknen are historically grounded in the fact that much of the region was subject to territorial disputes between the north-eastern kingdom of Lamakhitu and the kingdom of Lakmaras situated in the south of modern-day Lamkanen and strongly allied to Bunaq peoples in the south-west. For instance, Pélissier (1996:174 ff.) describes a series of battles in 1897 for lands in Lamaknen with Lamakhitu, while the changing ownership of the Maukatar enclave (described in the following section) was rooted in the dispute between Lamakhitu and Lakmaras.

Map 8.4 Bunaq villages in Lamaknen and Raihat

More recently, the Bunaq from the east have been establishing new lowland villages around Maliana. Although these villages were founded several generations ago, individual lowland villages still trace themselves back to a particular upland village and maintain ritual ties with it. For example, the upland village of Tapoʔ (< *taʔ* 'axe' *poʔ* 'holy') is the origin for a lowland village situated on the alluvial plains south-east of Maliana. The name of the village of origin is even reflected in that of the new village: Tapomemoʔ (literally: 'sweet Tapoʔ).

Conflicts of the past half-century have also brought additional waves of Bunaq from East Timor into West Timorese Lamaknen and Raihat. At the end of World War II, Bunaq people fearing reprisals due to their support for the Japanese arrived in Lamaknen from the East Timorese village of Lebos and established the village of Lakus after a grant of land from the then *loro* (king), A. Beretalo. Today Lakus people maintain distinct elements of a north-eastern dialect but often lexically coloured by Lamaknen dialect. For instance, Lakus has the North-East feature in which ' replaces r finally, but applies them to otherwise typical south-western/Lamaknen dialect items such as ʧieʔ for 'sleep' where the local Lamaknen dialect has ʧier.

More refugees arrived in 1975 when the Indonesian Army moved into East Timor. Fighting destroyed whole villages in Lamaknen; Friedberg reports that her field site, the village of Henes, had ceased to exist when she returned to Lamaknen after 1975 (personal communication). In 1999, following the vote for independence in East Timor, many more refugees arrived in Lamaknen and Raihat and set rambling bush huts on roadsides, many of which remain to this day.

Table 8.4 Examples of Tetun Ritual Vocabulary in Bunaq Lamaknen

Bunaq Lamaknen		Tetun	
molo lok	'offer betel'	*lok*	'offer in hospitality'
paʔol sau	'corn harvest festival', 'lift ban on eating corn'	*sau*	'lift a prohibition/ban'
muk ukon	'govern', lit. 'land rule'	*rai uku*	'govern', lit. 'land rule'
ukur	'power, authority'	*ukur*	'ritual, ceremony', lit. 'cords linking edges of loom'
uma metan	'ruling house'	*uma metan*	lit. 'black house', used in ritual contexts in reference to 'power'

According to oral traditions, the Bunaq of the north-west (as centred on Lamaknen) formed an autonomous region of the Wehali kingdom, a large southern Tetun territory (Therik 2004) and rival to Likosaen, discussed in the previous section. The influence of Wehali on the Bunaq of this region has been thoroughgoing, leaving heavy marks on all aspects of ritual practice. One illustration of this is the widespread adoption of Tetun terms for ritual practice. In the examples in Table 8.4, we see that general Tetun terms—typically with some (additional) use in ritual—have been borrowed by the Lamaknen Bunaq with a more restricted and specific ritual meaning. In this, the Bunaq show a historical willingness to accommodate and integrate the ritual concepts of another group into their own customary practice.

The South-West Bunaq Area: From Betun to Suai

In the south-west, the Bunaq extend in a corridor west from Lolotoen in the north and Suai in the south across western Covalima subdistrict almost reaching into southern Belu, West Timor.

In East Timorese Covalima, the Bunaq occupy the majority of the region that formed the Maukatar enclave (see Fox 2003:15, Map 2). Today, the Maukatar enclave makes up the villages (*suco*) of Covalima directly north of Suai, such as Holpilat, Taroman, Fatululik, Datotolu and Laktos. From 1860, the Maukatar enclave was recognised as part of the Dutch territory in Timor. The borders of the Maukatar enclave were defined with reference to local, and in particular Bunaq, states. The Dutch claimed Maukatar was theirs on the grounds that it was a part of the Dutch state of Lakmaras, in modern-day Lamaknen, and was joined by that state to other Dutch territories. The Portuguese, however, claimed that since 1859 Lakmaras had been taken over by the Portuguese state of Lamakhitu, another Bunaq kingdom situated in the area of Bobonaro.

Despite Bunaq dominance of the enclave both today and in the recent historical period, the majority of Bunaq villages in the area have placenames with Tetun etymologies—for example: Fatuloro < Tet. *fatu* 'stone' *loro* 'sun', Kusilulik < Tet. *kusi* 'pot' and *lulik* 'holy', and Lia naʔin < Tet. *lia* 'voice, language' and *naʔin* 'lord, father's brother'. This distribution of peoples to placenames suggests that the Bunaq have here too been successful in expanding into new lands and assimilating a previous (probably) Tetun population. In a scenario of displacement of an existing population rather than assimilation of it, we would expect to see significant re-coining of placenames, and thus admixture in the presence of Bunaq and Tetun placenames.

Linguistically, this South-West region of the Bunaq language area is the most phonologically conservative. That is, they have not undergone the sound changes that characterise the North-East dialect, retaining the original sounds of the proto-language instead. This means that the Bunaq must have settled the region before the sound changes began to take effect, thus placing it in the relatively remote past.

In the western border area of Covalima, the Tetun are in the majority. Bunaq villages are found interwoven amongst Tetun villages stretching south of Fohorem to the coast. The Bunaq in this area were established in the recent historical period in two distinct waves. The newest group is the Bunaq villages in the lower lands along the coast between Suai and the border. These people were resettled by the Indonesian administration from northern Covalima *suco* such as Fatululik and Taroman as part of a rice-agriculture development program.

The second, older collection of Bunaq villages is situated in the upland parts of the *suco* of Foholulik and Lalawa, immediately south of Fohorem. These villages have their origins in a massive collective flight out of Bobonaro away from the Japanese Army. Their flight comprises the most significant displacement of Bunaq dating from World War II. The Japanese invaded Timor on 20 February 1942 and within days had overwhelmed the small force of Australian and Dutch troops. Some of these troops managed to evade capture and withdrew into the mountains, from where they waged a guerrilla campaign against the Japanese. The guerrillas spent much of their time in the Bobonaro area and were at different times based in Bobonaro town and Lolotoen. In August 1942, the Japanese carried out a series of reprisals in the area of Bobonaro against the population who had assisted the guerrillas, with, it is believed, tens of thousands killed and many others displaced, as in the case of these Bunaq who settled south of Fohorem.

Across the border, in southern Belu, Bunaq occupy disparate settlements of the Kobalima, Malaka Timur and Raimanuk subdistricts (Map 8.5). Individual Bunaq villages are scattered amongst a majority Tetun population. At the western extreme of the Bunaq area are Haroe and Welaus (noted by Woertelboer 1955:172), a few kilometres east of Betun, while to the north is a handful of isolated villages (I: *desa*) of Faturika, Renrua and Babulu. Moving east, Bunaq villages are strung out along the road right up to the *desa* of Alas and Alas Selatan on the border with Timor-Leste.

A single village in this region, Namfalus, originates in the same flight from the Japanese that saw the establishment of Bunaq south of Fohorem. The remainder all trace themselves back to Bunaq villages in the Maukatar enclave. As mentioned above, the enclave was subject to ongoing border disputes between the Portuguese and Dutch colonial administrations, but, in 1904, it was agreed that the lands would be ceded to Portugal in exchange for other areas (Sowash 1948). Following the 1904 agreement, disputes continued over the demarcation of borders, and in 1911 when Portuguese troops moved into Maukatar, they were met by Dutch forces. Clashes continued throughout 1911, before the Dutch agreed to withdraw as per the agreement of 1904. During the fighting of 1911 and following the ceding of the enclave to Portugal, some 5000 of the population of Maukatar, mostly Bunaq, decamped to Dutch Timor, in what is now southern Belu. As in Lamaknen, each of these Bunaq settlements has seen new additions from East Timor during the upheavals of 1975 and 1999.

Map 8.5 Bunaq villages in southern Belu and south-western Covalima

According to local informants, the resettlement of the Maukatar Bunaq was fraught with difficulties due to land disputes with the local Tetun, the refugee Bunaq were forced to move from place to place in Belu until the 1930s when the administration was able to settle them peacefully in their current locations. Nevertheless, Bunaq in southern Belu proudly declare themselves the first refugees from East to West Timor. They trace themselves back to particular villages in Maukatar—for instance, the Bunaq in Raakfao trace their origins to

Fatuloro in Maukatar and those in Sukabesikun to Belekasak in Maukatar. This regard for their origins persists among this Bunaq diaspora in the face of their ongoing amalgamation into the Tetun majority.

The South-Central Bunaq Area: From Suai to Zumalai

Much of the southern coast of Timor-Leste was traditionally uninhabited. Bunaq villages in the region between Suai and Zumalai are of recent establishment. Each village traces itself to an older upland origin site. Connections between old and new villages run deep. For instance, inhabitants of Beco, a village situated on the coastal plain east of Suai, identify themselves as coming from Teda, an upland village to the east of Lolotoen. Yet, they had never been to Teda themselves and both they and their parents were born in Beco. This points to the continuing significance of origin place in these villages despite the geographical removal. Indeed, the dialect of Bunaq spoken in these villages also strongly reflects the upland origins in the Lolotoen region with all the typical phonological markers of the North-East dialect. Some dialect mixing with the South-West is apparent in the use of certain lexical items, such as *boʔal* in place of *tina* for 'big' and *habuhabu* in place of *tahoʔ* for 'cloud'. This reflects the fact that today the most contact these Bunaq have is with speakers of the South-West dialect.

Bunaq villages in the lowland areas of Zumalai district were similarly founded on the basis of upland villages. As in the north-western corner, in lowland areas upland placenames reoccur—for example: Zulotas (literally: 'civet village') has given rise to a twin just north of Zumalai town called Zulokota (literally: 'civet city'). Many of these villages were established during the Indonesian period, with whole villages being brought south to the road on the promise of housing. Linguistically, the villages around Zumalai display a dialect that is entirely consistent with that of the upland settlements—a homogeneity indicative of very recent movement.

The Eastern Bunaq Area: From Zumalai to Betano

To the east of Zumalai, a corridor of Bunaq villages stretches across southern Ainaro subdistrict into the western-most part of Manufahi (Map 8.6). The peoples of Ainaro and Manufahi both have their origin in the north-eastern Bunaq area. This is shown by the fact that the dialects must have had a glottal stop (ʔ) in place of the consonant r in words such as *mar* 'farm', as is characteristic of the North-East dialect. The glottal stop has since been lost in the eastern dialects to give forms such as *ma* 'farm'.

In this area, the Bunaq have intermingled significantly with Mambai, the Austronesian group native to the area. The Bunaq here are typically bilingual in Mambai, and their varieties of Bunaq show the impact of mixing with Mambai neighbours. For instance, the loss of the glottal stop mentioned above and the loss of *w probably occurred under the influence of Mambai, which lacks both these sounds (Hull 2003). Specific innovations of the Ainaro and Manufahi Bunaq groups are discussed below.

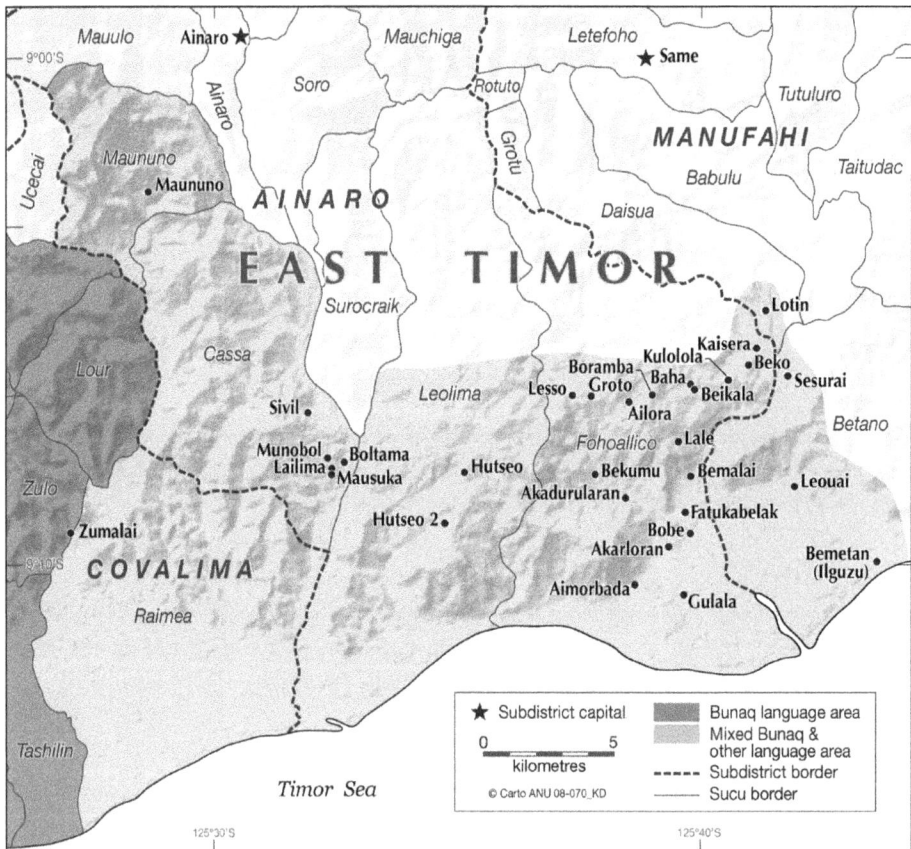

Map 8.6 Bunaq villages in Ainaro and Manufahi

The Bunaq in Ainaro

In Ainaro the Bunaq occupy the whole of the *suco* of Maununo. Originally, Maununo contained three discrete villages: Aileu, Mamalau and Mausuka.

During the Indonesian era, however, the villages were brought together to occupy the single location they do today. To the south of Maununo, Bunaq speakers are spread throughout the *suco* of Cassa. This group has close ties to the Maununo Bunaq (cf. Rawski 2002 on the bitter enmity between the Maununo and Cassa groups). Further east, the entire *suco* of Fohoailiku to the south-east of Ainaro is Bunaq. The Fohoailiku Bunaq claim to have moved from western Ainaro due to a dispute between rival Bunaq groups some time in the Portuguese era.

These three groups of Bunaq speakers share particular linguistic features distinct from other groups, which point to their having a single source. In particular, they have the first-person pronoun *au* 'I' from Mambai in place of Bunaq *neto* 'I'. Pronoun borrowing is cross-linguistically so rare that it is unlikely to have occurred three distinct times amongst the Ainaro Bunaq. More likely, *au* 'I' was borrowed once into an early group of Bunaq speakers in close contact with Mambai and has continued to be used by their descendents as later groups have branched off. Other innovations common to this group include the use of *gemel* to mean 'big'. This item is used to refer to a 'female animal' in all other Bunaq varieties and derives from *eme* 'mother'. The semantic innovation of this term in Bunaq Ainaro is again clearly calqued from Mambai *inan* 'mother', which is also used attributively to mean 'big/large'.

There are conflicting accounts of the origins of these three Bunaq groups, with some traditions claiming the Bunaq to be the original inhabitants and others that they arrived later. Placenames strongly suggest that the Bunaq here moved into an area with a pre-existing Austronesian population. The Bunaq villages in the region all carry Austronesian names. For instance, placenames with the formative *mau*, as in Mausuka and Maununo, abound; this formative is typical of placenames in the Mambai–Kemak–Tokodede-speaking areas, but is not present in the core Bunaq lands. The other placenames in the Bunaq area are clearly Mambai—for instance: Beikala, a Mambai binominal comprising Mambai *bei* 'grandparent' and *kala* 'ancestor', used in ritual speech.

In addition to these three groups with a common source, there are two small Bunaq groups that have different origins and accordingly different linguistic traits. First, the villages of Sivil and Lailima, which are strung along the road south of Ainaro town amongst Mambai settlements, were moved down from the Zumalai area during the Indonesian period. Second, east of Cassa there are two villages of Bunaq speakers amongst the sea of Mambai villages in the *suco* Leolima, Hutseo and its offspring of the Indonesian period, Hutseo Dua ('Hutseo II'). The Bunaq dialect spoken in these villages is still strongly north-eastern in flavour, consistent with a recent move from the region of Zumalai.

Bunaq in these areas show significant cultural entwinement with their Mambai neighbours. First, unlike the matrilineal western Bunaq, the Bunaq here have a patrilineal system of marriage and descent, following the pattern of the Mambai. Second, there is an inventory of shared myth between the two groups in the area. For instance, the Maununo Bunaq and Mambai both claim to be descended from the same pair of ancestors, and the mountain onto which the apical ancestors descended has both a Bunaq name (*lolo guzu muk po*) and a Mambai one (*manu aman parasa*) (see also Corte-Real 1998 for discussion of these terms). Such socio-cultural features set the eastern Bunaq off from the western Bunaq and point to not only a long span of linguistic contact with the Mambai, but also the Bunaq's acculturation to Mambai cultural norms and their view of the landscape and its ritual significance.

The Bunaq in Manufahi

In Manufahi, there are four Bunaq villages scattered along the road south of the main town, Same. The first Bunaq village established in this area is Lotin (also known as Loti). This group moved from Aiasa, near modern-day Bobonaro town, about 1891. According to oral histories, the move was prompted by a dispute with the ruler (*régulo*) of Bobonaro after the villagers of Aiasa killed his wife. The *régulo* called in Portuguese forces in August 1891, whereupon a series of bloody clashes took place (Pélissier 1996:119–20) and resulted in the flight of some of Aiasa village to Manufahi.

The original Lotin village was located to the north of the *suco* of Daisua—that is, isolated from other Bunaq-speaking communities to the west and in contact with speakers of the Mambai and Lakalei languages. The linguistic outcome of this isolation is that the descendents of the settlers from Aiasa speak a radically different dialect from that found in other parts of the Bunaq-speaking area. Lexically, the dialect is characterised by a range of semantic innovations whereby certain words have undergone significant shifts in meaning. What is more, in addition to borrowings from the local contacts' languages, entirely new words have been innovated in Lotin. Examples are given in Table 8.5.

Table 8.5 Some Lexical Innovations in Lotin Bunaq

Bunaq Lotin		Other Bunaq	
esu	'tree'	*esu*	'spine of palm leaf'
moel	'absent, not exist'	*muel*	'be thin'
hono	'present, exist'	*hono*	'be (ritual only)'
neun	'play'	--	--
ikir	'cassava'	--	--
be	'search'	--	--
kaman	'big'	--	--

Following the Boaventura rebellion, the Portuguese resettled some of the Lotin Bunaq in lower lands. The modern village of Lotin is some kilometres south of the original village, and two further villages, Il Guzu (literally 'black water' in Bunaq, also known in Mambai as Bemetan) and Leoai, were established for the Lotin Bunaq close to the coast. The three villages share a dialect distinct from all other Bunaq groups. Later, the remaining villagers of the original Lotin were resettled from the mountainous interior during the Indonesian period to the current site, marked on Map 8.7.

The fourth Bunaq village in Manufahi is Sesurai, located on the road between Lotin and Leoai. According to tradition, the Sesurai Bunaq fled from the Zumalai area to Manufahi some time in the Portuguese era. The dialect of Bunaq spoken in Sesurai has some characteristics consistent with the North-East dialect spoken in Zumalai, but has taken on some lexical traits of Lotin Bunaq, such as *esu* for 'tree' in place of *hotel*.

The Bunaq Expansions in Comparative Perspective

In the preceding sections I have sought to document the process of Bunaq expansion. Closely tracking placename dispersal, I show that the Bunaq have expanded from a core area in the mountains of central-eastern Bobonaro and north-eastern Covalima subdistricts. Corroborating evidence for seeing this area as the Bunaq homeland was presented in the form of Kemak/Mambai vocabulary across all Bunaq dialects. This suggests a mountainous homeland close to speakers of the precursors of modern-day Kemak/Mambai.

Using placenames, dialectal data and oral histories, three major types of Bunaq movement from the homeland can be discerned. They are: a) upland expansions; b) lowland expansions; and c) flights. How these different movements have shaped the Bunaq area is summarised in Map 8.7. Upland expansions appear to have come about as Bunaq have moved into an adjacent upland area, gradually overwhelming an incumbent Austronesian population. Placenames in these areas are of mixed origin, having both Bunaq and Austronesian etymologies. These expansions represent the oldest layer of retrievable movements for which only vague oral histories exist. Dialectally, such areas of old expansion are characterised by having a distinct dialect, such as that of Lamaknen, Maukatar (the centre of the South-West dialect expansion) and Maununo (the centre of the Ainaro dialect expansion). In lowland expansions, Bunaq have gradually moved into an adjacent lowland area that was previously or largely uninhabited. Placenames in these areas are Bunaq, either reflecting upland village names or being coined anew.[2] Oral histories for these expansions identify specific upland origins for a new village, and point to settlement having occurred within the past several generations. Due to the usual maintenance of ritual ties between the two areas, the dialects of new lowland villages remain consistent with those of the older source villages.

Flights are long-distance displacements of Bunaq, triggered by conflict in their area of origin. Placenames in regions settled by fleeing Bunaq typically reflect the language of the incumbent group. These movements characteristically represent recent historical events for which relatively precise historical records and/or oral histories exist. The dialects spoken by Bunaq villages established after a flight typically reflect the region of origin, but may be mixed with the speech of the incumbent people, speaking either another Bunaq dialect or a neighbouring Austronesian language group.

Towards an Understanding of Papuan– Austronesian Interaction in Timor

The conventional understanding of Austronesian history involves their expansion across the Philippine and Indonesian archipelagos, overwhelming pre-existing populations and transforming them into speakers of Austronesian languages (Bellwood 1998). McWilliam (2007) argues for the opposite scenario in far eastern Timor, suggesting that the Austronesian cultural features of the Fataluku point to their having taken over a prior Austronesian-speaking people. Following proposals in Wurm et al. (1975) and Hull (2004), McWilliam puts forward the argument that the Fataluku people may have arrived in Timor after the Austronesians, colonising them and taking on many of their cultural practices. A similar expansion of Makasai people is suggested to have occurred.

In this chapter, however, I have outlined a different manner of expansion for the Bunaq, one that has consequences for our broader understanding of the history of the Papuan groups in Timor. I have shown that detailed examination of placenames firmly locates the Bunaq in central Timor before the Austronesian arrival. This is significant since, if the Bunaq precede the Austronesians, the other Papuan languages must also be seen to have been prior. If not, we are unable to explain the cognate non-Austronesian vocabulary shared by the Papuans of eastern Timor and Bunaq in central Timor, examples of which are given in Table 8.6. The presence of such lexemes cannot be dismissed as having arisen through later diffusion by contact as the Austronesian languages

---

2 The exception to this is that new lowland villages created by administrators do not typically have Bunaq names.

intervene between Bunaq and the others. Instead, we must reconstruct the items to a 'proto-Timor' Papuan language from which the modern languages Bunaq, Makasai and Fataluku are all descended.

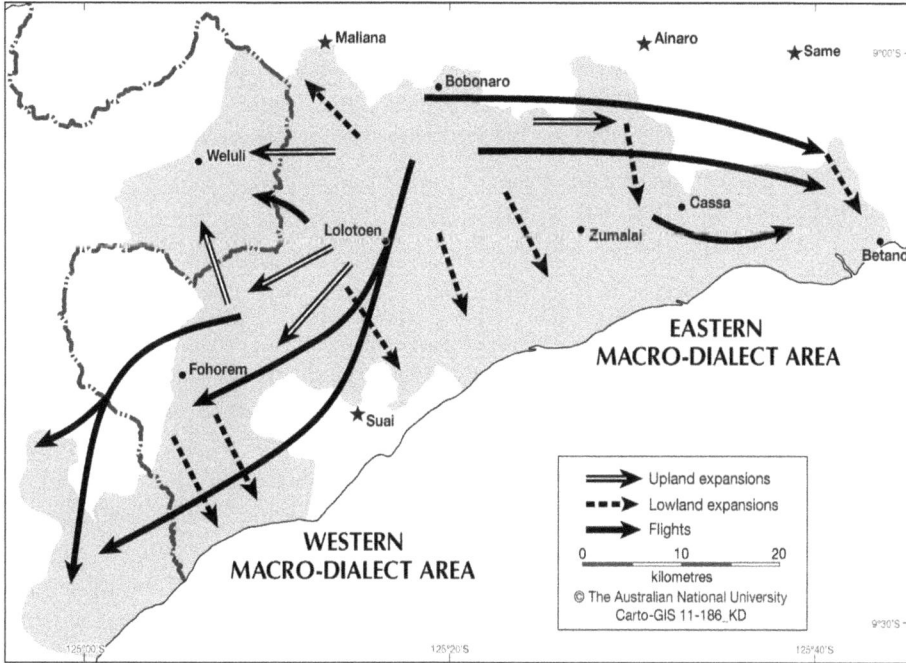

Map 8.7 Major patterns of the Bunaq expansion

This historical circumstance leaves us with the need to explain the presence of so many Austronesian cultural features amongst Papuan language-speaking groups in Timor. I pointed out in this chapter that Austronesian cultural influence on Bunaq in the form of Kemak/Mambai vocabulary can already be discerned even in the earliest times before the beginning of the Bunaq expansion. The Austronesian cultural stamp on the Papuan languages could then be understandable simply as the normal outcome of significant and prolonged contact with a more prestigious neighbouring cultural group. The greater question remaining for future comparative Timorese studies is by what mechanisms have the Papuan groups in Timor been subsequently able to turn the tables and successfully expand and assimilate established Austronesian peoples.

Table 8.6 Some Cognate Sets in Non-Austronesian Languages of Timor

Item	Bunaq	Makasai	Fataluku	Proto-Timor
'stand'	*net*	*etenaa*	*inate*	**(e)nate*
'woman'	*pana*	*pana*	*fana*	**pana*
'one'	*uen*	*u*	*ukan*	**kuna*
'earth'	*muk*	*muʔa*	*muʔa*	**muga*
'sit'	*mit*	*miʔi*	*mire*	**midʒe*
'sleep'	*tier*	*ta'e*	*taja*	**tade*
'give'	*-ini*	*gini*	*ina*	**(g)-ina*
'tree, wood'	*hotel*	*ete*	*ate*	**wate*
'fire'	*hoto*	*ada*	*aca*	**wata*
'mouse, rat'	*zul*	*cura*	*dura*	**dʒila*
'water'	*il*	*ira*	*ira*	**ila*

A full investigation of the various mechanisms that could have played a role in each of the Bunaq is beyond the scope of this chapter. I will, however, briefly discuss a general characteristic of the Bunaq that I propose has aided their expansion—namely, their readiness to incorporate aspects of Austronesian language and society. Throughout this chapter, I have outlined cases—primarily on the basis of different linguistic data—of Bunaq accommodation and adaptation of the cultural categories of their Austronesian neighbours. I tentatively suggest here that it is this inclusive cultural attitude that has enabled the Bunaq to successfully expand into new lands, whilst still maintaining a linguistic identity distinct from the incumbent Austronesian populations.

This pattern is particularly notable for the fact that it bucks the trend observed elsewhere in Melanesia, where differentiation is typically socially encouraged (Ross 1997; Thurston 1989). Numerous studies have shown that in Melanesia widespread bilingualism between neighbouring groups in contact is coupled with pressure within individual groups to differentiate from their neighbours. The result of these counter-forces is to promote on the one hand broad cultural and lexical isomorphism, but on the other hand heterogeneity. The structural parallelism results from bilingualism and the accompanying pressure towards the full translatability of concepts (Gumperz 1971), while the emblematic function of the lexicon drives formal differentiation of the words themselves.

That this kind of divergence drive has not occurred with the Bunaq in central Timor might be best explained by the fact that the Bunaq would have already been differentiated from the very start of their engagement with Austronesians. As mentioned at the beginning of this chapter, even today, after more than a millennium of contact, the Bunaq and their language are regarded as 'other' by their Austronesian neighbours. Thus, in restructuring their own cultural inventory and accommodating aspects of Austronesian language and society,

Bunaq groups must not have seen a threat to their own identity, but rather perhaps an opportunity to establish themselves and develop relationships with contact groups in new lands.

References

Australian War Memorial n.a., Independent Company war diary, AWM52/25/3/2: 2/2, Australian War Memorial, Canberra.

Bellwood, P. 1998, 'The archaeology of Papuan and Austronesian prehistory in the northern Moluccas, eastern Indonesia', in R. Blench and M. Spriggs (eds), *Archaeology and Language II: Correlating archaeological and linguistic hypotheses*, Routledge, London and New York, pp. 128–40.

Berthe, L. 1963, 'Morpho-syntaxe du Bunaq (Timor central)', *L'Homme*, (January–April), pp. 106–16.

Corte-Real, B. de 1998, Mambae and its verbal art genres: a cultural reflection of Suru-Ainaro, East Timor, PhD thesis, Macquarie University, Sydney.

Fox, James J. 2003, 'Tracing the path, recounting the past: historical perspectives on Timor', in James J. Fox and Dionisio Babo Soares (eds), *Out of the Ashes*, ANU E Press, Canberra.

Gumperz, J. J. 1971, 'Convergence and pidginization', in D. Hymes (ed.), *Pidginization and Creolization of Languages*, Cambridge University Press, Cambridge.

Hull, G. 2003, *Southern Mambai*, East Timor Language Profiles No. 5, Instituto Nacional de Linguística, Universidade Nacional Timor Lorosa'e, Dili.

Hull G. 2004, 'The Papuan languages of Timor', *Studies in Languages and Cultures of East Timor*, vol. 6, pp. 23–99.

McWilliam, A. R. 2007, 'Austronesians in linguistic disguise: Fataluku cultural fusion in East Timor', *Journal of Southeast Asian Studies*, vol. 38, pp. 355–75.

Pélissier, R. 1996, *Timor en guerre: le crocodile et les portugais*, Pélissier, Orgeval, France.

Rawski, F. 2002, 'Truth-seeking and local histories in East Timor', *Asia-Pacific Journal on Human Rights and the Law*, vol. 1, pp. 77–96.

Ross, M. 1997, 'Social networks and kinds of speech-community event', in R. Blench and M. Spriggs (eds), *Archaeology and Language 1: Theoretical and methodological orientations*, Routledge, London, pp. 209–61.

Ross, M. D. 2006, 'Metatypy', in K. Brown (ed.), *Encyclopedia of Language and Linguistics*, Elsevier, Oxford.

Sowash, W. B. 1948, 'Colonial rivalries in Timor', *Far Eastern Quarterly*, vol. 7, no. 3, pp. 227–35.

Spillet, P. G. 1999, The pre-colonial history of the island of Timor together with some notes on the Makassan influence on the island, Unpublished manuscript, Museum and Art Gallery of the Northern Territory, Darwin.

Therik, T. 2004, *Wehali. The Female Land: Traditions of a Timorese ritual centre*, Pandanus Books, Canberra.

Thurston, William 1989, 'How exoteric languages build a lexicon: esoterogeny in Western New Britain', in Ray Harlow and Robin Hooper (eds), *VICAL 1: Oceanic languages, Papers from the Fifth International Conference on Austronesian Linguistics. Part 2*, Linguistic Society of New Zealand, Auckland, pp. 555–79.

Woertelboer, W. 1955, 'Zur Sprache und Kultur der Belu (Timor)', *Anthropos*, vol. 50, no. 1, pp. 155–200.

Wurm, Stephen, Laycock, D. C., Voorhoeve, C. L. and Dutton, T. E. 1975, 'Papuan linguistic prehistory, and past language migrations in the New Guinea area', in Stephen Wurm (ed.), *New Guinea Area Languages and Language Study. Volume 1: Papuan languages and the New Guinea linguistic scene*, Pacific Linguistics, Canberra.

9. Tensions of Tradition: Making and remaking claims to land in the Oecusse enclave

Laura S. Meitzner Yoder

Introduction: Changing relations and landholding practices

This chapter explores how rural residential and agricultural land claims in Timor-Leste's Oecusse (Ambeno) enclave are established, maintained and transferred through various means including warfare, agricultural use, allocation by customary leaders and government programs, and migration. Settlement narratives illuminate some basic principles of claim making and explain how local customary leaders and early settlers preserve their favourable positions in relation to land control. This account analyses how landownership is linked to agricultural land use and village (*suco*) membership; the conditions in which both landowners and non-landowners acquire, borrow and use land; and how landownership and authority are transformed through agricultural change. This discussion also demonstrates how state land-titling policies that do not account for the causes and widespread incidence of land borrowing could inadvertently misidentify landowners, and might formally deprive a significant portion of the rural population of agricultural land access.

Recent property scholarship focuses on the human-relational aspects of ownership and use of land alongside other forms of claims to physical, cultural and intellectual property. There has been much attention to how definitions of ownership reflect or exclude the relational and identity factors at the core of many land claims (Hann 1998; Kalinoe and Leach 2004; Peluso 2003; Roseman 1998; Shamir 1996; Strathern 1998, 1999; Tsing 2003; Weiner 1999; Zerner 2003b). Different actors usually have different forms and evidence of claim; rural people, urban people, migrants, the state, those with natural resource-intensive livelihoods, and others with property interests have distinct expectations about what types and expressions of resource claims are appropriate or valid (Zerner 2003a).

The stunning complexity of customary land and forest regulation—in which ownership norms can be specific to each resource, lineage or location—is understandable when we consider that the bases of claims and the possibilities of ownership are embedded in social relationships and the identity of the would-be owner(s). Customary ownership norms are no longer viewed as a static 'tradition' (Hutchinson 1996), and specificity, mutability and responsiveness to social transformation are understood as intrinsic qualities in land use and tenure. Studying disembodied stated rights and practices is inadequate for understanding decision making regarding land if positions of relative power and relationships define the outcomes. Where 'claims rest on demonstrable relationships' (Strathern 2004:9), customary ownership is tailored to each case—better visualised as a constellation of practices or cases than as a single, coherent system. As 'ownership is a function of relations between persons with reference to things, and not between people and things' (Leach 2004a:43), this chapter examines how ownership is narrated and expressed in ever-changing modern land claims and use. Social relations in regard to land are often made visible through tales of relocation: settlement histories, accounts of moving towards roadsides and away from highlands to the coast during the years of Indonesian rule, as well as more recent shifts related to agricultural change.

Origins and Highland Settlement: Land claimed through warfare and agricultural use

The geographic focus of this discussion is on one roughly rectangular Oecusse[1] transect from the coastal lowlands to–highland interior, here named Lekot, drawing on data collected during ethnographic fieldwork conducted throughout Oecusse from May 2002 to November 2004. It outlines the development of landholding and land-use patterns contained within one administrative village (*suco*), covering approximately 43 sq km and inhabited by 1370 residents in 2004. Rivers largely define Lekot's eastern and southern borders, while the western border follows streams and ridges. Residents live in three areas: a large, concentrated coastal settlement, several small inland lowland settlements and an extensive village area at an elevation of about 700 m, 7 km inland from the coast. Ascending a north–south path that transects the length of Lekot in the dry season, travellers follow flat lowlands by a rocky riverbed 2 km inland before reaching water in the river. At that point, the path climbs steeply through 2 km of closed-canopy, seasonally deciduous forest, spotted with betel groves and meticulously irrigated with ditches and bamboo pipes. The forest abruptly

---

1   The primary language spoken throughout Oecusse is Uab Meto (also known as Baiqueno), which is used throughout western Timor, alongside Bahasa Indonesia. Terms given throughout are in Meto unless otherwise noted.

ends, leaving travellers on a very steep, treeless switchback gravel trail, which ends near the highland settlement. The southern half of Lekot comprises rolling hills and short climbs.

Lekot had its major origin settlements in the mountainous interior rather than on the coast.[2] The story below narrates original land claims and links early settlement to local authorities' roles in land allocation and ongoing oversight. The myth relates how the principal customary authorities, the *tobe* (ritual figures with specific authority over matters of land and forests, including conducting agricultural rituals, approving swidden sites, influencing natural forces that affect agricultural outcomes, and regulating sandalwood harvest) and *naijuf* (political figures who act as village heads within the boundaries of a suco),[3] came to be established by chasing out nearly all native inhabitants, with *tobe* domains named after warrior ancestors.[4] It describes how residential precedence is one aspect of land authority: the old *naijuf* (*naijuf mnasi*) and great *tobe* (*tobe naek*) were two of the original (re-)settlers, and the minor *tobe* (*tobe ana*) was given that land because he was the lone survivor of the original inhabitants. This narrative also explains the major family groupings for landholding and ritual responsibilities that presently exist in Lekot. The possibility of landholding and (in part) the current location of swidden fields still reflect this settlement history and *tobe* divisions. This story is compiled from multiple tellings of the history of Lekot settlement by different families.

> Long ago, there were only a few people in Lekot, but the Ambeno king [*usif*][5] told our *tobe-naijuf* ancestors to go attack the people who were then living in the area. So the *tobe* and *naijuf* and the people attacked these enemies and won, and the former inhabitants left because a lot of them had been killed.[6] When they had all fled, there was still one person left hiding in a tree, who also cooked and ate up in the tree. After our

---

2   Reid (1997:61–2) proposes that for most of Timorese history, the island might have been ruled from the 'inside out', and ethnographies from Timor describe pre-colonial interior political systems and relatively recent relocations to the coast (Fox 1977:63; Francillon 1980; McWilliam 1996; Schulte Nordholt 1971; Traube 1986).

3   The changing roles of these figures and their interactions with modern state processes regarding land and forest regulation are discussed extensively elsewhere (Meitzner Yoder 2007a, 2007b). The named, bounded domains of each of the 18–24 Oecusse *suco* are delineated by the customary leadership structure referred to as *tobe-naijuf*. During the fieldwork period, each Oecusse *suco* had one or two *naijuf* whose control defined the domain, with each averaging three to four *tobe* responsible for named, bounded areas nested within the *naijuf* domains.

4   The name of Lekot's *suco* derives from the words for 'settlement' and the onomatopoeic 'to dice/chop (meat) into small pieces', which villagers say substantiates the importance of warfare in establishing the current residents in the region.

5   For further discussion of the Ambeno and part-Portuguese kings in Oecusse, see Meitzner Yoder (2005:65–8, 96–102, 112–24). *Suco*-level authorities make frequent reference to their legitimation from the Ambeno king. In this case, the king commanded the people to eliminate any existing inhabitants and to settle the region from scratch; a combination of strength and precedence bolsters the great *tobe*'s power, exercised in selecting and appointing additional *tobe*, including the sole native survivor.

6   Note that the current authorities (*tobe-naijuf*) won their authority and do not claim to be autochthonous.

ancestors won, they went back to report to the king that the area had been cleared of enemies, but at night the king himself looked up and saw a fire burning in a tree, and asked, 'Whose fire is that burning in the tree?' The people answered, 'We don't know.' So the king ordered the people to go again to find the person building the fire, and when they did it wasn't a person at all, but a civet cat [*makan*] making the fire. The people caught it to question it, but once it was captured, it was no longer a civet cat but a person, so he answered them: 'Do not kill me, because I guard and control this area [*au es atukus ma anonot bi kuan bale*].' So the people did not kill him, and he alone was left alive after the other enemies had been killed or fled from Lekot. So that person originated from the animal, from nature, and the people made him the minor *tobe* [*tobe ana*] because he knew how to communicate very well with the spirits in the area.[7] However, our ancestors conducted rituals to ensure that he would not have many descendants who might chase us out in return; indeed, the minor *tobe* never has more than one son, usually born when he is already old.

In this war, the people of Lekot were successful in the struggle for land, so they settled it and made gardens [swiddens]. The great *tobe* [*tobe naek*] was chosen by the king and *naijuf* to control the largest land area, because he had a large family and they lost the most people during the battle.[8] The old *naijuf* [*naijuf mnasi*] was also there before other people came. Later, it was the *naijuf* and the great *tobe* who chose the small *tobe* and gave him his domain. Then both *tobe* received more newcomers [refugees], and those people followed the activities of each *tobe* in his domain. Land belonged to the person who opened a garden there, and their descendants, who divided up the various locations they inherited from their father, until Lekot was filled with fallowed garden sites. Each family may own many *seimu* [claimed land area used for agriculture], but separated in different locations. All landowners also received land in the *tobe* domains.

The area of Lekot is divided into three domains [*sopu*]. The first is controlled by the great *tobe*. The second is controlled by the minor *tobe* and the other *tobe* [*tobe tonene* (agriculture) or *tobe ulan* (rain)], who were chosen later. The names for the domain areas are those of the ancestors of each *tobe*, who fought their enemies and gained power over the area.

---

7 Note here some of the basic features of *tobe* authority: autochthony, supernatural origins, facility with ritual communication, and selection by the (newcomer) local residents to be the *tobe*. Throughout Oecusse as elsewhere in the Asia-Pacific region, settlement histories often feature total or partial displacements of autochthones.

8 One key basis for land acquisition is sacrifice or loss in warfare—a theme repeated after 1999 with auto-compensation for wrongs committed by militia families and individuals.

The third [the region as a whole] is controlled by the old *naijuf* and young *naijuf*, but has no land of its own. Each domain has other families which belong to it, and have most of their land there. All *tobe* and *naijuf* chose assistants, who became the warriors and defenders [*meob*] of the realm.[9]

The agriculture *tobe* [*tobe tonene*] was chosen during the Japanese time when the young *naijuf* took a wife from Suni-Uf in western Oecusse and the *naijuf* learned of new agricultural rituals from that region that would improve the harvests in Lekot. Returning to Lekot with his wife, the *naijuf* discussed gaining and using these rituals with the Lekot elders. They agreed, and each family contributed *mutin* [bead necklaces] according to the groups that divide meat [*sispa'*][10] at the great *tobe*'s ritual [*fua oel naek*]. They went there to learn these rituals and to buy seed,[11] giving a payment to the leaders there,[12] and the *naijuf*, great *tobe* and the people appointed one family as the *tobe tonene* to carry out these planting rituals henceforth.

This account illustrates some key principles of land authorities and land claims found throughout Oecusse. Amidst the wide variability present among Oecusse *suco*, in all cases a *tobe* with a defined land domain (for example, great *tobe* or minor *tobe*) is said to be of supernatural origin and/or among the earliest settlers to an area, which lends the requisite facility in communicating with ancestors and other spiritual elements in an area. This is not necessarily so for those *tobe* with ritual responsibilities but no domain (for example, *tobe tonene*). In these accounts, authority closely follows a pattern of precedence—

---

9   In Lekot, two sub-*kanaf* are known as the primary *meob* for the region. Their landholdings are concentrated in adjacent sections of a high mountain with a rock cliff base, originally chosen for settlement because of its inaccessibility and easy defence from approaching enemies. The *meob* kept their residence there long after other families settled the flat land where Lekot's highland settlement is today. That is where their first four generations are buried, and the *meob* families still take sacrifices or conduct prayers. Genealogies and oral histories from all Lekot *kanaf* agree that the *meob kanaf* were resident in Lekot before the *tobe-naijuf* structure described in this story came to be. The majority of their agricultural land borders an adjacent *suco*, in keeping with their roles as guardians. The warrior families have unique authority to call the people to warfare using a buffalo horn—a responsibility exercised during conflicts of 1987 and 1999.

10   See Meitzner Yoder (2005:339–40) on *sispa'*. Each family's ritual responsibilities are defined by groups visible in their participation at the great *tobe*'s main ceremony that closes the agricultural season.

11   The phrase used is '*sos pin* [*fin*] *pena, fin ane*': to buy the maize seeds, the rice seeds. Like the 'civilizing influence' of the part-Portuguese kings (Meitzner Yoder 2005:113–17), this is another example of new ideas coming from the outside—in this case, connecting rituals and seed, knowledge and material, to the marriage transaction. This linkage of cultural and agricultural knowledge is similar to the effort of the Oecusse district Agriculture Department's intentions regarding the (agri)cultural associations and *tara bandu* ceremonies (Meitzner Yoder 2007b).

12   The price paid for this knowledge was one *mutin* bead necklace and one horse. Strathern (2004:6) noted that for some groups in Papua New Guinea, displaying the 'foreign, exogenous—sources from which they have purchased the rights to perform a piece of ritual' in a festival adds value to the event, as it demonstrates the advantageous external relationship they formed.

inherently relational:[13] the first to arrive has the highest authority, followed by later arrivals. But settlers rarely encounter an uninhabited area; autochthones are eliminated or displaced to make way for the new settlers, and when they are permitted to remain (for example, in Lekot, the small *tobe* and the two warrior families), they only hold their present positions by virtue of the conquering settlers granting them those roles. In the story above, the remnant figure of the lone survivor who became the small *tobe* is feared, respected and controlled to avoid his rising to dominance.[14] Superiority in warfare trumps autochthony—but never completely.[15]

Origins and migrations are important aspects of land-claim establishment. The current generation is the ninth or tenth since the ancestors of the two oldest-recognised resident lineages (or family names, *kanaf*) moved to Lekot from Biboki, West Timor. These two families are now the primary warrior (*meob*) lineages of Lekot. It is now the sixth or seventh generation since the great *tobe*'s ancestor moved from Manatuto, a district in the main body of Timor-Leste, to Lekot.[16] When the great *tobe* lineage arrived, they gave the symbols of power that they brought with them from Manatuto (gongs and rattan) to the old *naijuf* lineage, because as *tobe* they were not permitted to keep those items.

Other settlers were accepted into the domains of the *tobe* and claimed land by opening gardens; the 11 landowning lineages present in Lekot all describe how their ancestors originally farmed the scattered areas now owned by members of the lineage.[17] Taboos (*nuni*) sometimes serve as a mnemonic device for the history of family migration. Hence, asking the history of a family's *nuni* array can evoke their geographic journey through various points, where events occurred and which taboos were acquired along the way.[18] The possibility of being included among the original—and thus current landholding—*kanaf* in highland Lekot was determined by at least the late 1800s or early 1900s. All *kanaf*[19] who moved into Lekot after the 1912 war are still considered newcomers, and are not permitted heritable land rights in the transect.

---

13   Fox defines precedence as 'an oppositional notion based on the assertion of a relational asymmetry…a socially-asserted claim to difference that generally involves an affirmation of some form of "superiority" and/or "priority"…invariably applied recursively to create a concatenation of relationships' (1996:131).

14   Relating the origin myth of Tunbaba, just east of Oecusse, Schulte Nordholt (1971:287) also noted 'a certain ambivalence inherent in this story, as the two founders came with Sonba'i…while on the other hand they "were already there"'—again indicative of the importance of autochthony in claims to authority.

15   There is no *terra nullius* in Oecusse settlement stories (cf. Griffiths and Robin 1997).

16   Several members of this lineage can name the male line extending back to the individual who left Manatuto to move to Lekot, but no further. Manatuto–Oecusse linkages of governance and military service are found in Portuguese sources as well (Silva 1897; Vaquinhas 1884).

17   Once claimed, land owned bears little relation to land farmed, as described further below.

18   Fox (1997:8) describes topogeny as 'the recitation of an ordered sequence of place names', which is used to transmit social knowledge and to preserve memory.

19   After this time, even in-migrants with the same *kanaf* name as an existing family were excluded from full membership and landownership. For example, there are multiple branches of two Lekot *kanaf* bearing the same name and distinguishable only by their taboos, which reflect their settlement histories; one branch of

The lineages' landholdings were established by various means: in a few cases, the *tobe* relegated areas to individuals or families to cultivate, but most accounts state that the *tobe* did not divide the land. The land became divided and claimed through the process of cultivation, without intervention or direction from any higher authority; a family selected, cleared and farmed a garden location, and, since that point, that land has been claimed by descendants of the original farmers.[20] Mechanisms of inheritance and land transfer[21] vary by *kanaf* and region, but this accounts for the island-like, patchwork pattern of land claims present today across the Lekot landscape. Clearly, the *usif* (ruler) and *naijuf* were not involved directly in dividing up large tracts of land to family groups or to individuals.

Land Transactions and the Perpetual Landlessness of Outsiders

In most of Oecusse,[22] upon marriage a woman leaves her birth *kanaf* to join that of her husband. Accordingly, *seimu* land is inherited by sons and remains largely within the *kanaf*.[23] Widows retain land rights to their husband's *kanaf* land, but for an older widow the land may pass directly to her sons. Unmarried daughters retain rights to their father's *kanaf* land. Women (regardless of their marital status) frequently inherit individually owned parcels of flooded rice land. In some areas of Oecusse (but not Lekot; this seems to occur in *suco* with more recent and numerous in-migration), a man who marries into a landowning *kanaf* and fully transfers his *suco* membership[24] to his wife's *suco* of residence

---

each *kanaf* may not own land, while the others may.

20   This is the most common means of establishing land claims (Rodman 1987; Vargas 1985; Ward and Kingdom 1995a; Zerner 2003a).

21   In general, male children inherit land, and a father's land is divided among all sons. The father determines the pattern of equal or unequal land division; while all sons often receive equal shares of subdivided land or equal rights to use undivided land, some fathers designate a larger share of land to the eldest son or the son responsible for maintaining the family's ritual house. Daughters rarely inherit swidden land; land from a couple without sons will be inherited by male relatives of the father.

22   An exception is the central flooded rice-growing region of Padiae (*suco* Cunha and Lalisuk), settled by Savunese and Rotinese in-migrants still called *kaes metan* (black foreigners/strangers) by Oecusse highlanders, in which most land is held and passed from mother to daughter. Until about 30 years ago, a new couple's residence was exclusively uxorilocal, and the wife's family took responsibility for providing the new family with land. Unlike other parts of Oecusse, Padiae inheritance frequently favours the youngest child with a larger share of family land and eventual ownership of the parents' house.

23   It is worth comment that the subject of land tenure has been barely mentioned in the vast and detailed ethnographic literature analysing marriage, bride-wealth and kinship alliances around Timor, perhaps influenced by van Wouden's (1968) influential study (Fox 1980).

24   In these cases, it is essential for the man to contribute animals to local ritual events, and sometimes give the local land authorities gifts of animals.

may be able to acquire heritable[25] rights to a strictly limited portion of his wife's *kanaf* land after multiple years of farming a plot and subject to approval by the *tobe* and/or *naijuf* with some payment to both figures.

Land access by male in-migrants is often problematic.[26] Before the new household of an external husband (not native to that *suco*) and local wife is allowed to settle in the *suco*, the local leaders and members of each landowning *kanaf* (*atoin kua tuaf*) meet to consider how the land requirements of the new family can be met. As land is almost never permanently transferred to in-migrants (referred to as *atoin anaomnemat*, wandering people), the new couple may be guaranteed rights to borrow—but never to own—land, sometimes for a specified number of generations (cf. McWilliam 2002:162–7).[27] As this disadvantages the couple's children, the new pair is encouraged to move back to the husband's home *suco*, where future land rights are secured.[28] When a couple does move to the husband's land, the wife's relatives might express relief that the couple and their children are 'freed' from their demeaning status as landless borrowers.

If the couple remains in the wife's *suco*, even for a generation, it is possible that their children or grandchildren might not be received as landowning '*kanaf* insiders' when trying to relocate to the father's home *suco*. This creates the most socially undesirable status with regards to land: a perpetual borrower—rejected as a *kanaf* landowner in one's paternal landowning *suco* and unable to acquire heritable land rights in one's *suco* of residence. Some villagers describe this state as '*atoin matustanab*', meaning someone being sent back and forth in the middle (as in a ball game), without a definitive home or stopping place. In 2004, 14 of highland Lekot's 120 households (12 per cent) were in these circumstances.[29] Twelve of these families (in two *kanaf*, each now with six households) are descendants of people who relocated (as 'political refugees') to Lekot during the 1912 and 1975 conflicts. They have attempted to return to their former *suco*

---

25   Even in these cases, the land retains links to the wife's *kanaf*.

26   Customary restrictions on outsiders' landownership have long been amply documented in Timor (Castro 1867; Metzner 1977; Sousa Xavier 1997; Vaquinhas 1883). Even access to unclaimed or common land can be unequal (Baumann 1997).

27   The wife's *kanaf* takes responsibility for ensuring that the couple will have access to enough land to meet their housing and subsistence needs, and the couple will participate in the same system of swidden land borrowing as *suco* members.

28   The difficulty of outsider men obtaining land is reflected in the numbers of local and outsider marriages even in coastal, peri-urban Lekot: 57 per cent of couples have both husband and wife from the same *suco*; 33 per cent are a local husband and an in-migrant wife; and just 9 per cent represent a local wife and an in-migrant husband, classified as *atoin anaomnemat*.

29   In addition to these 14 households, in 2004 highland Lekot had three cases pending since 2001–02. This is indicative of the villagers' reluctance to accept in-migrant males—called 'the seeds of land borrowing'—as members of their settlement. In one pending case of outside people being rejected, a widowed mother of a local married woman (now with her husband's *kanaf*) was not permitted to move in because she was accompanied by an orphaned grandson; village leaders said the woman's move would have been unproblematic if the orphaned child had been a granddaughter or if the woman had been alone, but a landless boy must not be permitted to settle in Lekot. Village authorities, including the hamlet head and *tobe*, served as gatekeepers to *suco* land access.

without success, and are now permitted to remain in Lekot only because they have intermarried with local women, but they still may not make permanent claims to any land. They have no swidden garden land (*seimu*) of their own. They do gain permanent rights to their house yards, even if local *kanaf* are reluctant to give them land.

The accepted disparity between *de facto* and *de jure* land availability is important in supporting the livelihoods of these landless people. With unlimited access to free borrowing of land for swidden agriculture in the present system, '*atoin matustanab*' are no more economically vulnerable[30] than their landowning neighbours. If, however, landholding formalisation through state-based regulatory reform or agricultural change reduced their access to land borrowing, this group would be economically disadvantaged.

Occasionally, people lose land due to debt incurred in emergency situations, and may regain land only by inflated repayments.[31] Families borrowing maize during hungry times might pay a high price in land lost that might take decades to regain—a debt they work steadily to cancel. In rare cases, landownership is not entirely place based, but might be linked to the actual *soil* of claimed land. Annual flooding rearranges landholding alongside seasonal rivers. Flooding might remove tens of metres of riverbank land for stretches of 100 m or more; where that soil is deposited further downstream, the upstream person who lost land may claim the 'new' land created, even on the other side of the river. This permits the highly unusual phenomenon of people owning land in an adjacent *suco*, when literal land transfer occurs on rivers that mark *suco* boundaries.

Local Authorities and Land-Use Regulation

Settlement narratives and subsequent land relations influence local political and ritual authorities' control over land parcels. The *naijuf* political authorities often were selected to serve as village head (*chefe do suco*) under the Portuguese colonial regime and much of their preferential landholdings were acquired in that role. There are two *naijuf* lineages in Lekot: one 'old', originally from Manatuto in eastern Timor, charged with oversight of traditional ceremonies; and the other 'young', which came later from neighbouring Manamas, West Timor, which is

---

30 On occasion, however, the *atoin matustanab* alone will clear the most marginal patch of unclaimed land (*naija sona*) in highland Lekot to plant low-yielding root crops—without converting that land to heritable *seimu* as a local *kanaf* would—when unable to get sufficient space in a group garden. Vargas (1985:18) demonstrated that non-landowning 'newcomers to the village made smaller fields [than other residents], indicating that they were not free to borrow as much land as long-term village residents were able to borrow'.
31 For example, during the 1960s, one man needed immediate assistance to fulfil his tax obligation: in exchange for about 2 kg of rice, he traded 1 ha of irrigated rice land, which was regained by his son only in 2003 for the price of two large cows (US$300).

concerned with *suco* governance including *suco* boundary conflicts. Regarding the *naijuf* landholdings, as an original settler, the old *naijuf* has landholdings, as do the other village member *kanaf*, and the lineage's land is treated the same as any other family's. The young *naijuf*, however, has very little land as a relative newcomer and, in most discussions about land, Lekot residents state that the young *naijuf* has no land, other than that taken from the people,[32] or other than what people gave to his lineage.[33]

As narrated above, the great *tobe* came to control the entire region, and subsequently divided the land with the (autochthonous) minor *tobe*. As the primary land authority, the great *tobe* maintains a level of control over the entire domain—for example, in 2003 the great *tobe* denied a farming group permission to open a garden in part of a claimed agricultural region (*seimu*) of the minor *tobe* area, on the grounds that the area was too steep and should be allowed to revert to forest.[34] Precedence confers special status: as a 'landholding *tobe*' with defined areas, individuals in these positions occupy them by virtue of their early residence; as such, people emphasise that they cannot be replaced with another lineage, unlike the *tobe*, who is responsible only for agricultural rituals concerning planting and rain/wind regulation.[35]

While precedence and the ordered hierarchy *usif-naijuf-tobe* hold for most cases, on matters relating to land and forests or within the ritual sphere, the *tobe* has more authority than the *naijuf*. Their landholding, however, reflects levels and spheres of their authority too: the *naijuf* may appropriate land from the people, while the *tobe* may not. Many say that the *tobe* had all the land and then distributed it to others, while the *naijuf* originally had no land but accumulated holdings from others. The *tobe* is clearly the primary land-use authority, but the *naijuf*'s political power enables him to usurp land and to keep it (Schulte Nordholt 1971).

32　Various young *naijuf* have appropriated some of the choicest land in Lekot, taking advantage of Portuguese labour practices and Indonesian land formalisation to acquire exclusive and permanent private rights to some of the most valuable land. This included declaring the largest-existing irrigated rice field owned by several local families, stone-fenced with village labour, to be his own during the Portuguese era; acquiring a private Indonesian title (while village head) to a large coconut grove planted with community labour while he was the Portuguese-era village head; and personally claiming a former public recreation beach site after 1999 by having his resident assistant construct a fence around the area.

33　The phenomenon of the landless *naijuf* is heard sporadically throughout Oecusse: in four other *suco*, the *naijuf* does retain a domain of his own, though small. *Naijuf* sometimes state that they have no land because they divided it all out to the *tobe*. One *naijuf* gleefully tells of how his lineage gave out all the meat and was left with only the bones, handing out all the land to the *tobe* and the population, except a sacred mountain adjacent to his house. This is a paradoxical display of power: owning it all so he does not need to own any.

34　When the group disobeyed this prohibition and opened gardens in that location anyway, mistakenly burning a portion of a betel grove, the great *tobe* assessed a fine subsequently paid jointly by all members of the group.

35　Since the ritual *tobe* do not have particular precedence in settlement legitimating their positions of authority, their places are more tenuous and they may be subject to removal if seen to commit ritual errors that cause calamity or fail to protect harvests.

There is a fundamental difference between the *tobe* and the *naijuf* with respect to landowning: while the *tobe*'s own land is treated just like that of other villagers, the *naijuf* reserves preferential tenure rights. In a 2001 example of land-tenure rearrangement when converting a swidden area to a new flooded rice field (see Meitzner Yoder 2005:218–20), land from the original landowners was redistributed in equal parts to the people who worked to build the irrigation and terraces. By contributing labour to the project, individuals previously without land in that area acquired heritable individual rights to a defined plot of land, equal in area to the land now held by the original landowners in the rice field. In this case and others, the *naijuf*, alone of all the original landowners (including the *tobe*) involved in this scheme, was exempt from dividing his land with contributing labourers. Seven people who joined the project late approached the *naijuf* and were granted rights to develop a given portion of the *naijuf*'s land, and in exchange for their labour were allowed to farm their plots for three planting seasons without any payment to the *naijuf*. In subsequent years they should give 10 per cent of their harvest as payment for use of the *naijuf*'s land.[36] Unlike all other farmers in the rice field, those planting on the *naijuf*'s land do not have heritable rights to the land, and should they discontinue using the land, it will revert to full control by the *naijuf*.

Irrigation development, and subsequent conversion to fruit-tree and/or flooded rice land use, inserts the layer of *cabo-oel* (literally, 'water chief/head') into the land authority framework. A *cabo-oel* is not an inherited position in the traditional hierarchy, but simply any person who proposes, originates and oversees an irrigation plan for a given flooded rice field or a fruit-tree grove. Importantly, the *cabo-oel* is not necessarily the landowner or even a *suco* resident, but secures broad, long-term use rights for the duration of an irrigated system.[37] Irrigation impacts on tenure in giving a measure of authority over land distribution to the *cabo-oel*, and in giving other non-landowners enduring rights to use the land for as long as the irrigation scheme is actively maintained and productive.[38] The *cabo-oel* obtains use of the land closest to the water source, followed (downstream) by the landowner. Beyond that, anyone interested in joining the irrigation scheme may be given space, subject to approval by the *cabo-oel* (not the landowner). Significantly, for land-use decisions in irrigated areas, the *cabo-oel*'s authority supersedes that of the customary landowner and the *tobe*.

---

36   Villagers note that his exceptional landholding status permits flexibility in cultivating these rice fields, allowing those without land or those with extra requirements to use his land under reasonable conditions.

37   In Oecusse, individual springs not used for agricultural purposes fall under the authority of the *tobe* rather than a *cabo-oel*, differentiating the *cabo-oel* from the Tetun *cabo-be'e* (*oel* = *be'e* = water) in other districts of Timor-Leste.

38   If the scheme fails or falls into disuse, all users' rights are fully relinquished to the original owner.

Coastward Migrations and Agricultural Change

Lekot, like much of Timor-Leste, has undergone dramatic demographic shifts during recent decades. Before World War II, most people in Lekot lived in dispersed sub-*kanaf* clusters in the highlands; only four households lived on the coast, including the great *tobe*. From 1945 to 1975, the Portuguese administration encouraged people to move to the coast for the purposes of schooling, but most were reluctant to do so for fear of physical punishments and additional labour demands made on coastal residents. A few families moved to the coast during the 1960s, but by 1975 the majority of the population was still living in family clusters in the highlands or inland lowland settlements. From 1976 to 1981, the Indonesian planned development of settlements, roads and schools attracted a few families, and there has been a steady trickle of migration to the lowlands since the mid-1980s. After every house but one in Lekot was burned during the post-referendum violence of September–October 1999, most people returned to their same places of residence to rebuild homes. By 2004, Lekot had 1370 residents, just more than half of them now in the lowlands: 120 households (640 residents) in an inland settlement at an elevation of 700 m, and 140 households (730 residents) in one peri-urban coastal and three inland lowland settlements.

Lowland Lekot residents still consider themselves mountain people who happen to live on the coast; few have lived there for more than a generation. Although some now rarely visit their former settlement area, many still regularly farm and worship in the highlands, and make weekly trips uphill to see family. Lowland land practices replicate the upland models in which the *tobe* and *naijuf* play key roles relating to land—at times unbeknownst to state authorities. In Lekot, the first hamlet head in 1976 was the minor *tobe*,[39] and although he was illiterate and from the mountains, he was responsible for an extensive lowland land allocation program, designating each highland family grouping a specified plot of land, which very few families took as their principal residence. Ten years later, the *naijuf* reallocated many of these plots to outsiders, including Indonesian civil servants and church workers, following the pattern of land allocation, in the form of grants (not sale) to outsiders. Methods of claiming uncultivated land (*naija sona*) and restrictions on landownership in the lowlands closely resemble these practices in the highlands.

---

39   Villagers joked that the Indonesian Government did not know that the man they selected as hamlet head was a *tobe*—an appropriate person to serve as overseer for the state-sponsored land-distribution program.

Ownership, Land Use and Changing Patterns of Rural Landholdings in Lekot

Land-use patterns are significant because they shape initial ownership claims, and are of broader significance through village membership that permits a family to become landowners. But for already claimed swidden agricultural land, ongoing use can be surprisingly unrelated to ownership or membership. This overview of everyday land-claim assertion and validation highlights how family (*kanaf*) identity, neighbourly relations, individual initiative, group membership and land authorities' permission circumscribe the possibilities for different forms of ownership in Lekot's varied agricultural landscape.

Lekot has both mountain and lowland inland settlements and peri-urban coastal areas. Land and resource tenure vary according to location and land use; each land-use category has specific patterns and norms of acquisition, purchase or temporary use, and levels of ownership and authority on decision making about that land.[40] Lekot's coast was almost unpopulated until the 1980s, leaving it with the uncommon phenomenon of unclaimed land even today. Much land has been converted from unclaimed land to individual holdings from the late 1990s onward. The significant, recent coastward migration demonstrates land claims that resemble upland patterns. As the growing coastal population addresses food needs and preferences by converting dry land to flooded rice fields, there is also conversion of land from periodic swidden to annual irrigated cultivation, with accompanying changes in landholding structures.

Much South-East Asian historiography posits a sharp divide between highland swiddening animists and lowland paddy-rice farmers who adhere to world religions, often implying a unidirectional move towards lowland livelihoods and identity (Burling 1965; Leach 1954, 1960; Wolters 1999). Scott (2009), however, notes that the migration moves in both directions—from hill to valley and valley to hill—and that there are intermediate cultural-ecological categories. Throughout this section, I highlight some of these factors that transgress these standard categories—that is, swidden farmers who start flooded rice cultivation on their own; highlanders who move to the lowlands and take their systems and norms of land claims with them, or live in the lowlands but still farm in the uplands; and how farmers' attempts to apply new land-division schemes can function or fail based in part on prior norms of land tenure. People in Oecusse use a range of classifications for land, described below.

---

40   Published land and tree tenure information for rural Timor-Leste is scant (for example, Metzner 1977; Saldanha and Guterres 2002; Sousa Xavier 1997; Susanto 1994–95; Ubbe 1995–96), and few accounts indicate the effects of migration and infrastructure development on changes in tenure patterns (Aditjondro 1994; Fitzpatrick 2002).

House Yards

In both mountain and coastal settlements, the land or yard closest to the house (*poa ume, uem balef*) is used for seasonal mixed gardens of root crops, maize and vegetables, as well as for fruit trees and animal pens. Individuals hold the house yard, and fenced border perimeters constructed of stone, branches, palm ribs or living fences are precisely maintained.

In highland areas (past and present), building a house and planting trees[41] associated with the house form one of the most enduring possible claims. Land and its planted trees remain *kanaf* property for several generations where one's ancestors were known to have lived on a given plot of land (*uem balef*). This convention applies even when descendants move to another *suco*—an action that normally diminishes claims to other (agricultural) types of land.[42] Allowing members of another *kanaf* to build a house on one's land usually permanently forfeits one's claims to that land, which then transfers to the new residents' *kanaf*.[43] Even when the new resident moves from that site, the former owner usually has no right to reclaim the land, and any other household subsequently wishing to build a house on that land would negotiate with the most recent residents (or their *kanaf* descendants).[44] In past times, *kanaf* clusters moved frequently, so there are many such residential sites for each *kanaf* across a *suco* landscape; frequent localised migration contributes to the patchwork nature of landownership in rural regions. The permanent nature of these land transfers makes landowners reluctant to release fertile or well-situated land to another *kanaf*, but requests for agriculturally marginal land for house building are usually still granted.

Despite the strength of the land claim resulting from residence, highland dwellers show no preference for living on their own *kanaf*'s land over asking for better-situated land from another *kanaf*. Until 1975, highland Lekot residents lived in widely scattered sub-*kanaf* clusters. During 1975–99, most families moved their houses two to four times to comply with changing government

---

41 Generally, trees remain the property of their planter (or descendants) for the life of the tree. In urban and rural land transfers, the original tree/landowner may choose to retain harvesting rights to the trees or to sell the trees, separately from the land, to the new landowner. Trees and land are always transacted separately, whether land is purchased or borrowed (cf. Peluso 2003; Rodman 1987; Van Trease 1987:11; Vargas 1985).

42 Over time, *kanaf* members remaining in the former *suco* will absorb the rights to the house land, but rights to the trees remain with the original owner (or descendants) even after that point.

43 In more densely populated rural areas (for example, southern Oecusse), such land grants for residential use are reportedly becoming less common, sometimes now replaced with outright sale as practised in urban areas.

44 There are exceptions, as happened in Lekot during 2003 when *Kanaf* A wanted to reclaim their hillside land below a spring that had been settled in the 1930s by *Kanaf* B, by now home to 30 households, in order to develop a nearby water source into flooded rice fields. The decision, mediated by elders from each *kanaf* and the hamlet head, involved *Kanaf* A giving an equivalent land area just above the water source for *Kanaf* B to relocate their houses, as well as a share in the new rice field. This was permitted because *Kanaf* B's relocation was necessary for the irrigation development that would benefit all Lekot *kanaf*.

requirements for proximity to roads (twice rerouted) and schools (relocated three times), creating a mixed-*kanaf* settlement. After independence in 2002, the hamlet head initiated a program to again relocate all residents adjacent to a new road and piped water system, mandating that each family select a 25 sq m plot on which to build a house along a stretch of road that primarily runs through land of four sub-*kanaf*.[45] As a result, most households are again relocating to another *kanaf*'s land. Transfers of residential land are made without any form of payment or ritual debt.

The Indonesian Government created Lekot's coastal peri-urban housing settlements on unsettled, densely forested land in the early 1980s. As products of state planning, they were subject to some formalisation.[46] Although the state oversaw the land allocation, people frequently selected a Lekot *tobe* to witness their formal land acquisition or subsequent transactions (following the *tobe*'s highland role). After the initial allocation, land that is sold follows state land administration conventions of permanent transfer. Residential land borrowing rarely happens in this region, with the exception of land used (rent free) by outside settlers during the Indonesian era that reverted to former claimants when vacated in 1999.

Swidden Fields

Seimu (land, *seimu*; actively swiddened fields, *lele*) refers to any land that has been used for swidden gardens, and therefore subject to enduring claim by a given lineage (or, as with first-generation swidden cultivation, an individual). Swidden gardens (*lele*) are the central food source for both highland and lowland residents; most Oecusse swiddens are cultivated for only one season, and are then left to fallow.[47] *Seimu* land can be left fallow for years or even decades, and returned to forest, without losing its status as claimed land of a given *kanaf*.[48]

---

45   The village head felt that formally limiting the plot size would reduce any potential complaints the original landowners would have about losing so much of their land, and the resettlement proceeded smoothly as all families received permission from the *kanaf* landowners for their proposed house site.

46   Of 67 households living in the coastal Lekot settlements since 1992, only 33 (48 per cent) reportedly held Indonesian land certificates, although most households (94 per cent) paid land tax annually from 1992 to 1997. Lekot highland residents report that there have never been land sales, land titling or surveying there.

47   Swidden agriculture is more prevalent in Oecusse than elsewhere on Timor. There are very detailed descriptions (cf. Conklin 1954, 1957; Dove 1981, 1985; Weinstock 1979) to complement overviews of swidden agriculture on Timor (Metzner 1977; Ormeling 1956; Panão 1915; Schulte Nordholt 1971).

48   Farmers usually establish original land claims through cultivation and maintain those claims through repeated cultivation, periodic maintenance of fallows, visits to the fallow site, establishing markers or fencing, and speaking about claimed land (or trees). The actual procedures, time to claim establishment or disappearance, and relative strength of claims are dependent on vegetation types, the status of the claimant and agricultural practices, as discussed further below (Conklin 1954, 1957; Dove 1981:88–101, 1985; Ormeling 1956; Vargas 1985; Ward and Kingdom 1995b). In Lekot, the largest contiguous forested area of *kanaf*-level land runs 2 km between the highland and coastal settlements, adjacent to a river. Individuals from seven *kanaf* farmed that land (that is, claimed and converted it to *seimu*) during Portuguese times, but early in the Indonesian administration the Forestry Department prohibited agricultural use by declaring the land

As the land underpinning the subsistence livelihoods in Oecusse, a large percentage of Oecusse's land area—approaching 90 per cent—is recognised as *seimu* (including both irrigated and dryland agricultural fields, fallowed and cultivated).

People usually make contiguous gardens, sharing a common perimeter fence with neighbouring farmers to reduce fencing labour.[49] Making the sturdy 1.5 m-high wood/stone fences required to protect gardens from free-ranging livestock is one of the most labour-consuming activities in creating a new garden (cf. Fox 1977:34).[50] Group gardening also confers yield benefits as neighbours assist in guarding ripening crops from birds and monkeys.[51] Throughout Oecusse, sometimes an entire village will plant on one small mountain in a given year, on contiguous land owned by several different *kanaf*, with a single fence constructed around the mountain's base. Each year, farmers form different groups that clear vegetation and burn, fence and plant a chosen area. Anyone may join a farming group, regardless of one's status as landowner or a kin relationship to others in the group. A household may have one large or several smaller garden locations per year.

Groups form when a landowner decides that a given area is appropriate for cropping and indicates this decision by chipping the tree bark along paths near the chosen area (*tae pait*), usually by May. This step is usually taken only after informing the *tobe* with jurisdiction over that land and receiving his assent. Seeing this sign of intention to open a swidden, others approach the landowner and may join the group until the planned area is full. Farming groups of 15–40 households are common throughout Oecusse. The landowner allocates

---

protected forest. The area was largely left to return to closed-canopy forest after the 1970s, but despite its return to forest, the *kanaf* maintain their respective claims and can still indicate the boundary markers of planted and non-planted trees, rocks or ravines between *kanaf* sections. In some families, land claimed by the *kanaf* bears some measure of internal, individualised, heritable division among family members over a given land area. With today's dense forest cover, the high population of monkeys makes agriculture difficult, so many family heads discourage family members who want to make swiddens in this region. In 2003, a customary authority (*tobe*) enforced the ban on farming in this area, stating that it should remain forested since gardens there were unlikely to meet with good harvests.

49   Those who do make gardens individually often take the unusual step of planting there for two or more years, to make the fencing labour worthwhile.

50   Mathematically, the labour savings in group fencing are substantial—for example, 10 people farming together must each build only 32 per cent as much fence when compared with farming (and fencing) the same land area alone. This strong preference for having a common perimeter fence contrasts with situations in which households prefer having separate, if nearby, gardens (see, for example, Dove (1981:113 ff.).

51   Other potential benefits of group gardening include pest saturation and labour exchange, as in shared fencing. Labour exchange for planting and harvesting is, however, minimal in Lekot (cf. Dove 1981:117; Vargas 1985:19, 112). In general, the planters are fully responsible for all aspects of land preparation, planting and harvesting within their own boundaries. Schulte Nordholt (1971) reported a greater degree of labour sharing in western Timor.

internal boundaries for each farmer, which the farmers mark in four ways.[52] Each household is then responsible for managing the crops within its plot, from clearing to harvest.

While new internal boundaries on swidden fields are created and marked each time people use land, *seimu* ownership boundaries between *kanaf* are permanent and usually follow landscape features, such as ravines, streams, paths or lines between prominent stones/trees. Individually owned fields, such as those surrounding the coastal settlement, are often farmed in shorter rotations of three years' fallow (using leguminous trees—for example, *Sesbania* sp., *gala-gala*, to improve soil fertility); these plots usually have constructed (palm rib) or planted (with living fence tree species—for example, *reo*) boundaries that owners maintain even while the fields are fallow.

Initial land acquisition is based on agricultural use, but on land with established *kanaf* claims, making a swidden garden on borrowed land confers no rights to the land user beyond that season's harvest (cf. Vargas 1985:74 ff.). With the labour advantages of this system, people more frequently join a group and plant on borrowed land than on their own; during fieldwork, about 30 per cent of highland swidden fields were farmed by the landowners.[53] There is no preference for planting annual swiddens on one's own land over planting on someone else's land.[54] Even individuals with extensive *kanaf*-level landholdings borrow land for swiddens if they favour a certain location (for example, proximity to another field or their home). It is common for groups to farm land even without the landowner as a member of the group. Group composition changes annually, but during the growing season the group members have responsibility to each other—for example, if one group member clears or burns a protected area, the entire group must assist in paying any fine assessed by the *tobe* and/or *naijuf*.

---

52 First, when clearing the land, vegetation along the boundaries is cut to 1 m high, while all other vegetation is cleared to ground level; second, after burning the field, farmers place wood or rock lines around their areas; third, farmers plant a row of maize or sorghum (different from the irregular spacing inside their plots) along the boundaries; and fourth, farmers might plant a short-season variety of maize along the borders of their area.

53 As population density increases, ease and frequency of land borrowing decrease. With 32 people/sq km (and 3.2 ha/person), Lekot's population density was less than half the average for Oecusse. In populous southern highland Oecusse, rotating swiddens are slowly giving way to the annual cultivation of settled agriculture, including tilling, not yet practised anywhere in Lekot outside some house yards. Swidden, permanent dryland and irrigated practices coexist throughout the region (Dove 1984).

54 This point becomes important when landholdings are subject to titling. For example, Ward (1995:219) noted how this problem arose in Fiji with the Government's 'assumption that the registered owners of the land would also be the users', when 'in fact ownership and use were often not in accord'. Since most Lekot farmers practice similar land preparation and none carries out improved fallow management, landowners do not identify soil problems or damage to their fields resulting from other people's use of the land; at this stage, no farmers were considered better than others regarding knowledge or skill in soil improvement.

When borrowing land for swiddens, residents of the landowner's *suco* pay no rent or harvest share to the landowner.[55] Where a swidden area is close to the *suco* border, members of the neighbouring *suco* are (reluctantly) permitted to join the farming group as they will contribute to the fence construction and help protect the swidden from grazing animals. In these cases, neighbouring *suco* members must pay a negotiated amount (for example, one small basket of rice and 120 ears of maize) to the landowner, even if they are members of the landowners' own sub-*kanaf*;[56] *suco* boundaries are stronger than any lineage affiliation. Multiple land-use or rental arrangements commonly exist within one fence. All farmers must participate in the harvest rituals of the *tobe* in whose domain they make gardens; contribution to this ritual activity depends on the physical location of one's garden, not one's residence or belonging to a given *tobe* or *naijuf* domain.[57]

A *seimu* may be owned at a variety of social levels—by single households, among siblings or at the sub-*kanaf* or *kanaf* levels[58]—according to the nature and frequency of its use. These classifications are not absolute, however, and no local language terms distinguish these levels. There are very few household-held *seimu* in highland Lekot, other than flooded rice fields. Household-held *seimu* in coastal Lekot include most land outside house fences but still near settlements, which are planted to maize, dryland rice and root crops in (minimally) three-year rotations, as well as flooded rice fields. *Seimu* held among siblings are usually planted to maize and rice in rotations of three years (with green manures planted) or more (bush fallow), and include fields further away from settlements than household-held land. Both household and sibling-held *seimu* are usually farmed by the landowners themselves and are rarely borrowed by others. Much *seimu* held at the sub-*kanaf* or *kanaf* level is farmed with rotations of 10 years or more. When *kanafseimu* are farmed, it is almost always as part of a multi-*kanaf* farming group.

Initial claims result in household ownership of a given plot of land, which the next generation may inherit and hold as sibling-level ownership, and with the increase of descendants after several generations may be recognised as *kanaf*-wide land. The prevalence of individual-level ownership near the recently

---

55   At most, each local resident in a group will contribute a small animal towards the planting and post-harvest feasts, but a land borrower's contribution is the same as a landowner's contribution in these events.

56   A sub-*kanaf* is a subset of a large *kanaf* that shares additional specific taboos (*nuni*), described above, and is distinguishable by an additional name, appended to the *kanaf* name, which refers to the taboo. Full sub-*kanaf* names, with the appendix, are not normally used in everyday settings.

57   As members of a neighbouring *suco* frequently farm part of Lekot, the number of participants in Lekot's primary harvest ritual usually exceeds the number of Lekot households.

58   In small families, sometimes all members of a *kanaf* or sub-*kanaf* are also siblings. *Kanaf* are small, well-defined units, limited to members of a group. It could be misleading to call this land 'communally owned', as all claims are within one (extended) family. See Fox (1999) for more on the intricacies of different ways to gain membership in a given *kanaf*. It is extremely complex for outsiders to correctly identify the socially relevant level of landownership (cf. Geertz 1972; Ward 1995; West 1998; West and Kloeck-Jenson 1999; Zerner 1994).

settled coast links to debates over whether this indicates an individualising trend in landholding, which has received much attention in ethnographies and land administration elsewhere (Healy 1971; Lea 1997; Martin 2004; Simpson 1971; ter Haar 1948; Ward and Kingdon 1995b). Observers have long reported, and legislated, a move away from (presumed) communal towards individual landholdings in Timor (Anon. 1924; Gonçalves 1937; Martinho 1943, 1945; Sumardjono et al. 1994–95; Suryosuwarno 1993; Ubbe 1995–96). In contrast, some lowland Lekot residents point out that individual claims are always the necessary first step to creating *kanaf*-level landholdings out of unclaimed land, and they expect that today's first-generation coastal household claims will over time evolve—communalising—into the sibling or *kanaf*-level claims that fill the highlands. The earliest residents of lowland Lekot have more *kanaf*-level claims than recent settlers, as an individual's claim is shared among his sons. Most Lekot people describe a *communalising–individualising cycle* in landownership, resulting from changes through inheritance, migration and other factors (cf. Hooper and Ward 1995; O'Meara 1995:113).

On sibling-held and *kanaf seimu*, different members may have unequal levels of authority over using land (for access to trees, cf. Peluso 2003). There are informal gradations of rights according to residential proximity to a given plot of land. For example, with coastward migration over the past three decades, people now living on the coast will usually ask permission or inform their highland-dwelling siblings before planning a garden on highland *kanaf* land. This would not necessarily be done among siblings who all live in the highlands. Land claims can diminish over time when an individual moves away from the settlement and there is competing use by other members of one's own *kanaf* who live closer to the land. An individual who voluntarily moves to another *suco* would not expect to return to reclaim full land rights after one generation of absence; that land[59] would have become controlled by the remaining members of the *kanaf*. *Seimu* held at the *kanaf* level are very rarely sold; most people take extensive measures to prevent land from leaving their *kanaf*.

Flooded Rice Fields

Irrigated rice fields (*aen oek*) are one class of *seimu*, but their tenure and use arrangements are quite different from unirrigated fields. Flooded rice fields (*ane* = rice, *oek* = water/wet) are not widespread throughout Oecusse, as most of the district highlands do not have sufficient water to support this use. There are extensive fields along the lowland rivers, especially in the centre of Oecusse's north coast, where the main crop grown is flooded rice.[60] These primary flooded

---

59   Planted trees, however, do not transfer to fellow *kanaf* members.
60   Significant rice-field development occurred using forced labour during the Japanese wartime occupation, with continued expansion to the present day.

rice fields occur in areas not previously settled by Oecusse natives, and in these regions the *tobe-naijuf* authorities are not as well defined as in the highlands. As these fields are always individually owned, people from distant *suco* may purchase or sharecrop land in these areas. Irrigated rice fields are surrounded by constructed wood/stone fences as for swidden gardens; internal borders are clear with the low irrigation ridges that bound each plot.

The unusually abundant water in Lekot allowed flooded rice expansion near both mountain and coastal settlements. Irrigation was initiated in one unterraced highland site during the 1960s, with the first irrigated terraced rice field constructed in 1975. In 1975, one highland Lekot farmer who observed methods of rice production in lowland central Oecusse decided to terrace a tiny plot adjacent to a spring. Despite ridicule from other villagers, he persisted and planted that area three years in a row, by which time others believed it was possible and began to make small terraces for flooding on their own land. The technology caught on and the community slowly converted several areas into flooded rice fields over the past decades.[61]

All of the flooded rice fields in Lekot were conceived and constructed entirely with farmer initiative; none has ever received outside financial or technical assistance.[62] By 1999, there had been many hectares of rice fields constructed in six locations in Lekot, but more than half of that area was not in use, as the terraced land or the irrigation systems had been made unusable by landslides.[63] Anticipating food shortages from 2000–02 onwards, existing sites were expanded and three new sites were opened; in 2004, a major new scheme was under construction in the highlands, with plans to convert more than 200 ha of former swidden areas to flooded rice fields, encompassing land held by all 11 of the landowning Lekot *kanaf*. People in Lekot expect that this will transform their farming systems and reduce dependency on swidden fields, which many view as more subject to the vagaries of weather that destroys their crops (especially drought and lodging in high winds). While irrigation construction and initial field terracing are labour intensive, subsequent cultivation is considered much easier—and more productive—than making swidden gardens.

---

61 Lekot villagers insist that they are still unskilled wet rice cultivators, and that their planting style is slow and cumbersome. They say that when working side-by-side with people from primary rice-growing areas of central Oecusse, their relative lack of familiar dexterity in transplanting the rice is humorously obvious. To them, it is still largely an outsider, lowlander (*kaes metan*) technology.

62 Oecusse Agriculture Department staff never visited Lekot during Indonesian times, and they were amazed to learn after independence of such extensive flooded rice development in the highlands. This lack of government intervention is notable, given Indonesia's many programs—from transmigration to agricultural subsidies and farmer incentives—designed to promote wet rice cultivation in places with swidden cultivation or other crop staples (Aditjondro 1994; Li 1999).

63 There are many abandoned terraces in highland Lekot—by some estimates, twice as many abandoned terraces as productive terraces. One farmer likened Lekot people's treatment of terraces to swiddens that, without purchased fertiliser, needed to be left fallow.

Highland and lowland flooded rice fields are individually owned and may be sold for cash.[64] In the extensive rice fields of central Oecusse (but not Lekot), there are no restrictions on ownership or transaction by outside-*suco* residents or natives of other *suco*. Flooded rice fields also have unique gender representation among owners: many individual Lekot women have their own plots in Lekot and in the rice-growing *suco* of central Oecusse.

Village Commons or Unclaimed Land

Unclaimed land (*naija sona*) is that which has not yet been claimed by any *kanaf*.[65] Land remains *naija sona* only if it is bare, grassland, inaccessible, infertile, landslide prone or otherwise unsuitable for farming; even steep ravines, if forested, are always claimed by a *kanaf*. There is very little *naija sona* in the Oecusse highlands—mostly small landslide areas or useless patches of infertile soil. Since Oecusse's coast was sparsely settled before the Indonesian era, some *naija sona* persists on mountain ridges near the coast—a relic of the former interior-centric settlement pattern, which left distant coastal lands unused while fully occupying the highlands. *Naija sona* is not necessarily distant from settlements. On the coast, *naija sona* land can be adjacent to houses, where it is gradually claimed by individuals (via farming, planting trees, building structures or fencing) and converted to *seimu*. In coastal Lekot itself, more than 2 sq km of *naija sona* has been converted to individually held *seimu* since 1985. Along the Oecusse coast, *naija sona* is receding inland as lowland settlers continue agricultural expansion. Some *naija sona* areas are considered dangerous—home to troublesome spirits and best left undisturbed.

Members of the *suco* use *naija sona* as common land for grazing animals and gathering firewood or construction materials; one *naija sona* patch in highland Lekot cannot grow annual crops but is the source for a hardwood (*tas tasi*) preferred in house construction. Non-village residents may not use *naija sona* or its products without explicit permission from local government or customary authorities. All this land requires a local authority to approve its use by those outside the village, or its conversion to *seimu* by village members. Aware that Timorese planting trees would later consider the planted land as their own, the Portuguese administration forbade villagers' unauthorised tree planting along coastal areas of Lekot until the late 1960s in an effort to reduce people's claims to lowlands areas the state wanted for plantations or other purposes. Once land has been claimed through use and thus gained the status of *seimu*, it does not revert to *naija sona*, even if left uncultivated for many years.

---

64   More detail on changing tenure for flooded rice fields can be found in Meitzner Yoder (2005:214–25).
65   This term is sometimes also used for infertile, unused claimed land that is left bare, so ownership status must be clarified with more detailed questions.

Conclusion: Customary rural landholding in the modern policy context

The customary features governing land claims and resource management in most of contemporary Oecusse remain more influential in everyday land-use decisions than state designations of land areas for different purposes. State land-administration efforts that do not account for existing land claims and ownership systems risk enacting programs or legislation that bear little relevance to the local situation. Recent policy studies highlight the dangers of de-contextualised land policy, and emphasise the need for land-administration structures and policies that reflect, rather than seek to supplant, existing customary patterns (Meinzen-Dick and Mwangi 2008; Mwangi 2006).

Customary landownership is inextricably linked to social identity, place, historical ties and ritual connections. These factors are not fixed, but are constantly redefined in tandem with migration and changing circumstances. Agricultural developments, including irrigation or tree planting, are significant factors in rural landholding transformations. Intra-village claims to authority and agricultural patterns have shaped landownership and land-use relationships among residents within a domain.

The layering of political and ritual authorities, in evolving forms responsive to agricultural change, is a central feature of land access and use. All rural land—claimed or unclaimed through agriculture—is under the responsibility of at least two customary and/or state authorities who mediate land use and acquisition. The *tobe* and/or *naijuf*, other members of a *kanaf* and irrigation overseer (*cabo-oel*) might all need to be included in making land-management decisions, in additional to local government officials. Even today in peri-urban areas, formal land transactions usually involve the approval and legitimation of the relevant *tobe* and/or *naijuf*. New customary authorities, whether for rituals or irrigation, are designated as needed to give oversight to land use.

Persistent land claims are established through agriculture, settlement and labour. While initial landholding patterns are determined by agricultural use, landownership is subsequently rearranged through investments such as house building and installing irrigation or planting trees. Migration histories can help distinguish whether individually held areas are individuating, or merely newly claimed and evolving towards group ownership. The validity of a given claim is contingent on evidence of a wide range of factors: the claimants' past acquisition and inheritance, recent use, customary or government positions, political allegiances during recent conflicts, skills, initiative and labour contribution to group projects.

In Oecusse, highland land use reflects current agricultural practices more than landownership. Early settlers have favourable landowning status, and there are ownership restrictions on in-migrants. Farming in groups that form to fence swidden gardens means that landowners often do not plant on their own land, and that non-landowners presently enjoy unproblematic borrowing of land for annual cropping. The ease and frequency of temporary land borrowing contrast sharply with the near-impossible permanent acquisition of land by outsiders. Early settlers became established as eligible landowners, but the range of eligible landowning *kanaf* has closed. Newcomers—defined as people not native to the local *naijuf*'s domain—can be excluded from acquiring heritable rights to land even after four generations of residence. State land policies must account for such features: a modern land-administration program that titles land based on agricultural *use* at a given point in time would frequently misidentify the locally acknowledged customary landowner, and a program that simply formalises existing customary claims would exclude a significant portion of the population from ever owning land.

This case illustrates how land tenure and concepts of ownership are responsive to agricultural and demographic change. As people moved closer to urban areas and developed irrigation, they modified underlying land tenure and practices to accommodate the different requirements of permanent settlements and settled agriculture. Increasing population density also leads to agricultural change, which in turn further modifies land use and tenure across this diverse landscape. Nascent land-administration programs must be able to accommodate the substantial changes that occur if they are to have relevance among a dynamic population.

Acknowledgments

Fieldwork for this chapter was conducted between July 2001 and November 2004. I extend thanks to the Oecusse Government and customary authorities, and to multiple reviewers for helpful guidance. Research was funded by: a Yale University Doctoral Fellowship; a Fulbright-Hays Doctoral Dissertation Research Abroad Fellowship; an International Dissertation Field Research Fellowship, Social Science Research Council and the American Council of Learned Societies; a Dissertation Research Grant, Yale Center for International and Area Studies; a Mustard Seed Foundation Harvey Fellowship; a Southeast Asian Studies Doctoral Fellowship at the Research School of Pacific and Asian Studies, The Australian National University; and a Language Training Grant, Yale University Southeast Asia Program.

References

Anon. 1924, *Provincia de Timor: Compilação da Legislação Geral e Privativa desta Provincia sobre Concessões de Terrenos (Mandada publicar por P.P. No. 40 de 8 de Março de 1924)*, Imprensa Nacional Timor, Dili.

Aditjondro, G. J. 1994, *In the Shadow of Mount Ramelau: The impact of the occupation of East Timor*, Indonesian Documentation and Information Centre, Leiden, Netherlands.

Baumann, P. C. 1997, 'Historical evidence on the incidence and role of common property regimes in the Indian Himalayas', *Environment and History*, vol. 3, pp. 323–42.

Burling, R. 1965, *Hill Farms and Padi Fields: Life in mainland Southeast Asia*, Prentice-Hall, Englewood Cliffs, NJ.

Castro, A. D. 1867, *As Possessões Portuguezas na Oceania*, Imprensa Nacional, Lisboa.

Conklin, H. C. 1954, 'An ethnoecological approach to shifting agriculture', *Transactions of the New York Academy of Sciences*, vol. 17, no. 2, pp. 133–42.

Conklin, H. C. 1957, *Hanunóo Agriculture: A report on an integral system of shifting cultivation in the Philippines*, Food and Agriculture Organisation of the United Nations, Rome.

Dove, M. R. 1981, Subsistence strategies in rain forest swidden agriculture: the Kantu' at Tikul Batu, volume 1, Dissertation thesis, Stanford University, California.

Dove, M. R. 1984, 'Man, land and game in Sumbawa: some observations on agrarian ecology and development policy in eastern Indonesia', *Singapore Journal of Tropical Geography*, vol. 5, no. 2, pp. 112–24.

Dove, M. R. 1985, *Swidden Agriculture in Indonesia: The subsistence strategies of the Kalimantan Kantu*, Mouton, Berlin.

Fitzpatrick, D. 2002, *Land Claims in East Timor*, Asia Pacific Press, Canberra.

Fox, J. J. 1977, *Harvest of the Palm: Ecological change in eastern Indonesia*, Harvard University Press, Cambridge, Mass.

Fox, J. J. (ed.) 1980, *The Flow of Life: Essays on eastern Indonesia*, Harvard University Press, Cambridge, Mass.

Fox, J. J. 1996, 'The transformation of progenitor lines of origin: patterns of precedence in eastern Indonesia', in J. J. Fox and C. Sather (eds), *Origins, Ancestry and Alliance: Explorations in Austronesian ethnography*, Research School of Pacific and Asian Studies, The Australian National University, Canberra, pp. 130–53.

Fox, J. J. 1997, 'Place and landscape in comparative Austronesian perspective', in J. J. Fox, *The Poetic Power of Place: Comparative perspectives on Austronesian ideas of locality*, Research School of Pacific and Asian Studies, The Australian National University, Canberra, pp. 1–21.

Fox, J. J. 1999, 'Precedence in practice among the Atoni Pah Meto of Timor', in L. V. Aragon and S. D. Russell (eds), *Structuralism's Transformations: Order and revision in Indonesian and Malaysian societies. Papers written in honor of Clark E. Cunningham*, Arizona State University Program for Southeast Asian Studies, Tempe.

Francillon, G. 1980, 'Incursions upon Wehali: a modern history of an ancient empire', in J. J. Fox (ed.), *The Flow of Life: Essays on eastern Indonesia*, Harvard University Press, Cambridge, Mass., pp. 248–65.

Geertz, C. 1972, 'The wet and the dry: traditional irrigation in Bali and Morocco', *Human Ecology*, vol. 1, no. 1, pp. 23–39.

Gonçalves, L. d. C. 1937, 'Adatrecht van Portugeesch Timor. I. Direito consuetudinário dos indígenas de Timôr', *Adatrechtbundel*, vol. 39, pp. 443–74.

Griffiths, T. and Robin, L. (eds) 1997, *Ecology and Empire: Environmental history of settler societies*, Keele University Press, Edinburgh.

Hann, C. M. (ed.) 1998, *Property Relations: Renewing the anthropological tradition*, Cambridge University Press, Cambridge.

Healy, A. M. 1971, 'Land problems and land policies in Kenya and Papua New Guinea: a comparative historical perspective to 1963', in M. W. Ward (ed.), *Land Tenure and Economic Development: Problems and policies in Papua New Guinea and Kenya*, New Guinea Research Bulletin No. 40, New Guinea Research Unit, The Australian National University, Canberra, pp. 63–124.

Hooper, A. and Ward, R. G. 1995, 'Beyond the breathing space', in R. G. Ward and E. Kingdon (eds), *Land, Custom and Practice in the South Pacific*, Cambridge University Press, Cambridge, pp. 250–64.

Hutchinson, S. E. 1996, *Nuer Dilemmas: Coping with money, war, and the state*, University of California Press, Berkeley.

Kalinoe, L. and Leach, J. (eds) 2004, *Rationales of Ownership: Transactions and claims to ownership in contemporary Papua New Guinea*, Sean Kingston Publishing, Wantage, UK.

Lea, D. 1997, *Melanesian Land Tenure in a Contemporary and Philosophical Context*, University Press of America, Lanham, Md.

Leach, E. R. 1954, *Political Systems of Highland Burma: A study of Kachin social structure*, Harvard University Press, Cambridge, Mass.

Leach, E. R. 1960, 'The frontiers of "Burma"', *Comparative Studies in Society and History*, vol. 3, no. 1, pp. 49–68.

Leach, J. 2004a, 'Land, trees and history: disputes involving boundaries and identities in the context of development', in L. Kalinoe and J. Leach (eds), *Rationales of Ownership: Transactions and claims to ownership in contemporary Papua New Guinea*, Sean Kingston Publishing, Wantage, UK, pp. 42–56.

Leach, J. 2004b, 'Preface: rationales', in L. Kalinoe and J. Leach (eds), *Rationales of Ownership: Transactions and claims to ownership in contemporary Papua New Guinea*, Sean Kingston Publishing, Wantage, UK, pp. x–xi.

Li, T. M. (ed.) 1999, *Transforming the Indonesian Uplands: Marginality, power and production*, Harwood, Amsterdam.

McWilliam, A. 1996, 'Severed heads that germinate the state: history, politics, and headhunting in southwest Timor', in J. Hoskins (ed.), *Headhunting and the Social Imagination in Southeast Asia*, Stanford University Press, Stanford, Calif., pp. 127–66.

McWilliam, A. 2002, *Paths of Origin, Gates of Life: A study of place and precedence in southwest Timor*, KITLV Press, Leiden, Netherlands.

Martin, K. 2004, *Land, Custom and Conflict in East New Britain*, Resource Management in Asia-Pacific Program, Research School of Pacific and Asian Studies, The Australian National University, Canberra.

Martinho, J. S. 1943, *Timor: Quatro Séculos de Colonizacão Portuguesa*, Livraria Progredior, Pôrto.

Martinho, J. S. 1945, *Problemas Administrativos de Colonizacão da Provincia de Timor*, Livraria Progredior, Pôrto.

Meinzen-Dick, R. and Mwangi, E. 2008, 'Cutting the web of interests: pitfalls of formalizing property rights', *Land Use Policy*, vol. 26, no. 1, pp. 36–43.

Meitzner Yoder, L. S. 2005, Custom, codification, collaboration: integrating the legacies of land and forest authorities in Oecusse enclave, East Timor, PhD dissertation, Yale University, New Haven, Conn.

Meitzner Yoder, L. S. 2007a, 'Hybridising justice: state-customary interactions over forest crime and punishment in Oecusse, East Timor', *Asia Pacific Journal of Anthropology*, vol. 8, no. 1, pp. 43–57.

Meitzner Yoder, L. S. 2007b, 'The *tobe* and *tara bandu*: a post-independence renaissance of forest regulation authorities and practices in Oecusse, East Timor', in R. Ellen (ed.), *Modern Crises and Traditional Strategies: Local ecological knowledge in island Southeast Asia*, Berghahn, New York, pp. 220–37.

Metzner, J. K. 1977, *Man and Environment in Eastern Timor: A geoecological analysis of the Baucau-Viqueque area as a possible basis for regional planning*, The Australian National University, Canberra.

Mwangi, E. (ed.) 2006, *Land rights for African development: from knowledge to action*, CAPRi Policy Briefs, CGIAR, Washington, DC.

O'Meara, J. T. 1995, 'From corporate to individual land tenure in Western Samoa', in R. G. Ward and E. Kingdon (eds), *Land, Custom and Practice in the South Pacific*, Cambridge University Press, Cambridge.

Ormeling, F. J. 1956, *The Timor Problem: A geographical interpretation of an underdeveloped island*, J. B. Wolters and Martinus Nijhoff, Groningen and The Hague.

Panão, A. F. 1915, 'Timor: agricultura indigena', *Revista Colonial*, vol. 3, no. 30, pp. 198–200.

Peluso, N. L. 2003, 'Fruit trees and family trees in an anthropogenic forest: property zones, resource access, and environmental change in Indonesia', in C. Zerner (ed.), *Culture and the Question of Rights: Forests, coasts, and seas in Southeast Asia*, Duke University Press, Durham, NC, pp. 184–218.

Reid, A. 1997, 'Inside out: the colonial displacement of Sumatra's population', in P. Boomgaard, F. Colombijn and D. Henley (eds), *Paper Landscapes: Explorations in the environmental history of Indonesia*, KITLV Press, Leiden, Netherlands, pp. 61–89.

Rodman, M. C. 1987, *Masters of Tradition: Consequences of customary land tenure in Longana, Vanuatu*, University of British Columbia Press, Vancouver.

Roseman, M. 1998, 'Singers of the landscape: song, history, and property rights in the Malaysian rain forest', *American Anthropologist*, vol. 100, pp. 106–21.

Saldanha, J. M. and Guterres, P. 2002, *Customary Property Rights and Agricultural Production: A tale of two sub-districts in East Timor*, Center for Economic Studies, East Timor Study Group, Dili.

Schulte Nordholt, H. G. 1971, *The Political System of the Atoni of Timor*, Martinus Nijhoff, The Hague.

Scott, J. C. 2009, *The Art of Not Being Governed: An anarchist history of upland Southeast Asia*, Yale University Press, New Haven, Conn.

Shamir, R. 1996, 'Suspended in space: Bedouins under the law of Israel', *Law and Society Review*, vol. 30, pp. 231–57.

Silva, J. C. d. 1897, *Relatorio das Operações de Guerra no Districto Autónomo de Timor no Anno de 1896, Enviado ao Ministro e Secretario D'Estado dos Negocios da Marinha e Ultramar pelo Governador do Mesmo Districto*, Imprensa Nacional, Ministerio dos Negócios da Marinha e Ultramar, Lisboa.

Simpson, S. R. 1971, 'Land problems in Papua New Guinea', in M. W. Ward (ed.), *Land Tenure and Economic Development: Problems and policies in Papua New Guinea and Kenya*, New Guinea Research Bulletin No. 40, New Guinea Research Unit, The Australian National University, Canberra, pp. 1–36.

Sousa Xavier, P. d. 1997, Studi tentang Hukum Pertanahan Adat Timor Timur di Kecamatan Uato Carbau Kabupaten Viqueque, Dissertation thesis, Sekolah Tinggi Pertanahan Nasional, Yogyakarta.

Strathern, M. 1998, 'Divisions of interest and languages of ownership', in C. M. Hann (ed.), *Property Relations: Renewing the anthropological tradition*, Cambridge University Press, Cambridge, pp. 214–32.

Strathern, M. 1999, *Property, Substance and Effect: Anthropological essays on persons and things*, Athlone Press, London and New Brunswick, NJ.

Strathern, M. 2004, 'Introduction: rationales of ownership', in L. Kalinoe and J. Leach (eds), *Rationales of Ownership: Transactions and claims to ownership in contemporary Papua New Guinea*, Sean Kingston Publishing, Wantage, UK, pp. 1–12.

Sumardjono, M. S. W., Suyitno Iswanto, H., Widodo, W., Sudjito Ismail, N., Bosko, R. E. and Listyawati, H. 1994–95, *Report on research into Adat land law of East Timor*, [Unofficial translation], National Land Agency and Faculty of Law of Gajah Mada University, Yogyakarta.

Suryosuwarno, P. 1993, *Pemilikan Tanah di Timor Timur (edisi II)*, Kantor Wilayah Badan Pertanahan Nasional, Propinsi Timor Timur, Dili.

Susanto, A. S. 1994–95, *Analisa dan Evaluasi Hukum tentang Transaksi Tanah Adat di Timor Timur*, Badan Pembinaan Hukum Nasional, Departemen Kehakiman Republik Indonesia, Jakarta.

ter Haar, B. 1948, *Adat Law in Indonesia*, Institute of Pacific Relations, New York.

Traube, E. G. 1986, *Cosmology and Social Life: Ritual exchange among the Mambai of East Timor*, University of Chicago Press, Chicago and London.

Tsing, A. L. 2003, 'Cultivating the wild: honey-hunting and forest management in southeast Kalimantan', in C. Zerner (ed.), *Culture and the Question of Rights: Forests, coasts, and seas in Southeast Asia*, Duke University Press, Durham, NC, pp. 24–55.

Ubbe, A. 1995–96, *Laporan akhir penyusunan monografi hukum adat di Timor Timur*, Badan Pembinaan Hukum Nasional, Departemen Kehakiman Republik Indonesia, Jakarta.

Van Trease, H. 1987, *The Politics of Land in Vanuatu: From colony to independence*, Institute of Pacific Studies of the University of the South Pacific, Suva.

van Wouden, F. A. E. 1968, *Types of Social Structure in Eastern Indonesia*, Martinus Nijhoff, The Hague.

Vaquinhas, J. d. S. 1883, 'I: Timor', *Boletim da Sociedade de Geographia de Lisboa*, vol. 4, no. 7, pp. 307–28.

Vaquinhas, J. d. S. 1884, 'O Sr. Major José dos Santos Vaquinhas', *O Macaense, Macau*, vol. II, no. 95, p. 210.

Vargas, D. M. 1985, The interface of customary and national land law in East Kalimantan, Indonesia, Dissertation thesis, Yale University, New Haven, Conn.

Ward, R. G. 1995, 'Land, law and custom: diverging realities in Fiji', in R. G. Ward and E. Kingdon (eds), *Land, Custom and Practice in the South Pacific*, Cambridge University Press, Cambridge, pp. 198–249.

Ward, R. G. and Kingdon, E. (eds) 1995a, *Land, Custom and Practice in the South Pacific*, Cambridge University Press, Cambridge.

Ward, R. G. and Kingdon, E. 1995b, 'Land use and tenure: some comparisons', in R. G. Ward and E. Kingdon (eds), *Land, Custom and Practice in the South Pacific*, Cambridge University Press, Cambridge, pp. 6–35.

Weiner, J. F. 1999, 'Culture in a sealed envelope: the concealment of Australian Aboriginal heritage and tradition in the Hindmarsh Island Bridge affair', *Journal of the Royal Anthropological Institute*, vol. 5, no. 2, pp. 193–210.

Weinstock, J. A. 1979, Land tenure practices of the swidden cultivators of Borneo, Dissertation thesis, Cornell University, Ithaca, NY.

West, H. G. 1998, '"This neighbor is not my uncle!": changing relations of power and authority on the Mueda Plateau', *Journal of Southern African Studies*, vol. 24, no. 1, pp. 141–60.

West, H. G. and Kloeck-Jenson, S. 1999, 'Betwixt and between: "traditional authority" and democratic decentralization in post-war Mozambique', *African Affairs*, vol. 98, pp. 455–84.

Wolters, O. W. 1999, *History, Culture, and Region in Southeast Asian Perspectives*, Southeast Asia Program, Cornell University, Ithaca, New York.

Zerner, C. 1994, 'Through a green lens: the construction of customary environmental law and community in Indonesia's Maluku Islands', *Law and Society Review*, vol. 28, no. 5, pp. 1079–122.

Zerner, C. (ed.) 2003a, *Culture and the Question of Rights: Forests, coasts, and seas in Southeast Asia*, Duke University Press, Durham, NC.

Zerner, C. 2003b, 'Moving translations: poetics, performance, and property in Indonesia and Malaysia', in C. Zerner (ed.), *Culture and the Question of Rights: Forests, coasts, and seas in Southeast Asia*, Duke University Press, Durham, NC, pp. 1–23.

10. Struggling Geographies: Rethinking livelihood and locality in Timor-Leste

Sandra Pannell

A Geography which Struggles I: Introduction

The island of Timor could be regarded—to borrow Edward Said's expression—as a 'geography which struggles' (1993:6). Our understanding of this geography is dominated by a discourse of destruction and degradation. Writings about the island and its people commonly talk about the 'Timor tragedy' or the 'Timor problem'. As James Dunn's account reveals, the tragedy of Timor (see Dunn 1983:xi) is a story of gross injustice and local suffering, linked to the dismal failure of the international community to respond to Indonesia's invasion of East Timor in 1974. Since independence in 2002, it seems that 'poverty and unemployment' are contributing to a 'new tragedy' in one of the world's latest nation-states (BBC n.d.).

Timor's 'problem', on the other hand, is said to be an island-wide ecological crisis, caused by swidden agricultural systems and population pressure.[1] While the notion that local shifting cultivation systems in the 'Outer Islands' were inherently fragile and maladaptive to increasing population was first identified by F. J. Ormeling in 1956, it was Clifford Geertz's study of ecological change in Indonesia that popularised the idea (Geertz 1963). While not intended as such, Geertz's conclusions about swidden agriculture appeared to reinforce existing and overly negative European perceptions of these systems as primarily 'attended by serious deforestation and soil erosion' (Geertz 1963:15–16).

The characterisation of local subsistence systems as 'voracious slash-and-burn agricultural regime[s]', with 'low agrarian production' (McWilliam 2002:1), responsible for Timor's environmental 'problem', has prompted a significant national and international development effort aimed at changing local land-use practices and improving the country's economic circumstances. Yet, as delegates attending Timor-Leste's first conference on 'Sustainable Development and the

---

1   As both Fox (1977) and Friedberg (1977) point out, however, colonial policies and actions in both East and West Timor played an important—often overlooked—role in the creation of this crisis, in symbolic and empirical terms.

Environment', held in Dili in 2001, identified, '400 years of colonization by Portugal, and 25 years of occupation by Indonesia' (Anderson and Deutsch 2001:11; see also McWilliam 2003:308) have also contributed to the process of ecological degradation and resulted in substantial changes to local subsistence practices. For example, Fox (2000:24) reports that during the latter part of the Portuguese colonial period, the Government initiated a series of agricultural extension programs in an attempt to 'induce a shift of population' to the least-populated southern coast of Timor. While the ecological and population density variability found across Timor-Leste was perhaps not an intended consequence of such social displacements, colonial resettlement schemes have, in part, contributed to the situation wherein the Lautem district in the far east of the country has one of the lowest population densities and some of the more extensive forested and coastal resources of all the regions in Timor-Leste. In the period of Indonesian occupation, as Soares (2001:20) points out, napalm bombing and forced resettlement practices by the military 'saw a mass destruction of the environment' and resulted in widespread famine. Dunn (1983:338) also comments upon the 'rapacious exploitation' of sandalwood and other forest-based resources, which the Timorese traditionally depended on for their livelihood, during this period. Speaking of livelihoods, both Soares and Fox report that traditional identities, constructed around particular modes of livelihood, have been severely eroded over the past 25 years as a result of population movements and a greater emphasis upon rice and commercial crops, such as coffee (Fox 2000:25; Soares 2001:19–20). Indeed, Shepard Forman (1981:87) goes so far as to conclude that for the Makassae of Timor-Leste, with the loss of their means of livelihood during the period of occupation, 'the cycle of production and exchange which reproduces life has been broken'.

While the Sustainable Development conference delegates emphasised the rampant 'destruction' (Anderson and Deutsch 2001:20) of the environment resulting from this history of colonisation and forced occupation, it is a history that also alerts us to the adaptive nature of Timorese subsistence practices. For many so-called 'farming' communities throughout Timor-Leste, critical to their survival throughout this turbulent history was a reliance upon a variety of resources gained from hunting-and-gathering activities in local forests and woodlands, waterways and inshore marine areas.

The anthropological and economic literature on East Timorese societies is somewhat silent about these practices, often depicting shifting cultivation as the sole means of subsistence or as the predominant 'life paradigm' (Forman 1981:96). Certainly, in some areas of Timor-Leste today—for example, in central Ainaro and in heavily populated areas of Bobonaro, where deforestation and extensive cultivation have led to an almost complete reliance upon swidden or seasonal dryland agriculture, and the concomitant attenuation of non-agricultural subsistence practices—this is increasingly the day-to-day reality (A. McWilliam, Personal communication). While historically local people in these areas might have pursued more diverse subsistence practices, population pressure and the expansion of the amount of land under intensive cultivation have effectively served to narrow local livelihood options.

As Fox (1977:17) points out, however, in characterising Indonesian ecological systems as based upon wet rice cultivation or swidden agriculture, other 'important ecological systems in the outer islands' are neglected. Some idea of the existence of these other systems is apparent in the written record where, as the pages of history indicate, an agricultural-centric model of Timorese life has not always predominated. For example, on the voyage of the Dutch brig-of-war *Dourga* to Portuguese Timor in 1825, Kolff, the commander of the expedition, commented upon the 'neglect' of agriculture in the districts around Dili. Kolff writes that while the land was 'highly fertile', it appeared to him that the Portuguese were too 'indolent' to turn their attention to agriculture, while the 'natives' were too engaged in the local, highly profitable slave trade to bother with such pursuits (Kolff 1840:38). From Kolff's account, it is clear that Portuguese Government officials derived a considerable portion of their income from the slave trade, and also from the commerce in beeswax and sandalwood, which local people were 'forced to deliver up at a small, and almost minimal price' (p. 35).[2]

On his visit to East Timor in 1861, Alfred Russell Wallace also reports upon this latter commerce, stating that 'almost the only exports of Timor are sandal-wood and bees'-wax' (1872:199). Identifying beeswax as the more 'valuable' and 'important' of these two products, Wallace provides a detailed and vivid description of native men harvesting honey and wax from a wild bee colony in the forests above Dili.[3] Sandalwood and wax are also mentioned as two of the products of Timor recorded by Pigafetta in 1522, while one of the first European references to Timorese sandalwood, dating from 1518, identifies 'sanders-wood, honey, wax, slaves and also a certain amount of silver' (Dames 1921:195–6) as traded items from the island.[4] Some 300 years later, George Grey, summarising the state of trade in the Indian archipelago, reports that the produce of Timor consists of 'goats, pigs, poultry, maize, paddy [sic], yams, plaintains, fruit, sandal-wood, bees-wax and tortoiseshell' (Grey 1841: vol. 1, p. 282).

---

2   Some 150 years later, a similar situation existed in Indonesian-occupied East Timor with respect to the small, but profitable coffee industry. As Dunn reports, the income from this industry 'became an important source of private gain to a group of senior [Indonesian] military officers' (1983:337).
3   Gunn (1999:115) reports that in the early nineteenth century, more than 20 000 *piculs* (a local measure of weight, equivalent to 137 lb, according to Echols and Shadily [1990:428]) of beeswax was exported annually from Portuguese ports in Timor.
4   Other products recorded by Pigafetta are 'ginger, buffaloes, pigs, goats, fowls, rice, bananas, sugarcane, organs, lemons…almonds, beans and gold' (cited in Glover 1986:11).

In the twentieth century, Ian Glover makes mention of non-agricultural subsistence practices in East Timor, and discusses how caves are used 'as temporary camps for parties out hunting in the dry season' (1986:206). According to Glover (1986:206–7), 'cave occupation reflected mostly the hunting and collecting aspects of life', which he believes did not reflect the 'total Timorese way of life'. In contrast, the Portuguese archaeologist Antonio de Almeida (1957:241) found that hunting and fishing by the inhabitants of East Timor contributed to a 'great part of their maintenance'. Almeida discusses at length communal hunting of deer, boar and buffaloes, and reports upon the local procurement of shrimps, eels, fish, lobsters, oysters, crabs, turtles and tuna from the rivers, fresh and saltwater lagoons and the seas of East Timor.

Like Almeida, McWilliam (2001:89) observes that so-called swidden agriculturalists 'continue to draw heavily on the existing diminishing forest resources'. He also suggests, however, that the exploitation of forest-based resources for firewood, building materials and natural medicines and for 'supplementary hunting' is contributing to the 'deteriorating condition of forest ecology' (2001:90). Other accounts—notably by members of the Government's forestry unit—give the impression that these activities are relatively recent, and that local people are forced to exploit forest resources as a result of unemployment and high prices for staple items (Martins 2001:32), producing even further environmental degradation.

The anthropologist Claudine Friedberg (1989) is one of the few writers to explore the relationship between the activities that take place in these forested areas and agricultural practices. As Friedberg discusses, among the non–Austronesian-speaking Bunaq, whose traditional lands fall around the southern border area, agriculture is dependent upon the ritual hunting of wild pigs and the gathering of forest fruits and medicinal plants. Critical to local ritual is the exchange of these non-cultivated items with the ancestors of the 'upperworld' and between members of the village community prior to the sowing and harvesting of the rice and maize crops. Friedberg's discussion points to a more integrated view of subsistence, where hunting and gathering and agricultural cultivation are interdependent and mutually linked to the reproduction of the village's social and territorial integrity. Critical to this view are the interpenetration of economic and cultural activities, and the role of such productive actions in the creation of cultural values and social identities.

In this sense, Bunaq farming rituals represent the ongoing work required in the 'production of locality' and a distinctive subjectivity or 'sense of place' (see Appadurai 1996). As Appadurai points out, place is produced through the intersection of social relations, expressions of identity and the practice of culture. As the Bunaq example illustrates, the production of locality thus involves various relationships to land and landed practices, not simply those designated as 'swidden agriculture' or characterised as 'hunting and gathering' in the dualistic framework of the 'subsistence economy' discourse.

Acknowledging the problem with isolating and packaging specific practices as such and thus disregarding the social and cultural context in which knowledge is generated and put to practical use, in this chapter, I propose to adopt a more holistic view of subsistence than previously reported. For example, in a recent paper focused on the Fataluku-speaking[5] districts of Com and Méhara, Pannell and O'Connor (2005:196–7) briefly reported on inshore reef fishing and littoral-zone foraging, and observed that 'various species of game birds, together with deer, wild pigs, monkeys, civet cat and cuscus are regularly hunted by local people'. Also commenting on the subsistence practices of Fataluku people in the Lautem district, McWilliam (2006:2) reports that hunting in the forests and coastal margins is regularly undertaken and he states that the local population relies on a 'wide variety of forest products'. While these references to Fataluku hunting-and-gathering practices constitute notable exceptions in the overall literature, there is a strong suggestion that these activities are merely secondary or supplementary to agricultural production.

Once again focusing upon the Fataluku-speaking district of Lautem, and more specifically the *posto* or 'subdistrict' of Tutuala, I aim to make more visible those livelihood practices eclipsed by the prevailing and materially visible picture of cleared fields and unproductive farmers.[6] In this chapter, I attempt to explore the more varied and dynamic nature of local patterns of 'making a living'.[7] An integral element in these patterns of productive action is the shifting and recycled nature of the Fatluku landscape, as a back-and-forth movement between garden and forest. As I discuss, this recursive movement is not confined to so-called 'subsistence practices'; it is also a key structuring leitmotif in local engagements

---

5   Throughout this chapter, I adopt the orthography identified by the Fataluku Language Project, a community-based project conducted under the auspices of the Instituto Nacional de Linguística at the Universidade Nacional Timor Lorosa'e. This project is sponsored by the Endangered Languages Program of the Netherlands Organisation for Scientific Research (NWO) and involves professional linguists from the University of Leiden. The orthography developed by this project differs slightly from the one used by researchers at the Language Documentation Center at the University of Hawai'i at Manoa for the Fataluku language.

6   Michael Dove (1983) provides an insightful critique of the view of shifting cultivation as a delinquent pattern of resource extraction and its practitioners as wasteful and unproductive.

7   Tutuala is one of five *posto* or subdistricts in the district of Lautem (the other *posto* are Iliomar, Lautem, Lospalos and Luro). The district of Lautem has a population of some 57 453 residents (as of 2004), and a population density of 33.8 inhabitants per sq km, making it one of the least-populated areas in Timor-Leste. Previously, the district capital was Lautem, but for some time now Lospalos has performed this function. Each subdistrict is divided into a number of villages (*suco*), which in turn might contain several hamlets (*aldéia*). The *posto* of Tutuala includes the *suco* of Tutuala, Mehara and Maupitine. The administrative head of the subdistrict, the *chefe do posto*, resides in Tutuala. In the nested structure of local government in Timor-Leste, each *suco* and *aldéia* also has an administrative head (the *chefo do suco* and *chefe do aldéia*, respectively). The *suco* of Tutuala comprises the hamlets (*aldéia*) of Pitileti, Ioro, Vero and Cailoro.

with a series of state regimes (that is, the Portuguese and Indonesian colonial administrations), and in the stories Fataluku people tell of how they survived these encounters.

Like the Bunaq context, in Tutuala, these projects of place making are mediated by a quotidian engagement with the non-human beings endemic to this part of the Timorese landscape. As Friedberg's discussion indicates, the 'life-force' emanating from these beings traverses social groups and 'cuts across village boundaries', blurring any sense of local places and livelihood practices as immutable, bounded or homogenous. These references to a sentient landscape alert us to the limitations of a strictly subsistence-focused discourse.

Unlike the Bunaq example, however, I also discuss elements of Fataluku productive action in the context of some of the political fields in which they reside and struggle. In this respect, I focus upon the strategic role of Fataluku hunting and gathering during the period of Indonesian occupation and the significance accorded these forms of indigenous labour within certain contested spaces by the newly formed Government of Timor-Leste. As I hope to demonstrate, to paraphrase Elizabeth Povinelli, Fataluku people's productive encounters with the landscape provide them with a way of 'attending to and ensuring the physical, mythical, and emotional production of the environment, the human body, and the social group in the midst of ecological adversity and sometimes horrendous historical upheavals' (Povinelli 1993:30).

As I discuss, the diverse nature of Fataluku economic practices—entailing and blending agricultural and hunter-gatherer type activities—provides the kind of subsistence flexibility that enables local people to deal with chronic environmental uncertainty. In this respect, Fataluku livelihood practices perhaps have more in common with the lontar economies of outer arc islands to the west of Timor than they do with swidden systems on the island itself (see Fox 1977).[8]

The diverse and flexible nature of the Fataluku system also provides local people with the means to cope with radical political change. This flexibility certainly facilitated local, forest-based resistance to the Indonesian occupation in the period 1975–99, particularly given the Indonesian military's 'search-and-destroy' missions, mounted with the 'deliberate aim' of destroying local food crops and domestic animals (Dunn 1983:307).[9] While local Falintil members relied upon their extensive knowledge of forest foods and medicines and their

---

8   As Fox discusses in his ethnography *Harvest of the Palm* (1977), the lontar-focused economies of Roti and Savu are 'marvelously stable and adaptive', in contrast with the 'slash-and-burn' agricultural economies found on the neighbouring islands of Timor and Sumba, which have 'led to steady ecological deterioration'.
9   Dunn (1983:336) reports that the water buffalo population of East Timor declined from 150 000 in the mid-1970s to less than 25 000 by 1981.

expert hunting skills to survive and defeat the numerically superior Indonesian forces, in post-independence Timor-Leste (see Collins et al. 2007; Pannell and O'Connor 2005), as I discuss in the concluding sections of this chapter, these once-regarded heroic elements of Fataluku subsistence are now, paradoxically, under threat from the nation-building activities of one of the world's newest democracies.

Alahu and Tahi

The agrarian image of Timorese society is reinforced by the overall impression presented in the literature that Timor-Leste comprises a 'harsh', drought-ridden landscape that has been cleared, cultivated and, ultimately, degraded by the actions of humans.[10] Yet, throughout this same countryside can be found extensive tracts of primary rainforest and montane cloud forest, as well as swathes of secondary vegetative growth, watered by the 'double monsoon' experienced in Timor-Leste and on the neighbouring islands of eastern Indonesia (McWilliam 2003:309, 311). Reported upon by several commentators from as early as 1885 (see Forbes 1989 [1885]:454), many of these forest 'groves' are said to persist into the present because of the 'lulic'[11] or 'sacred' status accorded them by the local custodial community (see also Glover 1986:21; King 1963:148–50; McWilliam 2001:90, 2003:311; Metzner 1977:98; Ormeling 1956:85; Therik 2000; Traube 1980:295). As the naturalist Henry Forbes discovered—much to his disappointment—a range of ritual prohibitions exists regarding access to and use of forested tracts designated as lulic.

'Sacred' or tei forests also exist throughout the district of Lautem, which is a fertile and well-watered region, supporting large expanses of primary and secondary-growth forest. In the Fataluku language, there are a number of terms used to describe forested spaces that do not specifically conform to the scientific classification of forest as 'primary', 'secondary', and so on.[12] The general term for forest is alahu. Hoto is a term that is also used to describe forest generally, but it also, more specifically, refers to 'wilderness', while forests containing wild

---

10 To some extent, this is a perspective based upon the more populous north coast and its hinterlands, which, in contrast with the extended periods of rainfall experienced in the mountain areas and on the southern coast, is visited by 'long stretches of seasonal drought' (McWilliam 2003:309).

11 Lulic is a Tetun word and equivalent terms exist in the other languages spoken in Timor-Leste (see McWilliam 2001).

12 In a similar manner, Friedberg (1979:85) observes that among the Bunaq, plants are classified according to a 'complex web of resemblances and affinities', rather than according to a 'tree-like system of hierarchical categories', as represented by the Linnaean system of taxonomy.

animals are known as *caikeri*. Forest containing large, closed-canopy trees is called *irinu*[13]—a reference to the mature or 'old' (*irine*) status of these trees, while young, regrowing brush is called *totoku*.

Throughout these forests grow economically important stands of bamboo (*liru*—four species are identified by informants), sugar palm (*tua ma'arau*), tamarind (*kailemu*) and timber (*ete*). The forest is also home to various species of game birds (*aca hoto*), together with deer (*vaka hoto*), wild pigs (*pai hoto*), monkeys (*lua*), bats (*maca*), civet cat (*pusa hoto*) and cuscus (*acuru*), which are regularly hunted by local people. Fataluku men collect, in addition to these faunal and floral resources, beeswax[14] (*vani capu*) and honey (*vani ira*), the nests of swallows (*lelilawu*), building materials, root dyes, and medicinal (*eteasa*)[15] and poisonous plants from the forest, and, in more recent times, graze buffalo (*arapou*) throughout this area.

Throughout the forest important subsistence resources such as lontar palms (*kakalu*), bamboo stands and coconut palms, as well as former garden sites (*pala*), are marked by ritual signs called *lupurasa*. *Lupurasa* signs, such as young coconuts and monkey skulls, warn others against using the marked object. Ignoring this warning is said to result in injury, sickness and sometimes death. According to informants, *ratu* groups possess their own distinctive *lupurasa* signs.

In the Tutuala area, the forested landscape extends to the coast, and embraces both the 'male sea' (*tahi calu*) in the south (the Timor Sea) and the 'female sea' (*tahi tupuru*) in the north (the Strait of Wetar). Fataluku men and women regularly walk down the series of uplifted limestone terraces to fish for both demersal and pelagic species, hunt for turtles, octopus and crustaceans, and collect various species of shellfish in the intertidal zone and on the fringing reefs. In late February and March, the Fataluku-speaking communities in the Tutuala area and beyond collectively participate in the ceremonial harvesting of sea worms (*meci*). While the reef-based subsistence activities of Tutuala residents were photographed by members of the Siboga Expedition more than 100 years ago (in January 1900) (Weber 1902), recent archaeological evidence, however, points to a local reliance upon marine resources spanning a period of more than 30 000 years (S. O'Connor, Personal communication; see also O'Connor and Veth 2005).

---

13 In his word list from Oirata, a 'Timorese Settlement on Kisar', Josselin de Jong (1937:24) records *irim(i)* as the word for 'forest, bush' and also the term for 'old'. *Iririmi* is given as the term for 'brushwood'.

14 Earl (1853:182–3) reports that in the 1850s 'quasi-Papuan tribes' from 'Kapalla Tanah' or the far eastern point of the island of Timor—in other words, Fataluku speakers—traded beeswax with traders from the 'Serwatty Islands' (the Southwestern Islands north-east of Timor, including Leti, Moa and Lakor).

15 A recent ethno-botanical study of medicinal and poisonous plants used by the East Timorese resistance, undertaken in the proposed Nino Conis Santana National Park in the Lautem district of Timor-Leste, identified more than 40 medicinal and poisonous plants (see Collins et al. 2007).

Hunting (*haware*) and gathering in the coastal zone are facilitated by the use of wooden canoes and boats (*loiasu*),[16] bamboo spears (*api coro*) and handlines, while dogs, blowpipes (*tutufa*), airguns, metal spears (*coro*) and twine traps (*hilu*) are used to hunt deer, monkeys and pigs in the forest.

In the forest and along the coast, Fataluku hunter-gatherers obtain water from a range of sources, including permanent springs (*ira ina*) emerging at an altitude of about 300 m in the uplifted limestone terraces; a number of spring-fed sources along the coast accessible only at low tide; seasonal rockholes (*piaru*) (often protected with a rock lid); ephemeral creeks and rivers (*veru*); temporary rain-filled depressions (*luri*); drip seepage (*cupucupu*) and drip-fed pools in caves.

Local people know the forested and coastal environment of the Tutuala region in terms of a series of named locales. Names for an identified area often derive from that of a former settlement located within the area. Conversely, some former, pre-Portuguese settlements, such as Tutuhala, take their name from a nearby mythological site, which also defines the identity of the general locale. In some cases, locality names derive from specific environmental features. Throughout the forests of the Tutuala region, locales might also be known by the name of an individual *tei* site.

Tei are seen as malevolent and motivated forces, which occupy pre-existing places within the local landscape. They are said to 'guard' an area and the people of the clan group or *ratu* associated with it. *Ratu* members perform rituals at the *tei* to ensure prosperity, fertility and good health. While *tei* are often described as 'wild' or *hoto*, and many are said to be located throughout the forest, *tei*-based rituals involve 'feeding' these non-human beings with domesticated foodstuffs, such as 'rice, eggs, pig meat and palm spirit' (Pannell 2006:208). To 'cool' the *tei*, however, it is necessary to 'feed' (*fane*) it uncooked (*u'ureke*) food. Ceremonies conducted at *tei* sites are not just for humans, but also for the environment as a whole. As such, the cultural beliefs and social practices associated with *tei* have wider ecological effects. As this suggests, for Fataluku people, nature and culture do not exist as separate realms of meaning or practice. The landscape of the Tutuala region bears testimony to the indivisible relationship that exists between the physical environment and local traditions. The existence of extensive tracts of forested land as an integral part of this landscape is not just, however, a function of the protection offered through the local value placed upon 'sacred groves'. As I discuss in this chapter, the concept of *lulic*, or *tei* in Fataluku, is inextricably linked to other cultural conventions, social relations and place-making activities.

---

16   *Loi* is the term for 'boat' in the Austronesian language spoken on the island of Leti (van Engelenhoven 1997:14). Josselin de Jong (1937:270) gives '*rusunu*' as the term for a 'native boat' or 'canoe' in the Fataluku language spoken in the village of Oirata on the island of Kisar. As McWilliam (2007:6) points out, there is considerable lexical borrowing from Austronesian languages in contemporary Fataluku speech.

As discussed in this section, in the Tutuala area, forests also persist because social identities are forged in these spaces and 'they take on the complexity of associations with the forest landscape as a fabric of diverse social and natural resources' (Tsing 1993:62). Thus, in post-independence Timor-Leste, despite a history of social dislocation, violent political ruptures and ongoing economic instability, the forests of Tutuala continue to support a range of traditional livelihood practices. Moreover, these spaces provide a tangible environment for the situated expression of Fataluku values about locality and local subjects. In the recent past, these values were also realised in the context of labile, forest-based communities, known as *lata*.

Lata

The popular characterisation of Timorese society as agrarian conveys a sense of stable human settlement, with social identities forged in domesticated villages. In the subdistrict of Tutuala, however, permanent village enclaves date mostly from the later period of Portuguese rule—post 1945—intensified during the first years of the Indonesian occupation, and are linked to the efforts of the governing authorities to practically control the populace through their resettlement on the edges of roads or along the coast. It is important to realise here that until World War II (and for some years afterwards) the occupation of the inhabitants of the Tutuala area was still focused upon foundation or ancestral centres located deep within the forest.

In contrast with the idea of fixed agrarian communities—heavily promoted and forcibly implemented during the Indonesian period (see Dunn 1983:336)—the oral histories of Tutuala-based *ratu* or 'clan groups' are stories about mobility, recalling as they do the establishment and abandonment of occupation sites by specific *ratu* as they moved throughout the forested upland areas of Tutuala. These sites include former walled and current open settlements (*lata*), caves (*veraka*) occupied by ancestral figures, and rock shelters and caves used in prehistory and during the Japanese and Indonesian occupations of the island. Several former settlements are also found on Jaco Island (Totina). *Lata* and other site types provided the ritual and occupation focus for dispersed kin groups exploiting the surrounding forests and tending nearby swidden gardens (*pala*). Former walled settlements also contain circumscribed ceremonial spaces called *sepu* and ancestral graves (*calu lutur* or *narunu*), while both settlements and the caves occupied by Fataluku ancestors contain guardian *tei* sites (*lata toton*). As additional elements to the stone walls that apparently served to fortify *lata*, several species of cacti (*latu*)—each possessing different repellent properties— were planted along and around the perimeter enclosure.[17]

A number of these stone-fortified settlements in the Tutuala area have been test pitted and/or material has been obtained from within the perimeter of the stone walls for dating. Results of radiocarbon dating on marine shell and charcoal and optically stimulated luminescence (OSL) dating of pottery from the test-pitted sites suggest that the fortified structures began to be constructed about 1300 AD.[18] They appear to have been erected and used into the historical period, and some were still in use until the middle of the twentieth century (Lape 2006). As McWilliam (2003:311) points out, 'inter-domain feuding and warfare… encouraged widespread settlement of small populations in strategic defensive locations on barricaded hilltops'. While these ancestral settlement sites are no longer permanently occupied, *ratu* members regularly perform rituals and ceremonies at the *tei* and gravesites located within these walled settlements.

These former, named settlements are often described by present-day Fataluku speakers as *lata irata*—not only a reference to the 'overgrown' (*irinu*)[19] status of these previous occupation sites, but also a statement about the integrated nature of forests and human settlement in this part of Timor-Leste. Like the situation described by Valeri (2000:15) for the Huaulu in Seram, the forest here also claims 'back the spaces that humans have managed, at one point, to cut out of it'. In this sense, the forests of the Tutuala district are imbued with a history of human movement, occupation and use. The history of these forests is not just a story about the journeys taken and settlements occupied by *ratu* groups, but it is also a story about gardens and gardening.

---

17   On a visit to the former settlement of Locami, informants identified five different species of cacti (*latu*)— *latu irinu*, *latu uku*, *latu pokala*, *latu lépenu* and *latu sériku*—growing along the perimeter walls of the *lata*.

18   While Lape links the emergence of fortified settlements in East Timor with a period of rapid climate change and inter-group conflict, it has also been well established that slavery flourished in eastern Indonesia following the introduction of Islam in the East Indies in the thirteenth century (Grant 1964:9). As Andaya (1991:83) observes, the demand for slaves from the east increased when the Dutch East India Company (Vereenigde Oost-Indische Compagnie: VOC) 'forbid the use of slaves from Butung, the Malay areas, Makassar, Bali and Java'. In a commentary on 'Papuans' in the Indian archipelago, Earl (1853:182) reports on the 'quasi-Papuan tribes' (I take this to be Fataluku speakers) of south-eastern Timor. He observes that these people are wary of strangers and have good reason to be so because the 'great slave mart of the Bughis and Macassar traders, Kapalla Tanah, or the Land's-end, is in their immediate neighbourhood' (Earl 1853:182). 'Kapalla Tanah' (Kepala Tanah or 'Head of the Land') is the name that appears on maps from this period for the easternmost point on the island of Timor (Weber 1902), which is occupied by Fataluku speakers today. As Earl's account indicates, slavery was certainly a real fact of life in the mid-1800s for Fataluku people.

19   The term *irinu* is also used to describe dense stands of primary rainforest.

Pala

In a recent article on Fataluku forest tenure, Andrew McWilliam (2006:3) identifies Fataluku people as 'a predominantly agrarian society', and states that they have 'for centuries pursued systems of...dry land swidden agriculture combined with irrigated rice production'. This said, Fataluku people from the Tutuala area associate wet rice production with the agricultural extension programs introduced by the Portuguese Government in the 1960s and the efforts of the Indonesian authorities, post 1977, to promote a more familiar idea of what constituted landed productivity and agricultural stability (see Fox 2000; Tsing 1993).[20]

The short history of irrigated rice production in this area stands in contrast with the relative antiquity of shifting cultivation.[21] For Fataluku people, this history (*rata*) of shifting cultivation is marked by the stone walls (*lutur*) of former gardens that crisscross the forest landscape and the particular history of plant succession associated with these areas. In a similar manner to the way in which former settlements—particularly those regarded as the earliest occupation sites—are associated with gigantic forest tress, especially strangler figs (*hama*), the memory of former gardens (*pala cenu*) is also linked to particular plants and plant communities. Long grass and bushy growth (mainly, *Imperata cylindrical*, *Chromolaena odorata* and *Lantana camara L.*), remnant fruit trees and lontar palms (*tua ma'arau*) often mark more recently abandoned gardens, while sites gardened in grandparental times have become forest again in the eyes of Fataluku people. As this suggests, forests in the Tutuala area are truly anthropogenic spaces, where old gardens become newly forested areas and mature forests in turn are potential garden sites. The memory of this transformation is articulated as a history of human use and social relationships, as people walk through the forest remembering the gardens of their kin and neighbours, and the stories associated with them.

Most people maintain at least one garden for several years, which is planted with a wide range of edible and non-food plants, including corn (*cele*), cassava (*ete lusu*), pumpkin (*tau*), various kinds of yams and beans, bananas, papaya, tobacco, and an array of herbs and spices. The emphasis on phased planting and multiple cropping in Fataluku gardens makes them similar to Hanunóo swidden plots (see Geertz 1963:19). As Clifford Geertz (1963:19) observes, these subsistence practices 'give an excellent picture of the degree to which this [type of] agriculture apes the generalized diversity of the jungle which it temporarily replaces'.

---

20   In a similar manner, Friedberg (1977:149) notes that among the Bunaq, irrigated rice paddy is identified as 'an innovation of the Japanese who forced the Timorese to use this method during the last war'.

21   Earl (1853:182) reports that in the 1850s 'quasi-Papuan tribes' from 'Kapalla Tanah' or the far eastern point of the island of Timor—in other words, Fataluku speakers—'grow maize and yams'.

In June and July, when the nights turn cold,[22] Fataluku people start to prepare their swidden gardens for planting later in the year. For existing gardens, preparation largely entails weeding, while for new gardens, extensive tree cutting and undergrowth clearing take place, enabling the burning and fencing of the garden, which take place about October or November. The period from July to November is called *mokurahunu* and is defined by the prevailing southerly winds and the eventual onset of the dry season. About November, the winds shift to the north, marking the commencement of the period known as *aianhisinu*—associated with the first soaking rains and the commencement of the phased planting cycle. This period continues through to April when *temuru*, or the wet season proper, as far as local people are concerned, begins.

Given the history of swidden cultivation in the area, and the long cycles of forest-plot rotation, most gardens in Tutuala are developed out of secondary-forest land that has been fallow for a number of years. In the Tutuala area, demarcated tracts of land are readily identified in terms of their ancestral *ratu*-based association. Individuals do not, however, confine their gardening activities to the lands linked to their particular *ratu* group. In this sense, gardening reflects a person's position in a diverse network of consanguineous and affinal kinship ties, which cut across clan group membership and the boundaries of *ratu*-identified lands. The mosaic landscape of gardens that emerges each year in the Tutuala region not only conveys a sense of current social connections, it also links present gardeners to the actions of previous users, and to the powerful beings that control fertility in this area.

The creation of a new garden or the opening of a fallowed plot entails making offerings (*siri ho catu fane*) to the *tei* being 'guarding' that particular area. When ritually fed, this being is said to ensure the fertility of the land and protect those involved in associated gardening activities. Gardening is an inherently social undertaking and the opening of a new garden and the subsequent harvesting of garden produce, particularly corn, involve the collective assistance (*lehen pala fai*) of other *ratu* members and collateral kindred. Like the situation described by Friedberg for the Bunaq, in Tutuala, the rituals associated with the cultivation and harvesting of gardens are accompanied by hunting and gathering and the shared consumption of mainly forest-based products by the extended kin groups formed on these occasions. The dual nature of 'harvesting' here, from forest and garden, together with the shifting and recycled nature of the landscape, as a back-and-forth movement between garden and forest, erode the neatly drawn semantic boundaries between agrarian societies and hunter-gatherers—a typological erosion dramatically illustrated by local occupation and use patterns during the period of armed resistance to the Indonesian occupation of East Timor.

---

22   This period of coolness is divided into *sakar lafai* ('big cold') and *sakar moko* ('small cold').

A Geography which Struggles II: 'Running to the forest, hiding in the mountains'

People interviewed in the Lautem district spoke of everyday survival and the years of armed resistance to the Indonesian forces as a constant movement between roadside village sites and the nearby forest or mountains. As Pannell and O'Connor (2005) report, at various times during the Indonesian occupation, entire villages in the Lautem district would flee to the familiar surroundings of the forest or to the mountains and take refuge in caves. For example, in 1975, in the *suco* of Méhara, part of *posto* Tutuala, most of the population fled to the forest and lived in a series of caves until 1977, when they returned to live by the side of the road again. A similar exodus occurred in July 1999, at the height of the militia violence. Only after the referendum did most of the villagers emerge from the forest. Even then, some chose to remain in the forest. After the Indonesian forces left Méhara, at least two families continued to live in the cave known as Piriluturu, near the village of Loikero. All of the hamlets within Méhara were looted and public buildings, such as the school, were destroyed by the Indonesian armed forces (Tentara Nasional Indonesia or TNI)[23] and the roving militia gangs during the lead-up to the referendum. A number of the local residents were tortured and some were also killed at this time. The violence and terror, however, were not confined to this period. For local people, the entire period of the Indonesian occupation is associated with such events and emotions, mediated by their experience of 'running to the forest' and 'hiding in the mountains'.[24]

In Indonesian nationalist discourse, *hutan* ('forest') and *gunung* ('mountains') are part of a social landscape signifying political marginality, cultural differences and economic imbalances. As Tsing (1993) points out, in this discourse, rainforest shifting cultivators and the inhabitants of upland areas are generally regarded as socially 'primitive' and economically 'backward'. For policymakers and Indonesian civil servants alike, these are people and places that are also associated with moral uncertainty and physical danger, where the boundaries between the natural and supernatural worlds are blurred. In contrast with the pan-Indonesian coastal culture—characterised by adherence to Islam—these interior and upland areas are regarded as being inhabited by headhunters, animists and all manner of non-human beings. Continuing the colonial tradition established by the Dutch, state development programs in Indonesia involving these allegedly 'isolated' groups (BI: *suku terasing*) are largely presented as

---

23   For most of the period that Indonesian forces occupied East Timor, the Army was known by the acronym ABRI (Angkatan Bersenjata Republic Indonesia). The Indonesian armed forces were renamed Tentara Nasional Indonesia (TNI) towards the end of the occupation.

24   Articulated to the researcher as *'lari ke hutan, sembunyi di gunung'*.

civilising missions aimed at promoting compliant, modern citizens. Often this objective is affected through the forced resettlement of forest and upland communities to more manageable terrains—to coastal lowlands or closer to regional administrative centres.

As Kenneth George (1996) observes for the upland Mappurondo group in Sulawesi, these distinctions between upland and lowland, the interior and the coast, also feature in local cosmographies, though the significance attached to these classifications is often an inversion of the official discourse. This is a point also made by Valerio Valeri in his discussion of the rainforest-dwelling Huaulu people of the mountain interior of Seram. For the Huaulu, the opposition between the superior upland groups and the weaker coastal peoples is not only underscored by Huaulu myths and perceived behavioural differences, but also pivots on a contrast between 'indigenousness and immigrant status' (Valeri 2000:22)—with the latter status less valued than the former. In Huaulu society, a further opposition exists between the forest and the village. As Valeri points out, this relationship between the village and the forest is a complex, 'fearsome symmetry': 'Humans are not only outside the forest and against it, but also of it. Like all creatures, they follow its law: hunting and being hunted, killing and being killed' (2000:16).

For the Huaulu, however, who are subject to this law of balance and retribution, 'there are ways to regulate, displace, or even repress its operation' (Valeri 2000:16).

And so it is the case for the people of the Tutuala area. The forest and the mountains are important sources of non-domesticated food and other resources traditionally utilised by local people. They are also the sources of ancestral and non-human power. These are spaces inhabited by people's ancestors and other named beings. Like the Huaulu, the people of this region recognise the need to engage with and, where possible, propitiate these beings. Their ongoing occupation of the forest is mediated by the maintenance of these relationships. Perhaps, at no time was this more important than during the Indonesian occupation, when local resistance entailed waging a guerilla war in the forests and upland areas of the region.

Like the situation in other villages throughout Timor-Leste, in the Lautem district, many of the able-bodied men became Falintil (an acronym for the Armed Forces for the National Liberation of East Timor)[25] resistance fighters. They

---

25   In July 2005, I was part of an ANU-based team that excavated a rock shelter in the Tutuala area known as Jerimalai. Analysis of the excavated materials is ongoing but the radiometric dating of the lower levels has demonstrated that it is the oldest occupation site in island South-East Asia, east of the Sunda Shelf. The basal level of Test Pit A is dated at 38 255 +/− 596 (Wk-17831). The basal date for Test Pit B is 37 267 +/− 453 BP (Wk-17833) (S. O'Connor, Personal communication).

spent years living in caves throughout the forests, often fighting the Indonesian forces with homemade rifles and bullets made from sharpened stones. Falintil's occupation of the forests in the Lautem district varied in duration. At times, caves were used for only a couple of hours at a time—for example, while the men cooked the game they had caught in the forest or slept briefly before moving on to the next cave site. At other times, caves were occupied for much longer periods, becoming temporary headquarters for Falintil's operations in the district. Timor-Leste President and former leader of the Falintil guerilla force, Xanana Gusmão, was among the freedom fighters who sought refuge in the many caves dotted throughout the *suco* of Méhara.

Talking to ex-Falintil members, it became apparent that creating a sense of disorientation and displacement within the forest environment was an essential element in their strategy of subverting the Indonesian forces. For these men and women, the covert and shifting nature of the guerilla war waged between local people and Indonesian forces was one that they were well equipped to participate in with their intimate knowledge of the local landscape. Contrary to the attempts of the Indonesian Government to homogenise people's experience of space in terms of a range of standardised administrative areas and boundaries, it is perhaps local people's understanding of their environment as a landscape of micro-differentiations that enabled them to disperse and ultimately dispense with the numerically and technologically superior occupying forces.

As the previous discussion indicates, an important element in the development and success of the East Timorese independence movement is its material and political recolonisation of the spaces demonised by the Indonesian authorities. Moreover, the command of the 'forests' and the 'mountains' by Falintil guerillas signalled a reclamation of local history and culture, discursively focused as it is upon caves, ancestral centres and other places within this geography. The emplacement of Timor-Leste's recent history of violence and resistance in this landscape of forests and mountains is also an important element in an emerging national identity. In the Lautem district, people's reoccupation of the forest during the Indonesian period is often invoked to illustrate the new relationship between citizenry and state—local villagers and the national president alike shared the experience of being forest-dwellers. As this suggests, forests and mountains feature in a national territorial strategy to memorialise and eulogise recent events and identities. In this situation, individual biography and collective history are seen to coalesce at various spatial intersections, to the point where forests and mountains represent monumental spaces in the unfolding terrain of the new nation-state (see Pannell and O'Connor 2005).

A Geography which Struggles III: Concluding remarks

In many respects, the livelihood practices of Fataluku people in the Tutuala area have more in common with the Meratus Dayaks of Kalimantan (Tsing 1993) and the Hualulu of Seram (Valeri 2000), who are more readily recognised in the literature as 'forest-dwellers' or 'hunter-gatherers', than as 'agrarian societies'. While much has been written about the 'ecological Eden' conjured up by overly romanticised, and ultimately primitivising, images of 'indigenous' peoples and lifestyles (Ellen et al. 2000), as my comments in the previous section indicate, we are also familiar with the political and rhetorical effects of a group or a people being labelled as 'traditional hunter-gatherers' or as a 'forest-dwelling community', as opposed to an agrarian society. The designation of a community as 'farmers' or their livelihood as 'agrarian' effectively erases their overlapping and multiple social interests and ancestral connections to forests and other non-cultivated spaces. As Anna Lowenhaupt Tsing (1993:xi) observes, in the context of 'expanding capitalisms' and 'contested cultural politics', such designations contribute to, and are part of, the construction of local marginality. In the new era of Timor-Leste's nation building, heralded by independence in 2002, Fataluku people are in real danger of being excluded from the very landscape that they and their ancestors have shaped and transformed over the course of thousands of years.

As previously indicated, the eastern region of the Lautem district contains one of the largest continuous tracts of lowland tropical and monsoon forest on the island of Timor. This forested region covers an area of some 300 sq km and features the steep-sided and densely vegetated Paichao Range along the southern coast, near the village of Loré. During the period of Indonesian occupation, 1975–99, a large proportion of this area was classified as a nature conservation reserve (*kawasan suaka alam*), while under the UN Transitional Administration in East Timor (UNTAET), the area was declared a 'protected wild area' (see McWilliam 2006). It is this area that the Directorate of Forestry (Government of Timor-Leste) seeks to protect as the country's first national park: the Nino Conis Santana National Park.

From a conservation perspective, the area proposed for the Nino Conis Santana National Park is not a pristine wilderness, nor does it contain rare or endangered fauna and flora. Rather, the so-called ecological values of the nominated park landscape are highly anthropogenic in origin. With the exception of birds, none of the animals found throughout the area encompassed by the park is endemic to Timor; they are all human introductions brought from areas to the east or west during the late prehistoric or historical periods. And, as I have already discussed, much, if not all, of the forested landscape of the park has been altered and shaped by thousands of years of human occupation and use. With very few exceptions, this is the situation found throughout Timor-Leste. For example, Metzner, commenting on the Baucau and Viqueque areas, states that '[a] very high proportion—probably as much as 90 per cent—of the vegetation of the area has been modified by man. As a consequence of repeated cutting, burning, cultivation and grazing it is hard to recognize the distribution of natural vegetation today' (1977:52).

To some extent, the identification of the proposed park as a 'Category V Protected Landscape/Seascape' is capable of recognising this human–environment interaction and its long history. According to the Guidelines for Protected Area Management Categories of the International Union for Conservation of Nature (IUCN 1994:22), 'Protected Landscapes/Seascapes' are defined as an '[a]rea of land, with coast and sea as appropriate, where the interaction of people and nature over time has produced an area or distinct character with significant aesthetic, ecological and/or cultural value'.

While key management objectives for 'Category V Protected Landscapes/ Seascapes' include the maintenance of the 'harmonious interaction of nature and culture', providing support for 'lifestyles and economic activities which are in harmony with nature' and the 'preservation of the social and cultural fabric of the communities concerned' (IUCN 1994:22), away from the noble intentions and rarefied spaces of the UN Educational, Scientific and Cultural Organisation (UNESCO) in Paris, and on the ground in Tutuala, the situation is not so harmonious or interactive. Fataluku people have already been told by local government authorities—obviously unaware of the UNESCO provisions regarding the preservation of lifestyles and support for economic activities— that hunting and gathering in the proposed national park area are now illegal. In banning this dimension of local Fataluku productive practices, the actions of the National Government appear to be focused upon producing the same social effects as previous colonial regimes—notably, the creation of dedicated agrarian communities. Government prohibition of hunting and gathering in the new national park not only has the potential to adversely affect the kind of subsistence flexibility that has enabled local people to deal with chronic environmental uncertainty and acute political instability, but it also seems to be blind to the important micro-strategic role this back-and-forth social movement between garden and forest played in securing the new nation-state of Timor-Leste. While it might seem that the establishment of the new national park, and the bundle of state regulations associated with it, has rendered the task of producing locality even more of a struggle for Fataluku speakers in the Tutuala area, to date the lack of an active management regime for the park and the near absence of enforcement measures have effectively meant continuation of many of the 'banned' activities, albeit now under a communal veil of clandestine operations. With recent talk of the decentralisation of state power, and with it the emergence of more opportunities for local input into policies and decision making at the regional level, the potential exists for Fataluku people to once again reclaim the spaces and places so intrinsic to productive action and cultural identity.

Acknowledgments

The research on which this chapter is based was supported by an Australian Research Council Large Grant, and, in Australia, was conducted under the auspices of The Australian National University and the Rainforest Cooperative Research Centre, James Cook University. In Timor-Leste, research was undertaken under the auspices of the Ministero da Educacau, Cultura, Juventude e Esporto, and I would like to extend my general thanks and appreciation to the ministry staff who assisted me in the course of this research. Particular thanks go to the Ministerial Secretary of State, Senor Virgilio Simith, for his warm and much-welcomed support. I would also like to acknowledge that without the support of the people of Tutuala this research would not have been possible. In this regard, I am particularly indebted to Senors Rafael Quimaraes, Custodio Quimaraes, Pedro Morais and Mecario de Jesus for their intellectual input, constant interest and warm friendship while in the field. I would like to acknowledge the invaluable support of my close friends and co-field researchers Sue O'Connor, from The Australian National University, and Peter Lape, from the Burke Museum, University of Washington. Finally, this chapter has benefited from the comments and suggestions made by the volume editor, Andrew McWilliam.

References

Almeida, A. de 1957, 'Hunting and fishing in Timor', in *Proceedings of the Ninth Pacific Science Congress, Bangkok 1957. Volume 3: Anthropological and social sciences*, Secretariat, Ninth Pacific Science Congress, 1963, Bangkok, pp. 239–41.

Andaya, L. Y. 1991, 'Local trade networks in Maluku in the 16th, 17th and 18th centuries', *Cakalele*, vol. 2, no. 2, pp. 71–97.

Anderson, R. and Deutsch, C. (eds) 2001, *Sustainable Development and the Environment in East Timor*, Proceedings of the Conference on Sustainable Development in East Timor, 25–31 January 2001.

Appadurai, A. 1996, *Modernity at Large: Cultural dimensions of globalization*, University of Minnesota Press, Minneapolis and London.

British Broadcasting Corporation (BBC) n.d., 'Country profile—East Timor', *BBC World News Service, Asia-Pacific.*

Collins, Sean, Xisto Martins, W. M., Mitchell, Andrew, Teshome, Awegechew and Arnason, John T. 2007, 'Fataluku medicinal ethnobotany and the East Timorese military resistance', *Journal of Ethnobiology and Ethnomedicine*, vol. 3, no. 5, pp. 1–10.

Dames, M. L. (ed.) 1921, *The Book of Duarte Barbosa*, The Hakluyt Society, London.

Dove, M. 1983, 'Theories of swidden agriculture and the political economy of ignorance', *Agroforestry Systems*, vol. 1, no. 3, pp. 85–99.

Dunn, J. 1983, *Timor: A people betrayed*, Jacaranda Press, Milton, Qld.

Earl, G. W. 1853, *The Native Races of the Indian Archipelago: Papuans*, H. Bailliere, London.

Echols, J. M. and Shadily, H. 1990, *Kamus Indonesia Inggris: An Indonesian– English dictionary*, PT Gramedia, Jakarta.

Ellen, R., Parkes, P. and Bicker, A. 2000, *Indigenous Environmental Knowledge and its Transformations: Critical anthropological perspectives*, Harwood Academic Publishers, The Netherlands.

Forbes, H. O. 1989, *A Naturalist's Wanderings in the Eastern Archipelago*, Oxford University Press, Singapore, Oxford and New York.

Forman, S. 1981, 'Life paradigms: Makassae (East Timor) views on production, reproduction and exchange', *Research in Economic Anthropology*, vol. 4, pp. 95–110.

Fox, J. J. 1977, *Harvest of the Palm: Ecological change in eastern Indonesia*, Harvard University Press, Cambridge, Mass.

Fox, J. J. 2000, 'Tracing the path, recounting the past: historical perspectives on Timor', in James J. Fox and Dionisio Babo Soares (eds), *Out of the Ashes: Destruction and reconstruction of East Timor*, Crawford House Publishing, Adelaide, pp. 1–30.

Friedberg, C. 1977, 'The development of traditional agricultural practices in western Timor: from the ritual control of consumer goods production to the political control of prestige goods', in J. Friedman and M. J. Rowlands (eds), *The Evolution of Social Systems*, Duckworth, London, pp. 137–71.

Friedberg, C. 1979, 'Socially significant plant species and their taxonomic position among the Bunaq of central Timor', in Roy F. Ellen and David Reason (eds), *Classifications in Their Social Context*, Academic Press, London, pp. 81–103.

Friedberg, C. 1989, 'Social relations of territorial management in light of Bunaq farming rituals', *Bijdragen tot de Taal-, Land- en Volkenkunde*, vol. 145, Part I: Nusa Tenggara Timur, no. 4, pp. 548–63.

Geertz, C. 1963, *Agricultural Involution: The processes of ecological change in Indonesia*, University of California Press, Berkeley, Los Angeles and London.

George, Kenneth. 1996. *Showing Signs of Violence: The cultural politics of a twentieth-century headhunting ritual*. University of California Press: Berkeley, Los Angeles and London.

Glover, I. 1986, *Archaeology in Eastern Timor, 1966–67*, The Australian National University, Canberra.

Grant, B. 1964, *Indonesia*, Penguin Books, Harmondsworth, UK.

Grey, G. 1841, *Journal of Two Expeditions of Discovery in Northwest and Western Australia, 1837–39. Volume 1*, T. & W. Boone, London.

Gunn, G. C. 1999, *Timor Loro Sae 500 Years*, Livros do Oriente, Macao.

International Union for Conservation of Nature (IUCN) 1994, *Guidelines for Protected Area Management Categories*, International Union for Conservation of Nature, Gland, Switzerland, and Cambridge, UK.

Josselin de Jong, J. P. B. de 1937, *Studies on Indonesian Culture. Volume I: Oirata—A Timorese settlement on Kisar*, Foris, Amsterdam.

King, M. 1963, *Eden to Paradise*, Travel Book Club, London.

Kolff, D. H. 1840, *Voyages of the Dutch Brig of War Dourga, Through the Southern and Little-Known Parts of the Moluccan Archipelago and Along the Previously Unknown Southern Coast of New Guniea Performed During the Years 1825 and 1826*, James Madden & Co., London.

Lape, P. 2006, 'Chronology of fortified settlements in East Timor', *Journal of Island and Coastal Archaeology*, vol. 1, pp. 285–97.

McWilliam, A. 2001, 'Prospects for the sacred grove: valuing lulic forests on Timor', *Asia Pacific Journal of Anthropology*, vol. 2, no. 2, pp. 89–113.

McWilliam A, 2002, *Paths of Origin, Gates of Life: A study of place and precedence in southwest Timor*, KITLV Press, Leiden, Netherlands.

McWilliam, A. 2003, 'New beginnings in East Timorese forest management', *Journal of Southeast Asian Studies*, vol. 34, no. 2, pp. 307–27.

McWilliam, A. 2006, 'Fataluku forest tenures in the Conis Santana National Park in East Timor', in Thomas Reuter (ed.), *Sharing the Earth, Dividing the Land: Land andterritory in the Austronesian world*, Pandanus Books, Canberra, pp. 253–75.

McWilliam, A. 2007, 'Austronesians in linguistic disguise: Fataluku cultural fusion in East Timor', *Journal of Southeast Asian Studies*, vol. 38, no. 2, pp. 355–75.

Martins, J. R. 2001, 'Development of forestry conservation', in *Sustainable Development and the Environment in East Timor. Proceedings of the Conference on Sustainable Development in East Timor, 25–31 January 2001*, pp. 31–3.

Metzner, J. 1977, *Man and Environment in Eastern Timor: A geo-ecological analysis of the Baucau–Viqueque area as a possible basis for regional planning*, Monograph No. 8, Development Studies Centre, The Australian National University, Canberra.

O'Connor, S. and Veth, P. 2005, 'Early Holocene shell fish hooks from Lene Hara Cave, East Timor establish complex fishing technology was in use in island South East Asia five thousand years before Austronesian settlement', *Antiquity*, vol. 79, no. 304, pp. 249–56.

Ormeling, F. J. 1956, *The Timor Problem: A geographical interpretation of an underdeveloped island*, J. B. Wolters, Groningen, The Netherlands, and Jakarta.

Pannell, S. 2006, 'Welcome to the Hotel Tutuala: Fataluku accounts of going places in an immobile world', *The Asia Pacific Journal of Anthropology*, vol. 7, no. 3, pp. 203–21.

Pannell, S. and O'Connor, S. 2005, 'Toward a cultural topography of cave use in East Timor: a preliminary study', *Asian Perspectives*, vol. 44, no. 1, pp. 193–206.

Povinelli, E. A. 1993, *Labor's Lot: The power, history and culture of Aboriginal action*, University of Chicago Press, Chicago and London.

Said, E. 1993, *Culture and Imperialism*, Vintage, London.

Soares, D. B. 2001, 'East Timor: perceptions of culture and environment', in R. Anderson and C. Deutsch (eds), *Sustainable Development and the Environment in East Timor*, Proceedings of the Conference on Sustainable Development in East Timor, 25–31 January 2001, pp. 18–21.

Therik, T. 2000, 'The role of fire in swidden cultivation: a Timor case study', in Jeremy Russell-Smith, Greg Hill, Siliwoloe Djoeroemana and Bronwyn Myers (eds), *Fire and Sustainable Agricultural and Forestry Development in Eastern Indonesia and Northern Australia. Proceedings of an international workshop held at the Northern Territory University, Darwin, Australia, 13–15 April 1999*, Australian Centre for International Agricultural Research, Canberra, pp. 77–80.

Traube, E. G. 1980. 'Mambai rituals of black and white', in James J. Fox (ed.), *The Flow of Life: Essays on Eastern Indonesia*, Harvard University Press: Cambridge, Massachusetts and London, pp. 290-317.

Traube, E. G. 1986, *Cosmology and Social Life: Ritual exchange among the Mambai of East Timor*, University of Chicago Press, Chicago and London.

Tsing, A. 1993, *In the Realm of the Diamond Queen: Marginality in an out-of-the-way place*, Princeton University Press, Princeton, NJ.

Valeri, V. 2000, *The Forest of Taboos: Morality, hunting and identity among the Huaulu of the Moluccas*, University of Wisconsin Press, Madison, Wis.

van Engelenhoven, A. 1997, 'Words and expressions: notes of parallelism in Leti', *Cakalele*, vol. 8, pp. 1–27.

Wallace, A. R. 1872, *The Malay Archipelago: The land of the orang-utan and the bird of paradise*, Macmillan, London.

Weber, M. (ed.) 1902, *Siboga-Expedite. Monographie I de: Uitkomsten Op Zoologisch, Botanisch, Oceanograpisch en Geologisch Gebied*, E. J. Brill, Leiden, Netherlands.

11. The Articulation of Tradition in Timor-Leste

James J. Fox

Introduction

When *The Flow of Life* was published in 1980, it was intended to identify some of the distinctive features of eastern Indonesia and to shift perspectives on how the region was viewed. In that volume, Timor figured prominently. Six out of 14 comparative essays—seven, if one counts Rote within this area—were focused on Timor. Previous comparative efforts had been limited and were largely confined to the influential study by the Dutch anthropologist F. A. E. van Wouden. His work, *Sociale Structuurtypen in de Groote Oost*, in 1935—translated as *Types of Social Structure in Eastern Indonesia* in 1968—was based largely on fragmentary materials reported by travellers, missionaries and government officers. While certainly perceptive in many of its particular analyses, the work advanced a single formal model that purported to provide the original underlying basis for societies in eastern Indonesia.

The Flow of Life challenged this model by presenting a diversity of social forms in eastern Indonesia and by convincingly representing the diverse conceptual bases of societies of the region. *The Flow of Life* was the first study of its kind to be based on substantial fieldwork. As the book claimed, it shifted focus from the study of models to the study of metaphors—the often highly poetic articulation of metaphors of life.

This book, *Life and Land in Timor-Leste*, follows a trajectory set out in *The Flow of Life*. Like *The Flow of Life*, all the papers in this volume are based on considerable fieldwork. This work is, however, more specifically focused and critically formulated to consider local polities in Timor-Leste and the way in which they have survived and adapted to the Indonesian occupation, the United Nations' presence and the present-day national development demands of an independent Timor-Leste.

Despite the great attention given to Timor-Leste over the past decade, few studies have sought to examine traditional social life as framed within particular traditional polities and in different rural areas. This book should therefore have a double impact—both theoretical and practical. It opens a new window on what is occurring in Timor-Leste. The initial question to ask of this volume is what comparative insights it provides and where do these insights lead.

Traditional Timorese Discourse

On Timor, traditions go deep. They are bound to the land—to specific places and to particular origins. Thus, the common comparative framework for all of the essays in this volume is their examination of Timorese traditional relations to the land and the significance of these relations. These relations—somewhat bewildering at times—are in fact the substance of life.

From these local attachments and sources of vested authority, a network of connections spreads throughout the island. Although Timorese traditions might be thousands of years old, these are not static. Engagement with the world involves continual adaptation and reinterpretation. This process has allowed the Timorese to both resist and assimilate. The capacity to do this, however, has never been properly realised by those who have come to change Timor.

The source of this capacity is a conception of the world embodied in a language of complementary categories, a discourse that constitutes a general rhetoric and a pervasive logic. This use of binary categories is most densely manifest in the ritual languages used in formal relations and in ceremonies, but the most critical of these categories are equally part of ordinary discourse. Many of the papers in this volume provide exegeses on these key categories.

The second chapter in this volume, Susana Barnes' 'Origins, precedence and social order in the domain of *Ina Ama Beli Darlari*', is a superb examination of various 'origin groups' that comprise a socially diverse community in Uato Lari. The chapter focuses on core origin groups, their ritual position among other groups that make up the local polity and the complex relationships among all these groups to particular tracts of land. The paper offers an exemplary exegesis of key complementary categories in Timorese discourse. While only a careful reading can do justice to Barnes' exegesis, I wish to highlight the main categories she examines.

The first categories she focuses on are the categories elder/younger (*kaka/wari*). Together, these terms define and, separately, they distinguish, relations within a descent group and among related descent groups. As a set, these categories collectively identify members of an origin group while individually each specifies a relative relationship to the other.

Barnes recounts an ancestral dispute between an elder and younger brother—ancestors of the Beli and Darlari origin groups—that resulted in an allocation of land and status whereby the younger brother became the 'lord of the land'. This position is described as 'rod of the land/rock of the land' (*rea mumu, rea uato*). The narrative of this dispute explains why, in this context, the category of 'younger' takes precedence over the category of 'elder'.

In addition to these categories, Barnes introduces the important categories of black and white—categories that both describe and differentiate the two most important sacred houses, the white and the black houses (*uma buti/uma ita*), of the Darlari, each of which has different ritual duties in supporting the lord of the land. As Barnes explains, in this context, 'white' takes precedence over 'black'.

Within Darlari, there are other categorical distinctions among those who 'guard the fields/guard the water' (*lai bosa/lai wai*): the *Makaer Luli* who watches over the *sacra* and the *Kabo Rai* who allocates access to the land. Both are involved in the performance of the rituals of 'rock and tree' (*uato no kai*).

Having described this core group, Barnes discusses the designation of other in-coming origin groups in terms of the ritual categories that define them and locate them on specific lands. This again involves the categories of black and white used to identify certain allied groups who are known as the 'people of the white children/people of the black children'. Yet other binary categories are applied to another vassal group to whom land was granted in return for the obligation to protect the borders of the domain. This is described as 'guarding the people/guarding the land', and the warrior group to whom this task of gatekeeper was allocated is referred to as the 'door and gate' (*ita mata/kai hene*) of the domain. Yet another group was incorporated into the Darlari domain as 'wife-taker' to the Darlari who as 'wife-giver' became committed to a continuing 'wife-giver/wife-taker' (*oa-sae/uma ana*) relationship. In all of this, only the Darlari elders possess the full knowledge of the elaborate historical construction of their domain from its origins to the present or, as it is described in Naueti, the knowledge that extends from 'trunk to tip' (*la'a-na/rae-na*). This is a critical feature of their centrality for the whole of the domain.

Although brief and directed specifically to aspects of ritual duties within a single domain, Barnes' paper provides a clear indication of the importance of Timorese binary discourse and how it is used to establish meaning and relevance to social relations. Other contributions to this volume are equally illustrative of this all-important discourse. This is particularly so in the case of the paper by Elizabeth Traube (Chapter 6).

All of Elizabeth Traube's writings exemplify a profound understanding of the Mambai based on careful and considered assessment of their discourse. Her fieldwork was first carried out in the 1970s prior to the Indonesian occupation and she has returned for further long fieldwork in the Aileu area. Her paper in *The Flow of Life*, 'Mambai rituals of black and white', is a thoroughgoing exegesis of 'the complementary opposition of two categories of ritual action, the "white" (*buti*) and "black" (*meta*)'. Her intention in that paper was not to describe a particular ritual sequence but rather 'to provide an outline of the total system by considering the set of ideas which underlie all ritual performance' (1980:291–2). Her book *Cosmology and Social Life: Ritual exchange among the Mambai of East Timor* (1986) extended the analysis of her paper in *The Flow of Life* into what is, without doubt, the most thoroughgoing and subtle examination of the thought world of an East Timorese population.

Her paper, 'Planting the flag', in this volume is no less brilliant because it is able to explicate Mambai intellectual engagement in interpreting categories of the past to confront realities of the present. Again, it is not my intention to repeat her analysis but rather to highlight the complementary categories she focuses on—many of which are those that Barnes highlights as well.

Traube's core narrative also involves a dispute between an elder and a younger brother that results in the movement of all the ancestral *sacra*—disks, necklaces, drums and gongs—to a second ritual house. This creates a division between cult origin villages: Raimaus associated with the elder brother and Hohul associated with the younger brother. Raimaus is represented as the northern 'door' that leads south to the 'innermost' sanctuary at Hohul. In this context, various categories are linked by association within the ambit of Mambai ritual life. They relate to the most important matters of ritual life. These matters are described in similar terms to those of the Naueti. They pertain to matters of 'rock and tree' (*hauta nor aia*).

The alignment of the categories that define the relationship of Raimaus to Hohul, as set out in the discourse of the narrative that Traube recounts, is as follows.

Raimaus	*Hohul*
Elder	Younger
North	South
Outer	Inner

This is not, however, the only use of the categories elder/younger (*kaka/ali*). These categories are also used to distinguish among the founding ancestors of the Mambai and thus differentiate between outsiders and insiders: rulers and ruled. Although the narrative involves a triad of founders, it is told from the vantage of the youngest and presented as a succession of separate dyadic relations.[1] Like all such origin narratives, it must be told from 'trunk to tip' and, like other narratives, its 'tip', which continues to develop, can be relied upon to provide an explanation of the present.

According to the narrative, a first-born brother, Au Sa, who is associated with the dark arts of blacksmithing, wanders off to the west and disappears thereafter from the narrative. A last-born brother, Loer Sa, 'rinses white, bathes clean', takes all regalia and departs to become the ancestor of the *Malaia* who are epitomised by the Portuguese. This leaves the middle brother, Ki Sa, to represent the Mambai who occupy Timor and who remain 'with only rock and tree'.

As told in dyadic formulation, Ki Sa is elder; Loer Sa is younger. Only by seeking the return of some of the sacred regalia from his *Malaia* brother is Ki Sa able to restore order: 'heavy rule and weighty ban' (*ukun rihu/badun mdeda*). Eventually the *Malaia* descendants of Loer Sa return to rule as the Portuguese. By this narrative, the Mambai are seen to retain their ritual authority and the 'base or trunk of rule' (*uku-fun*), while the Portuguese or their *Malaia* representatives are accorded political power—the 'tip of rule' (*fail tu uku-laun*).

What is most notable in this telling is the association of complementary categories that it entails. These are different to the telling of the narrative of Raimaus and Hohul in that in this narrative, the elder takes precedence by association with the inside and ritual authority whereas the younger brother is the outsider with political power. As Traube explains, this contrast can also be represented by the complementary categories 'male and female'.

Ki Sa	*Loer Sa*
Elder	Younger
Inside	Outside
Trunk of rule	Tip of rule
Female	Male

---

1   It is a common and perhaps critical feature of such origin narratives that they reduce triadic relations to separate dyadic relations. The Kemak of Marobo, for example, attribute the foundations of their community to three ancestors: the Dato Telu who divide power and authority among themselves but only after an initial breach and eventual reconciliation with the youngest (Renard-Clamagirand 1982:117–25). The two elder brothers are given 'hot' + 'male' identifications as opposed to the third brother who is considered both 'cool' + 'female'. Similarly, the Tana Ai of Flores recognise a triad of ancestors, two of whom travel together and eventually establish the domain of Wai Brama and are then reunited with their wayward third brother who travels separately (Lewis 1988:45–69).

Significantly, when pressed to categorise the Indonesian occupiers and to differentiate them from the Portuguese as *Malaia*, the Mambai invoke the figure of Au Sa—the neglected 'third' member of an original triad in the origin narrative—to represent the dark ancestor of the Indonesians. By the logic of the narrative, their attempt to rule represented an extraordinary categorical reversal in which the 'eldest' as 'outsider' attempted to rule.

As Traube demonstrates, there is a logic and subtle flexibility to the use of complementary categories that make possible the formulation of different contentions within Mambai discourse. Attention to this discourse opens vistas to our understanding of local developments in Timor.

Implicit in the categories of this discourse are ideas of governance—a conception of relationships the fulfilment of which is appropriate to wellbeing. At its core, there is the distinction between ritual authority and political power: authority is represented as an inner unity, symbolically 'feminised', silent, immobile but implacable, whereas political power can be diverse, symbolically 'masculine', active and invariably clamorous (see Fox 2008).

Common Timorese Categories of Discourse

The main categories of Timorese traditional discourse are similar throughout the island but their context varies. Recognising context is crucial. The use of complementary categories produces a relational dimension to all discourse. Together, any set of complementarities defines a unity while each of its components distinguishes within that unity. Similar binary categories can occur in different contexts; they may be applied recursively and, most pertinently, their subtle reversal is significant (see Fox 1989).[2]

Judith Bovensiepen's paper, 'Opening and closing the land: land and power in the Idaté highlands' (Chapter 3), focuses on narratives of origin that establish authority over the land. Various key complementary categories are invoked. As she explains, Laclubar is central land (*rai klaran*) and as such it is conceived of as 'the navel of the land, the liver of the land' (*larek usar, larek nau*). In this conception, 'the west of Timor-Leste represents the tail of the land (Idaté: *hiak*) and the east the head (Idaté: *ulun*)'. Her paper, as a whole, is an exegesis on the Timorese ideas associated with the categories of 'opening and closing' in relation to land.

---

2   The use of complementary categories allows for the formulation of relational propositions. Such categories may be applied recursively at different levels and the elements in any set of complementary terms may be reversed. This is why, for any interpretation, context is crucial. This use of complementary categories occurs widely in eastern Indonesia. I have discussed its use in greater detail in Fox (1989).

Similarly, Molnar's paper, 'Darlau: origins and their significance for Atsabe Kemak identity' (Chapter 5), examines a succession of origin narratives told from different perspectives beginning from the time when the sky and earth were joined and presided over by a 'Female Sun' and a 'Male Sun' (*Lelo hine/ Lelo mane*). The amusing (and somewhat confusing) details of these narratives are counters in a contestation over precedence within and beyond the Kemak domain of Atsabe. They foster a set of relations based on the common categories of elder/younger (*ka'ara/aliri*) and of wife-giver/wife-taker (*nai hine/nai mane*).

The various narratives that Molnar summarises are replete with binary categories but not all of these categories are of the same critical significance within the framework of Timorese discourse. A relatively small number of complementary categories function as 'operators'—propositional organisers that set out relations among other categories.

Some of these key 'operators' are the gender categories such as male/female; relative age categories such as elder/younger and, in some cases, first-born/ last-born; colour categories such as black/white or red/blue-green; directional categories such as east/west, north/south or inside/outside; various body categories such as right/left, head/tail or trunk/tip; conditional categories such as open/closed or hot/cool; and a number of verbs of placement such as lifting/ lowering or ascending/descending. Listing these categories as though they belonged to separate semantic domains is potentially misleading because of the overlap between them.

Perhaps the most important aspect of this discourse is its continuing use in assessing and reinterpreting current developments in Timor within a framework that relates the past to the present and is thus able to deal with a diversity of complex issues from land tenure to local governance. At the same time, this discourse is a tool for negotiating present, often contentious, relationships. It creates possibilities for achieving the resolution of problems based on reference to versions of the past that, depending on context, are accepted for present purposes. Moreover, traditions in Timor are flexible since they are not wedded to a single canonical view of the past but can draw on multiple perceptions of ancestral precedence.

Most important for understanding this traditional discourse is the recognition that the different populations of Timor who speak their own distinct languages share key 'operators' within this discourse. This would not be surprising among the related Austronesian languages of Timor. It is, however, remarkable that key elements of this discourse are also shared among non–Austronesian-speaking populations of the island. This is the particular significance of Andrew McWilliam's research among the Fataluku. He has demonstrated this most explicitly in his paper 'Austronesians in linguistic disguise: Fatuluku cultural fusion in East Timor' (2007), but he does so as well in his paper, 'Fatuluku living landscapes' (Chapter 4), in this volume.

Although the Fatuluku use their own distinctive complementary categories, they also share various key categories with their Austronesian neighbours. Thus, they describe their wife-giving groups as 'trunk and stem' (*ara ho pata*); they associate the 'head of the land' (*mua cao*) with east and the 'tail of the land' (*mua ulafuka*) with west and they rely on elder/younger categories to distinguish siblings but also to differentiate ritually among the posts on which the house is constructed (McWilliam 2007). In some cases, as, for example, with the term for 'elder' (*kaka*), an Austronesian word has been borrowed to create the appropriate set of complementary categories. Indeed the very fact that terms are borrowed to establish common categories of discourse signals the fundamental importance of these categories.

This sharing of common categories of discourse points to a further congruence of social categories among the populations of Timor.

The Congruence of Timorese Kin Categories

The papers in this volume give some idea of the remarkable diversity of the forms of local social organisation on Timor. This diversity is found both within groups with the same language and across groups with different languages— both Austronesian and non-Austronesian. Many of these differences are the result of a long history of adaptation and development including contact with neighbouring groups. Thus, as a result, there is, at an organisational level, a great variety of local practice that is distinctive and defining.

Despite this diversity, however, there is also a degree of commonality in kin relations. For example, all Timorese social systems are lineally organised and much of this lineal organisation across the island is based on similar categories. Thus, at a categorical level, father (F) and father's brother (FB) are equated but distinguished from mother's brother (MB) just as mother (M) and mother's sister (MZ) are equated and are everywhere, except among the Bunaq, distinguished from father's sister (FZ). This allows for the creation of 'lineally' organised groups—clans and lineages.

These clans and lineages might recognise either a maternal or a paternal lineality. The most striking case of this difference occurs among Tetun-speaking populations: the southern Tetun insist on maternal inheritance and descent whereas the northern Tetun and the Tetun in the east of Timor tend to rely on paternal inheritance and descent. The exception to this general rule are the

Bunaq who distinguish father and mother's brother but do not distinguish between mother, mother's sister and father's sister. This 'incomplete' lineality has implications in the organisation and fluidity of social groupings among the Bunaq.

Table 11.1 presents the kin categories that are used across the whole of the island of Timor for the first ascending consanguineal generation. (It is essential to consider the whole of the island to appreciate the borrowing of specific relational terms among different populations.)

Virtually all Timorese populations use the term *ama* for father and father's brother and *ina* for mother and mother's sister. The only exceptions are at the eastern end of Timor. Unlike other non-Austronesian populations who have borrowed terms from their Austronesian neighbours, the Fatuluku use an entirely different set of terms for father and mother, mother's brother and father's sister to the rest of Timor.[3]

Table 11.1 Lineal Distinctions in First Ascending Generation

Group	F =	FB ≠	MB	M =	MZ ≠	FZ
Rotinese	ama	ama	to'o	ina	ina	te'o
Helong	ama	ama	baki	ina	ina	eto
Dawan	amaf	amaf	bab mone	ainaf	ainaf	bab feto [Amanuban]
N. Tetun	ama	ama	bab	ina	ina	ki'i [Fehalaran]
S. Tetun	ama	ama	tua nai	ina	ina	ina feto [Wehali]
Bunak	ama	ama	baba	eme	eme	eme
Kemak	amar	amar	nair	ina	ina	ki'ir [Atsabe]
		amar kai		amar na'i	inar kai	inar ki'i [Marobo]
Beka'is	ama	ama [ama kai]	baba	ina [ina kai]	ina	ki'i
Isni	aman	ama	banin	inan	inan	ki'in
Tokodede	ama	ama	ama luli	ina	ina	bagi hine [Liquisa]
						ba'i [Maubara]
Mambai	ama	ama	na'i	ina	ina	kai (hinan)
Idaté	ama	ama	bani manek	ina	ina	bani mahinak
Isni	ama	ama	lobak banin	ina	ina lobak	ki'in
Galoli	ama	ama	ba'i	ina	ina	obu
Naueti	amau	amau	obu	inau	inau	in'tua
Waima'a	ba'a	ba'a	obu	woi	woi	in'tuo
Makassae	*baba*	*baba*	*boubo*	*ina*	*ina*	*ina hatu*
Fatuluku	*palu*	*palu*	*pienu*	*nalu*	*nalu*	*tamu*

3 The Waima'a, who are an Austronesian population now under heavy Makassae influence, appear somewhat anomalous in that they use the term *woi* for mother and mother's sister. They also happen to use another term, *mama*. Where the *woi* term comes from is not clear.

At a deeper level, the evidence in Table 11.1 points to a time when all of the Austronesian populations of Timor were previously bilaterally organised. The diversity of terms for the categories mother's brother (*to'o, baki, bab mone, baba, ba'i, tua nai, nair, banin, banin manek* and *obu*) and father's sister (*te'o, eto, bab feto, ki'i, inar ki'i, bagi hina, banin hina, kai* and *ina tua*) suggests multiple separate processes of creation. From this perspective, the partial, incomplete transition of the Bunaq to lineality is not particularly anomalous. It could be argued as well that other Timorese societies—the Kemak, for example—are still undergoing this transition.

This evidence, combined with similar evidence from elsewhere in eastern Indonesia, links the Austronesian social formations found on Timor to earlier bilateral forms of Austronesian social organisation that are still evident in Taiwan and much of western Austronesia.

The present-day similarity in the configuration of kin relations on Timor and the family resemblance of key terms used in this configuration contributes to defining a common ground for social interaction. This is even more so if one extends this perspective to the primary kin categories that define relations between siblings and cousins.

On Timor, as elsewhere in eastern Indonesia, gendered terms for siblings are also applied to parallel cousins—the children of one's father's brother and mother's sister. Relative age terms distinguish siblings but are applied only between members of the same sex. Thus, brothers and male parallel cousins will refer to each other as elder or younger and sisters and female parallel cousins will do the same among themselves. Other terms will be applied between siblings and parallel cousins of the opposite sex.

This configuration of relationships is found throughout Timor with two minor variations on this system. The majority of Timorese populations use two terms to distinguish between elder and younger (as, for example, *kaka/alin* among the Mambai). The Tetun and those populations influenced by the Tetun, together with some but not all Kemak, the Idate and the Bunak, use three terms for relative age. These three give rise to two dyads. Thus, among the Tetun, brothers and male parallel cousins use the terms *maun/alin* for elder/younger, while sisters and female parallel cousins use the terms *bin/alin* for elder/younger. It is particularly instructive that the Kemak of Marobo who are in closer proximity to the Tetun and more particularly to the Bunaq[4] use three terms whereas the Kemak of Atsabe who are at a greater distance from the Tetun and Bunaq retain a two-term (*ka'ara/alin*) configuration. Both the two-term and the three-term

---

4   The terms for relative age used among the Kemak appear to reflect borrowing from the Bunaq, their immediate neighbours. Thus, the Bunaq appear to have borrowed from the Tetun and the Kemak from the Bunaq.

patterns of relative age are transformations of similar Austronesian two and three-term relative age patterns. What is significant on Timor is that the non–Austronesian-speaking populations—the Bunaq, Makassae and Fatuluku—have all borrowed from their Austronesian counterparts to create similar relative age configurations.

A minor variation on the Timorese pattern of relations among siblings and cousins is found among the Bunaq and the Naueti. Instead of using gendered terms between siblings and parallel cousins of the opposite sex, both societies rely on a single reciprocal term. In the context of eastern Indonesia, this is in no way unusual. The use of a single reciprocal term between opposite-sex siblings and parallel cousins is in fact a common pattern variant, particularly among Austronesian societies in Maluku.

Table 11.2 Gender and Relative Age Distinctions in Ego's Generation

	Sibling/parallel cousin (Same sex)	Sibling/parallel cousin (Opposite sex)	
Group	Elder/younger	Brother (w.s.)	Sister (m.s.)
Rotinese	ka'a/fadi	na(k)	feto(k)
Helong	kaka/pali	blane	bata
Dawan	tataf/olif	nauf	fetof [Amanuban]
N. Tetun	maun/bin/alin*	nan	feton [Fehalaran]
S. Tetun	maun/bin/alin*	nan mane	fetosawa [Wehali]
Bunaq	*kaqa/nana/kauq**	*g-intili*	
Kemak	kaar/nanar/alir*	nar	mtor [Marobo]
Kemak	ka'ara/aliri	nar	toporo [Atsabe]
Beka'is	ka'an/walin	manek	fetok
Isni	ka'an/alin	naran	haton
Tokodede	bo/alin	na mane	moto hine [Liquisa]
Tokodede	kaka/alin	na	moto [Maubara]
Idate	bouk/bin/alin*	nara	hitoo
Mambai	kaka/alin	nara	tbo
Waima'a	wa'i/ware	bo'u	mae
Naueti	kaka/wari	mae (ana)	
Makassae	*kaka/nook*	*bo'o*	*topo*
Fatuluku	*kaka/noko*	*nami*	*lereno*

These relationship categories are, as it were, the basic building blocks on which different configurations of social organisation on Timor are structured. Although these particular categories are similar to one another, they each occur in different overall configurations of social relationships—a wider kin terminology, thus allowing for a diversity of social organisation across the island.

The Dynamic of Unity and Division Among Uma Lulik

Just as this volume provides critical insights into Timorese traditional discourse, it also provides valuable documentation on the resurgence of traditional institutions and practices. Few commentators expected this reaffirmation of local tradition to emerge after the decades-long disruptions of the Indonesian occupation and the devastations that occurred in 1999. In the first flush of freedom under UN auspices, attention was directed to the formulation of new forms of democratic governance. In this process, the rural populations of Timor-Leste were left to reshape their own local identities and, remarkably, across the island, great emphasis was given to the rebuilding of traditional houses—what are generally referred to as *uma lulik*.

Restoration of *uma lulik* occurred throughout Timor-Leste at a remarkable pace. The anthropologist Alexander Loch, who began his fieldwork in the Baucau area in 2002, was one of the few outsider observers to attempt to document the building of *uma lulik*. In his book *Haus, Handy & Halleluia* (2007), in which he examines the building of three such *uma lulik*, he estimates that between 1999 and 2004 in the area around Baucau alone, there were 150 to 200 *uma lulik* constructed or reconstructed. This number meant that there were 30 to 40 *uma lulik* restored each year over the period he was able to survey (Loch 2007:291).

According to Loch, the physical construction of these houses required from two to five months' work and demanded at least 1000 man-days of labour—some needed twice this amount. The particularity of construction—the choice of timbers and other materials and the necessity that all work should follow a particular ritual order—was paramount.

Yet this considerable labour was not the main focus of effort. More important for the construction of any single *uma lulik* were the negotiation, re-establishment and celebration of the specific social relationships that underpinned the house as a ritual entity—as a named sanctuary and locus of identity. Loch notes that this complex negotiation to reconcile relationships among the living was mediated through ritual invocation and a precarious dialogue with the spirits of the ancestors of the parties involved.

An essential feature of every *uma lulik* is its name, its narrative of origins and thus its grounding in the past. Physical structures can be destroyed—and indeed were destroyed during the Indonesian occupation—but not the idea of these structures, embodied in name and origin. This was retained in local consciousness and was given re-expression as soon as circumstances allowed.

In this volume, Traube's discussion of the importance of the relationship between the two origin villages Raimaus and Hohul gives a glimpse of the centrality of these structures within a larger orbit of relationships. Barnes' examination of relations among the various specifically named branch houses of the main 'origin' group of Darlari and their further relations with other migrant houses provides an even clearer indication that *uma lulik* do not exist as entities on their own but as a part of a nexus of relationships. Similarly, Molnar's discussion of the contentious efforts at the re-establishment of precedence within the domain of Atsabe through the renewal of relations between different constituent houses, each with their own ideas of precedence, points to the ever widening framework within which any particular *uma lulik* is located. Perhaps most telling of all is Palmer's contention in her paper, 'Water relations: customary systems and the management of Baucau City's water' (Chapter 7), that managing the town's water supply would be best achieved by a 'mapping' of the *uma lulik* within the watershed to determine and then to negotiate usage rights with ritual custodians.

Increasingly, the role of *uma lulik* can no longer be ignored in local governance. Their social prominence is apparent, even as their role in Timor-Leste continues to develop. It is instructive to see the way that members of urban communities are being drawn into participation in the ceremonies of their *uma lulik* of origin. A return to the countryside for celebrations is coming to be seen as a social obligation even for city dwellers. In particular, the generation of 1999—the so-called *geração foun*—especially those deeply influenced by education in Indonesia and overseas, have begun to rediscover their local 'roots' and are now more willing to link themselves with particular ancestral *uma lulik*. It is possible—indeed probable—that in the future, a link to an *uma lulik* will be an essential component of East Timorese identity.

From a sociological perspective, the resurgence of *uma lulik* is still in its early phase. As emphasised by virtually all of the papers in this volume, an *uma lulik* does not exist on its own but in relation to other *uma lulik*. As more *uma lulik* come into being, the connections between them are extended and articulated, making every ritual celebration of a house's origins a political event. This opens up another aspect of Timorese tradition: the tracing of paths between houses.

For all of the attention given to local relations, autochthony and the spirits of place, there is no paper in this volume that does not also point to the ambulatory nature of Timorese society. In the past, as in the present, individuals and groups are associated with particular paths across the landscape. Thus, for example, Sandra Pannell in her paper, 'Struggling geographies: rethinking livelihood and locality in Timor-Leste' (Chapter 10), emphasises the importance of the oral histories of mobility among the Fataluku, and Antoinette Schapper in her paper, 'Finding Bunaq: the homeland and expansion of the Bunaq in central

Timor' (Chapter 8), provides a detailed examination of Bunaq expansion. For individuals and groups, the tracing of pathways is part of the creation of social identity.

In her paper, 'Tensions of tradition: making and remaking claims to land in the Oecusse enclave' (Chapter 9), Laura Meitzner Yoder describes the nature of these 'paths'. She writes: 'Taboos (*nuni*) sometimes serve as a mnemonic device for the history of family migration. Hence, asking the history of a family's *nuni* array can evoke their geographic journey through various points, where events occurred and which taboos were acquired along the way.'

The term *nuni*, which Yoder translates as 'taboo', is the Dawan or Atoin Pa Meto equivalent of the Tetun term *luli(k)*. Here Yoder notes that in their narratives of mobility, the Dawan evoke locations along a path of migration marked by events of ancestral significance. The formal invocation of these locations, which commonly occurs in ceremonies on Timor, constitutes a 'topogeny' (Fox 1997)—a recitation that functions much like a genealogy to locate individuals and groups within an ordered past.

The topogenies of different groups can intersect at different strategic locations, providing linkages similar to the linkages created by common ancestors. Key locations might be associated with physical features of the landscape but they might also be represented by houses or the remains of previous settlements. The reconstruction of *uma lulik* that are associated with significant locations and formative events thus come to mark out prominent paths in narratives of social mobility.

An *uma lulik* does not exist on its own but in relation to other *uma lulik*. Each *uma lulik* is part of a network. With the re-establishment of *uma lulik*, various local networks are being created and, as these networks expand, they are beginning to draw links to one another. Paths are being drawn within these networks, allowing groups and individuals to trace and create relationships that were previously obscure (or perhaps never before existed). Molnar, for example, notes that the Kemak network of Atsabe did not, at the time of her fieldwork, extend to embrace the Kemak of Marobo, but she is able to point out a connection between Atsabe Kemak and Marobo Kemak through the origin houses of the Atsabe-oriented villages of Boboe and Obulo. Connecting the Atsabe houses to houses in Boboe and Obulo and from these houses to Marobo creates a path that can then extend to the Bunaq with whom the Marobo Kemak are intermarried. Such paths are the makings of a new form of social integration for Timor-Leste.

Conclusion

For more than a decade, overwhelming attention in Timor-Leste has been given to the creation of new modern democratic instruments and institutions of governance. Under UN auspices, this emphasis was understandable and appropriate. The consequence of this, however, is that less attention has been directed to understanding elements of tradition that serve and preserve Timorese social life. Often, as was the case during the Indonesian occupation, the persistence of tradition has been regarded as a limiting factor for the development of a modern nation-state.

Despite this emphasis, an increasing number of researchers, including a number of East Timorese, have pointed to the importance of tradition in shaping national consciousness and local-level governance. They, too, have also noted the conflict among 'paradigms' of governance and the administration of justice in Timor-Leste (Babo-Soares 2003, 2004; Hohe 2002; Lutz and Linder 2004; McWilliam 2005, 2008; Traube 2007; Trindade 2008).

Writing on what he describes as 'local authority systems', McWilliam has stressed both the lack of attention given to different conceptions of governance and the lack of engagement between developing local social formations and state regulatory systems.

'Recognition and understanding of these local authority systems remains both undervalued and poorly understood particularly at the national level of government in Timor-Leste, but their vitality and relevance to local contexts and to the fundamental strength of the nation state is undoubtedly significant' (McWilliam 2008:179).[5]

The Timorese possess centuries-old conceptions of governance that, as I have tried to indicate in this chapter, they continue to articulate. The discourse phased in complementary categories that they rely upon to frame these ideas is both subtle and flexible. It has served to accommodate Portuguese colonial impositions and an Indonesian occupation and it continues its engagement with the present.

The effort to understand snatches of localised Timorese dialogue and thus tune into what is occurring among a majority of the population poses a challenge to policymakers. A first step in making this effort requires a change in attitude and calls for what the Timorese would call *respeitu*—a genuine respect for what is valuable in local traditions and a willingness to acknowledge this valued heritage in forging new, possibly unique, forms of social governance. One can only hope that this volume will serve to clear a path towards such respect.

---

5   This paper by McWilliam appears in a volume edited by David Mearns (2008) with other papers that touch on these same issues.

References

Babo-Soares, Dionisio da Costa 2003, Branching from the trunk: East Timorese perceptions of nationalism in transition, Doctoral dissertation, The Australian National University, Canberra.

Babo-Soares, Dionisio da Costa 2004, 'Nahe Biti: the philosophy and process of grassroots reconciliation and justice in East Timor', *Asia Pacific Journal of Anthropology*, vol. 5, no. 1, pp. 15–34.

Fox, James J. 1980a, 'Models and metaphors: comparative research in eastern Indonesia', in James J. Fox (ed.), *The Flow of Life: Essays on eastern Indonesia*, Harvard University Press, Cambridge, Mass., pp. 327–33.

Fox, James J. (ed.) 1980b, The *Flow of Life: Essays on eastern Indonesia*, Harvard University Press, Cambridge, Mass.

Fox, James J.1989, Category and complement: binary ideologies and the organization of dualism in Eastern Indonesia' in David Maybury-Lewis and Uri Almagor (eds), *The Attraction of Opposites: Thought and Society in a Dualistic Mode*, University of Michigan Press, Ann Arbor, pp 33-56.

Fox, James J. 1997, 'Genealogy and topogeny: toward an ethnography of Rotinese ritual place names', in J. J. Fox (ed.), *The Poetic Power of Place: Comparative perspectives on Austronesian ideas of locality*, Department of Anthropology, Comparative Austronesian Project, Research School of Pacific and Asian Studies, The Australian National University, Canberra, pp. 91–102.

Fox, James J. 2003, 'Tracing the path, recounting the past: historical perspectives on Timor', in James J. Fox and Dionisio Babo Soares (eds), *Out of the Ashes*, ANU E Press, Canberra.

Fox, James J. 2008, 'Repaying the debt to Mau Kiak: reflections on Timor's cultural traditions and the obligations of citizenship in an independent East Timor', in David Mearns (ed.), *Democratic Governance in Timor-Leste: Reconciling the local and the national*, Charles Darwin University Press, Darwin, pp. 119–28.

Hohe, Tanja 2002, 'The clash of paradigms: international administration and local political legitimacy in East Timor', *Contemporary Southeast Asia*, vol. 24, no. 3, pp. 569–89.

Lewis, E. Douglas 1988, *People of the Source: The social and ceremonial order of Tana Wai Brama on Flores*, Foris Publications, Dordrecht.

Loch, Alexander 2007, *Haus, Handy & Halleluia: Psychosoziale Rekonstruktion in Osttimor*, IKO—Verlag für Interkulturelle Kommunikation, Frankfurt am Main.

Lutz, George and Linder, Wolf 2004, *Traditional Structures for Local Governance for Local Development*, University of Bern, Bern.

McWilliam, Andrew 2005, 'Houses of resistance: structuring sociality in the new nation', *Anthropological Forum*, vol. 15, no. 1, pp. 27–44.

McWilliam, Andrew 2007, 'Austronesians in linguistic disguise: Fataluku cultural fusion in East Timor', *Journal of Southeast Asian Studies*, vol. 38, no. 2, pp. 355–75.

McWilliam, Andrew 2008, 'Customary governance in Timor-Leste', in David Mearns (ed.), *Democratic Governance in Timor-Leste: Reconciling the local and the national*, Charles Darwin University Press, Darwin, pp. 129–42.

Mearns, David (ed.) 2008, *Democratic Governance in Timor-Leste: Reconciling the local and the national*, Charles Darwin University Press, Darwin.

Renard-Clamagirand, B. 1982, *Marobo: Une société ema de Timor*, Langues et Civilisation de L'Asie du Sud-Est et du Monde Insulindien 12, SELAF, Paris.

Traube, E. G. 1980, 'Mambai rituals of black and white', in James J. Fox (ed.), *The Flow of Life: Essays on eastern Indonesia*, Harvard University Press, Cambridge, Mass., pp. 290–314.

Traube, E. G. 1986, *Cosmology and Social Life: Ritual exchange among the Mambai of East Timor*, University of Chicago Press, Chicago.

Traube, E. G. 2007, 'Unpaid wages: local narratives and the imagination of the nation', *Asia Pacific Journal of Anthropology*, vol. 8, no. 1, pp. 9–25.

Trindade, José 'Josh' 2008, 'Reconciling conflicting paradigms: an East Timorese vision of the ideal state', in David Mearns (ed.), *Democratic Governance in Timor-Leste: Reconciling the local and the national*, Charles Darwin University Press, Darwin, pp. 160–88.

van Wouden, F. A. E. 1968, *Types of Social Structure in Eastern Indonesia*, R. Needham (trans.), Koningklijk Instituut voor Taal-, Land- en Volkenkunde, Translations Series Vol. 11, Martinus Nijhoff, The Hague.

Index

Afaloicai 26, 31n.26, 33, 34, 35, 36n.36
agricultural
    change 155, 187, 188, 195, 198, 206,
    207, 208, 209
    development 35, 168, 175, 206n.62,
    208, 218, 228
    economy 135
    productivity 135, 189, 221, 228
    prohibitions 74, 97n.15, 201n.48
    rites 31n.26, 70n.21, 74, 120, 135,
    155, 189, 191, 196, 204, 220
    see also land—agricultural, ritual—
    agricultural, ritual—harvest
agriculture 1, 13, 23, 30n.23, 43, 145,
    168, 197n.37, 201n.48, 202,
    206n.62, 209, 219, 222
    rice 9, 24, 27, 33, 35, 48, 97n.15,
    148, 149, 150, 151, 152, 175, 193,
    196n.32, 197, 199, 200n.44, 204,
    205–7, 218, 219, 220, 228
    subsistence 14, 24, 48, 64, 202, 217,
    218, 219, 220, 221, 222, 224, 228, 234
    swidden 24, 25, 64, 89, 189, 190,
    193n.21, 195, 197, 199, 201–6, 209,
    217, 218, 219, 220, 221, 222, 226,
    228, 229
    see also hunting
Aileu 3, 16, 99, 119, 123–9, 131–7, 178, 244
Ainaro 89, 92, 93, 96n.14, 98, 136, 166,
    167, 177, 178, 179, 181, 218
ancestors
    communication with 12, 29, 37, 40,
    42, 191, 252
    offerings to 42, 43, 72n.28, 73, 74,
    155n.4
    see also ritual—engagement with
    ancestors
ancestral
    burial sites 23, 24, 27, 29, 42, 51,
    76, 88, 226
    centres 226, 232
    connections to land 14, 24, 58, 233
    conventions 79
    entitlements 13, 67

    jurisdiction 15
    knowledge 37–41
    leaders 17
    narratives 10, 14, 17, 27, 29, 30,
    48–54, 87, 94–5, 96, 97, 98n.19,
    99–105, 106, 189–90, 243
    obligations 31, 43
    origin places 2, 10–11, 13, 226, 227, 254
    origin villages 11, 12, 87, 90, 93, 94,
    100, 111, 128
    precedence 247
    protocols 4
    sacra 12, 28, 29, 32n.31, 36, 37, 41,
    47, 65, 92, 120, 244
    settlements 17, 24, 66
    shades 62, 69, 71, 72, 73, 74, 75
    see also land—ancestral
ancestry 27, 42, 72n.29, 110, 111, 112
Armed Forces for the National Liberation
    of East Timor, see Falintil
Australia 9, 55, 69n.20, 175
Austronesian
    and Papuan languages 19, 163, 164,
    182–5
    borrowings from 164, 168–70, 171,
    181, 225n.16, 248, 249, 251
    comparative analysis 4, 5, 19, 82, 88
    culture 5, 10, 11, 14, 15, 16, 19, 50,
    63, 77n.42, 89, 110, 117, 121n.3,
    122n.6, 169, 251
    distribution 6, 168–9, 178, 179, 181
    heritage 3, 4
    history 6, 182–3
    languages 48, 182, 225n.16, 247, 248
    studies of 5, 82
    speaking societies 12, 32, 64, 80, 81,
    88, 141, 164, 168, 250
authority 10, 88, 89, 93, 97–9, 105–6,
    108–12, 187, 208
    customary 15, 53, 54, 56, 67, 151,
    187, 189, 201n.48, 207, 208
    emplaced 12, 14, 17, 30, 41, 74, 81
    landed 15, 62, 64, 66, 68, 70, 75,
    79–82, 189, 191, 195–7, 199, 205
    local structures of 12, 13, 62, 242, 255
    moral 18, 61, 69, 71, 75
    of descent groups 25, 27, 28, 29, 32

www.ingramcontent.com/pod-product-compliance
Lightning Source LLC
Chambersburg PA
LVW061227270326
CB00025B/3400

9 781921 862595